THREE YEARS IN THE

Bloody Eleventh

THREE YEARS IN THE

Bloody Eleventh

The

Campaigns

of a

Pennsylvania

Reserves

Regiment

Joseph Gibbs

The Pennsylvania State University Press • University Park, Pennsylvania

Library of Congress Cataloging-in-Publication Data

Gibbs, Joseph, 1965–
    Three years in the "Bloody Eleventh" : the campaigns of a
Pennsylvania Reserves regiment / Joseph Gibbs.
        p.   cm.
    Includes bibliographical references and index.
    ISBN 978-0-271-05838-2 (pbk : alk. paper)
    1. United States. Army. Pennsylvania Infantry Regiment, 11th
(1861–1865) 2. Pennsylvania—History—Civil War, 1861–1865—
Regimental histories. 3. United States—History—Civil War,
1861–1865—Regimental histories. 4. United States—History—Civil
War, 1861–1865—Campaigns. 5. United States. Army—Reserves—
History—19th century. I. Title.

E527.5 11th.G53 2002
973.7'448—dc21

                                                        2001035926

It is the policy of The Pennsylvania State University Press to use acid-
free paper for the first printing of all clothbound books. Publications on
uncoated stock satisfy the minimum requirements of American National
Standard for Information Sciences—Permanence of Paper for Printed
Library Materials, ANSI Z39.48–1992.

Contents

Maps and Illustrations

Maps

Illustrations
following page 78

Maps
and
Illustrations

■

Abbreviations

FSNMP	Fredericksburg and Spotsylvania National Military Park
GNMP	Gettysburg National Military Park
HSP	Historical Society of Pennsylvania
MOLLUS	Military Order of the Loyal Legions of the United States
NA	National Archives and Records Administration
NA-RG15	National Archives and Records Administration, Record Group 15 (Records of the Veterans Administration, 1773–1976, pension files); cited along with veteran's name and certificate number. (Although the soldier's name is cited herein, many pension folders are filed in the archives under the names of widows or dependents.)
NA-RG92	National Archives and Records Administration, Record Group 92 (Records of the Quartermaster General's Office)
NA-RG94-CMR	National Archives and Records Administration, Record Group 94 (Records of the Adjutant General's Office), entry 534, Carded Medical Records
NA-RG94-CSR	National Archives and Records Administration, Record Group 94 (Records of the Adjutant General's Office), entry 519, Compiled Military Service Records, Volunteer Organizations: Civil War
NA-RG94-11MR	National Archives and Records Administration, Record Group 94 (Records of the Adjutant General's Office), Eleventh Pennsylvania Reserves Miscellaneous Regimental Papers (box 4236, 8W3/R6/C17/SC)
NA-RG94-11P	National Archives and Records Administration, Record Group 94 (Records of the Adjutant General's Office), Eleventh Pennsylvania Reserves Personal Papers (boxes 117 and 118, 7W2/R6/C19/SE)

NA-RG94-MOF	National Archives and Records Administration, Record Group 94, Medical Officers Files, box 630
NA-RG94-VSF	National Archives and Records Administration, Record Group 94 (Records of the Adjutant General's Office), Volunteer Service File, P-696, V.S. 64, box 579
NA-RG153	National Archives and Records Administration, Record Group 153 (Records of the Judge Advocate General's Office [Army]), entry 15, court-martial case file
NA-RG156	National Archives and Records Administration, Record Group 156 (Records of the Office of the Chief of Ordnance)
NPS	U.S. Department of the Interior, National Park Service
Official Records	*The War of the Rebellion: A Compilation of the Official Records of the Union and Confederate Armies,* 128 serials (e.g., volumes) in four series (Washington: Government Printing Office, 1880–1901). All entries are from series 1 unless otherwise indicated.
PSA	Pennsylvania State Archives (Harrisburg)
PSA-RG19	Pennsylvania State Archives (Harrisburg), Record Group 19 (adjutant general's correspondence)
RNBP	Richmond National Battlefield Park
USAMHI	United States Army Military History Institute, Carlisle, Pennsylvania

Long before most of them had ever heard a shot fired in anger, the soldiers of the Union army's Eleventh Pennsylvania Reserves called their regiment the "Bloody Eleventh." The moniker likely stemmed from bravado—a "bloodied" unit had seen action and earned a measure of battlefield glory—and like most recruits of 1861, the men were eager to get at and "whip" the Rebels.[1] Regardless of how it emerged, the name was prophetic. Of 2,144 Union regiments raised during the war, the Eleventh Reserves suffered the eighth highest percentage of men killed in battle. The unit carried 1,179 soldiers on its rolls during three years of service, and 196 of them (11 officers and 185 enlisted men) became combat fatalities—16.6 percent of its total. Not counting its many wounded, the Eleventh Reserves was one of those regiments that, as William Fox observed in his 1889 study of Civil War casualties, could "fairly claim the honor of having encountered the hardest fighting in the war." Factor in 1 officer and 112 enlisted men killed by disease, plus the fact that hundreds of its members spent time in Rebel prisons, and the unit's tour of duty becomes even grimmer.[2]

The regiment's ten companies, about a hundred men each when at full strength, were raised in seven western Pennsylvania counties: Cambria, Indiana, Butler, Fayette, Armstrong, Westmoreland, and Jefferson. Mostly farmers and common laborers, leavened with a mix of back country lawyers, wagonmakers, blacksmiths, and students, the rough-hewn men of the Eleventh proved to be good soldiers. They were led in the field by equally tough Regular Army figures, such as George Meade, George McCall, Truman Seymour, John Reynolds, and Samuel Crawford.

The Pennsylvania Reserves organization as a whole comprised fifteen regiments, thirteen of which were infantry, most of which remained grouped as a division throughout the war. Save for stretches spent in two short-lived Union formations—Irvin McDowell's Army of the Rappahannock and John Pope's Army of Virginia—and a stint in the Washington defenses early in 1863, the division was always part of the Army of the Potomac.[3] Accordingly, the Eleventh Reserves was present at most of the eastern flashpoints of 1862–64. Preceded by a skirmish at Great Falls on the Potomac, its combat tour began with the Seven Days' Battles on the Peninsula. It ended in the middle of Ulysses S. Grant's grinding 1864 campaign of attrition against Robert E. Lee's Army of Northern Virginia.

These battlefield actions started at Mechanicsville in late June 1862, at which a fraction of the regiment was engaged. The Eleventh fought as a whole the next day, at Gaines' Mill, and was nearly destroyed. With the Union line pierced in several places, the unit held its ground alongside a New Jersey regiment while the rest of its wing of the army withdrew. Forced to surrender, its troops were marched to Richmond's Libby Prison, the enlisted men later taken to the Belle Isle stockade. The prized regimental flag (or "colors") became a Rebel trophy. Yet if capture could be marked by humiliation, the Eleventh's performance at Gaines' Mill earned only praise.

While most of the regiment was in Confederate prisons, a fragment remained in service, losing more than 30 percent of its numbers at the vicious 30 July 1862 action known as Glendale, Frayser's Farm, White Oak Swamp, or Charles City Cross Roads (among other names). Two members of this ad hoc force earned the Congressional Medal of Honor for gallantry during this battle, marked by one of the few times in the war when participants fought hand-to-hand.

Reconstituted after the war's first major prisoner exchange, the Eleventh Reserves saw hard service during the remaining months of 1862. It was routed along with the rest of its brigade on the second day of Second Bull Run, and the victory at South Mountain a few weeks later came at the cost of most of the regiment's officers, killed or wounded by a single Confederate volley. The Eleventh Reserves suffered several more killed at Antietam, where it fought at the edge of the infamous cornfield on the Miller farm. At Fredericksburg it, along with the rest of the Pennsylvania Reserves division, had a hand in the day's only successful Union assault on Rebel lines.

Following the Fredericksburg disaster, the shattered Pennsylvania Reserves division was sent to Washington to rest and thus missed the Union defeat at Chancellorsville. With the Rebel army subsequently on the move into their home state, the division's officers petitioned headquarters to be sent back into action. Their return to the Army of the Potomac climaxed on Gettysburg's second day, when the Eleventh Reserves was involved in the counterattack that started from the slopes of Little Round Top and surged into the Wheatfield, breaking the Confederate advance.

The next spring, though its term of enlistment was soon to end, the regiment took an active role in Grant's Overland Campaign toward Richmond. It fought its way out of entrapment in the Wilderness and lost more men at Spotsylvania Court House and elsewhere. Its final engagement, repelling a Confederate attack at Bethesda Church, about two years after but only a few miles distant from Mechanicsville, arguably brought the Eleventh Reserves full circle.

Some high-casualty units earned notoriety from a single, disastrous engagement. The Eleventh Reserves had many terrible fights—Gaines' Mill, Second Manassas, Fredericksburg, and the first day of the Wilderness, especially—but its high losses ultimately represented steady attrition. Its men were less colorful than other units of its division—the famous "Bucktails," for example, of the Thirteenth Pennsylvania Reserves, who earned a superb reputation and habitually led the advance as skirmishers. Yet judged by casualties suffered, few units in the Army of the Potomac endured more fighting over time.

Few also earned less postwar notice. Aside from the diligent Samuel P. Bates, who allotted about ten pages to the Eleventh in his multivolume 1869 *History of Pennsylvania Volunteers,* no contemporary historian seems to have seriously chronicled the unit. A weighty 1865 account of the Pennsylvania Reserves as a division of the Army of the Potomac makes only occasional mention of the Eleventh. Such terse attention explains why many works on the eastern theater include only brief references to the regiment.[4]

In this book I try to tell the story of the Eleventh Pennsylvania Reserves using a variety of sources. These are undeniably fragmented and incomplete, as only a scattered amount of relevant contemporary material has survived. Letters, diaries, and other first-person writings provide a starting point, and others will likely emerge from private collections over time and be useful to researchers.

To cite some examples, multiple letters survive by two members of Company A—the "Cambria Guards"—Andrew Lewis and Philip Lantzy; both died in separate battles in 1862. A single letter by "Brady Guards" (Company K) Pvt. Thomas W. Sallade describes some of the scenes in the regiment's early training; one by regimental chaplain the Reverend Adam Torrance details service at Gettysburg.[5] Several missives exist penned by Sgt. Harvey Fair of Company B, the "Indiana National Guards," who like Lewis died at Gaines' Mill. Late in life, Aaron Kepler of Butler County's "Dickson Guards" (Company C) penned an unpublished memoir of life in the Eleventh up to his wounding and capture at Gaines' Mill, following which he was eventually exchanged and then discharged. Another Butler County unit, Company D (the "Connoquenessing Rangers") is represented by diaries kept by young corporal Jesse Fry and fifer Charles H. Minnemeyer. Their comrade Robert E. McBride published a memoir of army life—the first four months of which were spent in the Rangers—entitled *In the Ranks*.[6]

James X. McIlwain, a sergeant in Armstrong County's "Independent Blues" (Company G), survived three years in the regiment, and his letters have found their way into archival collections. The family of Samuel Jackson, who was originally McIlwain's captain and later commander of the regiment, found his 1862 diary among his papers after his death and published it. As this book was being finished in 2000, letters by Pvt. Andrew Ivory of the Independent Blues and a single letter by Robert McElhaney of the Dickson Guards came onto the collectors' market. Other stray items from members of the regiment will likely emerge in the future.[7]

Further illumination comes from the notebook-diary kept by Indiana County's James McGinley, a corporal in Company E, one of two companies in the regiment that originally called themselves the "Washington Blues" (the other was Westmoreland County's Company I). McGinley's volume had a few adventures itself when its owner lost it after writing his 1 May 1864 entry. A Confederate captain found the book, writing his own name on the flyleaf but fortunately not eradicating the earlier notations. A Union cavalryman recovered it and in 1890 finally located McGinley, who had moved to Fort Collins, Colorado, and returned the diary to its rightful owner.[8]

Contemporary periodicals are another valuable source, and they are generally more trustworthy than postwar accounts, always potentially tinged by a rearrangement of facts. Kepler's 1900 memoir told of his captain confronting an Irish private who had brought a rattlesnake to camp. "Begorra ai'm a goin' to schwear 'im an' let 'im go!" the soldier replied jokingly, citing the practice of releasing prisoners after the latter had taken the Oath of Allegiance to the Federal government. But the tale echoes an anecdote published in at least one western Pennsylvania newspaper in 1861; it must have circulated many times during the war. And by the time the regiment unveiled a memorial at Gettysburg, the veterans' remembrance of what they did on the battle's second day bore little resemblance to either contemporary accounts or their former colonel's 1877 letter on the subject.[9]

Firsthand soldier accounts found their way into newspapers through several channels. Relatives shared camp and battlefield missives with local editors, and some soldiers wrote directly to the papers, often employing initials or pen names. Such accounts are invaluable, but papers from several of the Eleventh Reserves' component counties have had a poor survival rate for parts of the war. And as the conflict progressed, fewer literate pens remained in the ranks to send letters back. Finally, a caveat must be attached to published letters, because editors who cleaned up spelling and punctuation may also have removed details deemed unimportant at the time.[10]

Not every letter home following a fight, whether kept private or made public, contained details of a battle. Many who survived the shock, gore, and chaos of war sought only to scrawl a few words to let the homefolks know that they had survived. And as the war progressed and they became desensitized to combat, soldiers spent less time in their letters dwelling on particulars of battle.

On a more official level, the National Archives and Records Administration is home to an illuminating set of miscellaneous and personal papers from the Eleventh Reserves, contained in Record Group 94. And although the regimental and company books are not part of the archives' collection, ordnance inventories in Record Group 156 provide data on weapons and equipment starting with the fourth quarter of 1862. Additionally, as the government granted pensions to veterans and their survivors, applications housed in Record Group 15 detail the service, wounds, and personal and family data for veterans of the Eleventh. These pension folders may hold a handful of pages or hundreds. They can include government forms, surgeon's certificates, responses to annual questionnaires, letters written home from the field, and even notes scribbled on scraps of paper. Because of their varied contents, some judgment had to be exercised when citing pension file materials. In many cases, particularly when data was culled from a series of documents, it seemed best to simply give the certificate number assigned to the soldier's (or his family's) pension folder.

Some pension folders from members of the Eleventh Reserves were unavailable for study. They had remained in the Department of Veterans Affairs' records holding facility in Suitland, Maryland, which was subsequently damaged by a February 2000 fire. It is unclear at the time of this writing what records were affected by the fire.[11]

Sources outside the regiment itself also help flesh out a picture of the conditions affecting the Eleventh. Meade and Reynolds, for instance, wrote home about their experiences in the Pennsylvania Reserves division, and the former commanded the Eleventh's parent brigade for a time. Then there is the U.S. government's omnibus collection of wartime reports and correspondence, the *Official Records,* in which the regiment's movements and battles were summarized and chronicled by its field commanders.[12]

All Civil War sources need to be used with care, and many disagree over details. A historian perusing the 1861 files of Warren, Pennsylvania, newspapers highlighted the rare occasion when "rival editors substantially agreed in their descriptions" of an event.[13] Confusion is most noticeable—and should be expected—in recounting battle action. Battle accounts and maps only approximate the chaos; an author can at best synthesize a mass of conflicting data. Many Civil War survivors deemed accuracy an impossible goal. One Confederate veteran-turned-brigade historian noted: "No one soldier sees all that occurs in the battle in which he participates; it is impossible he should. Officers and privates do not see alike even when observing the same occurrence, for they look from different angles and standpoints."[14] A dozen years after the war, when Union Col. Kenner Garrard responded to a request for his memories of Gettysburg, he did so acknowledging that "no doubt others may differ widely from me in these matters." He also volunteered: "There is little truth . . . in the details of wars as recorded in history."[15]

That said, these soldiers' stories were vivid ones, and it seems strange that no hefty postwar regimental history came from the Eleventh Reserves' veterans. Some definitely thought they deserved one. "Other regiments were as good, but none better," former officer Hannibal Sloan remarked when the unit unveiled its granite memorial in the Wheatfield at Gettysburg. He continued: "it is meet and proper that the survivors should gather the testimony and show that this regiment did its duty. Otherwise history will record [only] that . . . it was organized, mustered into the service, served three years and was mustered out. This won't do—we must brighten our memories, refer to our diaries, look up and write up our history, and demand that the truth be told of us and justice be done to our dead and to the survivors of our regiment."[16]

None of his comrades seem to have taken up Sloan's challenge. Many potential chroniclers of the three years of service, of course, had been left in graves across Virginia, Maryland, and Pennsylvania. The survivors may have avoided writing about the unit immediately after the war, when their recollections were freshest, because their service had been hard and they may have wanted to put the conflict behind them. For these men, reminders of the war might be only a few houses away, in the form of neighbors who came back mangled. In late summer 1863, when the Pennsylvania Reserves division presented an elaborate sword and sash to

Meade, he acknowledged not only those "now sleeping their sleep in lonely battlefields" but also wondered "how many others are now limping over the country mutilated cripples."[17]

The Eleventh Pennsylvania Reserves provided many of the latter. Pension applications reveal men who lost limbs or were partially blinded or deafened in battle. Some stopped musket balls with their teeth, others survived gunshot wounds in the genitals. Yet many soldiered on rather than seek discharges. As medical historian Jack D. Welsh wrote of the people of the era, "They did not consider themselves victims but accepted what happened and carried on with their lives."[18] Some suffered in mind as much as in body. One veteran struggled with fits of dementia every time he heard a loud noise. Another was locked in an insane asylum with the war still raging. Released from the service, he promptly signed up in another unit, unable to exit the conflict despite its horrors.

Such stories underscore the rigors of service in the Eleventh Reserves. One newspaper account of the men discharged following the Fredericksburg and "Mud March" campaigns noted: "They, with but two exceptions had all visited Richmond as prisoners, and some of them twice; they were discharged in consequence of sickness and wounds—the majority for wounds received in the hard fought battles in which the Pennsylvania Reserves generally took a conspicuous part. Several were wounded thrice, some twice, and others being more lucky only happened to be in the path of one ball shot by traitors to the best Government the sun ever shown upon."[19]

A year and a half later, another writer commented on the regiment's return following its 1864 muster-out. "The remnant of the 11th P.R. reached Pittsburg[h] on Wednesday last, their three years term of enlistment having expired. . . . The Regiment went out over one thousand strong, and although we did not count them when they got off the cars in Pittsburg[h], we think that only about one hundred and fifty returned."[20] The "Bloody Eleventh" had more than earned its self-appointed, self-fulfilling nickname.

Any Pennsylvania Reserves unit challenges a researcher, as it did the Civil War–era administrator, because of the organization's confusing numbering system. The regiments received two designations: a "reserves" number reflecting the state formation in which they originated; and a "line" number corresponding to their integration into the Federally mustered Pennsylvania Volunteers. Hence, the Eleventh Pennsylvania Reserves was also known as the Fortieth Pennsylvania.[21]

In spite of the attempt to impose a standard numbering system on the Pennsylvania regiments, the Reserves continued to call themselves (and be called) by their Reserve number. Accordingly it was (and remains) easy to confuse Reserves and non-Reserves units. Consider the 1864 plight of Frederick Rexroud, then a thirty-six-year-old Philadelphia-born machinist. At a recruiting station in New Brighton, on 26 February, he signed papers for three years, or the duration of the war, in the Eleventh Pennsylvania Volunteers. Due to a clerical error, he was sworn into Federal service as a member of the Eleventh Reserves. One regiment was not as good as another for Rexroud, who probably had friends or relatives in the Eleventh Volunteers. The officer who signed him up, district provost marshal Capt. John Cuthbertson, tried to get the adjutant general's office to fix the mistake, but it refused as the mustering had already taken place. The conscientious Cuthbertson kept at it, and the secretary of war finally issued special orders correcting Rexroud's enlistment status.[22]

The spelling and grammar of the primary sources used herein varies widely in quality. I have tried to closely transcribe the materials, using brackets when clarification seemed necessary. Please note that deciding whether a nineteenth-century writer's cursive character indicated capitalization was often a judgment call, as was my decision to use the modern spelling of Butler County's Connoquenessing Creek throughout the main text.[23]

The companies that formed the Eleventh Reserves had their own identities and characters. In this work, their original nicknames have been used interchangeably with their letter designations. Several tables within the text give both identifications, as does the following:

Company	County	Original Designation
A	Cambria	Cambria Guards
B	Indiana	Indiana National Guards
C	Butler	Dickson Guards
D	Butler	Connoquenessing Rangers
E	Indiana	Washington Blues (I)
F	Fayette	Union Volunteers
G	Armstrong	Independent Blues
H	Westmoreland	Westmoreland Guards
I	Westmoreland	Washington Blues (II)
K	Jefferson	Brady Guards

(Note that the letter J was not used in U.S. Army company designations.)[24]

Although much of this book deals with battles, I have tried to focus on movements and activities directly involving the Eleventh Reserves. Accordingly, strategic-level overview has been kept to a minimum, with many important details in Civil War history summarized or omitted altogether.

I long ago took to heart Civil War historian Robert K. Krick's maxim "Good books about the war contain good and plentiful maps on their specific subjects; bad books contain few or none."[25] That said, production realities unfortunately limited the number of maps that could be included here. Readers further interested in individual battles may wish to examine those contained in the general works—as well as the highly detailed National Park Service troop movement map sets, when available—cited in the notes and bibliography.

Nor was it possible to include a complete regimental roster—a staple of many nineteenth- and early twentieth-century regimental histories. Fortunately, each company's rolls are transcribed in pages 854–75 of volume 1 of Bates' *History of Pennsylvania Volunteers.* This standard reference work was republished, in a slightly different volume configuration, by Broadfoot Publishing, Wilmington, North Carolina, in 1993.

Like many modern Civil War books, this project originally sprang from personal genealogical research, and my first thanks go to several distant relatives who put good fortune to historians' use. In 1978, Vernon Krug and his wife, Lovelle (née Lantzy), learned that the Lantzy family had saved a cache of nineteenth-century documents, including twenty-eight letters sent home during 1861–62 by Philip Lantzy, Company A, Eleventh Pennsylvania Reserves. With the help of Lovelle's cousin, genealogist and history buff Charles Lantzy of Mechanicsburg, Pennsylvania, the Krugs transcribed Philip's writings, then sent copies of the transcripts and photocopies of the letters themselves to several research centers, including the United States Army Military History Institute at Carlisle, Pennsylvania. The originals are now deposited with the Department of Special Collections at Mugar Memorial Library, Boston University.

Enthusiastic support came as well from Madeline Paine Moyer of Raleigh, North Carolina, a descendant of Andrew Lewis, first lieutenant and later captain of Philip Lantzy's company. She passed along significant genealogical and anecdotal information about the officer and his family, gave feedback on portions of the manuscript, and also made available family photographs.

I owe a great debt to Michael Musick of the National Archives and Records Administration, who aided me immensely in finding data sources in the collection he oversees. David Wallace of the same institution was also instrumental, as were private researchers Vicki Killian of Takoma Park, Maryland, and Ronald L. Waddell of Lebanon, Pennsylvania, and author Thomas P. Lowry, whose Civil War works have set a standard for using the National Archives.

Many National Park Service historians offered constructive criticism and insight. They include Alan Marsh and Joan Stibitz at Andersonville; Ted Alexander and Keith Snyder at Antietam; Frank O'Reilly at Fredericksburg/Spotsylvania; John Heiser at Gettysburg; Chris Bryce at Manassas; and Robert E. L. Krick at Richmond. I am also indebted to author and historian Steven R. Stotelmyer of Sharpsburg, Maryland, for sharing data acquired in his research on the Maryland campaign of 1862.

Thanks goes to Pam Cheney, David Keough, and Michael J. Winey at the U.S. Army Military History Institute at Carlisle, Pennsylvania, for invaluable access to documents and photographs from their various collections. I also drew upon the resources provided by the staff of the Brandeis University Libraries; Katherine Kominis of the Department of Special Collections, Mugar Library, Boston University; Michael Lear and Ann W. Upton of the Archives and Special Collections Department of the Shadek-Fackenthal Library, Franklin and Marshall College, Lancaster, Pennsylvania; Elinor Hernon of the Newton (Massachusetts) Free Library; and Richard Hill of the State Library of Pennsylvania. The maps reproduced here came courtesy of David DiBiase and Mark Wherley of the Peter R. Gould Center for Geography Education and Outreach at Penn State University. Additional photographs came from Ronn Palm of Kittanning, Pennsylvania, and Ziegler Studios in Gettysburg, Pennsylvania.

Various Pennsylvania historical societies and government officials contributed time, advice, and resources. I am grateful to Connie Mateer of the Armstrong County Historical Society; Leslie Conrad of the Cambria County Historical Society; Cindy Pierce of the office of the Cambria County Register of Wills; Carla Wright of the Capitol Preservation Committee, Harrisburg; John J. Craft of the Civil War Library and Museum, Philadelphia; Carol Bernie and Colleen Chambers of the Historical and Genealogical Society of Indiana County; Jennie Benford and Linda Pelan of the Historical Society of Western Pennsylvania; Marianne Heckles of the Lancaster County Historical Society; Ron Gancas, senior curator at the Soldiers and Sailors Memorial Hall in Pittsburgh; and James Steeley and Jennifer Wilson of the Westmoreland County Historical Society.

Outside of the Keystone State, I owe thanks to James Greve and Sandra Peterkin of the Library of Virginia; Donna J. Williams of the Maryland Historical Society; Bonnie Wilson of the Minnesota Historical Society;

Carolyn S. Parsons, Mark Winecoff, and Katherine Wetzel of the Museum of the Confederacy, Richmond; Crista LaPrade of the Virginia Historical Society; and Barbara Billings of the Western Reserve Historical Society, Cleveland. I also gleaned important feedback and support from friends and colleagues Niall and Eva Heney, Tanya Karpiak, Richard K. Lodge, Les Masterson, Marina Parsons, and Ann Ringwood.

I have special regard for the editors and staff of Penn State University Press (including their anonymous peer reviewers) and am grateful for their confidence in accepting and working with my manuscript. Last but not least, my wife, Tatyana, was a true partner, and her patience and love was essential to my undertaking and finishing this project.

With those thanks given, please note that any errors herein are the author's responsibility.

Chapter 1

A County Divided

At the time John Brown led his abortive raid on the Federal arsenal at Harpers Ferry, Virginia, residents of Pennsylvania's Cambria County enjoyed the attentions of at least four newspapers. These papers shared an identical typeface and design and contained like mixes of fiction, poetry, farming advice, and local news. Yet each had its own brand of politics, and readers of any one paper could find editorials critiquing—sometimes bludgeoning—a competitor's views.

This local war of words echoed one going on at a national level in the eighteen or so months preceding the Civil War.

Similar situations could be found in many western Pennsylvania communities. A look at contemporary Cambria County, which produced the unit destined to become Company A of the Eleventh Pennsylvania Reserves, offers a glimpse into what was taking place across the state.

Cambria County—like much of western Pennsylvania—was in its infancy as an organized region. Nestled against the Allegheny Mountains, it was first settled near the end of the eighteenth century. Early inhabitants included Catholics moving from Maryland and eastern Pennsylvania; German Dunkers and Amish; and Welsh emigrants. The latter named their settlement using the medieval Latin name for their homeland. The title was given to the county as a whole in 1804.[1]

Ebensburg, the centrally located county seat, was an up-and-coming borough in 1859. Its growth came, wrote a contemporary observer, despite a location "such as to preclude the possibility of its ever becoming a place of extended business or large population. Situated upon high ground, without any water power, its increase must be owing entirely to the enterprise of its people, and the necessities of the neighborhood." With a thousand inhabitants, it was big enough to host three weekly newspapers, though "whether they all find it profitable might be a grave subject of inquiry."[2]

Each weekly was partisan, listing party committee members and candidate endorsements below its second-page masthead. The two Democratic organs favored different wings of the party, which had split after the emergence of Illinois Senator Stephen Douglas as a national figure. The *Democrat & Sentinel* was conservative on slavery and supported President (and Pennsylvanian) James Buchanan's laissez-faire handling of the issue.[3] The Douglas-aligned *Mountaineer,* on the other hand, often criticized the Washington administration, attacking Buchanan's perceptible weakness in dealing with the national crisis.[4] Across town, the *Alleghanian* was Republican and abolitionist, as was the county's most established paper, the *Cambria Tribune,* published in Johnstown, seventeen and a half miles to the southwest.[5]

The banter between the three Ebensburg papers varied in tone and taste. The *Mountaineer* had no trouble breaking party ranks over issues, referring at one point to "the muddy brain of the *Dem. & Sent.*"[6] The real rivalry was between the *Alleghanian* and the *Democrat & Sentinel.* As the latter once wrote of the former: "A Jack-ass, if we may credit the story, once undertook to criticize and find fault with the song of a Nightingale. Why then should we feel offended at the editor of the *Alleghanian* for pointing out the typographical errors he happens to discover in the columns of the *Democrat & Sentinel?* We are old enough to know the difference between the braying of an Ass, and the roaring of a Lion."[7]

The same paper charged, just before the 1860 election, that Republican presidential candidate Abraham Lincoln believed in equality between the black and white races, a bold position at the time even among slavery's opponents. The *Alleghanian* denounced the statement as a lie. In its hot-tempered rebuttal, replete with an excerpt from a Lincoln speech, the *Alleghanian* seemingly lost its composure: "There, Mr. *Dem. & Sent.*, are his [Lincoln's] views. What do you think of them? And ain't you a reliable family newspaper, going about with such a brazen-faced and cast-iron-countenanced falsehood on your unprepossessing exterior, endeavoring to diddle voters in the support of your candidates? Now ain't you?"[8]

Though abolitionist, the *Alleghanian* employed the stereotypes of the day. Consider its attack on "the defunct, irresponsible editor of the *Democrat & Sentinel*"—Charles D. Murray—presented in the form of a black preacher's "sarmint."

> *A sarmint delibbered on de occasion ob de def of Mister Charley Dizzard Murray, de frend ob Slavery and de villifire of de nigger. By de Reverend Mister Sambo Saffron. Before de cullud peeple of Hard Scrabble.*
>
> BELUBBED BREDDERN:—It fords me much pleasure to form you dat de individooal you see layin yander is ded agin; an it am my dooty as your much respectable pasture, to say a few words on dis melancholic occasion.[9]

How much real bitterness existed between the two papers can today be only a matter of conjecture. When Murray actually did die—eight months after the "sarmint" was published—the *Alleghanian* eloquently eulogized him, acknowledging his talents and closing its obituary with "We ne'er shall look upon his like again."[10]

Such politeness may have been forced. If Pennsylvania as a whole was divided on slavery, Cambria County had active abolitionists willing to back opinion with action. They had made the town a stop on a branch of the Underground Railroad, the path escaping slaves used to flee northward. In Johnstown in 1837, slave catchers succeeded in wounding and capturing two runaways. Townsfolk delayed the captives' immediate return, arguing that they needed nursing, then whisked them farther north. When the pursuers tried to follow, a troop of rock-throwing boys slowed them down. The hunters gave up the chase, unaware that adults were arming themselves to put up more lethal resistance. Similar antislavery sentiments existed in varying levels in nearby regions. Brown's raiding party included Albert Hazlett, a resident of neighboring Indiana County, who was captured at Harpers Ferry and later executed by the Virginia authorities.[11]

Brown's raid, his capture, trial, and hanging, and the issues the episode aroused gave each Cambria County paper a chance to stake out political turf. The *Democrat & Sentinel* celebrated the "even handed justice meted out to John Brown, the punishment justly due to the double crime of Treason and Murder. . . . Will not all sensible, unionloving patriotic and conservative American citizens, whether Democrats or Republicans, agree with us in saying that the world is well rid of such a monster?"[12]

The *Mountaineer* of the same date was more cautious in its assessment. Brown's conviction and hanging were judicial triumphs, but "let not human malignity follow him beyond the grave." More important, the South needed to be aware that Northern Democrats could not long overlook threats to the Union, nor guarantee political support should secessionist talk continue. "Let them . . . be just to the conservative men of the North, who have so earnestly sustained them of late, by being true to the constitution," the *Mountaineer* observed. "Let them be just; then can they with confidence look forward to the earnest assistance of the North in their tribulation, should it come."[13]

On the Republican side, the *Alleghanian* coupled attacks on slavery with assaults on the Democrats. Its first take on the Harpers Ferry episode cited the "wild insanity" of the raid to point out the folly of the Douglas-supported Kansas-Nebraska Act, which held that local elections would determine if those incoming states would allow slavery or prohibit it. This platform had sparked a migration of pro- and antislavery zealots to the territories, leading to violence and opening up a "Pandora's box of evils." The tragedies that followed unhinged men like Brown, reported the *Alleghanian*. "Those who suffered in person, in the sanctity of their houses, became, like Brown of Osawatomie, frenzied with the scenes of diabolical horror thro' which they had passed. Reason fled her throne, and the idea of resistance to the supposed cause of all the tumult and outrage became a religious fanaticism."[14] The *Cambria Tribune* echoed the *Alleghanian*'s point of view.[15]

Within a few weeks, both Republican papers shifted tack and began to focus on the raid as a necessary assault on slavery. In Johnstown, the *Tribune* reprinted a piece that painted the hanging as meant to send a larger message: "Attempt to disguise it as you may, . . . John Brown was executed not as a traitor, not as a murderer, but that his death might be a terror to the Abolitionists of the North."[16] The *Alleghanian* meanwhile reprinted an opinion piece that foresaw the end of "the bold hypocrisy of our boast of being the freest government on earth, whilst the notorious denier of fundamental rights to millions on our own soil. . . . Will any one . . . be found in the North ready to exult in the final doom of a man whose only crime was the desire of realizing to the oppressed the initial truths of the immortal Declaration? We believe, sincerely, that the death of Brown will do more for the final overthrow of the system of Southern slavery than any single fact of the century. It has already done far more than even Brown and his followers ever dared to hope."[17]

The prediction proved right. And when Cambria County went for Lincoln in the presidential election of 1860, the *Alleghanian* saw it as vindication. "Republicans of Pennsylvania! There is a good time coming. The Augean stables are to be cleansed all over the country.—Peace and prosperity are again to shine upon our nation, and the people will again enjoy a season of repose from the storms of slavery agitation which have been thrust upon us by the Slave Oligarchy."[18]

The *Democrat & Sentinel,* which had backed John C. Breckenridge for president, blamed its party's defeat on mavericks like Douglas who had fissured the organization. If they "and their followers had stood by the administration, the Black Republican Party would not have attained its present strength," the paper observed in late 1860, just after South Carolina seceded.[19]

On the latter controversy, the editor added a warning: "We have been surprised several times recently, at hearing gentlemen who ought to know better assert that the South Carolinians are nothing but cowardly braggarts, and destitute of the courage necessary to sustain them in facing an enemy in the field of battle. Their history proves exactly the reverse of this." The paper cited examples of Carolinian heroism in the Revolution, the War of 1812, and in Mexico. "We do not wish to be understood as maintaining that the citizens of South Carolina are braver or better men than those of the other States," it carefully noted. "Our object is merely to show the absurdity of the charge of cowardice brought against them."[20]

A few months later, those same South Carolina forces besieged Fort Sumter, which surrendered on 14 April 1861. The news arrived in western Pennsylvania by the next day, sparking rallies and flag-raisings across the region. In Ebensburg on Wednesday, 17 April, two hours' notice brought five hundred people—about half the town's population—to the courthouse for a mass meeting featuring patriotic speeches and songs. Two days later, Ebensburg's courthouse saw another impromptu gathering, held "to take into consideration the propriety of organizing a military company to be tendered to the Government for the suppression of Treason." Thirty-three men put their names forward.[21] The role of organizing and leading this emerging unit fell to two politically connected local businessmen, Robert Litzinger and Andrew Lewis. Both had military experience, having served together in the Mexican War in a unit raised in Cambria County.

Litzinger's life thus far had already touched upon each faction represented by the town's papers. Born 28 November 1830, his ancestors were German Catholics who originally settled in Adams County. In Ebensburg, he gained a certain status from Mexican War service in a locally raised military unit, the Cambria Guards. Drawn from the region's mix of Welsh, German, and Swiss stock, it served as Company D in the Second Regiment of Pennsylvania Volunteers during the Mexican War. Another Cambria County unit, the "Highlanders," formed Company C of the same regiment. (Although young, the county already had a military tradition, having furnished two four-month companies for the War of 1812.) Litzinger was only sixteen when he enlisted in January 1847 as a fifer, alongside his older brother John, who turned nineteen that month and served as a drummer. Dennis Litzinger, twenty-three at the time of enlistment and possibly a cousin of the others, signed on as a private. The unit started the long march south with eighty-five men. It left eighteen dead in Mexico, and three more died in New Orleans. John Litzinger did not make it back home, dying at San Angel, Mexico, in April 1848.[22]

The campaign earned Robert Litzinger the reputation of "a brave and gallant soldier." He came home to Cambria County's Black Lick township—he later settled in Belsano—and married. By 1860, his wife Mary had given birth to four children. For work, Litzinger learned the printing trade and served briefly as the publisher of the *Democrat & Sentinel* when it emerged in 1853. His politics apparently led him to sever ties with that paper; in 1858 he became de facto publisher of the *Mountaineer,* though he did not formally assume the title until the middle of the following year. Up to that point, Litzinger seems to have put out the *Mountaineer* without salary, an arrangement that further indicates a political motivation. The paper's editorial slant hurt it financially; Buchanan loyalists shunned it when it came to advertising and printing work. Hence, the *Mountaineer* proclaimed that "on the people, and the people alone, we rely for our success in the future."[23]

In early 1860, Litzinger left the *Mountaineer* to form a business partnership with Ebensburger Abraham A. Barker, Esq. The *Mountaineer* appears to have suspended publication at this time. Like his earlier shift from the *Democrat & Sentinel* to the *Mountaineer,* this move may have been politically motivated, and it may have reflected Litzinger's feelings on the role slavery was playing in national troubles. His new partner, Barker, born in 1816 in Lovell, Maine, had been a leading abolitionist in his native state, as well as a temperance advocate. Barker moved to Cambria County in 1855 and prospered in both the lumber and mercantile trades. Within a year he became a major figure among the state's Republicans—known in Pennsylvania at the time as the "People's party." By 1859, he held a seat on Ebensburg's board of school directors; the next year he led Lincoln's election campaign in western Pennsylvania. He would take over the *Alleghanian* in September 1861 and successfully run for Congress three years later.[24]

While Litzinger's partnership with Barker hints at the former's abolitionist sentiments, the politics of his Mexican War comrade Lewis are less distinct. Born in Philadelphia in about 1812, Lewis had moved to Columbia, in Lancaster County, and had a trade as a house plasterer by the time he arrived in Ebensburg in 1840. When troops were raised for service south of the border, Lewis signed up alongside the Litzingers, even though at thirty-five he was relatively old for the ranks. Of his time in Mexico, the *Democrat & Sentinel* reported that "he participated in the battle of Chapultepec, and assisted in planting the Flag of our Country in triumph on the walls of the Mexican fortress." After the war, the veteran became active in local affairs, and by 1859 he sat on the Ebensburg town council.[25]

He also settled back into domestic life with his wife Maria, born in 1821, whom Lewis married in mid-1838. Their union was described as happy. One friend described Lewis' character as "without a stain," and others characterized him as "an excellent husband and father, a kind friend, an esteemed citizen, and a man in every attribute of the word." He appears to have shared Barker's views on drink, as the officers of the local temperance union called him one of their "most active, devoted and zealous members." Personal letters that have been preserved from Lewis to his family show affection and humor.[26]

Yet the Lewises also endured tragedy. In common with many nineteenth-century families, the mortality rate of their offspring was appalling; four of six children died in infancy. The effect of their deaths may have been reflected in Lewis' struggle with what he termed "an unconkerable passion," which despite his efforts to hide had nonetheless "somwhat sowered" his personality. As he wrote to his daughter Mary Frances—born in 1845 and called "Melley" and "Fanny" by her family—he was unable to control it: "My passion for an hour or too is worse on me than a whole yeare of hard work. . . and often after it has subsided apearentaley to evry observer I hav beene sore from the effects of it . . . and often hav I thought afterwardes I would try and conker it but I never wase able."[27]

Military life appealed to the gray-eyed Lewis, whose hair was a matching color at the time of the post-Sumter rallies. He wanted his small surviving son—Andrew Jackson Lewis, born in 1857, and called "Jackey"—to attend West Point "should [he] live to become a man."[28] Being a town council member at the time, it is possible that Lewis played a role in a September 1859 effort to organize a new Ebensburg militia unit. The *Alleghanian* reported "that a meeting of citizens of Ebensburg and vicinity will be held at the Court House . . . for the purpose of taking into consideration the propriety of raising and organizing a military company. . . . Our town has been long enough without a military company. Johnstown boasts of several, and even Hemlock is ahead of us. This should not be." The piece added: "The Cambrians who served in Mexico, whether they be dead or living, have brothers and sons and admirers who are not ready to let the military spirit die out entirely in this community."[29]

At that time, enthusiasm for a company had been lacking. But now outrage over Sumter uncorked intense passion and Ebensburg, like much of the rest of the country, was ready for war. Armed with the list of thirty-three men who had volunteered during the 19 April meeting, Litzinger and Lewis took part in a more formal session on the next Monday. A band played and a reporter noted, "the ladies turned out *en masse* and graced the occasion with their presence." Local lawyer Robert L. Johnston chaired the session, giving "a brief but thrilling address." Part of it stated "that the families of the volunteers would be cared and provided for during their absence, in all cases where pecuniary aid would be necessary and acceptable." Forty-seven more names were added to the muster roll, bringing the fledgling unit to approximately company strength. Litzinger and Lewis were elected captain and first lieutenant, respectively. Perhaps at their suggestion, the "Cambria Guards" name was resurrected for their unit.[30]

Lewis' decision to re-enter the military may have been influenced by financial need as well as patriotism. He owed varying amounts of money to many Ebensburg residents, including a mortgage, interest on the mortgage, and bills for foodstuffs. Likely fearing his advanced years might disqualify him, the forty-nine-year-old Lewis gave his age as forty-four on the enrollment papers.[31]

Robert Abbott McCoy was chosen as the unit's second lieutenant. A onetime candidate for county register, McCoy was described as: "a young and promising member of the Bar of this County. Brave, energetic and intelligent, he will doubtless cover himself with glory in the battle field, should an opportunity for doing so offer itself." McCoy, soon to turn twenty-six, himself enlisted another law student as the company's first sergeant: Rowland M. Jones, a blue-eyed, dark-haired, fair complexioned bachelor born circa 1839. With these selections made and the ranks filled, Litzinger dutifully notified Pennsylvania governor Andrew Curtin of the company's availability. The offer was one of hundreds received by Curtin, and though not accepted into state service immediately, Litzinger's company was advised "to be in readiness to march at an hour's warning."[32]

Litzinger and Lewis drilled their recruits daily and added ten more men by the beginning of May. "They are," wrote an observer, "a noble, good-looking body of men, and will do honor to Little Cambria in the 'tented field.'" At the same time, other companies were being formed in the county for three months' service, pursuant to Lincoln's initial call for 75,000 volunteers. Several had already headed off for training camps and depots hastily set up near Pittsburgh. Litzinger's approximately ninety men were therefore disappointed when Curtin's office informed their commander that despite earlier hopes, their "services cannot be accepted immediately, as the present requisition has already been filled, but that another requisition will probably be soon made, when they will be among the first ordered to shoulder arms and take up their line of march for the seat of war." Ebensburg's contingent impatiently awaited a new call-up and orders to march.[33]

There are no contemporary accounts of significant antiwar sentiments in Cambria County in 1861, although Johnstown produced one man who reportedly bore arms unwillingly for the Confederacy.[34] That said, as in much of the North, the issue of fighting for union versus fighting to end slavery was and would remain a sensitive one.[35]

Yet if Cambrians were divided as to why they were shouldering arms and heading off to war, for most there was no doubt about going. "The war fever is increasing instead of abating in Cambria," the *Democrat & Sentinel* noted at the start of May. The paper had responded to the fall of Fort Sumter with a new logo—an American flag inscribed "The Union forever"—on its second, editorial page. But it also stressed that it was supporting the war on the basis of preserving the union, not as a crusade to free the slaves.

> None are more determined and enthusiastic in the good cause than the members of the Democratic party. But in doing this they entertain no intention of endorsing the principles of Abolitionism. . . . At this time, when the Democracy of Cambria are responding to the call of the President for volunteers with as much promptness and alacrity as their Republican fellow citizens, it is very wrong for the Johnstown *Tribune* to announce that we are called up to war against the "Slavery propagandists of the South" and for the Ebensburg *Alleghanian* to proclaim that the contest is between freedom and slavery. Have they become so wedded to the one idea of the party, that they cannot ignore it at a crisis like this. Slavery has really nothing to do with this contest.[36]

Perhaps it was this kind of editorial policy that incited the *Blairsville Journal,* in neighboring Indiana County, to include the *Democrat & Sentinel* on a list of alleged pro-secession papers. The *Democrat & Sentinel's* initial response was to call the *Journal's* "obscure quack" editor "a low, vile, infamous liar and scoundrel." When the *Journal* amplified its charges by invoking the *Democrat & Sentinel's* 1860 support of Breckenridge—since gone over to the Confederacy—the latter paper took pains to note that its candidate "was run as a Union, not as a secession candidate, and 'the Union and the equality of the States' was the rallying cry of his friends during the campaign." In this spat, the *Alleghanian* supported its rival, acknowledging that "in the matter of Union vs. Disunion [the *Democrat & Sentinel*] is eminently sound."[37]

Although the *Democrat & Sentinel* itself called for just such local bipartisanship, it frequently attacked Curtin's administration. Appealing to state pride, it faulted the way Harrisburg equipped its soldiers, many of whom lacked arms and uniforms when they arrived in Washington. "We learn that wherever our gallant volunteers appear, they are laughed at and pointed out as the ragged Pennsylvanians," the paper charged. "Now is this not humiliating . . . to every citizen of the State?" A legislative committee eventually looked into the poor-quality issues of clothing, blankets, and rations and decided that Curtin was not directly at fault. Public opinion eventually blamed the men to whom he had entrusted the mobilization effort.[38]

Interparty wrangling compounded the logistical problems. In this case, it was between Curtin and fellow Pennsylvanian Simon Cameron, Lincoln's secretary of war and the senior political boss of his home state's Republican party. Lincoln's campaign managers had promised the powerful Cameron a cabinet seat in return for his support in 1860; Lincoln never authorized the bargain but followed through on it.[39]

Cameron's rift with Curtin, which predated this episode, stemmed in part from prewar business connections with rival railroads. It came to a head after Cameron bested Curtin for a Senate seat in 1856. Curtin recovered his political fortunes through hard work as Pennsylvania's secretary of state and in 1860 announced his candidacy for governor. Cameron at first put his weight behind a rival candidate in the "People's party," but an eventual compromise was worked out. Under its terms, Cameron's allies supported Curtin for governor and made him head of the party delegation to the Chicago Republican convention. In return, they wanted Cameron nominated for the presidency, apparently a sop to his pride though he conceded having only dark horse status. In spite of the ability to work out such deals, Pennsylvania's rough-and-tumble political atmosphere left a void between the two sides.[40]

It is ironic that the bad blood remained in 1861. Curtin was among the first Northern governors to offer troops to safeguard the nation's capital, whose safety was Cameron's priority. The day before the attack on Fort Sumter, Curtin persuaded the Pennsylvania legislature to pass a bill that, among other things, set up a state military bureau and enabled state-owned arms to be issued to local militia formations. Yet regardless of the looming national emergency, Cameron and Curtin reignited their squabbling—their first dispute was over which railroad the volunteers would be sent.[41]

The situation worsened as the enthusiasm greeting Lincoln's appeal for volunteers taxed Federal resources. While the president's April call set Pennsylvania's quota at sixteen regiments, many more companies came forth, and were accepted into state service, than were needed. Within two weeks of the call-up, Pennsylvania had assembled twenty-five regiments for three months' service. But Cameron refused to accept more soldiers into Federal service than those requisitioned. Historian William Heseltine has perceived this refusal as an extension of the Cameron-Curtin animosity. Cameron's motive would have been to embarrass Curtin in the eyes of what a different historian, Bruce Catton, called "all of the indignant voters who wanted to go to war and could not be accepted." Curtin's nineteenth-century biographer saw the repercussions of refusing volunteers in a different prism; the governor "feared the evil effect such a course would have if more troops were needed in the future." Yet Federal resources were undeniably limited, and Cameron in fact rejected surplus volunteers from other states.[42]

At the same time, Curtin was wary of transferring all the state's available militia over to service in eastern Virginia, especially given Pennsylvania's long southern border. To ease the problem, immediately after Fort Sumter he decided to form a new state force, to be called the Pennsylvania Reserve Corps. At Curtin's urging, the legislature passed a bill to create it, with its soldiers enlisting for three years. The volunteers would "be clothed and equipped as similar troops in the United States service, and . . . be liable . . . to be called into the service of the United States or National Government." The legislation, which Curtin signed on 15 May 1861, provided for thirteen regiments of infantry, one of cavalry, and one of artillery.[43]

The three-year proviso dovetailed with the new set of needs the War Department had begun to formulate. The day before Curtin signed the bill, Cameron asked the governor to furnish at least ten three-year regiments as part of the state's quota. Still mindful of scanty resources, Cameron stressed that Pennsylvania was to respect the overall requisition limit: "It is important to reduce rather than enlarge, and in no event to exceed it," Cameron wrote. He added: "If it should be agreeable to Your Excellency it would be especially gratifying to this Department to have some of those regiments offered for three-years' service from Allegheny and other western counties . . . brought into service under the quota for your State."[44]

Within five days of the creation of the Pennsylvania Reserve Corps, Curtin informed Cameron that he knew "of eight or ten regiments so organized and about 300 companies pressing upon me for admission, all apparently eager and willing to serve for any period you may see fit to indicate." Two days later he notified Cameron that "we are about to forward fifteen regiments under our late law and desire to muster them into service." The Cambria Guards became the sixth unit which Curtin formally accepted from that county. Litzinger, Lewis, and company were about to go to war.[45]

In spite of the exigencies of war, it took until 7 June for Ebensburg's company to be formally requisitioned for state service. "The official command to report at camp was so tardy in arriving that very many were inclined to believe that they would never be ordered into service," wrote one observer. The delay had such a demoralizing effect that some edgy recruits "attached themselves to other companies." Their places were filled once the Cambria Guards' marching orders became known. On the eve of departure, a crowd filled the Ebensburg courthouse to bid the unit farewell. "The room was densely packed, and a large number of fair ladies graced the occasion with their presence. . . . [Several speakers] delivered eloquent addresses, telling the soldiers that next to their God their first obligation was to their country; that on them devolved a portion of the duty of perpetuating the institutions of the greatest and best government existing; and bidding them all 'Be Brave.'"[46]

Litzinger's men assembled again at daybreak on Wednesday, 12 June. Escorted by friends and relatives, and with its captain's relative (though not his son) Thomas Litzinger serving as drummer, they marched or were driven to the Pennsylvania Railroad station at Wilmore, a borough about ten miles south, situated in a narrow valley. Wilmore, "a few miles east of Summerhill . . . was once a brisk village," noted a contemporary account, "but is now decaying rapidly. There are many beautiful and productive farms in the vicinity." Here the company boarded an express train headed for Pittsburgh, 102 rail miles away. "Many bitter tears were shed," observed a witness to the scene. "But amidst all the sorrow manifested, it was pleasing to observe that no one sought to restrain another from going."[47]

Their destination was a state military facility, Camp Wright, set up about ten miles from Pittsburgh, where the men would transfer to the Allegheny Valley Railroad, detraining at Hulton station. The journey took about eight hours and probably passed pleasantly. A writer traveling on the Pennsylvania Railroad of the era, at about the same time of year, compared the line's services favorably against those of other companies. He praised the light and ventilation in the cars and marveled at facilities for passenger comfort. Of the journey over the Alleghenies, the same traveler wrote: "The mountains are finished up to the top with the richest green in the world, and the beauty of summer flows down the gorges as if it were water."[48]

After marching into camp from Hulton station, the Cambria Guards settled in for what for many was probably their first night away from home. Of the accommodations, a member of the company observed: "Here we dined for the first time, on crackers and pies. This operation over, we commenced putting up tents, and by 5 or 6 o'clock had ourselves pretty comfortably fixed for a camp sleep. We next partook of a regular old supper of beans, pork, beef, potatoes, crackers and coffee, served up on pine boards—all but the coffee, which was distributed in tin cups. We were minus plates for a couple of days but that didn't lessen the novelty of camp life—on the contrary, it rather added to it."[49]

Camp Wright was well provisioned and orderly, with the nearby Allegheny River providing water. "The camp is situated on gently sloping ground," wrote one visitor, "which successfully prevents the formation of mud-puddles within it. Trees are scattered throughout and around the enclosure, affording a grateful and luxurious shade from the heat of the sun. The strictest cleanliness is required as to the camp and surroundings, and no intoxicating liquor is allowed within gun-shot."[50]

Named for Curtin's aide John A. Wright, the camp was set up at the beginning of June and was by all accounts an improvement over the first Pittsburgh-area military facility, Camp Wilkins, about a dozen miles away. Named for William Wilkins, the leader of the Pittsburgh Citizens Committee for Defense, Camp Wilkins grew around some privately owned fairgrounds off Penn Avenue, adjacent to the Pennsylvania Railroad tracks. The onrush of volunteers quickly overcrowded the site. Sanitation was poor, and men slept four-abreast in what had been fairground cattle pens. The camp commissary stocked only salt beef, hardtack, and coffee, and officers had appealed to the public for donations to improve the fare.[51]

Although Camp Wright was better stocked than Camp Wilkins, worries about the Cambria Guards' food situation led Ebensburg residents to start efforts to keep the absent men well supplied. Early presents included at least one 100-pound keg of butter, and the *Alleghanian* urged the community to send one every week. To mark the Fourth of July, the paper solicited donations for "a box of provisions of various kinds, in sufficient quantity to afford the entire company a luxurious 'feed.'" The paper also reminded its readers that soldiers appreciated mail from home: "If you have a son, or a brother, or a cousin, or a friend in the army, write to him as often as possible. Nothing is more highly prized by the soldier than a letter from the dear ones at home."[52]

Regardless of such attentions, military life did not sit well with all members of the Cambria Guards. It is unclear exactly how many men filed out of Ebensburg in early June. But a company roll published on 20 June shows a total of seventy-six men, down from the early May total of approximately ninety. One enlistee had second thoughts as soon as he left home and "vamosed" after arriving at Camp Wright. Within a few days, at least four more followed, probably mindful that leaving after being sworn into state service would make them subject to desertion charges.[53]

Other causes thinned the ranks. A medical board rejected seven members of the unit "on account of physical imperfections." One wanted it known that "nothing but circumstances over which he had no control prevented [him] from going forth with the company." Per his request, the

Alleghanian reproduced the certificate Litzinger gave him. It certified "that Clinton R. Jones is honorably exonerated from accompanying the Cambria Guards in their campaign."[54]

Litzinger easily found a dozen replacements when he returned to Ebensburg late in June. Likely acting quickly lest more fit men change their minds, once he got back to camp on 26 June he called the company together to be sworn into state service by a Lieutenant Hall of the Pennsylvania militia. Here the Cambria Guards faced their first battle with army red tape: they learned they had more soldiers than could be processed.[55]

The episode is puzzling. As a soldier-correspondent described it in a letter to the *Alleghanian,* "Upon counting noses, we found that we numbered 81 men—four more than could be received." But U.S. Army regulations, which guided volunteer units, then set company strength as between 64 and 82 privates—between 83 and 101 men when all ranks were included. In spite of this fact, Hall tried to intimidate a few into backing out of soldiering, stressing the serious consequences of taking the oath. He read portions of the Articles of War, emphasizing that desertion was punishable by death. Hall invited those with misgivings to step out of the ranks. None did.[56]

"Gentlemen," Hall was quoted as saying, "four of you must withdraw, and you can now do so honorably, and be passed to your homes free of expense." When no one stepped out of the line, Litzinger selected four "whom he considered least able to endure the hardships of camp life, and had absolutely to order them from the ranks." Hall administered the oath for three years to the remaining men, who gave several cheers for the Union. The next day, the Cambria Guards marched to the camp's hospital to be vaccinated, officers included.[57]

The four-men-over-the-limit story becomes stranger when juxtaposed with a soldier's late June letter to the *Democrat & Sentinel*. The letter reads: "On last Tuesday the Cambria Guards, numbering 77 men, were 'sworn in' by Lieut. Hall." Nothing is mentioned of soldiers being ordered from the ranks. The writer added: "It is said by some that, before going into active service, every Company must number 101 men; in that case some more of our friends will have a chance to join us." Barring some mistake, perhaps Litzinger staged the episode in order to diplomatically remove four men he knew to be unfit.[58]

If so, the tactfulness would seem to be in keeping with Litzinger's character. The new captain showed himself to be industrious and conspicuously attentive to his soldiers' needs. During a heavy shower on one of the first days at Camp Wright, Litzinger braved the rain and went to each tent, instructing occupants on how to keep the water out. "He spares neither time or means to make the men comfortable," one correspondent wrote home. "He is a favorite of the whole company, and the men are proud to call him Captain."[59] The approach boded well. Save for one man, who bolted from Camp Wright the day of the battle of Bull Run, the Cambria Guards appear to have endured the war without a single desertion.[60]

Chapter 2

Soldiers in Dead Earnest

Camp Wright to Camp Tennally

Robert Litzinger's and Andrew Lewis' mobilization efforts in Cambria County were among hundreds taking place in western Pennsylvania. The units which, along with the Cambria Guards, eventually coalesced into the Eleventh Pennsylvania Reserves formed in six other counties during the same period. All started moving toward Pittsburgh-area camps in June 1861.

Two units emerged west of Ebensburg, in Indiana County, which in 1860 had a widely scattered, largely agrarian population of 33,735. The county seat, Indiana borough, had only four streets, though it was slightly larger in population—1,329—than Ebensburg. A spur linked it and the county's second largest town, Blairsville (population 1,018) to the Pennsylvania Railroad. According to the 1860 census, 95 percent of the county's population, largely of English and Scots-Irish heritage, had been born on American soil.[1]

A recent work has noted that, despite its Republican majority, not all of its residents were abolition-minded. Yet Indiana County had a martyred link to John Brown, and a history as a station on the Underground Railroad. Local militia units—the "Saltsburg Guards" and the "Black Hornets" among them—were in place at the time of the Harpers Ferry raid. As in Ebensburg and elsewhere, efforts were afoot in the months before Sumter to form additional ones. One such venture started in January 1861, led by thirty-year-old James R. Porter and his brothers, Daniel, twenty-one, and Robert, twenty-three.[2]

The Porters were influential figures in the area. Their Adams County-born father had moved first to New Alexandria, then Clarksburg, then finally Saltsburg, where in 1829 he bought a salt works. Sixteen years later he started a store there, James Jr. eventually joining him in business. The pair worked together until January 1853, when the younger Porter bought a canal packet, the *Indiana,* and struck out on his own. Four years later he was elected county prothonotary on the Know-Nothing ticket. By the time he and his brothers met to discuss forming a militia company, James Porter was a recognized Republican leader.[3]

Their pre-Sumter volunteer effort "failed ignobly" in James Porter's words, but he was a natural choice to lead recruitment when war came. On 18 April, a meeting in Indiana borough authorized "Captain" Porter to form a company. A dozen men, James' brother Daniel among them, signed on to the "Indiana National Guards." One of the day's speechmakers, Richard Harvey Fair, then in his mid-twenties, was named sergeant, and twenty-two-year-old Hannibal Sloan, a six-foot-tall aspiring lawyer, became a lieutenant.

While waiting for his company to be called into state service, James Porter kept busy. Officials in Harrisburg authorized him to round up the county's stores of publicly owned arms. The rest of the time he spent drilling his growing force, his recruits apparently including relatives of Albert Hazlett, John Brown's unlucky comrade from Indiana County. A postwar account described Indiana National Guardsmen William M. and Henry C. Hazlett as Albert's brothers. If so, they varied widely in age. William was about thirty-six at this time, according to documents in his pension file; Henry was later remembered as being about seventeen in 1862.[4]

Meanwhile, in Blairsville, another Indiana County company, calling itself the Washington Blues, was forming under twenty-six-year-old Nathaniel Nesbit. (A second local Nesbit, twenty-eight-year-old James, probably a relative of Nathaniel's though not his brother, organized a company that saw action in the Fifty-fifth Pennsylvania.) Described posthumously as a resident of Livermore, Nathaniel Nesbit's residence was given in regimental documents as Conemaugh township. He would be remembered as "a devout sincere christian, a remarkable affectionate brother, an obedient son, a liberal friend, an upright citizen and a dauntless soldier." These and other qualities prompted Blairsville's ladies to present him with a silk national flag on the steps of the Evans Hotel at the time his company was set to march.[5]

Daniel R. Coder and Hugh A. Torrance, both about six feet tall, served as Nesbit's first and second lieutenants, respectively. Born in or about 1830, Coder had a ruddy complexion, dark hair, and gray eyes. Later described as a "man of high character and intelligence," Coder was working as a schoolteacher when he signed on with the company. Blairsville's Torrance was a blacksmith like his father. Born in 1832, the younger Torrance (clerks often spelled his name as "Torrence") was generally calm and quiet but was noted for his strength. He displayed the latter in wrestling matches with his friends as well as in his work beside the forge. Heading for war, Torrance left behind his wife Harriet, whom he had married the previous January. Now twenty-two, Harriet had just become pregnant with the couple's first child.[6]

By the time of the ladies' flag presentation, a large number of Indiana County companies had formed alongside those of Porter and Nesbit, each jockeying for recruits and authorization to join state service. Hoping consolidation would increase their chances of being called to Harrisburg, nine of the units—the National Guards among them, though not the Washington Blues—tried combining themselves into a 600-man Indiana County regiment. The new organization formed on 10 and 11 May, with James Porter named lieutenant colonel. When Curtin declined to accept the entire regiment, its component units split up again. The companies held together, however, and Porter and Nesbit eventually received word to rendezvous at Camp Wright.[7]

Two more companies destined to join the Eleventh Reserves emerged to the south, in Westmoreland County. Here, another set of county "Guards" came together, as did a second company that adopted the "Washington Blues" name favored by Nesbit's unit.

On 19 April, Greensburg resident Daniel Kistler Jr. started assembling the Westmoreland Guards. Like Litzinger's unit, it resurrected the name of a Mexican War company. Born circa 1811, Kistler came from a German Lutheran family that had been among the area's earliest settlers; his father was a founding deacon of Zion's Evangelical Church in Greensburg, the county seat. The younger Kistler was living in Hempfield township in July 1843 when he married an Adamsburg woman, Sarah Ann Probst. She gave birth to a son, Morris, about five years later. By 1856, when the future captain joined a group improving and renovating the town's cemetery, he ranked among the "men of the highest standing in Greensburg." A year later, he began service as one of the town's assistant burgesses and councilmen.[8]

Kistler's counterpart at the head of the Westmoreland County Washington Blues, organized early in May, was Thomas H. Spires, a burly, six-foot-two, 220-pound officer with gray eyes and auburn hair who gave his occupation as "laborer." Spires' first lieutenant, Eli Waugaman, born circa 1834, stood nearly the same height and had been a wagonmaker since 1855. For a second lieutenant, the Washington Blues reached across the border into Indiana County's Black Lick township and secured another one of the area's blacksmiths, David Berry, born circa 1818. He left behind his wife, Olive, to whom he had been married twenty years.[9]

Butler County, which provided another pair of units fated to fall in with the Eleventh Reserves, was on a war footing well before April 1861. When South Carolina seceded, so many students and faculty from the county's West Sunbury Academy joined the militia that, student Aaron Kepler recalled, the exodus "practically closed the school." The six-foot-tall, brown-eyed, black-haired Kepler also wanted to join, but his parents dissuaded him. Apparently for a change of scene, they sent him to the Shippenville Academy in Clarion County. He was there when Fort Sumter fell, and "The cry was 'War, war!' on every hand." Back home in Sunbury, Samuel Louden was organizing a new company, the "Dickson Guards," named for the West Sunbury Academy's principal, the Reverend William T. Dickson. Kepler was still not allowed to join, but his parents eventually agreed on a compromise: he could sign up provided he first helped gather the fall harvest. When that work was done, fate or perhaps design led him to Louden's unit, by then already a part of the Eleventh Reserves, with Dickson, aged fifty-six when sworn into Federal service on 1 September, serving as its chaplain.[10]

At about the same time Louden formed the Dickson Guards in Sunbury, in the town of Butler a twenty-six-year-old bachelor farmer named William Stewart was organizing the Connoquenessing Rangers, named for the local creek. Made captain of the unit on 1 June, Stewart was the oldest of four children—two sons and two daughters—of Andrew Stewart, a farmer whose fields yielded a hand-to-mouth living. William's brother David signed up in a different Butler County unit; he would die the following summer.[11]

After being accepted for state service, the eighty-two Connoquenessing Rangers marched to Camp Wilkins, where surgeon Franklin Irish examined the recruits. His report has survived in the regimental papers, giving a wealth of data on the original unit's demographics. Its members' given ages ranged from seventeen to forty-three. Most gave their occupations as farmers and laborers, but the roll included wagonmakers, carpenters, tanners, clerks, blacksmiths, coal diggers, stage drivers, and shoe makers. First Lieutenant J. S. Kennedy was a tailor; twenty-three-year-old privates Jacob Kinsell and Thornton Fleming were, respectively, a schoolteacher and a dentist. Dr. Irish rejected several men on medical grounds. One had a maimed hand, two had defective vision, and seventeen-year-old John Johnston suffered from a hernia. A forty-three-year-old farmer whose name appears to have been Peter Debillion was rejected on account of being "short." Taller men who passed the examination still proved susceptible to the rigors of army life and close-quarter living. Pvt. Vernon Johnston died from "meazles" in early July, by which time the company had been transferred to Camp Wright and integrated into the Eleventh Reserves.[12]

The roll in Stewart's company also included a twenty-four-year-old Evansburg tanner named John Gansz, whose name is spelled in various forms in government and regimental documents. Gray-eyed, dark-haired Gansz had been born in Harmony, Butler County, in 1837. He signed up as a corporal in Stewart's company, notwithstanding that earlier he had served as a lieutenant in a local militia unit known as the Connoquenessing Whites. Dr. Irish initially disqualified Gansz on medical grounds, but the word "rejected" was eventually inked over with "passed." Gansz later told Governor Curtin why: "I enlisted June 14 [18]61 and was examined by the Surgeon and rejected on account of my left Arm[.] Our Capt[ain] then got got [sic] a Man examined in my Name and smugeled me in to the Co[mpany]. I have been an Invalid and an expense to the Government ever since for every time the weather changed I got a terrible pain in my arm (which stands at a right angle) and was unfit for duty."

Gansz, promoted to sergeant late in 1861, wrote the above in mid-1862, by which time he was unsuccessfully seeking a discharge. If the allegation about Stewart falsifying the medical record was ever investigated, it does not seem to have affected his army career. Rather it was Gansz who had troubles with the provost marshal before the war ended.[13]

For service in the Eleventh Reserves, Fayette County offered up the Union Volunteers. Its captain was Everard Bierer, a well-connected Uniontown lawyer whose military career would be marked by an eagerness for promotion, accompanied by a penchant for going over his immediate superiors' heads. Born in Uniontown early in 1827, Bierer studied at private schools. After leaving Madison College in 1845, he learned the law under a local jurist, then roamed the frontier territories for a few years. By October 1850, he had returned to Uniontown, where he was elected district attorney as a Democrat. Two years later he married Ellen Smouse at Brownsville. She ultimately bore eight children, each living into adulthood. Bierer was a devoted Bible student and was galvanized as the slavery issue grew in intensity. He switched parties in 1856, backing John C. Frémont for president. An ardent Lincoln supporter in 1860, he developed close connections with Andrew Curtin and other Republican politicians.[14]

Bierer's first lieutenant, Peter Adolphus Johns, also brought a legal-political background to his service. He was born in Wilmington, Delaware, in 1817, moving to Fayette County sometime before Christmas Day 1842, when he married Susan Marietta before a minister in Connellsville. He saw service in Mexico, where he served as a corporal (and was promoted to sergeant) in the Fayette County-raised Company H of the Second Pennsylvania Volunteers. In 1848, he became one of three county auditors, and three years later he was voted into the multifaceted post of register of deeds, recorder of wills, and clerk of the orphans' court. He was elected to the state legislature in 1856 and was living in Uniontown by the time he and Bierer formed their Fayette County unit. Like Hugh Torrance, Johns left behind an expectant wife; Susan Johns gave birth to a son, Peter Jr., in the fall of 1861. The company's second lieutenant was another Uniontown lawyer, John W. DeFord, who spent most of his time in the Eleventh detached to the Signal Corps.[15]

Volunteers from Jefferson County organized the Brady Guards, named for their captain, Evans R. Brady, of Brookville, hitherto editor of that town's *Jeffersonian* newspaper. The year of Brady's birth does not seem to have survived in the available government records, but early in 1845 he married Frances A. Magee, born circa 1824, and five years later the couple celebrated the birth of a daughter, Grace. Like many of his counterparts, Brady became disillusioned with the war. He also grew tired of a captain's responsibilities. "A private soldier," he wrote his mother a week before his death at South Mountain in September 1862, "has much less to do, less risk to run, and has better times every way than the commander of a company."[16]

Brady seems to have brought his employees into the war with him. His first and second lieutenants, James P. George and Edward Scofield, both gave their occupation as printer on their enlistment forms. The darkhaired, gray-eyed George was twenty-nine years old when he signed on as first lieutenant. At the time he joined he had been married for two and a half years to Jane E. Clark, whose first husband had died only a month after their nuptials in December 1854. The new officer left behind the Georges' first child, only a few months old at the time the Brady Guards were organized. Clearfield-born Scofield was black-eyed, dark-haired, had turned nineteen in March 1861, and was still a bachelor. By the time this newspaper trio formed their unit, another member of the local printing brotherhood, Joseph P. Miller, born circa 1835, had already established himself as a Union veteran. The sandy-haired, blue-eyed Miller signed up 18 April in what became Company K of the three-month Eighth Pennsylvania Infantry. The stint was apparently a positive experience for Miller, who in September joined the Brady Guards.[17]

The final element in the Eleventh's mix originated in Armstrong County, from where Samuel McCartney Jackson brought the Independent Blues in tow to Camp Wright. Nearly six feet tall, Jackson had been working as a merchant in Apollo, running a store with his brother James, before war came. He left behind the former Martha Byerly, whom he married in January 1860, and their daughter Gertrude, born on the subsequent New Year's Eve. Jackson seems to have been both competent and popular, important characteristics as volunteer regiments at this time elected most of their field officers. From being captain of the Independent Blues, Jackson would rise to the posts of major, lieutenant colonel, and ultimately colonel of the regiment. His company's first lieutenant, James P. Speer, born circa 1826, also rose through the ranks before illness forced him from the war. Speer was a florid-complexioned bachelor with brown hair and blue eyes and had previously been manager of a Kittanning mill.[18]

Andrew Curtin's first choice to command the Reserves was Pennsylvania-born George B. McClellan. But the governor's offer reached the future Army of the Potomac commander after he had accepted a command from Ohio, where he had served before the war as a railroad executive. Curtin then gave the job to George Archibald McCall, an experienced field officer born in 1802 and educated at West Point.

McCall served in the Seminole and frontier Indian wars; he earned two brevets while commanding an infantry battalion in Mexico. Chronic neuralgia led to his retirement from the army in 1853, but McCall settled in Pennsylvania and stayed active in the militia, in which he was a major general at the time Curtin tapped him for the Reserves. He also retained his military bearing. McCall was, as one member of the Eleventh wrote following a late June review, "a fine looking old gentleman, of the real soldier stamp."[19]

Ranking as a brigadier in the new U.S. volunteer army, McCall was intent on bringing the Reserves into Federal service as a whole, and as one observer noted, "by succeeding he made [them] the only entire division to keep its geographical identity throughout its three years of fighting." His first organizational task was to form the coalescing infantry, cavalry, and artillery formations into the fifteen regiments called for under the Reserves statute. In mid-June, while forming the Second, Third, and Fourth Reserves at Camp Washington in Easton, Pennsylvania, McCall invited the independent companies to align on their own initiative. As no firm groupings emerged within the five-day deadline McCall set, he ultimately organized the regiments based on the order in which companies arrived in camp.[20]

It is unclear if McCall employed the same organizational methods at Camp Wright, where he arrived on Friday, 29 June. Regardless, on 1 July the Eleventh Reserves came into existence. The Cambria Guards became Company A, considered a choice assignment and a designation that delighted the men. Robert Litzinger's Mexican War service may have earned the Guards the first spot, because companies were usually lettered to correspond with their captains' seniority. As one of the Cambrians observed in a letter home: "The members of the 'Guards' were unanimous in desiring to get Co. A., before they received it, and as a natural consequence all were jubilant when Capt. Litzinger announced that we held the first post of honor." James Porter's Indiana Guards drew the Company B designation, perhaps in recognition of his lieutenant colonelcy of the makeshift Indiana County regiment.[21]

The new regiment's makeup at this point was:

Company	Captain	County	Original Designation
A	Robert Litzinger	Cambria	Cambria Guards
B	James Porter	Indiana	Indiana National Guards
C	Samuel Louden	Butler	Dickson Guards
D	William Stewart	Butler	Connoquenessing Rangers
E	Nathaniel Nesbit	Indiana	Washington Blues (I)
F	Everard Bierer	Fayette	Union Volunteers
G	Samuel Jackson	Armstrong	Independent Blues
H	Daniel Kistler	Westmoreland	Westmoreland Guards
I	Thomas Spires	Westmoreland	Washington Blues (II)
K	Evans Brady	Jefferson	Brady Guards[22]

This lineup of officers was not final; the regimental staff had yet to be named. In volunteer and militia units, while company officers typically voted to fill most posts from within, colonels were usually appointed by higher authorities. Curtin evidently directly commissioned his choice to lead the Eleventh Reserves—thirty-nine-year-old Thomas Gallagher, a Westmoreland County native who, if he arrived at camp with his county's units, had no official hand in raising either.[23]

Born near Pleasant Unity on 17 January 1822, Gallagher worked as a merchant, owning a large store in New Alexandria. In 1849, he and Elizabeth K. McBride were married by the Reverend Adam Torrance, who later served as chaplain of the Eleventh Reserves and was possibly a distant relative of Second Lieutenant Hugh Torrance from neighboring Indiana County. By the time the rebellion started, Gallagher had long been active in the county's militia and, said a contemporary account, "had by experience acquired a knowledge of company and regimental drills and maneuvers." Within the state militia, he progressed from lieutenant to brigadier general. At the time the war began, he was serving as brigade inspector for Westmoreland County, and it is possible that fellow militia general McCall recommended him to Curtin. He left the New Alexandria store "in the hands of strangers," he later wrote, and headed for Camp Wright.[24]

A noted disciplinarian, Gallagher came from a military family. His lineage included a grandfather who had served as an army captain in

Ireland before bringing his family to America in 1810. The Eleventh Reserves' commander was quoted as observing that "if some men will have no character themselves, one will have to be established for them." Yet he maintained a gruff flexibility. One day at Camp Wright, the tent-dwelling Cambria Guards on their own initiative settled into some recently vacated barracks. Lt. Robert McCoy subsequently went to Gallagher to get belated permission for the move. Gallagher refused. "But the men have already done so without orders," McCoy was quoted as saying. Gallagher, in the words of a correspondent, "after giving it as his opinion that 'we'd do,' said that we might as well remain." A similar episode occurred a few months later when the regiment was inundated in spring rains while camped near Alexandria, Virginia. Again without permission, the troops shored up their leaking wooden barracks with tent canvas. "The Col. complains a little, but shows no definite resistance to their actions," Samuel Jackson, by then lieutenant colonel, wrote in his diary.[25]

Gallagher, who fathered three children, also showed some paternalistic traits as an officer. This emerges in postwar correspondence between his widow and one of the regiment's enlisted men. Christopher Herbert, who grew up not far from Gallagher's home, arrived at Camp Wright in 1861 just shy of his seventeenth birthday. U.S. Army regulations held that recruits had to be at least eighteen; those under twenty-one needed a parental certificate authorizing their enlistment. Apparently in ignorance of this rule, Captain Daniel Kistler added Herbert, who did not have parental permission and was under eighteen anyway, to Company H.

Herbert's angry father soon turned up to claim his underage son. But by the younger Herbert's account, his father "allowed me to stay upon Col[.] Gallagher promising to take care of me." Gallagher, who like many officers seems to have turned a blind eye to the age proviso, evidently kept Herbert on as a "striker" or orderly. He "looked after me," Herbert wrote the colonel's widow in 1885, "and kept my money and evry day I was with him and in his tent. . . . Your husband was like a father to me."[26]

The new colonel started a pattern of daily training: company drill from 8 to 9 A.M.; regimental drill from 10 A.M. to noon; and afternoon company drill from 3 to 4 P.M., followed by a 6:30 P.M. dress parade. Part of the training dealt with such basics as the "position of the soldier" in parade line and the various motions of the manual of arms. Significant time was spent teaching the men how to load and fire while standing or kneeling—loading took multiple motions which the men were expected to do in unison—and how to line up and execute turns or changes of front.[27]

The Cambria Guards and the Brady Guards—Companies A and K—were designated as flank units, stationed on the ends when the regiment was in a line of battle. In keeping with Winfield Scott's tenets of military thinking, such companies were to be trained as specialists in the art of skirmishing, forming the advance troops deployed a short distance in front of the rest of the regiment when necessary. It is likely that much of the daily company drill involved teaching the Cambria Guards and the Brady Guards to break ranks quickly and fan out in pairs across an area representing the regiment's front. Other companies might also to be trained to answer such a call in certain circumstances; the tactical manuals of the era contained many skirmishing drills.[28]

The regimental and company books of the Eleventh Reserves never made it to the National Archives, but Gallagher's orders regarding skirmisher training probably resembled the one described in this entry from the order book of another Pennsylvania unit: "The two flank Companies of the Regiment will hereafter at least once a day (in the morning) be instructed in the movements of *skirmishers* viz: to deploy forward and by the flank, to extend intervals and to close them, to reliefe skirmishers, to advance and retreat in line, to change Direction and to march by the flank, to fire at a halt and marching, to rally and to assemble."[29]

The Brady Guards' designation as the Eleventh's other flank unit hints that Gallagher formed his battle line at variance to the tactical manuals of the day. As companies were normally named alphabetically in order of their captains' seniority, most tactical manuals put companies A and B on the flanks. One 1860 manual specified an order from left-to-right of B, G, K, E, C, H, I, D, F, A. The same lineup was repeated in later influential military handbooks. Given that A and K anchored the Eleventh's flanks on the right and left respectively, it is possible that Gallagher trained the companies to line up in alphabetical order, a system which would be easier for recruits and inexperienced officers to remember.[30]

Gallagher also regularly prescribed target practice, mostly to benefit the rifle-equipped flank companies. Tactical manuals of the day stressed the individuality of each piece. "A perfect arm can only exist in theory," noted one text. "A soldier always firing the same piece will become acquainted with its defects, and will be able to make such allowances when firing as experience teaches him to be necessary."[31]

The same book prescribed giving recruits a pair of two-hour drills to teach the principles of aiming. Instructors set a partly filled sandbag on a bench placed on a table. Making an indentation in the sandbag with the back of his hand, the instructor cradled a musket or rifle into the slot and brought a sample target into line with the muzzle and breech sights. After his trainees looked through the sights, the instructor turned the gun out of alignment and had each man in turn rectify the aim. A later drill taught the men the principles of trajectory, line of sight, and line of fire and how to use a raised sight to aim at targets beyond the weapon's "point-blank." In one aiming exercise, recruits fired using only percussion caps, trying to extinguish a candle placed a yard from the muzzle. Some drills called for using blank cartridges, the purpose being to teach new soldiers to preserve their aim despite the hammer's jolt and the recoil from the black powder discharge. One manual stressed that "The instructor should make the soldier understand that a good marksman is known by the steadiness with which he preserves his gun when it misses fire."[32]

With the colonelcy set, the companies assembled to elect the rest of the field officers. For the lieutenant colonel's post, the men selected James Porter of the Indiana National Guards. His old unit promptly raised his brother Daniel, previously their first lieutenant, to succeed him as captain. For major, the regiment selected Jackson, succeeded in his Company G by Speer. Mexican War veteran Johns, first lieutenant of Company F, became adjutant, the officer charged with overseeing daily administrative tasks. Ex-blacksmith Torrance of Company E was elected quartermaster, responsible for meeting general supply and transportation needs. "These officers," a soldier wrote home, "have the confidence of those under their command."[33]

Although the Eleventh would have at least two more regimental elections, as the war continued voting for officers was increasingly discouraged. John Reynolds, originally a Pennsylvania Reserves brigadier and later its division commander, urged ending the system because it tended to advance politically gifted officers rather than militarily skilled ones. The rank and file also sometimes elected poor officers as a form of protest. A soldier in the Seventh Pennsylvania Reserves once noted that his newly elected lieutenant colonel "is very unpopular with the Col. That is the reason of his election, not because he is fit for the office. The Col. is now airing his wrath on the men by piling on duty wherever he can."[34]

The day after the Eleventh named its field officers, the unit celebrated the Glorious Fourth in a grove outside Camp Wright. The event featured a reading of the Declaration of Independence, musket volleys, and cannon salutes. Now told that companies could have a maximum strength of 101 officers and men. Litzinger started back to Ebensburg on 5 July to drum up more recruits for Company A.[35]

By this time, Gallagher's regiment had received its first government issue of shoes. In the case of the Cambria Guards at least, this appears to have been the first bit of uniform clothing its members had received since the ladies of Ebensburg presented them with havelocks on their departure. A piece of headgear worn over the army's standard visored forage cap, havelocks shielded the neck from the sun. Dorothea Dix, appointed to oversee the Union's nursing corps within a few weeks of Fort Sumter, particularly championed the article. Dix was quoted as saying: "I never can have too many. Should any one ask what they shall do for the soldiers at a cheap rate, say, make Havelocks." And an article in the *Alleghanian* concluded, "The ladies should respond to this request."[36]

After First Bull Run the paper called for a mid-course correction: "Havelocks are said to be a failure from the fact that the white material of which they are manufactured renders them conspicuous marks for the enemy to fire at. Therefore, ladies, use muslin of a darker shade in your labor of love."[37] A harsher verdict came after the war. "The ladies of our native county sent us a full complement of Havelocks, and a useless appendage they were," wrote the historian of Company K of the First Pennsylvania Reserves. "[One soldier] said they were 'Moighty noice to corrie me tobaccy in.' We sent home thanks and threw the 'head-bags' away."[38]

The references to "Blues" in some unit monikers hints that at least those companies arrived in some kind of uniform. Perhaps, as was the case with a unit from Warren, ladies' societies turned bolts of blue cloth into soldier apparel. Whether any of the Eleventh's companies actually left their homes in something other than civilian clothes and havelocks has been lost to history. Yet at some point following the shoe distribution in Camp Wright, the men received a formal issue of army togs. They would get knapsacks and haversacks later.[39]

Pennsylvania's codes specified that soldiers called up for long-term service "shall severally receive a full suit of uniform, consisting of one cap or hat, one stock and clasp, one vest, one uniform coat, two shirts, one pair of woolen overalls, one pair of linen overalls, one pair of stockings, one pair of socks, one frock [coat], and one pair of shoes." There was often a large difference between what regulations called for and what was actually issued—or used. The stock, a kind of giant leather collar meant to keep a soldier's head up and facing forward, was universally discarded.

Nor did all Pennsylvania volunteers get regulation blue coats in 1861. Cadet gray was issued to some regiments until the confusion of First Bull Run forced standardization.[40]

There was general dissatisfaction with the clothing Pennsylvania's soldiers drew in the early months of the war. A Johnstownian called the situation "a shame and disgrace. . . . Some of the shoes furnished are of the coarsest kind, poorly made, and often go to pieces in a few days. I have seen the whole sole drop off, if a sole it could be called, being composed of a piece of oak shingle between two pieces of thin, inferior leather. . . . The pantaloons are not much better. I have seen them actually torn by drawing them on. . . . The blouses or roundabouts are made of very thin and flimsy material, being nothing more nor less than heavy blue flannel."[41]

If Gallagher's men received such poor items at Camp Wright, their letters home understated problems. Hinting that the troops did not make a smart appearance, one soldier referred to regimental drill as "ragamuffin drill." There was at least sufficient quantity. A recruit who joined the unit in late July wrote home that "we have Plenty Clothes more then we Nead." Problems with quality seem to have vanished by the end of the year, when the same soldier observed, "I have more Clothes Now than Ever I had At one Time yet and our Pants are made of fine stuff." He may have been writing about an issue doled out in late October at a different encampment—Camp Pierpont—which a private in another Pennsylvania Reserves regiment described as "first rate," and of "a dark blue collar [color]. The coat is a frock coat worth a bout 8 dollars."[42]

A more critical equipment issue, about which the Eleventh's members mightily complained, involved weapons. Put very briefly, the Civil War's appalling casualty rates stemmed in part from the development of *rifled* arms—those with their barrels grooved so as to put a spin on the projectile. These could shoot farther and more accurately than smoothbore muskets and artillery, and their ultimate dominance of the battlefield made Napoleonic concepts of linear warfare obsolete. Although one analysis has argued against attributing changes in the era's military thinking to the rifle alone, defenders nonetheless gained enormous tactical advantage over attackers. Soldiers protected by even modest entrenchments and armed with rifles could punish attackers at long range, and even after gaining this costly experience, some commanders of assault columns failed to apply it.[43]

The weapon that brought about this situation evolved from the first-generation rifled arms brought from Europe by German and Swiss immigrants. By the mid-1700s, the designs had evolved into what history termed the Pennsylvania or Kentucky rifle. This long-barreled weapon made a mark in the Revolutionary War, even though few actually saw service. That war was largely a musket affair—rifles tended to be highly individual pieces of craftsmanship. Smoothbore arms, easier to make and maintain, fit the military's need for cheap, standard weapons that could be bought in quantity and easily maintained.[44]

Frontier tall tales overstated the case for the rifle's accuracy, but sober examples of battlefield performance showed that the weapon had military merit. In 1792, George Washington authorized the creation of a 325-man rifle battalion, and by 1803 Harpers Ferry craftsmen were building rifles in limited quantities. But even as rifles became more standardized and their components interchangeable, technical drawbacks kept the smoothbore in favor. The flintlock igniting system's jolting action, unpredictable timing, and frequent misfires reduced any firearm's accuracy and reliability. And for a lead ball to meet the grooves of a rifled barrel, it had to be rammed deep into the breech from the muzzle and partly flattened or deformed, a time-consuming act compared to the smoothbore's loose-fit loading.[45]

Pennsylvania gunsmiths worked out a simple solution to the latter problem. They wrapped the ball in a greased patch, which easily slid into a grooved barrel and had the added benefit of cleaning powder buildup on its journey to the breech. When the gun was fired, the patch contacted the rifling, spinning the projectile.[46]

The gunsmiths also replaced flintlock ignition with the more reliable percussion system—a tiny metal "cap" of mercury fulminate that sparked when the hammer fell, touching off the powder charge. More research brought perhaps the deadliest improvement: the famous "minié ball," or bullet. This tapered cylinder with a hollow base could be easily tucked into an unfouled rifle barrel; the gunpowder burst forced its chassis to flare out, contacting the rifling while also sealing the bore against a loss of pressure and at least partially scouring the barrel. The bullet's aerodynamic shape increased range and accuracy; its soft lead body habitually flattened on impact, creating gaping wounds.[47]

Although the Civil War was fought in this era of the modern rifle, few Yankees or Rebels had them at the start. Because it took months for the North and South to expand or establish arms-making industries, ordnance officers at first relied on anything at hand in state arsenals. An early shipment of arms to Pennsylvania volunteers—the invoice was dated 20 April 1861—was deemed "totally unfit for service" by their commanding general. One of his colonels reported, "Some five or six have had the springs broken in cocking them." Another stated that most of the muskets had "either broken locks or holes through the barrels, bayonets not to fit the pieces, &c." He underscored his protest by remarking "that in one of my companies alone fifty-four muskets had to be repaired, perhaps at my own expense." His regiment's situation was still preferable to that in the Second Pennsylvania. There the colonel reported: "The number [of muskets] thus defective and useless are two hundred and forty-six. The balance are reported to be only in tolerable condition, and if taken apart and critically examined would no doubt be found to be unsafe and useless."[48]

Similar feelings abounded at Camp Wright when a trainload of arms was unloaded at Hulton station and passed out on Monday, 15 July. As noted in the *Alleghanian,* "They are the old style flint-lock muskets altered to percussion, and the [*Pittsburgh Dispatch*] says that considerable dissatisfaction existed among the men on ascertaining their quality."[49]

Curtin was probably relieved to be able to deliver even these. At the time the worn guns were being issued at Camp Wright, a major of the Pennsylvania militia was scouring the western counties for "such old style and imperfect U.S. war implements as may be scattered among the people of this community." As the *Harrisburg Telegraph* noted: "As the arms are gathered, they are deposited with contractors in Lancaster and Philadelphia," where they were to be "remodeled in a manner to make them the most effective weapons in the service." Besides upgrading flintlocks to percussion systems, plugging any empty screw holes with melted brass, gunsmiths could re-bore and rifle some smoothbore barrels to accept the new standard .58-caliber minié bullet.

Yet many old weapons were simply worn or rusted beyond the point of being made serviceable by modification, and Camp Wright seems to have landed a supply of these. Also lacking was any sign of the pay the men had been promised. When, within a few weeks, the unit moved on toward Washington and the seat of war, "the most exciting topics of discussion in our camp now, are the probability of . . . receiving the amount due it from Pa., and the same uncertainty as to whether we get better arms than those furnished us at Camp Wright."[50]

The soldiers at Camp Wright at least had plenty of diversions. "Soldiers must and will have fun," a correspondent wrote home, "and to have it every device is resorted to—dancing, card-playing, boxing, and almost every other 'ing.'" Not every offer of amusement was welcome, however, and the recruits seem to have been quick to turn out traveling charlatans. "Last week a couple of impostors came into camp with 'blowing' and 'lifting' machines," the same correspondent continued, "for the purpose of fooling foolish soldiers out of a little 'change' that they needed badly though for other uses; but they left in 'double quick time,' amid groans and hisses. Since that we have not been bothered with any more of that class."[51]

Recruits had little trouble obtaining brief furloughs to return home. Civilians made frequent trips to deliver gifts and practical items. Cambria Guardsman Thompson Carney, a gray-eyed, brown-haired carpenter born about 1837, brought his violin along and proved himself a virtuoso entertainer. "Carney, our fiddler, contributes largely to the general good humor of the boys," a correspondent wrote home. "He is death on cat-gut." His Company A audience swelled when Litzinger brought four recruits back from his early July visit to Cambria County; Lt. Robert McCoy rounded up seven more on his own trip home. Some in the unit were disappointed more had not joined, but the *Democrat & Sentinel* noted "that this is the harvesting season with our farmers, and that all the young men in the country are engaged in assisting them in getting in their crops."[52]

Irvin McDowell's 21 July repulse at Manassas—First Bull Run—hastened the Eleventh's movement east. Originally ordered to leave for Camp Curtin, at Harrisburg, on 25 July, the departure date was moved ahead by two days. Entraining at Hulton station, the unit proceeded from Pittsburgh through many soldiers' native counties. In Cambria County, the train stopped at Wilmore for fifteen minutes, at which time friends and relatives of Company A's members "had a full opportunity to bid the gallant soldiers farewell. Many affecting scenes, we learn, occurred." Some boarded the train and stayed with the company until Altoona, about twenty-four rail miles.[53]

Several stayed for good, signing up with the regiment. Twenty-one-year-old Philip Andrew Lantzy was one of them. He hailed from Carrolltown, a coal-rich, hilly region north of Ebensburg. Its population in 1860 was about 1,400, and it was considered a fast-growing area.[54] A contemporary description gives a sense of the town:

> Carrolltown is eight miles north of Ebensburg, and is connected with it by a plank road. It is located on an eminence. The original Carrolltown lies on the south side of the hill; but the part of the village more lately built extends over the crest of the hill,

down the northern slope into the valley beyond. It is about half a mile in length. The Catholic church is a large brick building, situated on the highest ground in the village, and about midway between the extreme ends. The public school-house is similarly located, and stands on the opposite side of the street from the church. It contains a thriving population, and is surrounded by a productive country and thrifty farmers.[55]

Lantzy's parents met on shipboard when traveling to America from Wallbach, Canton Aargau, Switzerland, in 1816. Philip's father, Joseph Lenzi, had apparently been married before, as he brought a one-and-a-half-year-old daughter, Theresa, with him to America. The child's mother presumably died during or shortly after giving birth. Exactly a week after arriving, Lenzi married Mary Ursula Bitter in Philadelphia's Holy Trinity Catholic Church. They settled first in Lancaster County, then moved to Cambria County, building a hillside home in what by 1840 became Carroll Township. Joseph Lenzi became a prosperous and respected farmer. Theresa was joined by eight siblings, with Philip, born in December 1840, being the youngest. Their last name was anglicized to various spellings: Lantcy, Lancy, Lantzey, and Lantzy. The family used the last.[56]

Carroll township's German-speaking population was education-conscious. It had established six schools by 1860, when one writer noted that "The inhabitants, tho' the German is the language of their firesides, manifest a praiseworthy desire to give their children a good English education." This was the case with Philip Lantzy's family, for his surviving letters are all in English.[57]

Lantzy left home with a trunk and carpet sack, but without his parents' approval. "Tell Father and Mother," he wrote to his brother about a week after joining the regiment, "that they Should Not take it hard for it is to Late Now for to think hard of me going A way for I was Not Contended A bout home Eny more."[58]

He did not address slavery in his letters, but he made it clear that he abhorred secessionism. "I am gone to Fight for the Stars and Stripes of our union," he wrote at one point, "whitch must and Shall be preserved[.] our Country is in great Disturbence and I think it is gods will that the Rebels Should be made [to] Come under our Stars and Stripes[.] God save the UNION."[59]

Crowds greeted the train from Camp Wright, with Lantzy onboard, at every large station along the way. It arrived at Camp Curtin at 10 P.M. Although this was the principal collecting ground for Pennsylvania soldiers, the Eleventh stayed there for only about a day and a half, the men receiving knapsacks, haversacks, and other small accoutrements to complete their kit. They then boarded cars for Baltimore, again arriving at 10 P.M. The next morning, the unit marched through that once turbulent city to the Baltimore & Ohio depot. Their latest train brought them early that evening to a new campsite just north of Washington. "Tents were soon furnished but not in time for Company A to pitch theirs," one correspondent wrote, "hence we slept on the ground with the canvass for covering."[60]

After a week here, the new camp "seems almost as much like home to us as Camp Wright did," in the words of one soldier. He allowed, however, that "we have been obliged to dispense with many of the comforts and conveniences of our former abode. In the woods here no one has any boards that we can 'take' to floor our tents with. Then we have no stoves, but do all our cooking over regular camp fires, which is all very nice—when it don't rain. And last, but not least, we must eat our dry bread without the aid of mountain butter."[61]

More was missing than butter. Pay still was not forthcoming, and the poor arms remained an issue. On Monday, 29 July, the regiment was sworn into Federal service, and several soldiers vented their feelings. One correspondent wrote: "In some companies the men refused to leave the State service until they were paid off, but by Tuesday evening all except three or four had taken the required oath. We have received a promise of our pay the last of this week, or the first of next. We are also promised better arms than those we now have."[62]

Finding and issuing those new weapons were among McCall's first tasks once the Reserves concentrated near Washington. Morale was boosted by the appearance of the first shipments, weapons turned in by three-month regiments on muster-out, but the wait for their distribution was frustrating. The Cambria Guards and the Brady Guards were especially impatient; as flank companies they expected to receive rifles. Yet McCall was evidently misinformed on the condition of the newly received arms and got his first look at them only when Captains Litzinger and Brady formed their companies outside the camp arsenal on Saturday, 3 August. Finally seeing the weapons, McCall decided on the spot that they needed thorough refits, and Litzinger and Brady marched their disappointed men back to their camps. A small mitigation, perhaps, was the paymaster's arrival on Tuesday, 6 August. "Our company was paid off by the State, and the balance of the regiment was paid the day following," one soldier wrote home. "Each private received $15.03." Federal pay started arriving late in the month.[63]

A few days later, the Eleventh marched through the city of Washington proper to a new camp on the Potomac River. The site was a small Maryland village named Tennallytown (later Tenleytown), located about three miles from Georgetown. Sited at the junction of the Rockville, Poolesville, and Georgetown Roads, Tennallytown was about a mile and a half from the impressive Chain Bridge, which spanned the Potomac River and over which a Rebel assault was constantly feared. The bridge came to be a heavy fortification of its own: contemporary pictures show a well-screened smoothbore gun emplacement on the Maryland side positioned to blast canister shot across the bridge causeway.[64]

Tennallytown, according to a piece in the *Alleghanian,* got its name because "in lieu of streets, [it] has alleys laid out hither and thither through its limits. These alleys are to the number of ten—hence the name, Ten-alley-town." In fact, the town was named for John Tennally, a late-eighteenth-century resident and tavernkeeper. The large new military facility, situated "on an open, elevated piece of ground," was officially called Camp Tennally.[65] Here the soldiers entered a new, more serious phase of their army careers. One letter-writer noted that the men "have dispensed with their Camp Wright pastimes and amusements, and are beginning to play the soldier in dead earnest." The August weather was hot but good water was nearby.[66]

The men had lots of company because the various regiments of the Pennsylvania Reserves were being collected here to be further drilled and eventually organized into brigades. They were also learning how to perform on the parade ground. On 20 August, the regiments thus far collected were reviewed by General McClellan, commander of the newly formed Army of the Potomac, and President Abraham Lincoln, the latter accompanied by cabinet members. McClellan was decked out, as he described it in a letter to his wife, "for the first time in full tog, chapeau, epaulettes, etc—& flattered myself 'we' did it well." A member of the Seventh Pennsylvania Reserves wrote home how McClellan, escorted by a company of Regular Army dragoons, passed "up and down before each line, nothing escaping the notice of his clear keen eye."[67]

Philip Lantzy wrote of the scene: "We was out on Parade on the 20th and and [sic] we was in spected By General McClelen he is the Commander of the Penna Reserved Corps and there was A Bout 9 thousand Soldiers in the field of infantry and A Bout 20 pieces of artillery and A Company of Cavalry." The view was, Lantzy noted to the home folk, "A Nicer sight than Ever Eny of you will See on the Mountain I am shure." He added: "General McClelen . . . Rode a Round us But we was A

Lined with in A Bout 25 yds and A Bout 2 thousand in Each Roe and the President of the united states was A Long I Seen Aberham Lincoln To[o] and there was so many men there that I Cant Tell you how many Generals was there."[68]

The Pennsylvania Reserves had passed their first examination. In an address to his troops read at a dress parade the next day, McCall observed that "both the General and the President have expressed to me their unqualified approval of your soldierlike appearance on review, and of the discipline thus manifestly shown to exist in the corps."[69]

In common with many regiments at the start of the war—before hard campaigning taught otherwise—the Pennsylvania Reserves were overloaded with equipment, all of which required transportation. "There is A Bout 25 wagons to Each Regiment," Lantzy noted, "and There is A Big Road Runs A Long A Bout 100 yds from our Camp And there is So manny wagons and Bugeys Running A Long ther the Road is thick with them." At this stage of the war, regiments were allowed five wagons for headquarters gear and a pair for each company. The numbers stayed the same until August 1863, when the army cut the wagon allotment to between three and six, depending on a regiment's musket strength.[70]

To Lantzy, soldiering at this point seemed idyllic. "it is Nice and Cool here Now," he wrote home. "I think that there will Not Be Eny Danger Now Eny more we have Plenty to Eat and Drink here and we Need Not go out in the wet onlly when we are on Gard But we onlly Get on gard A Bout 1 Time in A weak and that is Not hard if I Like it as well on as I have So far." He added, perhaps in response to appeals from home, "I Could Not Think of coming home unless we were [h]onorably Dis Charged which I Think will Be be fore Long."[71]

Andrew Lewis was often thinking about his own family. His daughter Mary Frances' letters stressed how much she missed him. "I hope that this dreadful war will soon be over and you will get home safe," she wrote in one missive, "for oh papy should eny thing happen I know it would kill mammy and when I was sick I was so fraid I would die and not get to see you but I am spared and I hope to see you again." She detailed how "thare is some soldiers in town and you ought to hav seen Jackey the first time he seen them he thought one of them was you."[72]

Himself musing of little Jackey, Lewis wrote to his wife that he was "determined . . . to send him to West Point to giv him a milentry education So my mind [is] maid up on that scoor and I hop[e] you will not hav eny objections . . . and that you will try and bend his mind in that way whilst he is young and tell him Pap is agoing to make [a] soldier of him . . . and that Pap will fetch him a big drum for him."[73]

With Mary Frances' help, Jackey scribbled out a drawing for his distant father. "Jackey sends you some flowers," was written alongside. Older hands also helped him form a plaintive message on another sheet. "Dear Pappy," it read, "come home to Jackey."[74]

Though far from home, the new soldiers did not have to deal with hunger. The Union camp ration was the envy of many a European soldier and, from 1862 onward, of many hungry Confederates. At the start of the war, soldiers every day received three-fourths of a pound of pork or bacon, or one and a fourth pound of fresh or salt beef. Each man was further entitled to eighteen ounces of bread or flour, or a pound of hard bread, or one and a fourth pounds of corn meal. Companies further shared regular issues of beans and rice or hominy; these were sometimes substituted with dehydrated potatoes and mixed vegetables. Additionally, every day each company divided ten pounds of coffee (or one-half pound of tea), fifteen pounds of sugar, four quarts of vinegar, and two quarts of salt; units also received issues of soap and candles. When the regulations were revised in August 1861—the same time the Eleventh set up camp in Tennallytown—the bread/flour issue was upped to twenty-two ounces, and individual soldiers were to receive a pound of potatoes three times per week.[75]

One Cambria Guardsman's letter to the *Democrat & Sentinel* showed that the early war commissary was in line with regulations. "Our rations still continue to be of the most substantial kind; viz, soft and hard bread, beef, pork, beans, rice &c," he wrote. "A few days since the commissary commenced issueing hominy, which when well cooked makes an excellent dish for a soldier. Potatoes and molasses have also been added to our rations." Despite twenty-five wagons' worth of equipment, there was a lack of good utensils and stoves. The same writer added that "If our arrangements for cooking what we receive were as good as the quality of the articles received, no one could fare better either in or out of the service of Uncle Sam."[76]

The situation may have been better in Company B—the Indiana National Guards—one of whose anonymous correspondents wrote home, "The Guards have the best cook in the Regiment." But a comrade assessed the situation differently. "Every day it is the same," he complained. "Bread, meat, coffee, and bean soup. If you can send us some elderberries, corn, tomatoes, or anything of that sort . . . a little butter when the weather gets colder, would be very pleasant."[77]

A Dickson Guards veteran remembered long after the war that his rations sometimes included "compressed vegetable soup," likely a reference to what quartermasters called "desiccated vegetables," and which attained varying levels of popularity. A Massachusetts volunteer later described this ration as a two- or three-inch-wide cube, weighing about an ounce, "of a sheet or block of vegetables, which had been prepared, and apparently kiln-dried, as sanitary fodder for the soldiers." Soaked in water, the individual vegetables swelled to almost their natural size: "It seemed to show . . . layers of cabbage leaves and turnip tops stratified with layers of sliced carrots, turnips, parsnips, a bare suggestion of onions—and some other known vegetable quantities."[78]

In spite of the abundance of camp food, the men frequently bought victuals from residents living nearby. "Plenty to eat can be obtained from the inhabitants, at reasonable prices," one soldier wrote. "We usually fill our knapsacks when leaving Camp, with crackers &c. but these are scarcely ever all eaten, the soldiers preferring to buy while out." The men also learned to forage. Company A spent one Saturday "making a grand charge on a 40-acre cornfield, which is at this season readily conceded to be contraband, by the boys."[79]

Elements of each regiment at Camp Tennally were detailed for manual labor known in army parlance as "fatigue duty." A major project involved building Fort Pennsylvania, a set of earthworks between Tennallytown and the Chain Bridge. It was erected on property owned by one Giles Dyer, whose house was razed to make room for the fort. After removing the building, details went to work with axes to clear acres of adjoining timber. Watching the men work, an observer was reminded "of a large set of hands at work cutting wheat, so fast and steadily does the work progress. The large trees falling in such quick succession appears to rouse the men to be seized with a mania for destroying more, merely for the fun of seeing them fall; and then they labor very hard." Engineers then marked perimeter outlines, around which a twelve-foot-wide, eight-foot-deep ditch was dug, the dirt from it packed into ten-foot-high, fifteen-foot-thick walls with "no foothold . . . left between the ditch and embankment." Within the Eleventh Reserves, the earth-moving job fell to pairs of men detailed from each company, one equipped with a spade, one with a pick. For an abatis, "large limbs and tree tops are placed around on the outside of the ditch, pinned to the ground, the small branches being cut off, which causes [the fort] to present a very formidable appearance." It initially housed fifteen cannon, mounted *en barbette*, that is, able to "fire over a parapet without an embrasure." At least one of them was rifled and could hit targets in Alexandria, across the Potomac, if necessary. The site was deliberately chosen for its height; at 420 feet above sea level, it commanded the river and the Fredericktown and Old Brookeville Roads. More guns were expected. Andrew Lewis wrote home that the fort "will hav about 40 cannon and hold about five thousand men and I defy the Devil to take it." Although the heavy forests might hide approaching troops, observers counted on spotting huge clouds of dust kicked up by any enemy force marching on the fort.[80]

After completing this project, details went to work constructing two forts northeast of Tennallytown. Their construction would make "a complete chain of forts around Washington, which command the whole country in a manner that defies access from any point." Fort Pennsylvania later figured in history as one of those Confederate Maj. Gen. Jubal Early attacked during his July 1864 raid on Washington. By then, however, it had been renamed in honor of Maj. Gen. Jesse L. Reno, killed at South Mountain in September 1862.[81]

The rifles were finally distributed at Camp Tennally early on Wednesday, 7 August. The Eleventh's flank companies shouldered their altered flintlocks and marched to McCall's headquarters. There, wrote one correspondent, Brady's and Litzinger's men "exchanged their old guns for rifled minie muskets, of the most improved pattern." Another added that "the rest of the regiment will be furnished with the best improved Springfield musket."[82]

Civil War references to arms are often imprecise, but the description indicates the flank companies received the government-made "rifle musket," either the Model 1855 or the Model 1861. As the latter was brand new at the time, and the Eleventh's flank companies were getting arms turned in by three-month men, it is likely that Litzinger's and Brady's charges received the older model. Both weighed about nine pounds, were fifty-six inches long, and used the new army standard .58-caliber minié bullet.[83] The 1855 had a brass patch box built into the butt stock, an anomaly after the Minié's introduction made patches unnecessary, whereas the 1861 eliminated the feature. The 1855 also had a chamber routed under the lock-plate to house the Maynard tape-primer system, essentially a roll of paper "caps" similar to those found in later toy guns, which could substitute for standard percussion caps. But the waterproof metal caps hung on through the war, and the 1861 eliminated the tape-primer system altogether.[84]

The reference to the "best improved Springfield musket" being given to the nonflank companies identified the Model 1842, the U.S. Army's first percussion shoulder arm as well as its last smoothbore. This was essentially an update—but only via its firing method—of earlier flint-locks, including those converted to percussion systems distributed at Camp Wright.[85] The Model 1842 had an overall length of 57¾ inches; its 42-inch-long barrel was held in place on the walnut stock with three polished iron bands. Like the flank companies' rifles, it weighed about nine pounds and accepted an angular bayonet, which fit over the muzzle and was clamped in place. Its accuracy was conceded to be poor. An 1860 manual noted, "in a general action, where accuracy of fire is not attain-able, it may be made effective up to 300 yards; beyond 400 yards it is use-less." Tests a century later indeed yielded zero hits in fifteen tries aiming at a six-foot-square target 400 yards away. The model was, however, preferable to an old modified flintlock. And if smoothbores in general lacked the range of rifles, they were still lethal in close combat, more so when loaded with a common ammunition mix called "buck and ball," a .69-caliber ball topped with three buckshot. The result was, a later writer noted, that "At short range . . . you had four chances to hit someone." Some soldiers improved those odds. At Gettysburg, a New Jersey regi-ment discarded musket balls completely and simply filled up new car-tridges with ten to twenty-five buckshot apiece. The idea even took hold among bullet manufacturers, one of whom devised a three-piece missile that saw limited service.[86]

Word that they were to receive Springfield muskets must have been welcome news to the men outside Litzinger's and Brady's companies. McCall reported to General McClellan on 2 September: "The Eleventh regiment, Colonel T. F. Gallagher, nine hundred and forty-two strong, is armed with the altered flint-locks, except the flank companies, which have rifles. . . . The members of this regiment have great aversion to their old muskets."[87]

By this time, Camp Tennally hosted a wide variety of weaponry, McCall's report showing a mix of arms distributed across different com-panies in each regiment. Like the Eleventh, several regiments—the Third, Fourth, Tenth, and Twelfth Reserves—had their flank companies armed with rifles, the rest with muskets of varying quality. Company A of the Ninth Reserves was superbly armed by 1861 standards, its men wielding

Sharps breechloaders. The flank companies of the First Reserves, which were "promised the Belgian rifle" according to McCall, were destined for disappointment. Once introduced, this shoulder arm earned a reputation as unreliable, even useless.[88]

In the case of the Eleventh, the Springfield muskets were apparently distributed to the nonflank companies on Thursday, 19 September. They had a good effect on Gallagher's men. McCall noted in a later report that "This is a well drilled regiment, and with the improved arms, with which it is now supplied, would be very effective."[89]

Most new soldiers resented fatigue details and fortification building. One Camp Tennally unit used melted bullets to fashion a regimental "badge" portraying a pickaxe, shovel, and broom. Many recruits had signed on to fight and win what they thought would be a quick war and were impatient to get to grips with the enemy. Gallagher, who sensed a hard road ahead, tried to instill realism. Long after the war, an acquaintance remembered him telling some of the men that by the time their three years were up, they would be doing their best to avoid combat. He was also quoted as predicting that perhaps only half of the regiment's thousand men would return home.[90]

In spite of the drudgery, the natural excitement of the times translated into many false alarms. At Camp Tennally drums frequently called the regiments to quarters in the middle of the night, followed by orders to stand down. "We resign ourselves to our blankets again," a soldier wrote, "and dream of the fierce fighting we didn't do." Faulty intelligence was usually the culprit. One evening in early August a staff officer told McCall of seeing a Confederate force nearby. After a tense night, a morning reconnaissance showed that what were "supposed to be camps of the insurgents proved to be, under the scrutiny of the glass, only clusters of whitewashed houses, negro cabins, and fences on the opposite side of the Potomac."[91]

Amid the confusion of these phantom assaults, Gallagher kept his men drilling. With an eye on preventing the spread of disease, he instructed each company to police the campground to ensure sanitation. A letter to the *Democrat & Sentinel* detailed a slightly different daily itinerary than that put in place at Camp Wright: "At 4½ A.M. reveille, Co. drill 5 to 6; breakfast at 7; regimental drill from 7½ to 9 or from 9 to 10½; dinner at 1 P.M.; company drill from 2 to 3[;] regimental from 4 to 5½; guard mounting at 6; 6½ dress parade; retreat at sundown; 7 supper[;] 9 tatoo, and at 10 taps."[92]

When not training or doing fatigue duty, companies were detailed two at a time to go on picket, patrolling the areas outlying the Fort Pennsylvania area. They also spent some time guarding the principal Potomac crossing near their camp. John M. Loor, a musician in Company H, wrote home on 8 August that "we are agoing to the Potomac river today to guard the chain Brige," adding that Gallagher's regiment was to relieve the Ninth Reserves.[93]

Loor, who hailed from a home on Maple Avenue in Greensburg, was about seventeen at the time he signed up as a drummer in Daniel Kistler's company. As his family was poor, he probably saw the pay as an incentive—he sent most of his salary home. Before the war, he helped his ill father run a small confectionary store. His thoughts in his letters occasionally turned to his father's health, as well as to that of his younger brother Frank, only six at the time the war began, deaf since infancy and unable to talk. "[I] would only want to know how you are a getting along," he wrote his mother at one point, "wether Frank has lerned how to talk or Knot and how dody is getting a long." He acknowledged occasional bouts of stomach trouble but emphasized that his health was good. Loor cautioned his parents to disregard stories about sickness in camp unless he confirmed them. "If you have here any thing like that about me you must never belive it," he wrote, "knot unless I write it my Self for there is a good many sorry fellows that don't do any thing else but raise fallse reports[.]"[94]

Standing guard was—and presumably still is—one of the great rituals of soldier life. The new troops found it a predictable mix of boredom and excitement. A soldier in a Schuylkill County regiment left an account of sentinel duty near Washington at about the time the Eleventh was being formed. The guard "permits a person to come to within twelve or fifteen paces of his post, and then commands him to 'halt?' and asks, 'who comes there?' The answer will generally be, 'a friend.' The sentinel commands, 'advance, friend, and give the countersign.' The person advances, and leaning over the point of the bayonet of the sentry, gives the password, (the guard must always receive it a [*sic*] 'charge bayonet,') and proceeds on his way."

A visitor's failure to know the countersign caused the sentry to call for the sergeant of the guard. Should an intruder refuse to stop "after being warned several times . . . you draw trigger on him and of course kill him if you can." New sentinels made memorable mistakes, especially at night. The Schuylkill soldier described how one comrade on evening guard saw "some twenty yards from him, what was apparently a man, standing and silently gazing at him. He demanded 'who came there,' but received no reply. He called the attention of a sentinel near him to the matter, and together they marched with charged bayonets against the immovable and silent 'what is it,' and, with true soldierly courage, gallantly ran their bayonets in a small cedar tree."[95] An Ebensburger serving in Missouri early in the war wrote home of a stump near camp with fifteen bullet holes in it, the victim of nervous sentries with "great imaginative powers."[96]

Fort Pennsylvania companies were usually detailed as pickets in twenty-four-hour shifts, platoons taking turns on watch. Soldiers from the Eleventh Reserves found their early watches uneventful. "We started out on Friday evening, and returned to camp at 8 P.M. on Saturday," a Cambria Guardsman wrote home of one experience. "Co. A guarded about a mile and a half of a road. None of the pickets were in any wise disturbed, and we returned without even a sight of a secesher."[97]

Within a week, however, the same company's pickets stopped two men driving a herd of eighty-five cattle, evidently trying to cross the Chain Bridge. Something about them excited suspicion, for the pair were arrested and the cattle confiscated. The latter allegedly "were designed for the use of [Confederate Gen. Joseph] Johns[t]on's command, along the Potomac," a soldier wrote home. On their turn at guard duty, Company C pickets stopped and arrested two men who turned out to be deserters from a New York regiment.[98]

Gallagher kept the Eleventh's officers equally busy. Regimental commanders were supposed to establish officer-instruction schools among their company commanders, and Gallagher's met twice a week, presumably with tactical manuals in hand. The colonel sent McCall regular reports on each officer's proficiency and attendance. Another institution Gallagher established in August was that of the court-martial. Three soldiers of Fayette County's Company F were tried and convicted for insubordination stemming from an incident in which an officer—his name was not given in soldier letters—was kicked and subjected to "offensive language," including a threat on his life. The sentences varied, but all sent a message. At the close of regimental drill on the morning of Tuesday, 20 August one of the trio—Pvt. Thomas Jackson—was drummed out of the service. The others wore a ball and chain for ten days; one also had his pay stopped for that period. "Punishing these offenders has had a very salutary effect on the insubordinate spirits in the Reg't.," a correspondent noted.[99]

Possibly with the same incident in mind, Gallagher began to strictly enforce sections II and III of the Articles of War, which prohibited the use of profanity. Officers were fined a dollar and privates sixteen cents for the first offense. Repeat offenders were liable to a day's confinement. The punishments were put into place after a speech on the subject by the Reverend Dickson failed to have the desired effect.[100]

If pastoral counseling could not stamp out profanity, religion still played a prominent role in the lives of the men of the Eleventh. At Camp Wright, in the days before Gallagher's regiment was formed, ministers from other regiments had tended the soldiers. Some of the Cambria Guards attended services held by the chaplain of the three-month Erie Regiment in that unit's quarters. Eighteen others sought out a Catholic church four miles distant, their faith apparently undiminished even after learning they had walked in the wrong direction. "Quite a number are reading religious books" for diversion, one soldier-correspondent wrote to the *Alleghanian* from Camp Wright.[101]

Philip Lantzy frequently affirmed his religious conviction in his letters home: "My health is Good I hope we will all meet, if Not on Earth I hope it will Be in heaven. . . . I Do Not forget to Say My Prayers Every Evening and morning . . . I Got A Mettal from the Priest and I got a Scapular from [Lantzy's] Sister Maryann and she told me that you wanted me to Say the Five Wounds of our Savior I Do Say them Every Day and the Angel of the Lord Adored, and the Priest Gave me A Prayer and told me if I Said it Every Day that there would be No danger to say one our father to the Blessed Virgin Mary."[102]

Faith ran strongly in Lantzy, who sometimes knelt and prayed while on guard duty. "You must Not think That I have forgoten what the Misionery made us Promis under the Cross," he wrote home, "that we will Live as Catholics and die as Catholic[s] and I will Do What I Promised." Many contemporary Americans shared such a depth of faith; some Northerners attributed the Union defeat at First Bull Run to the Federal advance taking place on a Sunday.[103]

Given Gallagher's concerns with discipline, he and other officers at Camp Tennally must have especially eyed liquor as a troublemaker. There had been problems with drink even at Camp Wright, where alcohol was readily available outside the perimeter. A soldier in the Eleventh recalled a memorable June episode: "A fight occurred at Hulton station . . . ; some of the Erie boys made a charge on a lager beer saloon, tearing down the sign and handling the proprietors in a very promiscuous manner. In less than five minutes about two thousand men had congregated in the vicinity of the muss. The guard had to be called out . . . [and] several of the men received a bayonet gouge apiece before they could be quieted."[104]

Litzinger's Ebensburgers seem to have been well behaved during their Camp Wright stay. The Cambria Guards were summoned "several times to disperse crowds and quell riots," one member wrote home only four days after detraining at Hulton station.[105]

Even sober, some soldiers were clumsy or unlucky. Two men of the Eleventh Reserves—their names and companies were not given in the *Alleghanian's* account—were killed during the train journey to Camp Curtin. Riding on top of a rail car, they were "either crushed or knocked off" by a low bridge near Altoona. If alcohol did not have a hand in that episode, it certainly played a part when a drunken Second Pennsylvania Reserves private fell through a South Easton train platform onto a coal pile; he escaped without serious injury. One liquor merchant plagued that regiment for weeks. He followed the unit as it traveled, setting up shop a mile or so out of camp. Officers finally secured his banishment from the neighborhood.[106]

Sobriety was essential, particularly as the new soldiers had a habit of firing their weapons at inappropriate times. Riding through once-turbulent Baltimore on their way to Camp Tennally, soldiers of the Twelfth Pennsylvania Reserves fired an estimated twenty-five to thirty shots out of the train car windows. When the train stopped and their colonel investigated the shootings, every man denied firing. In the last car, however, the officer happened upon a private deliberately raising his musket and discharging it out the window. Ironically, the rough discipline the colonel handed out to the man resulted in the officer's court-martial. A witness for the prosecution—a comrade of the private whose ears had been boxed—testified that his friend asked him if it was alright to shoot out the window. He responded affirmatively, he testified, because "I knew nothing of an order prohibiting firing guns in the railway cars." In cross-examination, the colonel asked the witness: "Since you entered the service, and a gun was put in your hand, have you understood that you could fire it off when you pleased?" The witness answered no; the officer was eventually acquitted of this and other allegations of unofficerlike conduct.[107]

There were numerous accidental shootings. A Cambria County soldier serving in a three-month regiment "had his arm dreadfully shattered by the accidental discharge of a musket, while on the march to Martinsburg, Va., on the 2d inst.," the *Alleghanian* reported early in July. "Dr. Jackson, the Surgeon of the [Third] Regiment [Pennsylvania Volunteers], without a moment's delay had the wounded man carried off the road, and under the shade of a tree amputated the limb."[108]

Such accidents became an epidemic at Camp Tennally in late August. "Not a day passes that there is not more or less shots discharged in Camp by the careless handling of loaded muskets," one soldier wrote. "Thus far only two men has been injured, and that there has not been more accidents of the same kind seems like a miracle." Fatalities quickly followed this report. A soldier in the Tenth Reserves, while on guard duty, dropped his musket in such a way that it discharged into his own head, "killing him almost instantly." A Seventh Reserves soldier handling a loaded revolver shot himself in the forehead—the episode was not considered a suicide. In the Eleventh itself, a sentry accidentally shot Colonel Gallagher's horse in the neck. "The wound is not fatal and the animal will probably recover," a soldier-correspondent noted.[109]

The Pennsylvania Reserves would be kept together as a division— McCall's—with the fifteen regiments divided into three brigades. The First Brigade was headed by Brig. Gen. John F. Reynolds, later to die at Gettysburg in command of the Army of the Potomac's I Corps. The Third was led by Brig. Gen. Edward Otho Cresap Ord, a Regular Army artillery captain since 1850. A native Marylander, Ord had earned a West Point appointment from the District of Columbia. He played a role in the capture of John Brown at Harpers Ferry.[110] The Eleventh Reserves was placed in the Second Brigade commanded by Brig. Gen. George Gordon Meade.

Born in Spain of American parents in 1815, Meade was a hot-tempered, highly intelligent West Point graduate. Because he had received his appointment to the academy from Pennsylvania, he was put at McCall's disposal when the Civil War started. Although he brought service in Mexico and engineering credentials to his job, in late summer 1861 he had almost no pedigree as a field commander. This would change, of course: Meade was destined to lead the Army of the Potomac in its greatest hour, Gettysburg, and during its dark moments in the severe campaign of 1864. After the war, Rebel Gen. D. H. Hill called Meade "one of our most dreaded foes; he was always in deadly earnest, and he eschewed all trifling."[111]

But when the war began Meade was a relative nonentity, his looks a disappointment in a culture that tried to idealize its army officers. "His face is almost covered with beard, and his neck displays a leather stock that might have been used in the days of his ancestors," a newspaper correspondent wrote of him. "He is otherwise collarless, and his face is colorless, being of a ghastly pale, with thought, study, and anxiety marked upon his every lineament. . . . His nose is of the antique bend, [and] is the most prominent feature of the face."[112]

Meade soon made his presence felt. Gallagher had already drummed men out of the service and sent others to wear the ball and chain, but the Eleventh Reserves' experience of Regular Army discipline dated from the moment Meade took command. "Brig. Gen. Mead is very strict with his orders," a soldier-correspondent in the Eleventh Reserves wrote in September. "A soldier cannot go fifty rods along any of the roads, from his quarters, unless he has a pass, without being arrested by the patrol." Within six weeks, Meade himself was countersigning the passes hitherto issued by Gallagher. His signature came "provided that respectable personage be in a good humor and has pen and ink handy; otherwise it is not."[113]

A senior War Department official described Meade as "agreeable to talk with when his mind was free, but silent and indifferent to everybody when he was occupied." In such moments, Meade was "totally lacking in cordiality toward those with who he had business, and in consequence was generally disliked by his subordinates." Over time, Meade earned the enmity of some of the Eleventh's officers; Samuel Jackson once noted in his diary, "Reprimanded by General Meade very unjustly for having property destroyed." Meade's temper was such that after some soldiers complained about the general within his earshot, he allegedly promised "to get even with them come the next battle." A Massachusetts artillerist claimed that when an exhausted infantryman once accidentally bumped into Meade near a roadside campfire, the general drew his sword on the man.[114]

Part of the problem was that, like many Regular Army officers, Meade had little patience with volunteers. But nobody questioned Meade's courage, and if he seemed like a martinet, at least some of his bad temper stemmed from concern for his soldiers' lives. He felt that the training the Reserves received was insufficient, especially as most of the division's officers were elected. By and large, the Reserves officer corps was not deemed stellar, observers alleging that most commissions resulted from recruiting abilities rather than knowledge of tactics.[115]

Yet these men were risking their lives, and Meade avoided mentioning his lack of confidence in their skills in his first letters from Camp Tennally. When he finally vented his doubts, he railed that "They do not any of them, officers or men, seem to have the least idea of the solemn duty they have imposed upon themselves in becoming soldiers. Soldiers they are not in any sense of the word. Brave men they may be, and I trust in

God will prove themselves; but at this very moment . . . I doubt if any . . . realize in the slightest degree what they may have to meet."[116]

In addition to the Eleventh, Meade's brigade initially included the Third, Fourth, Seventh, and (briefly) Thirteenth Pennsylvania Reserves. The Third hailed from Philadelphia and Berks, Bucks, and Wayne Counties and was formed at Easton in June, as was the predominantly Philadelphian Fourth. The Seventh Reserves, formed at West Chester, was another regiment made up largely of recruits from Philadelphia and eastern Pennsylvania counties.[117]

The Thirteenth was placed with Meade for only about a week before being posted to Ord's Third Brigade. Recruited from the state's mountainous north, the regiment had several semi-official monikers. It was nicknamed Kane's Rifles after its founder and first colonel, Thomas L. Kane, and was referred to at times as the First Pennsylvania Rifles. It is best remembered as the "Bucktails," because each soldier pinned one—as evidence of marksmanship—to the side of his hat.[118]

The Bucktails were always superbly armed. At recruitment, each man brought his own rifle; they later received Sharps breechloaders and ended the war toting seven-shot Spencers. Active service for the Bucktails, who would be considered the cream of the Pennsylvania Reserves, began in June with a skirmish near Cumberland, Maryland; they (along with two other Pennsylvania Reserves regiments) were then attached to Nathaniel Banks' force near Harpers Ferry. They were sent to Tennallytown only in early October, though some elements may have arrived earlier in order to represent the regiment on the parade ground.[119]

It is likely that at least one Bucktails company or its color guard was at Camp Tennally for a grand 10 September review and ceremony when Curtin gave each regiment its "state colors"—large (70½ by 77¼ inches), yellow-fringed silk United States flags. Pennsylvania's coat of arms was painted in the center of the blue field, between groups of stars representing the thirty-four states of the complete Union. Each regiment's numbers— its separate Reserve Corps and Pennsylvania Volunteers designations— were also rendered in gold paint. The flags were made by Horstmann Brothers & Co. of Philadelphia and cost $65 each.[120]

There had been reviews and parades before, but the artillery salute given Curtin on this occasion was unforgettable to Philip Lantzy. In a breathless letter home he wrote:

> we was All out on Review the Day of the 10th of this month and There was Govener Curtin of Pennsylvania. . . . There was

A Bout Ten thousand of infantry There and there was A Regiment of Cavalry There and there was Twenty Four Pieces of Cannon There and we was in A Field A Bout A half A Mile from our Battery and so when Govener Curtin Came in they Fired the Cannons of The Battery[.] I Tell You that they made The Earth Trimble and they Fired A Bout 25 Times At the Battery[.] the Cannons were 12 Pounders . . . and then they Shot 25 times with the Cannons in The field . . . they were 6 and 12 Pounders[.] But it was A Nice Sight as Ever I Seen.[121]

The view was equally impressive at the other end of the regiment where the Brady Guards were stationed. Writing to a friend's father, Clarion County–born Thomas W. Sallade, now a private in Company K, opined like Lantzy that "I never saw a prettier sight[.] there was 12 regiments and one of artillery and two or three companies of cavalry." The farmer added that "Governer Curtan presented each regiment with a nice silk flag and when he was coming they fired ten shots from a battery which we have erected That was handy to where we was in the field and when he came the artillery fired 20 rounds as a salute."[122] General McClellan and President Lincoln also turned out for the ceremony, but the artillery salute and the day belonged to Curtin and the force he had created. For the latter the period of ruminating over "the fierce fighting we didn't do" was coming to a close.

Chapter 3

No More Bull Run Affairs

Great Falls, Dranesville, and the March to the Rappahannock

The Eleventh Pennsylvania Reserves' initiation to frontline soldiering came at Great Falls, Maryland, a site on the Potomac to
the northwest of Washington about fifteen miles from Camp
Tennally. It had been a tense spot since a day-long early-July
skirmish in which a Union soldier was killed. By late summer
1861, watching Great Falls became George McCall's responsibility. The Pennsylvania Reserves commander stationed regiments there for about ten days at a time. The men divided their
time between picketing and building field gun emplacements.

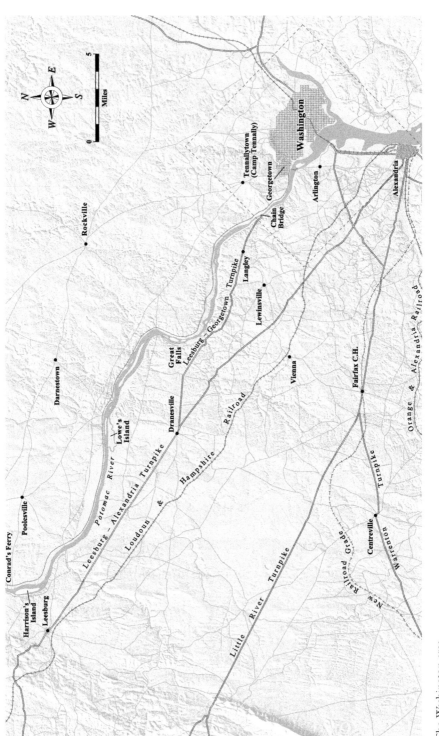

The Washington area

On this duty the soldiers received "marching rations" rather than camp fare. "While here we receive neither soft bread nor fresh meat," a member of the Seventh Reserves wrote home during his regiment's turn at Great Falls, "but live on hard pilot bread, and fat mess pork, and salty beef." If the rations were poor, the same soldier found the scenery "exceedingly wild and romantic. We are surrounded by dense pine forests. Very little of the land is cleared, as it is too barren to produce anything." Because of the latter factor, "a majority of the inhabitants in this vicinity are very poor, and do not live as well as the poorest persons in Pennsylvania."[1]

Before Gallagher's men had their turn at Great Falls, the Confederates again made their presence felt there. At daybreak on 4 September, when the Seventh Reserves were on picket duty, a detachment from the Washington (La.) Artillery quietly set up a battery—a three-inch rifled cannon and two 12-pound "Napoleon" howitzers—on a wooded hill on the Virginia bank. The artillerists trained the guns across the river, targeting a clutch of houses used as barracks about 1,500 yards away, adjacent to the Seventh's campsite. At about 8 A.M. they opened fire.[2]

The gunners had loaded ammunition known as "common shell," hollow rounds filled with black powder, which cast a shower of metal shards when they exploded. Those being fired from the Napoleons were probably equipped with an early time fuze, a hemp wick precut to a length that would burn for the estimated time desired. Shells fired from the three-inch rifle could have used the same type of fuze or a percussion one that ignited the internal charge when the projectile's nose hit something solid. Both were unreliable for a variety of reasons, but the ammunition was undeniably lethal.[3]

The Rebel barrage took the Seventh Reserves by surprise, one member of the regiment wrote home, "as we did not suppose they had any cannon near." Many Federals at first thought the sound of exploding shells were reports from nearby Union guns. "However, some of our men, who had run out of camp to see the fun soon returned in hot haste, informing us of various shot and shells, that had dropped in rather close proximity to them." Incoming rounds scattered the men inside the barracks; when someone waved a yellow hospital flag from one building, the Rebel gunners obligingly shifted aim to the adjacent tents. The Federal cannons tried to respond, but being smoothbores they lacked the range to reach the rifled gun on the opposite bank. Arriving on the field, McCall ordered up rifled artillery of his own. Before these could get into action the Confederates limbered their guns, having fired more than a hundred rounds in about forty-five minutes. No Union fatalities were reported, but one man in the Seventh Reserves "received a deep flesh wound in the arm, and several . . . made very narrow escapes, from the pieces of flying shell."[4]

Gallagher's men and the rest of the Pennsylvania Reserves had a week to ponder this episode before combat again visited units stationed near Camp Tennally. On 11 September, elements of the Seventy-ninth New York and the Fifth Wisconsin Infantry, under Union Brig. Gen. William Smith, reconnoitered across the Potomac, crossing the Chain Bridge and marching to Lewinsville. There they skirmished with cavalry under the command of then-Brig. Gen. J. E. B. Stuart, who was in charge of the Rebel army's outposts. Fire from a Confederate battery killed and wounded a few Union soldiers, and Smith withdrew in orderly fashion, a fact McClellan celebrated. "They behaved most admirably under fire," the latter wrote General-in-Chief Winfield Scott. Invoking the memory of July's rout at Manassas he added: "We shall have no more Bull Run affairs."[5]

In their quarters the Eleventh Reserves could hear the cannon fire from the fight at Lewinsville. Many wanted to join the action, some having already christened their untried regiment the "Bloody Eleventh," apparently hoping for battlefield acclaim. But as Philip Lantzy noted in a letter, "we was Not Called on for we had to Go out on Picket That Evening and we had to stay till The Evening of the 12th." Lantzy allowed that "that Battle was Not A Large one" though he emphasized the Federal perception that the attackers "Run of[f] as they allways Do."[6] This eagerness for a fight extended to the officers as well. Lieutenant Andrew Lewis chafed at what was essentially garrison duty: "I . . . would rather help to go after the rebbles than to be housed up in the citey."[7]

Lewis had shaved years off his age when signing up, but others reversed the process. Company F Capt. Everard Bierer reported that on 30 September 1861 his company received several Fayette County recruits whom state mustering officers had "inspected and Sworn into Service, uniformed and Equipped at Harrisburg. . . . At this time I did not know their ages nor whether their Parents were willing for them to join the army or not, but supposed they were, for various Reasons." Upon arriving at Camp Tennally, an officer prepared to muster them into Federal service. But "after ascertaining that those persons above named were minors, he refused to administer the oath to them, and said they must be discharged and sent home unless the written consent of their Parents could be obtained." For some reason, Bierer brought this matter straight to Meade, going over Gallagher's head—not the last time he would circumvent the regular chain of command.[8]

Gallagher ultimately had to deal with half a dozen such underage volunteers at Camp Tennally. Close to home, at Camp Wright, Gallagher had been able to deal successfully and directly with Christopher Herbert's situation, but his options were more limited on Washington's outskirts. He had two of the six discharged as minors, three others on surgeon's certificates. The last was eventually able to produce evidence of parental permission.[9]

The Eleventh Reserves' first violent encounter with the enemy started about ten days after the Lewinsville skirmish. The regiment packed up and started out from Camp Tennally to take its turn picketing Great Falls on a chilly 23 September. The long march wore out many soldiers, and wagons bearing their rations, tents, and overcoats failed to arrive. Two dozen unlucky men from each company drew the task of marching a further six miles upriver for guard duty.

The first night was eventful for Company A. One of its members spotted a rowboat nearing the Maryland shore and challenged the four men inside. They told him, "Go to hell." What happened next, as another soldier described it, was that the picket "preferred sending a substitute to his satanic majesty's domains and accordingly furnished his man with a letter of recommendation, in the shape of a minie ball, which no doubt secured proper attention for him at the high court of Pandemonium." In other words, the Cambria Guardsman shot one of the intruders. The boat did not land, so the extent of the man's injuries was not recorded. He seems to have been the first "secesh" tallied by the regiment.[10]

Whether or not the wounded man was a Confederate soldier, genuine Rebel troops were nearby. At daylight pickets stationed at a narrow part of the river got their first look at the enemy. There was no trouble getting close enough to stare, as by this time Generals McClellan and Johnston were said to have informally agreed "that the pickets of the two armies were not to fire on each other, as it was a barbarous practice, and contrary to the usages of modern warfare." What the Eleventh saw initially was disappointing. The Confederates ambling around on the opposite bank "are not very well uniformed," one sentry wrote, "it being a rusty, ugly cloth, and apparently quite well worn." After a few hours, the pickets started to do more than gawk, the Rebels inviting the Pennsylvanians over to share whiskey. "A number of our boys swam across by special invitation to take a smile of 'O be joyful,'" one correspondent wrote, "at the same time offering a toast to the Union which a Lieut. in the rebel army considered extremely bold." A lucky member of Company A allegedly swam across "at the solicitation of a couple of Virginias fair daughters . . . and enjoyed quite a sociable chat with the two beauties, and before leaving them he made bold to ask if they would have any objections to a Union kiss. They replied in the negative, whereupon their mugs met, producing a succession of sounds like an enraged parent spanking a stubborn youngster."[11]

The offer of a drink came from members of the Thirty-fourth Virginia, which was guarding this portion of the Potomac. Some other courtly Rebels introduced themselves as members of the Fourth Virginia Cavalry, known since Bull Run as the Black Horse Cavalry. The two sets of pickets "talked with all the familiarity of friends," one Pennsylvanian recounted. "Most of those with whom we were talking appeared like respectable men, and seemed to regret they were compelled to be our enemies.—They do not like the New England Boys, nor the Zouaves, but can 'go' Pennsylvanians." Philip Lantzy spoke to some who had expected the war to end within a month, that being how long they originally enlisted. "The Rebels," he wrote home, "Said that they wished to God that we would Not Nead to fight Enny mor it Looked hard to hear them say that they would Just as soon shoot Jeff Davis and [Confederate General P. G. T.] B[ea]uregard as Abe Lincoln or General Scott."[12]

Aside from the man shot in the rowboat incident, the only casualties of the stay had been eel and catfish the soldiers hauled from the Potomac. The men also had time to note the area's beauty, one of the Cambria Guards writing home of "majestic hills rising up almost to the clouds, with the projecting cliffs on which an occasional shrub or evergreen shakes its lonely head in the calm breeze. The murmer of the troubled stream beneath as it is precipitated over a descent of 70 feet laving its rocky enclosure with sparkling spray, renders the scene most grand and attractive."[13]

The peaceful atmosphere was fleeting. Still in a fraternal mood, pickets from the Thirty-fourth Virginia on Sunday, 29 September, told their Union counterparts that a South Carolina regiment would replace them overnight. The Eleventh may have received the news with strong emotions, for the siege of Fort Sumter sparked a particular distrust, even hatred, for Palmetto state troops. "The Federals charge them with being the instigators and beginners of the war," a Texan observed in an 1863 letter, adding that the Yankees "always exclude them from the benefit of truces between the pickets."[14] The Eleventh may have been wary of South Carolinians, but a week of sharing moonshine with Rebels and kissing pretty girls—coupled with faith in "the agreement entered into by the commanders"—made them complacent about the enemy's presence. Early on 30 September, a Company G soldier went to wash himself in the river. A Confederate picket shot him.

The Eleventh Reserves' first real action was under way. Previously placid soldiers grabbed muskets or rifles and took aim across the Potomac. Maj. Samuel Jackson led thirty men from his old unit to retrieve their wounded comrade. Charging to the riverbank, the smoothbore-equipped Company G men opened fire, which would have filled the air with thick gray smoke. They reported hitting at least three Rebels, but the exchange ended when a Confederate battery opened up and sent Jackson's scratch force reeling back.

For the next half hour, the Rebel guns fired into the Eleventh's campsite, set up around cabins originally built to house workers on the nearby Washington Aqueduct. The barrage included fifteen shells, only three of which exploded, an early indication of Confederate munitions problems. Fragments from a live round, however, wounded a second member of the Eleventh in the shoulder. A Rebel cannonball also struck and "bent double" another's rifle or musket while its owner, a German immigrant, was affixing a percussion cap. "Now, by Gott I cannot shoot any how," he was quoted as saying; the weapon was wrecked but he escaped without reported injuries. Union artillery eventually responded, and the Rebel fire subsided.[15]

The "Bloody Eleventh" had passed through its long-anticipated baptism of fire and received its first casualties. After the guns died down, Gallagher's men stayed on duty until relieved. No more skirmishing took place during the regiment's tour at Great Falls, but no more fraternizing is on record.

The shelling taught the men a few things about the effectiveness of cannons. Robert E. McBride, who joined the regiment in late 1863, later wrote a description of the general experience of being under artillery fire.

> "Shelling" is usually quite harmless, except when the guns are served by skilled artillerists, and under favorable circumstances. Unless the shell is exploded at the proper distance and altitude in front of a line, it is not likely to do any injury. A cannonade which, to the uninitiated, would seem sufficient to destroy every thing before it, will be faced with the utmost equanimity by veteran troops, if the artillerist[s] have the range too "long." It is always very annoying, however, as there is no telling when a shell may prove a little "short," and distribute its fragments for rods along the line. The men are usually ordered to lie down,

unless directly engaged. The shell cleaves the air with a frightful
sound, that is but faintly described by the word "shriek." Few
men can refrain from "dodging," as the dangerous missile comes
over with its unearthly sound.

McBride deemed the sound of grape and canister far worse, "a grinding,
groaning, gnashing sound, that chills the blood of the listener."[16]

Back at Camp Tennally after the stay at Great Falls, Gallagher learned
the entire division was scheduled to move. On the afternoon of Wednesday, 9 October, their strength on paper at 11,255 men, the three brigades
of the Pennsylvania Reserves crossed the Chain Bridge and took up
positions in northern Virginia proper, forming the far right flank of the
Army of the Potomac. The day was unseasonably hot, according to the
later recollections of Aaron Kepler, who had joined the Dickson Guards
earlier in the month, along with his cousin William Halderman and two
friends from Butler County. He wrote of a ten-mile march during which
he struggled with a knapsack weighed down by blankets, an overcoat, and
three days' rations. The trek brought the regiment about three or four miles
from the river, to a new site to be named Camp Pierpont after the Union-
loyal governor of breakaway West Virginia. A soldier-correspondent placed
it west of Langley and south of the Georgetown-Leesburg Pike, "within
one mile of Lewinsville, eight miles from Fairfax Court House, and fifteen from Leesburg." Kepler recalled the regiment setting up camp on a
wooded rise called Prospect Hill. After "clearing away the undergrowth"
so that they could pitch their tents, the regiment set to work "to cut and
slash down the large timber between us and the enemy, so that they could
not surprise or take undue advantage of us in our new quarters. Later on
this timber came in good for building our winter quarters, and for fuel,
and by the next spring there was not a vestige of it left. The once beautiful forest was a thing of the past." Officers marked out a parade ground
and kept the companies drilling constantly.[17]

In their few free hours, curious soldiers from the Eleventh visited a
nearby plantation. The owner was a former naval officer who had left to
join the Confederate army. A few servants remained, looking after a house
that, a correspondent observed, contained "a large and well selected
library, several pianos, and other luxurious appurtenances, showing the
recent occupants to have been of refined and elegant tastes." The visitors
may have carried off some mementos; McCall received complaints that
his soldiers were ransacking nearby homes and barns, the booty including
fowl, vegetables, and a small pig. The offenders who were caught were

probably punished by a spell in the guardhouse and loss of pay. Recovered articles were returned to their owners.[18]

The Rebel army was nearby but elusive. In mid-October, amid rumors of a Confederate withdrawal from Leesburg to lines near Manassas, McClellan decided to aggressively scout in his army's front. The venture would provide cover for topographical engineers creating or updating maps. The Pennsylvania Reserves division was to form the vanguard of the first reconnaissance-in-force. On 18 October, orders came for McCall to march west the next day to a small hamlet in the direction of Leesburg called Dranesville.[19]

Gallagher's men learned of the impending move that night and were told to pack two days' rations and be ready to march in the morning. At eight o'clock on the 19th, the division started down the Leesburg Pike. Reynolds' brigade, accompanied by artillery and cavalry, was in the lead, with Meade's and Ord's commands following.

McCall set a cautious pace, and it was one o'clock by the time the Eleventh Reserves halted outside Dranesville. Reynolds' men entered the town, surprising pickets belonging to a Louisiana Zouave regiment, killing five while suffering no Union losses. Aside from that dustup, Meade reported the area quiet.[20]

The operation entered its next phase on the following day when General Smith's division advanced on McCall's left to take up positions near Vienna, southeast of Dranesville. While this was in progress, McClellan received a telegram from Maj. Gen. Nathaniel Banks' headquarters, north of the Potomac. "The signal station at Sugar Loaf," it read, "telegraphs that the enemy have moved away from Leesburg." Hoping to seize Leesburg without a fight, McClellan contacted Brig. Gen. Charles Stone, commanding a division headquartered at Poolesville, Maryland, located to McCall's right, north across the Potomac. "General McCall occupied Dranesville yesterday and is still there," the telegram to Stone read in part. "The general [McClellan] desires that you will keep a good lookout upon Leesburg, to see if this movement has the effect to drive them away. Perhaps a slight demonstration on your part would have the effect to move them."[21]

Unfortunately for Stone and McClellan, the subsequent "slight demonstration" on 21 October resulted in a Union rout known to history as the battle of Ball's Bluff. The Pennsylvania Reserves started the day within marching distance of the action but did not participate. Instead, McClellan ordered their withdrawal to Camp Pierpont, because, he later explained, "it was not foreseen or expected that General McCall would be needed to co-operate with General Stone in any attack." Actually, when McClellan first learned that Stone was engaged he considered canceling McCall's orders to return, but by then the Pennsylvania Reserves had already been on the road to camp for several hours. By the time the division arrived, McClellan had no negative reports yet from Ball's Bluff but told McCall to stay ready for a forced march.

Meade kept the brigade on alert but had only a sketchy idea of what was happening on Stone's front. At 9 P.M., he dashed off a quick note to his wife. "All is now excitement and bustle, though it is night-time," he wrote. "I do not know the meaning, except that something is being done on some other part of the line and we are wanted to support the movement." Half an hour later, Stone telegraphed McClellan that he was "occupied in preventing further disaster." He noted that "Any advance from Dranesville must be made cautiously," words that ended any ideas about putting McCall's men in the fight.[22]

Like Meade, most of the Pennsylvania Reserves had little intimation that the Ball's Bluff fight was in progress. "We marched back to camp, without anything of peculiar interest occurring," a soldier in the Eleventh noted. For his part in bringing on—and losing—the fracas at Ball's Bluff, Stone was imprisoned and held for months without trial.[23]

Once Meade learned the particulars of the engagement, he decided that the "worst part of the business" was that McCall's division was a bare ten miles from the action. "Had we been ordered forward, instead of back, we could have captured the whole of them," he wrote home. He allowed, however, that "we were in ignorance of what was going on, and I presume McClellan was not fully advised of what was taking place, or he would have undoubtedly sent us on." Stone's performance remains a source of historical controversy. From Meade's point of view, the defeat came about in part because Stone "concealed from [McClellan] the true state of the case, and made such reports that induced him to believe all was going well."[24] A harsher analysis prevailed in the ranks: "Our men would not [have] Lost that But our men had A General and he was A Tra[i]tor," Philip Lantzy wrote home, "and he run them men on our Side in to that Plase so they would get whiped."[25]

The Eleventh Reserves' officers had their own troubles. Former blacksmith David Berry, second lieutenant in Company I, was plagued by chronic diarrhea contracted as early as the regiment's stay at Camp Wright. At one point at Camp Tennally, he "passed nothing but blood" and earned a month-long furlough. He returned with the diarrhea lessened but with new health issues, including pain in his left breast, dizziness, and hearing loss.[26]

Illness also plagued Berry's captain, Thomas Spires, and led to other problems. In the early hours of 16 October, Company I was on picket outside camp when firing started on the left of the line. With the sleepy men falling in and preparing to repulse an attack (which ultimately did not develop), Reynolds rode out to investigate. The no-nonsense Regular Army veteran was unimpressed with what he found at Spires' outposts. As Reynolds expressed it in the ensuing court-martial charges, the captain "did fail to parade with the portion of his company acting as Reserve . . . but instead thereof was found lying down." He further determined that Spires "did neglect to properly instruct the pickets under his command in their duties, and when spoken to upon the subject . . . showed ignorance of his duties and great indifference upon the subject."[27]

A few days later, Spires was ordered to report to a military court headed by another tough Regular, Brig. Gen. Winfield Scott Hancock, which ordered Spires' discharge from the military. He appealed the decision, and McClellan on 21 December reinstated Spires "to the service from the date he was ordered to be discharged, that he may be examined anew." There the document trail grows cold in the regimental papers, but Spires kept his command.[28]

Meanwhile, rheumatism aggravated by living outdoors plagued Lt. Col. James Porter. On 3 September he received a thirty-day furlough meant to help him recuperate. He returned on time, but the rheumatism was so severe that on 22 October he gave up the struggle to stay in the army and resigned his commission. He did not, however, leave the war, returning next August as colonel of the nine-month 135th Pennsylvania. Another unit raised from western Pennsylvania counties, the regiment formed part of Washington's garrison in late 1862 and served at Fredericksburg.[29]

James Porter's resignation caused a slight reshuffling of field and staff officers. Maj. Samuel Jackson was promoted to replace him on 28 October, the move authorized by a regimental election in which Jackson tallied 657 votes; the figure reported to Meade mentioned only votes cast for Jackson. Robert Litzinger was named the new major, Andrew Lewis becoming the new captain of the Cambria Guards.[30]

The latter's elevation occasioned another promotion within Company A, the commissioning of twenty-three-year-old Cpl. James C. Burke to second lieutenant. Wilmore resident Burke had already overcome what the era might have viewed as an unfortunate social background. The new officer was the illegitimate son of Veronica A. Maguire, born circa 1818, and one James L. Burke, who by one account had to be taken to court to support the child.

As a youth, Burke worked as a carpenter for a while then taught school. He had been preparing for a legal career in Ebensburg when Fort Sumter fell; then, as one account put it, he "changed his Blackstone for a blanket, musket and knapsack." He enlisted as a private, but his education and ambition helped mark the "gallant looking" Burke for promotion.[31]

Litzinger, and Jackson before him, probably enjoyed the major's post. Capt. Evans Brady described the rank as "The easiest place in the army," adding that "the most laborious [is] that of Captain." Yet Litzinger soon would have to deal with his own illnesses, as would Gallagher. The colonel was being troubled by kidney stones, which became more debilitating as the spring campaign got under way.[32]

Many Civil War soldiers' health broke down because of poor food, but the Eleventh Pennsylvania Reserves seem to have at least had quantity, if not necessarily quality. Besides standard army rations, Gallagher's soldiers benefited from separate accounts kept by each company. These "company funds" were compiled from savings on unused rations, the latter probably arising due to food packages from home or the soldiers' penchant for buying from sutlers or civilians. This cash, controlled by a "company council," was used for special foods or small luxuries or necessities. The Brady Guards, for example, reported savings of almost $50 on rations between 1 November and the end of 1861. The Cambria Guards' savings were enhanced by unloading fifty cents' worth of "condemned coffee." They put their company fund toward extra firewood and cooking utensils. Capt. Daniel Porter turned over $69 in company funds to Company B's cooks. At the regimental level, Robert McCoy served as treasurer of a "post fund" used to pay for, among other things, mail service. An enlisted man was detailed to serve as a mail carrier, at $20 monthly—a significant sum, which when added to the standard private's pay more than doubled his salary. And every man benefited when Meade established a brigade bakery; Gallagher signed over vouchers authorizing weekly payments of about $25 for soft bread for the regiment. As the enterprise itself needed bakers, Gallagher complied with an order to detail men "who have some experience in that business."[33]

Other expenses involved musicians. Civil War companies marched to drummers and fifers, but early in the war regiments assembled full bands to serenade the troops after drilling or to enliven dress parades. In the fall, the Eleventh Reserves began forming its own ensemble, from both the regiment's existing ranks and from among specially recruited musicians. The band, which eventually included at least sixteen men, needed new instruments; as horn makers of the era did not employ a pitch standard, units often had to buy complete brass sets from a single manufacturer. Shortly before Christmas, Gallagher approved a bid by the "post council"—represented by Lt. Col. Jackson and Maj. Litzinger—to spend $132.42 on musical equipment. The same three signatures appear on a mid-January 1862 voucher for $1.50, "being freight on instruments for the Band of the 11th Rgt PRVC."[34]

Camp Pierpont received an issue of winter clothing in early November. It included distinctive black "Hardee Hats." These "are of regular army style," one of McCall's soldiers wrote home, "and when six of them are put into one of our small tents there is very little room left for the men." Lantzy wore his in regulation fashion with the left brim pinned against the crown. He also placed his company letter and regiment number on the front, along with the infantry's bugle insignia.[35]

The heavier uniforms were needed because at about the time of Ball's Bluff northern Virginia started to experience the cold. "We had frost here A Bout A week A Go," Lantzy wrote home near the end of October. "We can feel winter Come on Now." At the same time, the soldiers noted how war had changed the local civilians' lot. "Grain of all Kind is Taken," Lantzy wrote, explaining that his regiment had been gathering "Some Corn That the virginia Boys Left when we chased them off there farms[.] It looks hard to see the Corn fields that the Secesions Left and did not husk. . . . our men husk it and feed our horses." There was also a shortage of the era's main food preservative. "The Rebels Cant Get Enny Salt at all for there army," Lantzy observed. "They hafto eat there Beef without A Bit of Salt and there was some of our men in A house in virginia and the man of the house told them that he had to pay seven Dollars A Bushel for Salt and very Glad that he could get it for that Price." Another soldier in the Eleventh wrote of a local farmer who "informed me that he had paid nine dollars per bushel for salt, and as for sugar and coffee, it was impossible to procure these articles for either love or money. Corn-bread, pork and butter were all they had on the table."[36]

Even though McClellan was now sounding out Secretary of War Simon Cameron on putting the army into winter quarters, scattered action continued to take place on the Pennsylvania Reserves' front. Late in November, McCall learned of a Confederate picket force at Dranesville. He ordered Col. George D. Bayard to take his First Pennsylvania cavalry—one of the units authorized under the bill creating the Pennsylvania Reserves and directly attached to divisional headquarters—out to dislodge them.

Born in 1835, West Pointer Bayard had seen action on the frontier and bore a scar on his face from an arrow wound. McCall's orders to him, delivered at about 9 P.M. on 26 November, included a list of area men to arrest. The suspects had allegedly killed two pickets on Lowe's Island, then stripped the bodies and left them to be eaten by hogs.[37]

By five in the morning on 27 November, Bayard's men had taken up positions around Dranesville. Two companies under a major went into town by the Georgetown Pike while Bayard brought the rest into the other end via the Leesburg Pike. The troops captured two Rebel pickets—privates from the Thirtieth Virginia Cavalry. Then they searched the town and arrested six men named as suspects in the Lowe's Island attack.

With eight prisoners secure, the command mounted up to return to Camp Pierpont. But as the head of the column passed a pine forest, a volley rang out. A private and the regiment's assistant surgeon were seriously wounded. Another surgeon had a musket ball stopped by his overcoat, and a shot killed Bayard's horse. The Pennsylvanians dismounted, encircled the woods, then entered, carbines in hand. In the ensuing fight, Bayard's force killed two Confederates and captured three more. Two of the latter were members of the Seventh South Carolina; the third was an officer attached to the staff of Rebel Brig. Gen. Milledge Luke Bonham, whose brigade was attached to the division of then-Maj. Gen. James Longstreet. Inside the wood, they also captured a Dranesville resident who had evidently summoned or guided the Rebel squad. The ambushers, who had arrived on mounts, had between them five shotguns, two pistols, and a Hall's rifle or carbine.

The column made it back to camp without further incident. The wounded Federal doctor died a few days later. "He was only twenty-six years old, and leaves a young wife, who reached here three hours after his death," Meade wrote home. "Such afflictions should reconcile us to our lesser troubles."[38]

One of the principal "secesh" Bayard bagged in Dranesville was a local slave-owning farmer named R. H. Gunnell. He was said to have invited the Rebel army to buy or otherwise appropriate crops from his farm, located about two and a half miles northeast of the town. His nephews were also on McCall's arrest list but had eluded capture by Bayard. As a result, McCall planned a second march to Dranesville, this one to involve all of Meade's brigade.

The second expedition's goals included arresting Gunnell's nephews, and Meade was also to clean out whatever still lay at Gunnell's farm. At daybreak on 6 December, the Eleventh fell into route step with the rest of the brigade and retraced Bayard's route. Fifty-seven wagons creaked along to bring in the forage. Expecting resistance, the task force included a battery and a cavalry squadron, and McCall stationed Ord's brigade and another battery within supporting range.

In Dranesville, Meade's troops captured Gunnell's nephews as well as three other residents described as "rank secessionists." Meade then deployed elements of the brigade in a defensive posture around the area and put others to work stripping Gunnell's fields and barns. "We Loaded all of the wagons with Corn and wheat and oats hogs potatoes and everything we could Get," Lantzy wrote home. "We got A Bout 15 Horses and A Yoke [of] Oxen." Another writer put the take at "2,000 bushels of corn, 30 fat hogs, 10 horses, 2 buggies, one yoke of oxen." The wagons were filled by 6 P.M., and a light snow was either imminent or already falling when the brigade started back on the Leesburg Pike. Two of Gunnell's slaves accompanied the soldiers back to camp, where they would find work as cooks. No enemy soldiers had been seen, though unknown to Meade a small Rebel force had retreated when it saw the Union brigade approaching.

The charges against the prisoners on McCall's arrest list ultimately broke down. Kepler recalled that most of those picked up during Meade's expedition were released after taking the oath of allegiance. Gunnell himself sat in prison until March 1862, at which point he too was sent home after swearing loyalty to the Federal government.[39]

To Meade, arresting disloyal citizens was one thing; ransacking farms was another, and he had not gone to West Point for actions like this. "I never had a more disagreeable duty in my life to perform," the brigadier wrote home. "The man [Gunnell] was absent, but his sister, with his farm and house servants, were at home." Meade confessed to having had difficulty restraining the foragers: "The men and officers got into their heads that the object of the expedition was the punishment of a rebel, and hence the more injury they inflicted, the more successful was the expedition, and it was with considerable trouble they could be prevented from burning everything. It made me sad to do such injury, and I really was ashamed of our cause, which thus required war to be made on individuals."[40]

Yet such official foraging filled Camp Pierpont larders at no cost to the Federal government. It also denied tons of supplies to the Rebels. Confederate Brig. Gen. D. H. Hill, in command of the troops near Leesburg, stepped up picket activity hoping to discourage what he termed the "successful foraging parties of the enemy [which] constantly depredate around Dranesville."[41] This Confederate restlessness showed the men of the Eleventh Reserves that the raid on Gunnell's farm had struck a nerve. "It appears to be a prevalent opinion among our officers that the enemy are going to make an attack," Sgt. Harvey Fair of Company B wrote home. "I hope they may decide on aggressive measures for then they will soon be whipt and as it has to be done the sooner the better."[42]

The confrontation Fair envisioned took place just a few days later, although it was not the decisive battle for which many hoped. The skirmish stemmed from D. H. Hill's interest in salvaging whatever Meade's troops had left behind. On 20 December, Hill dispatched a wagon train to Dranesville with orders to comb the area for food and forage. For protection, he sent Stuart, commanding 150 horsemen, four cannon, and about 1,600 troops.[43]

At Dranesville, Stuart's troops met with a larger Union force intent on beating the Confederates to the punch. Word had reached McCall the night before of Rebel pickets entering the town. Their apparent intention was to secure the area before the foraging party arrived. For good measure, they "carried off two good Union men and plundered and threatened others."[44] In response, at 6 A.M. on 20 December—at about the same time Hill's task force was under way—McCall dispatched his own well-armed foraging party. The wagon train was escorted by Ord's brigade and several artillery sections. Each man carried forty rounds and a day's rations. "We guessed we were on a foraging expedition—but could not explain the presence of Battery A," a participant wrote years afterward. Some troops started singing but Ord hushed them. "Boys, you make too much noise," he told them, adding, "When you meet the enemy pounce upon them like a wildcat." Reynolds' brigade started out after Ord, halting within supporting distance at a waterway called Difficult Creek. Meade's brigade stayed near Langley, the Eleventh doing picket duty.[45]

What became known as the battle of Dranesville began at about noon. As soon as he spotted the Federal artillery, Stuart sent the wagons back to camp, then attacked, hoping to turn the Federal left. He failed to do so, and the two sides were locked in a firefight which ended in the outnumbered Stuart's withdrawal. The Rebel cavalryman reported 43 of his men killed, 143 wounded. He estimated Union losses much higher. Factoring in the enemy's superior numbers, Stuart reported, "we may rightly call it a glorious success." McCall in fact reported 7 killed and 61 wounded.[46]

From the Union point of view, McClellan considered the battle of Dranesville a "brilliant" affair. Ord gave a more sober assessment. He told Meade, the latter recounted in a letter home, "that there was much shirking and running away on the part of both officers and men. . . . One regiment he could do nothing with." Yet the success helped defuse Bull Run's stigma. In Harrisburg, Gov. Andrew Curtin arranged for the word "Dranesville" to be painted on the silk standards carried by the regiments involved.[47]

Once again, the Eleventh had listened to the sounds of battle but was spared its sights. "Our men whiped them last Saturday A bout 12 miles from our camp," Lantzy wrote home. "We Could hear the Cannons and Guns go off Plain for we was on Picket Guard and we Could Not Go." Lt. Col. Jackson, in command of that picket force, laconically reported to Meade "that all was quiet along my line of Pickets during the 24 hours I had commanded." The regiment's entry into "real" battle was still to come.[48]

As he formulated it during the winter of 1861–62, McClellan's strategy for the new campaign constituted making an indirect attack on the Rebel capital, Richmond. He would float the Army of the Potomac down its namesake river and the Chesapeake Bay to Fort Monroe, a Virginia site the Federals retained on the tip of the peninsula between the James and York Rivers. From here, McClellan envisioned a quick northwest march to Richmond, allowing him, he hoped, to sidestep Johnston's army, positioned to block a direct advance from Washington.

In the meantime, his troops settled into camps straddling Washington. The original plan was for the Army of the Potomac to start building winter quarters after New Year's Day. In December, however, the army's medical director learned that some regiments "were excavating pits in the ground and covering them with their tents." Because these "excavations . . . could not be kept dry or well ventilated, and certainly would not be kept in good police," he put the men to work instead building "inclosures of rails or palisades some three feet high, to be roofed over with the tents." The Eleventh Reserves followed his advice and erected snug huts. Of the cabin constructed by his mess, Aaron Kepler wrote home that "we built it about four feet high with poles, and chunked and daubed it as well as we could, and then put our tent on it for a roof. We have two bunks in it and a little sheetiron stove, which we bought for $4.00."[49]

The surgeon's concerns were merited—more men died from disease than bullets during the Civil War. The Eleventh Reserves was more fortunate in health respects than other regiments. The day after the early December expedition to Gunnell's Farm, Lantzy wrote home: "There is Not Much Sickness here yet." But he noted that when one man in his company got sick, the journey to the hospital, probably made via springless wagon, did more harm than good: "They took him to the hospitle and on the Road they upSet and hurt him and he Died in A Day or two," he wrote. The victim was probably Private John Wise, who died at Washington on 28 November. His illness is unspecified in company records.[50]

Deaths and illnesses back home also haunted the men. In a letter to his brother's family back in Indiana County, Harvey Fair of Company B tried to console them for the loss of a daughter. "I was sorry indeed," he wrote, "that the dear little visitor which was sent for you to entertain should be taken home so soon, but such is life the dearer the object of our affections the sooner they fade. Your Ella, young though she was, dear friends, caused you many a ray of sun shine, and although she has now been taken away yet for her sake you should not mourn, but be satisfied, and bow submissively to the Hand that took your little angel home 'To where sweet flowers ever bloom.'"[51]

As a young volunteer, flush with the fever for war that greeted Indiana County in April 1861, Fair had leapt over the county courthouse's railing in his enthusiasm to sign up inside. He messed with his company captain, Daniel Porter, and their discussions frequently turned to family and friends back in Pennsylvania. "I never saw a man more attached to home than he was," Porter later remarked about Fair. "Often and often he would refer to the scenes of home, and seemed to long for the time when he could return."[52]

Yet men could die tragically back home too. An Ebensburg paper recounted a fatal accident at the Susquehanna sawmill owned by Philip Lantzy's brother John. Working on a frigid day in late January, John Lantzy started the mechanism unaware that his partner, Silas Ballou, had "had occasion to descend to the lower portion of the building, to remove a mass of ice which impeded the revolutions of the wheel. . . . The result was, that he was caught and drawn in by the wheel, thereby being crushed and bruised so badly that he survived but a short time. The deceased was probably fifty years of age, and was, we believe, unmarried."[53]

Headquarters constantly demanded men from the individual regiments. Soldiers were detailed "temporarily" to serve as teamsters, cooks, pioneers, and so on, occasionally to serve with artillery batteries. In February 1862, five men from each of Meade's regiments were detailed for gunboat service. The previous August, Lt. John W. DeFord of Company F was detailed to serve in the newly organized Signal Corps, and the same orders also applied to an enlisted man in the same company, Pvt. James McKerns. DeFord learned the craft well enough to become an instructor, but McKerns fell prey to other interests. On 13 January 1862, he sneaked out of camp in Georgetown and spent the evening on the town. He turned up at reveille the next morning, but his absence had been noted and he was thrown into the guardhouse. He managed to have some liquor smuggled into the stockade, and his condition became known to the camp's officers. The charges against him exist in the regiment's papers, but the disposition—likely a loss of pay and/or brief confinement—was not recorded. Whatever the result, McKerns served out his three years and was mustered out with his company in 1864.[54]

Some detail requisitions had repercussions within the regiment, particularly when a needed specialist was taken away. Gallagher was placed in the uncomfortable position of asking Meade to rescind an order detailing the regiment's hospital cook to serve in the brigade commissary. His note acknowledged having already lost a skilled man—"a regular Baker and the only one in the Regiment"—to the same duty.[55]

Cooks and bakers aside, Meade clearly sought to have more than one marksman in each unit. On 27 January, Lt. Col. Jackson noted in the pocket account book he used for a diary that he had "Received orders from Headquarters to expend 40 rounds of ball cartridge at target practice and report the result each evening to Brigade Headquarters." Surviving records confirm a span of target practice, involving each company of the regiment, from 28 January to 20 February. The target distance varied among companies, reaching a high of 300 yards on 8 February for rifle-equipped Company A.[56]

Perhaps the target practice was meant in part to keep the men busy, for there were problems with discipline in the weeks before Jackson received his orders. John Alt, a blue-eyed, black-haired private in the Brady Guards, abandoned his post one day while on picket guard. His lieutenant reported that Alt had "left the post of his company and returned to Camp contrary to orders and prior instructions of his Captain." Nine days later Alt brawled with another Company K private, William Morrison. The fight may have been sparked by boredom. The dreariness of winter quarters was marked by alternate days of rain and snow creating what Jackson described as "mud worse than ever." Heavy snow probably caused the regiment's stable to collapse at five o'clock one morning, killing two horses. To keep the men's minds occupied while waiting out the winter, some members of the regiment organized debating clubs, a correspondent who signed his letters as "Mitch" wrote home to an Indiana County paper.[57]

The harsh weather brought on more sickness, including some typhoid cases. Robert Litzinger fell ill in early February after a round of picket duty. Regimental surgeon James Seguin DeBenneville diagnosed the problem as "pleurisy and nephritic irritation," and it kept the major continually sick in quarters from the fourth of that month. DeBenneville, who reportedly "prescribed quinine for everything," handed out enough doses of that bitter medicine to make him unpopular with the rank and file. Kepler later described the surgeon, then about thirty-six, as "a conceited, pompous little fellow, full of airs and red tape." Hostility to DeBenneville evidently made its way to headquarters, for in early February Samuel Jackson accompanied him "to Division Hospital to have some false reports settled up in reference to the character of the Doctor. Got the matter settled." Enlisted men who distrusted the surgeon may have instead sought out six-foot-tall James A. Fulton, a private in Westmoreland County's Company H but a practicing physician before the war. Born circa 1834, Fulton worked as a doctor in Salem Crossroads until he enlisted in August 1861. His education served him well in the army, and by the time of Gettysburg, where he was wounded badly enough to be discharged, Fulton would be a lieutenant.[58]

If DeBenneville relied on quinine, Assistant Surgeon D. W. Ballantine prescribed stronger medicines for himself. Late on 8 February, Gallagher alleged, he found Ballantine "so drunk in the camp of the 11th Regt. as to be unable to perform his duty." When Ballantine sobered up and learned of the charges pending, he tendered his resignation and was honorably discharged.[59]

Litzinger's condition failed to improve, and on 12 February, the day after Ballantine resigned, he received a twenty-day medical leave. His fellow Cambria County residents hoped the major could take care of some small errands for them on his return to Ebensburg. Philip Lantzy asked his family to send his watch to Litzinger in Ebensburg via "some of the teams from Carrolltown." He wanted the major, when he returned, to "Bring it to me for I can Sell it hear for what I paid for it and so I could Rais some money." Litzinger evidently left the hospital tent with little advance notice; Lantzy acknowledged that he had missed speaking to him personally but felt sure of his cooperation.[60]

Yet Litzinger never returned to the regiment as an officer. Once home in Belsano, he lay seriously ill, and the *Alleghanian* reported that "serious doubts were . . . entertained for a time as to his recovery." On 7 March his leave was extended thirty days, with twenty more days soon added. Late in that month, he wrote Gallagher offering his resignation. He stated that the "abscess, formed upon my liver, is now discharging into the lungs, and hence, in the opinion of my physician, it will be impossible for me to take the field for many months if at all." Gallagher forwarded it to Meade, who scrawled "acceptance recommended" on the back and passed it on to divisional headquarters. The major's resignation was accepted on the first of April.[61]

Surprisingly, eighteen days later Litzinger stunned and gladdened his men by showing up at the Eleventh Reserves' camp. As Lantzy recounted it: "We was much excited to day we saw our good old Major Litzinger from Ebensburg come in to our camp he looks bad yet he came to see us he is going home to morrow and we was paid to day and so I can send you Some money."[62] Litzinger's visit showed especial determination due to the travel involved. At the time of the visit, made presumably in civilian clothes, his old regiment had long been on the march in Virginia. The Peninsula Campaign had already begun.

On 17 March, McClellan started embarking elements of his army for Fort Monroe. The Army of the Potomac by then had been reorganized into several *corps d'armée*. The Pennsylvania Reserves found their division placed in the I Corps, commanded by Maj. Gen. Irvin McDowell.

Many were unenthused about their commander, the loser of Bull Run. Indeed, the I Corps' progress as part of McClellan's invasion force would be halting, though not due to the corps commander. Lincoln, worried about the presence of Rebel Maj. Gen. Thomas "Stonewall" Jackson in the Shenandoah Valley, ultimately decided he wanted the I Corps kept near Washington. The move infuriated McClellan, who fumed with good reason from Meade's viewpoint. Lincoln eventually suggested McDowell might advance, over land, to link up with the rest of the army between the James and York Rivers. But the bulk of McDowell's troops never reached the Peninsula.[63]

The strategic map of northern Virginia started changing even before McClellan began the expedition to Fort Monroe. On 9 March, Johnston withdrew his army of 43,000 from Centreville to positions about thirty miles southwest, across the northwestern finger of the Rappahannock

River at Culpeper. The next day, McCall's division joined other elements of the Army of the Potomac in a limited pursuit, which McClellan let go as far as Centreville itself.

The march from Camp Pierpont started at 11:30 A.M. for Gallagher's men. One of them was Company G Pvt. Andrew Ivory, about thirty-seven at this time, an ex-farmer with blue eyes and dark hair. He had married the former Catherine Schroeder in 1848, and by the time war came the couple had at least six children. According to Ivory, on a typical march like this the soldiers carried "a knap sack on our back and in it one blanket, 2 shirts, 3 pairs of socks and 20 rounds of cartriges and some other little things. then our haversack with three days rations in it. then the gun and cartrige box with 40 rounds in it and canteen for water."[64]

Heavily laden like this the men were soon on a forced-march pace up the Leesburg Pike, following it for eight miles, then shifting southward onto "a by-road ankle deep with mud." At about 10 P.M., the exhausted regiment, having tramped "through woods, mud and water," camped at a spot on the Orange and Alexandria Railroad two miles north of Vienna, Virginia, on high ground next to a place called Hunter's Mill. Next morning, 11 March, the men were disappointed to learn of Johnston's withdrawal, news that nixed their hopes of having "a brush with the F.F.V's"— the First Families of Virginia. On 14 March, the regiment veered back the way it came on an especially hard, rain-soaked trek toward a new camp-site in Alexandria. The first leg brought it within three miles of Camp Pierpont, near which it turned eastward before encamping for another frigid, wet night. A soldier in another of McCall's regiments wrote home that to light fires here, "Two soldiers would hold a rubber blanket by the corners while a third would kindle the fire beneath it. The fires served to warm us, but it was impossible to dry our clothing, as the rain fell during the whole night. . . . To add to our discomfort, the atmosphere was so dense that the smoke did not rise above the tree tops." The march reportedly killed two men of the Fourth Reserves, one of whom was found dead by the roadside, the other "fell dead in the ranks." Samuel Jackson spent the miserable night huddled by a campfire but unable to sleep. The rain let up the next day, however, and the trip was brightened by what Jackson chronicled as a "Great Union demonstration by the ladies" as the unit passed through Falls Church.[65]

On 16 March, Gallagher's men staggered into a camp on Seminary Hill in Alexandria. The two-day trek, survivors told historian Samuel P. Bates after the war, "was ever remembered . . . as the severest test of their endurance to which they were called upon to submit." It also marked a further deterioration in Gallagher's condition. By Christopher Herbert's postwar account, the fiery colonel began openly to talk about his discomfort. "While marching in the spring of 1862," Herbert wrote Gallagher's widow, "he suffered severely and complained of his kidneys to me but never gave up—It was a wet and very muddy season and often when we would stop we would build a big fire to warm the lower part of his back as he would tell me there the trouble was."[66]

The regiment remained in Alexandria almost a month. To combat the weather's effects, the men received occasional rations of medicinal whiskey. Gallagher tried to keep them busy by drilling twice a day. Washington's bars and other distractions loomed nearby, and Jackson noted that it was "hard work to keep our men out of the city." As the embarkation for the Peninsula got under way, the troops assumed they would be part of the invasion fleet. "This letter will be short," Lantzy wrote home on 22 March from Seminary Hill, "for we will leave in a few days on A boat to go down south farther." Yet the Eleventh Reserves had about a month and a half to wait for its river ride.[67]

President Lincoln, acting for the time as his own general-in-chief, eventually clarified the role assigned McDowell's force. On 4 April, as McClellan's siege of Yorktown was getting under way, the I Corps was redesignated the Army of the Rappahannock. The name reflected Lincoln's plan for McDowell to make a separate, overland advance to a point near Fredericksburg on the Rappahannock River, virtually midway between Washington and Richmond. This would threaten the Rebel capital from the north, presumably drawing away some units from Johnston's army now facing McClellan on the Peninsula. From there, McDowell's roughly 40,000 men could support the Army of the Potomac as it advanced on Richmond proper. Should Stonewall Jackson remain a threat, McDowell could still be withdrawn toward Washington or the Shenandoah.[68]

McCall's orders to move south with the rest of McDowell's army came in early April, at a time when the troops were struggling under unseasonably severe conditions of snow and hail. Some Pennsylvania Reserves regiments got rail transport to Centreville. Meade's were not so lucky. His units set out toward Centreville at 7 A.M. on 11 April, the Eleventh seeing much evidence of war. A soldier-correspondent described once-thriving Fairfax Court House, near which the Eleventh camped for the night, as "looking considerably delapidated." An hour's march the next day brought the regiment to Centreville. There, Johnston's army had evacuated "a long line of earthworks thrown up in front of the village, commanding the road and all the adjacent country." Meade considered the works "quite strong," but a soldier in the Ninth Reserves saw them differently. "It was the most forsaken place ever I saw," he wrote home. "Their fortifications didn't amount to anything. Some places they had logs of wood set up and painted to look like cannons."[69]

Besides the maple ordnance, known to history as "Quaker Guns," the Eleventh found empty winter cabins which "were greatly superior to ours, the huts being large and well constructed." Marching further, the brigade came to the old Bull Run battlefield. At noon on the 12th, the Eleventh rested at the Stone Bridge where the fight had started nine months earlier, using Bull Run water to make coffee. By 3 P.M., the brigade settled at Manassas Junction. The Eleventh stayed there two nights until shifting camp about a quarter mile to a drier spot.[70]

The soldiers found much of Manassas burnt. They explored a nearby Rebel cemetery, with about 200 graves, and spent time walking over the battlefield. Meade felt that "[a] more beautiful ground for a battle never existed; country open, with rolling ground of gentle slopes, offering equal advantages to the attacking and attacked." Writing four decades later, Kepler remembered finding "it very different from what I had expected. It is a beautiful place—about 400 acres of land cleared, a nice field for a fight—and looked like a fine farm that no person had lived on for some years." A contemporary soldier-correspondent described the battlefield as "about a mile square, intersected with numerous ravines and covered with small hills and surrounded by dense thickets of stunted pine and oak." A tangle of sun-bleached horses' bones marked the spot where the Black Horse Cavalry—friends of the Eleventh on the Great Falls picket line—charged a line of Zouaves. Some of the latter lay partially buried nearby, "the bones of several of them protruding from the mold." Kepler also remembered the shallow graves. "Owing to the frosts of winter, and settling of trenches, many feet, legs, arms and heads were sticking up out of the ground, and some had never been buried at all." They also saw "a number of very fat hogs roaming over the field and fattening on the dead." Manassas would be known to the Eleventh Reserves as ground where "the dead would not stay buried."[71]

As the Rebel pickets had told members of the Eleventh across the Potomac, they had come to especially dislike Zouaves. Now a correspondent relayed, "We were told by an old negress, whose house stood near by, that Rebel soldiers, and particularly the Georgians, used to visit the battle-field, and, through hatred of the Zouaves, pry their bodies out of the graves!" The historian of the Second Pennsylvania Reserves later alleged that the regiment found a human skull and crossbones nailed over the door of a hut in an abandoned Rebel campsite. "Leg bones were also found with the marrow but partially dried up in them, from which finger rings had been sawed off."[72]

If true, both sides desecrated graves at Manassas. Reynolds administered a tongue-lashing to a brigade surgeon caught digging up a grave, presumably out of medical curiosity. "When I called him up to ask him about it," Reynolds wrote home, "he did not deny it, acknowledged that he had brought away some of the bones, but excused himself by saying they were rebels!" The bones, in fact, belonged to a Union soldier, a point the surgeon was allegedly aware of when he started digging. A soldier in the Seventh Pennsylvania Reserves confirmed the stories when he wrote his sister, observing that because of the shallow graves, "I could have easily gathered a bushel of human bones." He allowed that "the remains of one man have been treated with criminal neglect by the rebels"—perhaps a reference to the skull-and-crossbones reportedly found by the Second Reserves. But he added: "it pains me to know that the morbid curiosity of our own men has led them to unearth the bones of the slain in some places. A man who would do such an act . . . must have lost all feeling of humanity, but what will we say of those who do so to the remains of those, who, we have great reason to believe, were our own comrades. A demon must influence him at the time."[73]

On 18 April, the march resumed, with Bayard's cavalry leading the way for McCall. Johnston's army had retreated on the line of the Orange and Alexandria Railroad, along which the Pennsylvania Reserves followed. The quarry took steps to hinder any pursuit. "They have burnt all the Rail Road bridges A Long this Road when they Retriated from mannssus and so our men must fix all the Bridges," Lantzy noted in a letter, written from near Warrenton. Bayard's cavalry arrived at Falmouth, north of Fredericksburg across the Rappahannock, to find one bridge unburned. The horsemen advanced, but into the fire of concealed Mississippi troops. The result was twenty-two Union casualties, and Bayard was again unhorsed. His men re-formed and charged and made headway against the Rebels, who retreated across the bridge and set fire to it. The Union cavalry, however, were able to douse the flames and save most of this badly needed way across the Rappahannock. Again, the Eleventh was far from the action. It remained ten days in camp near Warrenton, a quarter mile from Catlett's Station and about ten miles from Manassas, until the general march toward the Rappahannock resumed.[74]

The stop at Catlett's Station allowed Gallagher to resolve the issue of replacing Litzinger. After the ill major handed in his commission, an election was scheduled to fill his post. The officers met on 7 April to see if they could put forth a particular candidate, which the rest of the regiment would presumably vote to confirm. Some favored the regimental adjutant, Peter A. Johns, but others preferred Capt. Daniel Porter. Both names went to a vote.

Contemporary sources disagree on exactly what happened on the first election between Johns and Porter. By one soldier-correspondent's account, Porter was elected major, but owing to "some informality in the proceedings," the decision was not allowed to stand. Yet Jackson in his diary wrote cryptically: "Johns elected Major by 50 majority over Porter. The returns disagreed to by General Meade on account of not receiving a majority of all the votes cast." The presence of a plurality rather than a majority indicates that Johns and Porter were not the only vote-getters. The second vote, held during the stay at Catlett's Station, ended in Johns receiving a suitable 124-vote majority. Lt. Robert McCoy of the Cambria Guards succeeded him as adjutant.[75]

In spite of continual rain, the stay at Catlett's Station had some excitement other than unit elections. Aaron Kepler recalled one morning when the regiment was ordered out to picket across Difficult Run. The men were issued three days' rations and sixty rounds of ammunition. On their second night on duty, Captain Louden's company was "pacing back and forth on our lonely beats, [when] pickets on the opposite side opened a lively fire on us, sending Minnie balls hissing around, seemingly in every direction, which kept us dodging. But we stood our ground and gave them back the best we had, until our reserve came up to reinforce us, when we made them 'skedaddle' on the double quick." The next morning, Gallagher complimented the company on its bravery, "which made us feel pretty good." Later that day, the Confederates again probed the Difficult Run line, pushing the Eleventh's pickets back to the now rain-swollen creek. The rest of Meade's brigade was summoned to help, and the threatened pickets eventually crossed on crude bridges formed from fallen trees. One member of Company C lost his balance and tumbled off a log into the "wild and roaring" water. He lost his gun underwater but clung to the rough bridge, the current drawing his feet and legs under it until they stuck out of the water on the other side of the log. Kepler pulled him out feet first, a technique he conceded gave his friend "a complete ducking, and seemed a little rough, but was the only way to save him." His comrade reported having "'never felt so scared in all my life as when I went under the log.' Then he gave a lusty 'Three cheers for the Union,' which seemed to be a panacea for his hard luck."[76]

On Monday, 28 April, the Eleventh Reserves hit the road for another grueling march. Reynolds, a veteran of Mexico and the western frontier, called the roads here the worst he had ever encountered. Company A was initially detailed as the brigade's rear guard, picking up stragglers and helping stuck or toppled wagons, at one point dragging a cart along after its horse team played out. The next day was easier on the whole regiment, the Eleventh forming the brigade's advance. The units were on marching rations of hardtack (Ivory called them "government pies"), salt meat, and coffee, the last in many ways a Civil War soldier's best friend. "It is a highly picturesque sight," one soldier wrote home at the time of this trek, "to see a brigade on the march, at the dinner hour. After the arms have been stacked and knapsacks thrown aside, in less than five minutes, as if by magic, a thousand or more little fires spring up . . . and fifteen minutes later, you [see] every man with a cup of hot, smoking coffee to his lips." The brigade reached Falmouth, north of Fredericksburg across the Rappahannock, at 4 P.M. on 29 April. "The 'darkeys' appeared excessively pleased at our debut in their midst," one correspondent wrote home. Meade's brigade entered Falmouth with "colors flying and the bands playing."[77]

Like other towns through which the Eleventh Reserves had passed, Falmouth showed signs of war's effect. A good part of its prewar population of about 1,000 had apparently followed the Rebel army south. A large cotton mill still operated, but overall the local economy was depressed. Elements of the army eventually crossed the Rappahannock and entered Fredericksburg itself. McDowell set fatigue details to work repairing the railroad line that connected the town with the landing at Aquia Creek, an offshoot of the Potomac River. In the Eleventh Reserves, a sergeant from Company G and thirteen enlisted men were detailed to work on building bridges. Reynolds was named Fredericksburg's military governor and handled the office well. In Fredericksburg itself, soldiers from the Eleventh learned, the few men who had stayed claimed to be pro-Union in sentiment, though the women were not so loyal. "The poor white population are not half so intelligent as the same class in the North," one correspondent wrote home, "and many of them do not even know the cause of the war now being waged between the two sections." To his wife, Meade wrote that "The men are away, and the women are as rude as their fears will permit them to be."[78]

The post did not lack excitement. "We are encamped in a very pretty place now, the prettyest we have been in since we commenced soldiering," a soldier in the Ninth Reserves wrote home during this time. "But the country is full of Guerillos and they commit depradations every chance they get. . . . In daylight they step around and are good union men but when night comes they gather together in bands and turn Secesh and do all the devilment they can." The Pennsylvania Reserves would meet these nighttime raiders during service in northern Virginia throughout the war.

In the meantime, Meade anticipated orders for the division to march to Aquia Creek, and from there to embark for West Point on the Peninsula, now McClellan's base of operations on the York River. Ivory was expecting good things. "I think before this reaches you our troops will be in Richmond," he wrote home on 7 May from Falmouth. "I want you to prepair a fourth of July dinner for me for I think I will be home again then."[79]

Figure 1
A Union regiment drilling. Scenes like this must have been common at Camps Wright, Tennally, and Pierpont. (Minnesota Historical Society)

Figure 2
A high-ranking figure in the prewar Pennsylvania militia, Thomas Gallagher led the Eleventh Reserves from its inception until he was promoted to brigade command prior to South Mountain. (Roger D. Hunt coll./ USAMHI)

Figure 3
Samuel Jackson originally captained the Independent Blues of Armstrong County, which became Company G of the Eleventh Reserves. He succeeded Thomas Gallagher as the regiment's commander. (Roger D. Hunt coll./USAMHI)

Figure 4
A Union company in line. (Library of Congress)

(a)

(c)

(b)

Figure 5
Three captains of
the Cambria Guards
(Company A):
Robert Litzinger *(a)*,
Andrew Lewis *(b)*, and
James Burke *(c)*.
(Ronn Palm coll./USAMHI;
Madeline Payne Moyer; Ronn
Palm private coll.)

Figure 6
Robert McCoy, the onetime Cambria Guards lieutenant later attached to Gen. Samuel Crawford's staff. (MOLLUS/USAMHI)

Figure 7
Cambria Guards Pvt. Philip Lantzy, killed at Antietam. (James Beck coll./USAMHI)

Figure 8
Indiana National Guards (Company B) Capt. Daniel Porter was the ranking officer in the Eleventh Reserves between Gaines' Mill and the August 1862 prisoner exchange. By the time he resigned early in 1864 he was the regiment's lieutenant colonel. (Ronn Palm private coll.)

Figure 9
George McCall was the first commander of the Pennsylvania Reserves division. (NA)

Figure 10
Future Army of the Potomac commander George Meade led the Eleventh Reserves's original brigade. (NA)

Figure 11

John Reynolds led a brigade of the Pennsylvania Reserves and later commanded the division itself. He was killed at Gettysburg while leading the Army of the Potomac's I Corps. (Archives and Special Collections/ Franklin and Marshall College)

Figure 12

The march through Manassas in early 1862 brought the Eleventh Reserves through abandoned Rebel winter quarters like these. (Western Reserve Historical Society)

Figure 13
An 1865 view of Mechanicsville near where part of the regiment saw its first battle. (MOLLUS/ USAMHI)

Figure 14
A Union bridge across the Chickahominy River. (Library of Congress)

Figure 15
At Mechanicsville, Rebel Col. M. S. Stokes died leading the First North Carolina against Union lines held in part by the Cambria Guards. (Western Reserve Historical Society)

Figure 16
Confederate Gen. John Bell Hood. Troops from his commands (at brigade and division level) fought the Eleventh Reserves several times in 1862–63. (Museum of the Confederacy, Richmond; copy photography by Katherine Wetzel)

Figure 17
The Gaines house served as Rebel headquarters during the Battle of Gaines' Mill; wounded Union prisoners were treated here after the fight. (Library of Congress/Museum of the Confederacy, Richmond)

Figure 18
Lt. J. S. Kennedy of Butler County's Connoquenessing Rangers (Company D) was among many Eleventh Reserves officers wounded in a single volley at South Mountain. (D. Scott Hartzell coll./USAMHI)

Figure 19
Sgt. William Timblin of Butler County's Dickson Guards (Company C) carried the regiment's flag at Antietam and Fredericksburg. He ended the war a captain. (USAMHI)

Figure 20
Pvt. James X. McIlwain of the Independent Blues shown wearing Zouave trappings, probably belonging to the portrait studio. (Richard Waechter coll./USAMHI)

Figure 21
Independent Blues Capt. James
Speer, later the regiment's major.
(MOLLUS/USAMHI)

Figure 22
Indiana County blacksmith
and regimental quartermaster
Hugh Torrance before he was
shot in the face at South
Mountain. (Ronn Palm
private coll.)

Figure 23
Jefferson County newspaper editor
Evans Brady, whose Company K was
known as the "Brady Guards." He
was killed at South Mountain.
(USAMHI)

Figure 24
Capt. Everard Bierer of Fayette County's
Union Volunteers (Company F), who spent
much of his time in the Eleventh Reserves
seeking promotion elsewhere. (Mary B.
Shannon coll./USAMHI)

Figure 25
Capt. William Stewart led the
Connoquenessing Rangers until he
was mortally wounded by cannon fire
just before the attack at Fredericksburg. (Ronn Palm private coll.)

Figure 26
The Eleventh Reserves crossed pontoon bridges like these across the Rappahannock twice in mid-December 1862—before and after the repulse at Fredericksburg. (Minnesota Historical Society)

Figure 27
The original colors of the Eleventh Reserves. Captured along with much of the regiment at Gaines' Mill, the flag was recovered after Richmond's fall. (Capitol Preservation Committee, Harrisburg)

Figure 28
Where the charge began: the view toward the Wheatfield at Gettysburg, as seen from the northern slopes of Little Round Top. (Ziegler Studio, Gettysburg)

Figure 29
The Eleventh Reserves' monument in the Wheatfield. The Maltese cross motif represents the badge of the V Corps, to which the Pennsylvania Reserves division was attached at the time of the battle. (Ziegler Studio, Gettysburg)

Figure 30

Gen. Samuel Crawford commanded
the Pennsylvania Reserves division in
its battles of 1863 and 1864. He
ordered and led the successful 2 July
1863 charge to the Wheatfield. (NA)

Figure 31

With the Confederacy on the verge of
surrender in April 1865, a photographer
captured this image of rain-washed Union
graves on the Gaines' Mill battlefield.
(Western Reserve Historical Society)

Chapter 4

One of the Awfulest Battles the World Has Ever Witnessed

The Road to Gaines' Mill

Irvin McDowell never joined George McClellan on the Peninsula. Yet his army's presence at Fredericksburg sparked two
Confederate counteroffensive thrusts, both with implications for
the Eleventh Pennsylvania Reserves. The first came in late May,
when McDowell's threat to Richmond prompted Stonewall
Jackson to take the initiative in the Shenandoah Valley, which
was guarded by Nathaniel Banks' troops. Jackson's fast-moving

assault resulted, as the Rebel commander had hoped, in part of McDowell's command being shifted to support Banks, thus preventing the Army of the Rappahannock from joining McClellan's force.

This factor played into the second counteroffensive. McClellan never gave up hope that McDowell would eventually be dispatched overland to meet him near Richmond. Accordingly, he kept part of his army north of the Chickahominy River, outside the Rebel capital, to facilitate a junction should McDowell march. This left the Army of the Potomac in an unsafe position: its halves on either side of the Chickahominy could not easily communicate or reinforce each other. McClellan kept the army thus deployed even after it became clear to most that McDowell wasn't coming. In so doing, he created a situation that invited an attack. And the Eleventh Pennsylvania Reserves was near the center of the fighting when Robert E. Lee started a series of offensives that ultimately took most of Gallagher's men out of the war for a while.

If First Bull Run stifled optimism that the war would end in a few months, the Rebel withdrawal from Yorktown and McClellan's gradual advance up the Peninsula convinced McCall's soldiers, on the Rappahannock sidelines, that the Confederacy was doomed. The feeling was compounded by Federal victories in the west: Forts Henry and Donelson, Island No. 10, and Shiloh, the latter more a tactical draw than Union triumph.

Cambria Guards Capt. Andrew Lewis wrote from Falmouth: "Every one has their eyes turned now towardes Richmond and Mclenend and thinks that a battle will soone be fought their that will desid the fat[e] of the Suthern Confedrasy." He noted sardonically that a swift Union victory could even be anticlimactic. The Eleventh would "most likley . . . be the first or among the first that will be discharged and then wont we hav done the Devell and all toward puting down the rebelion." He allowed, "It almost makes me laugh to think how we hav bene used and now we hav beene a year in the U S servis and as yet hav never had a fight." Lewis also passed on the time-honored soldier belief that business interests conspired to prolong the war: "I think that if it was now pushed it soone could be finished and an end put to it," he wrote, "but it payes some to [*sic*] well to let it be finished so soone." The Rappahannock was quiet, according to Lewis: "Their is no danger of eney of us ever falling in battle, for the enimey seames to keep a good distance of[f] from us all the time." However, he added, if McClellan was unable "to manag[e] them at Richmond we will git a chance of going down their yet."[1]

Many in the ranks hoped that would happen. Pvt. Philip Lantzy wrote home that "our division is ancious for to get in a little fight," though he doubted McCall's brigades would see action "for there's so many troops ahead of us." Drummer John Loor was less concerned about fighting, enjoying the interlude and remarking that he was eating "plenty of hoe cakes here and I tell you now they eat nice." He also soaked up the sentimental campfire songs of the era, the title of one echoing in a letter he composed on 6 May. "I don't care how long the war last[s]," he wrote his father, "for I will be gay and happy still."[2]

Optimism about the war's progress apparently affected even staid Colonel Gallagher. On 11 May, he reported to Meade that he had detailed men to recruit 58 soldiers needed to replace those taken sick or transferred to other duties. But he cryptically volunteered an opinion that "from the Progress the Army of the Union has made . . . further recruiting is not advisable." He did not specify the number of men absent at this time, but by the time the regiment became engaged on the Peninsula, Adjt. Robert McCoy was aware of 190 detached or ill, the equivalent of almost two full companies.[3]

By mid-May, McClellan had reached his position astride the Chickahominy River, one which remains fodder for historical analysis and criticism. The portion of the army on the southern bank relied on newly built bridges to keep linked to the main body, which drew its supplies from the depot at White House Landing on the Pamunkey River.[4] Hanging on to the north side of the river still made sense on 18 May, when McClellan was told to expect McDowell's overland arrival. Counting on Stonewall Jackson staying quiet, Lincoln had decided to reinforce the Army of the Rappahannock with elements from Banks' department, then start the whole heading southward on 26 May. Three days before the march was to start, Lincoln, accompanied by Secretary of War Edwin Stanton who had replaced Cameron, came to Falmouth to review the troops. Meade found time to chat with the president, who remarked that in running the war "I am trying to do my duty, but no one can imagine what influences are brought to bear on me."[5]

Of the dress parade before the distinguished guests, Lantzy recounted: "There was about 32 shots fired by the cannon for a salute when the President came on the review ground. It was a nice sight to hear the troops give him three Rousing Cheers he rode a Common Cavalry horse and he was dressed in very poor clothes if I had not known him, I would have thought he was a citizen he rode along in front with the [*sic*] general McCall with his old Stove pipe hat in his hand and his long nose Sticking out before him. the president said that we all looked well and he wanted us to move on towards Richmond."[6]

On the same day, Stonewall Jackson struck at Front Royal, routing Banks' roughly 8,000 men. Fearing for Harpers Ferry and points north, Lincoln quickly suspended McDowell's orders to join McClellan. The bulk of the Army of the Rappahannock, between 35,000 and 40,000 men by this time, was shifted in an effort to check Jackson. Only McCall's division, between a quarter and a third of McDowell's strength, remained at Falmouth. It would, Meade noted wryly, "have now the honor of holding Fredericksburg and the railroad from thence to Acquia [*sic*] Creek." He expected no Rebel strike from the south, the Confederates having destroyed so many bridges between Fredericksburg and Richmond as to prevent fast movements by either side.[7]

McClellan later claimed that he had kept his force split along the Chickahominy only because he hoped that Jackson could be dealt with, following which the Army of the Rappahannock could proceed as originally intended. He therefore had to keep elements of the Army of the Potomac north of the river to effect a linkup when McDowell's arrived. As he wrote in 1863, he wanted all along to concentrate south of the Chickahominy, establishing a new base on the James River, but "It will be remembered that the order for the co-operation of General McDowell was simply suspended, not revoked."[8]

Whatever the case, when Confederate commander Joseph Johnston learned that Stonewall Jackson had indeed delayed McDowell, he decided to strike McClellan's weaker, southern wing, consisting of Maj. Gen. Samuel Heintzelman's III Corps and Maj. Gen. Erasmus Keyes' IV Corps. The Rebels hit Keyes on 31 May in a battle to be known as Fair Oaks or Seven Pines. The engagement involved about 41,000 men on each side, the largest yet fought in Virginia.

Hampered by weather and mud, Johnston's uncoordinated attacks were repulsed, but only after the Rebels nearly routed Keyes, whose force was bolstered by one of Heintzelman's divisions. Meanwhile, three Federal corps sat largely inert across the river, rain-swollen to the point of rendering its few bridges unsafe. Union II Corps commander Maj. Gen. Edwin Sumner probably saved Keyes, and Heintzelman after him, by sending a division across one of the perilous crossings on his own initiative. Union losses were 790 killed and 3,594 wounded, with 647 missing. Rebel losses were higher: 980 killed, 4,749 wounded, and 405 missing.[9]

The battle showed the danger of the trans-Chickahominy deployment, but McClellan afterward opted simply to strengthen his southern wing, shifting almost all of the army across the Chickahominy bridges. However, he maintained the White House Landing base on the Pamunkey, leaving only the V Corps under Brig. Gen. Fitz-John Porter on the Chickahominy's north side to keep communications open. But Porter would have support in this key position. Early in June, Lincoln decided to detach McCall's division from McDowell's army (Brig. Gen. Abner Doubleday's brigade would take its place at Falmouth), float it from Aquia Creek to White House Landing, and assign it to Porter. This addition made the V Corps the largest entity in the Army of the Potomac, and McClellan counted on it to keep his supply line safe while he pondered his next move.[10]

Gallagher's men could sense a more active role in the campaign coming. Lantzy predicted that "one more large battle will bring this war to a close," and he expected to be in it. He took stock of his spiritual situation in a missive just before the regiment received orders to embark for the Peninsula. "God only knows whose lot it may be to fill," he wrote, "but whatever comes I am sadisfied for I pray to God every night and I hope that you all at home do the same and I do pray for you all." He confessed disappointment that his regiment lacked a Catholic priest. "There is what they call a Chaplin in our Regt.," he wrote, referring to the Reverend Dickson, "But I do not care for him for he is a Methodist." He was resigned to the possibility of death but not despairing of survival: "I have just quit all my dreaming and am preparing myself to die, but I think that if I live you will all see me home for Christmas."[11] His captain, Andrew Lewis, was also setting his affairs in order. In a letter he detailed his debts and instructed his wife as to whom to pay and how much. Yet he stressed that he expected to return, and "I will hav a big spree of some sort when I come back."[12]

The orders to move came on 8 June. McCall the next day marched his three brigades of Pennsylvania Reserves to Gray's Landing, about six miles below Fredericksburg on the Rappahannock. From there steam transports were to take them via Chesapeake Bay and the York River to the base on the Pamunkey.[13]

The troops filed onto the ships late on the 9th, but a lack of pilots and stormy weather delayed progress. Six-foot-tall, sandy-haired, blue-eyed James McGinley of Indiana County's Washington Blues embarked on a steamship called *John Brooks*. The twenty-year-old Clarksburg farmer had McCall and his staff for traveling companions, along with eight companies of the regiment, "30 horses, 10 wagons and a larg[e] quantity of Ammunition." The *John Brooks* was grounded at one point on 11 June, "stuck fast two hours" McGinley noted, until a gunboat pulled it free. As day broke on 12 June, the boat reached the entrance of the York River, on its way to the Pamunkey. At about 4 P.M. the men on the *John Brooks* began disembarking at White House Landing. The area was crowded with supplies, soldiers, and teamsters, and the new arrivals saw the signs of imminent fighting. A "canvas town" of hospital tents stood ready for a new influx of casualties. Professional embalmers had also set up shop and handed out advertising leaflets to troops marching past.[14]

On 13 June, Rebel cavalry leader Jeb Stuart began his famous three-day ride around the Army of the Potomac, unnerving McClellan with the ease by which he pierced the long flank. At this time the Pennsylvania Reserves were still spread between the Rappahannock wharves and White House Landing. Meade's brigade had gone ahead of him; he remained at Gray's Landing, having given up his space on the *John Brooks* to McCall. Several more days would pass before the arrival of the Third Brigade and its new commander, Brig. Gen. Truman Seymour, a Fort Sumter veteran and recently a Reserves artillery officer. He had come to the position in early May when Ord, the hero of Dranesville, was promoted to a divisional command.[15]

Reynolds, whose own brigade had arrived intact and was camped near Dispatch Station on the York River Railroad, started after Stuart on the day the raid began. By nightfall his men had marched about eight miles in pursuit to Tunstall's Station. A burning bridge and rail car illuminated the ransacked depot. Telegraph poles had been knocked down, the wires cut. A man who had evidently been a civilian laborer was found dead on the tracks, run over by a train. Another body lay in nearby woods, shot in the head.[16]

The Eleventh Reserves did not take part in the chase. Rather, it spent 13 June marching from its first camp, about a half a mile from White House, to Dispatch Station. McGinley noted in his diary that Richmond was only 13 miles away. The men spent 16 June gathering cherries, and the next day they prepared for an expected review by the army commander. "Brigade in line twice to receive General McClellan," McGinley noted, "but he did not make his appearance."[17]

McClellan was busy worrying about his Chickahominy-Pamunkey flank. He decided he would shift the army's main supply and administrative site from White House to Harrison's Landing on the James River. Using this site would allow him to concentrate all of his troops south of the Chickahominy, eliminating his need to protect the long line back to the Pamunkey.[18] In the meantime, until Fitz-John Porter's V Corps could be shifted across the Chickahominy, the Pennsylvania Reserves formed the Union army's extreme right.

From Dispatch Station, the next destination for Gallagher and his soldiers was a plantation owned by Dr. William Gaines. His nearby mill gave its name to the spot where the Telegraph Road crossed the Powhite Creek, itself an offshoot of the Chickahominy, the latter lying about a mile and a half to the south. A secessionist unintimidated by the Yankee army's presence, Gaines let the Pennsylvanians know that they were unwelcome. Angered by the burial of Federal fever casualties on his land, he railed that he would later disinter the corpses and use them as hog food. His dramatic threat honored a "secesh" theory that, as a Manassas farmer stated it, held that "one Yankee body will kill an acre of land whereas a Southerner's bones will enrich it for all time to come." Following the upcoming battles, one historian has noted, Gaines "witnessed far more interments on his property than he could have ever imagined."[19]

On the afternoon of 19 June, Porter ordered McCall to move the Reserves from the angry doctor's farm. They marched two and a half miles to Mechanicsville, a town which, a soldier recalled, "lies on the high ground, overlooking the Chickahominy on its north bank. . . . It consists of a church and some fifteen houses, all of which were deserted and perforated by shot and shell." It was only about four miles from Richmond, and it was possible to stand on shed roofs in Mechanicsville and see the Rebel capital's spires.[20]

The bulk of the division stayed east of the town, behind another swampy Chickahominy offshoot, Beaver Dam Creek. Pickets were posted—a regiment at a time, plus a battery—across the creek in Mechanicsville itself to prevent Rebel gunners from setting up on the high ground there. Pickets also watched Meadow Bridge, two parallel spans crossing the Chickahominy upstream about a mile northwest of the town.

McCall reported that his Beaver Dam Creek position, about a mile to the east of Mechanicsville, was "naturally a strong one, the left resting on the Chickahominy and the right extending to thick woods beyond the upper Mechanicsville road, which were occupied." Seymour described the creek as "a stream of small size, and would everywhere be passable but for its marshy edges, and, in its lower course, for a mill-race and deep ditches." The banks were steep, "covered with thick brush and woods, behind which extend broad fields." Covering the creek and two roads that approached it, McCall positioned Reynolds' First Brigade on the right,

Seymour's Third Brigade on the left. Sixteen heavy guns backed up the front line, and Meade's brigade, the Eleventh Reserves included, was kept in reserve. To McCall's right, Federal cavalry under Brig. Gen. George Stoneman screened the eight miles between Beaver Dam Creek and the wide Pamunkey, which formed the Army of the Potomac's northern flank.[21]

Gallagher's men quickly came face-to-face with the Confederates. The pickets were "within musket range of each other," Meade wrote home after his brigade took up its new position. Cobb's Legion, a Georgian mounted unit in Stuart's division-sized cavalry command, was visible in its camp across the river. The Rebel "Light Division" of Maj. Gen. A. P. Hill was positioned about a mile behind. These troops "held two redoubts and an extensive line of rifle pits along the crest of the highlands overlooking the river." McCall's men cut down trees in front of their lines, using the wood to build an abatis on the creek's steep western bank. The Reserves had benefited from their fort-building experience, for a Rebel artillerist considered this part of the line "absolutely impregnable." With these preparations made, McCall later wrote, "I awaited any movements the enemy might initiate."[22]

The movements were coming. Joseph Johnston had been wounded during the battle of Fair Oaks. Robert E. Lee, hitherto acting as Jefferson Davis' main military adviser, replaced him in command of what would now be styled the Army of Northern Virginia. Like his predecessor, Lee found McClellan's unorthodox deployment along the Chickahominy tempting.

By now, McClellan's weaker wing was the northern one—Porter's lonely-though-large and well-entrenched V Corps. Lee envisioned a bold maneuver to flank the fortifications, involving the withdrawal of Stonewall Jackson's three divisions from the Shenandoah Valley. These swift-marching troops were to brush aside Stoneman's pickets, come up behind the V Corps' right flank, and strike McCall's rear. Once Jackson was engaged, A. P. Hill's Light Division would hit McCall head-on, with support from the divisions of D. H. Hill and James Longstreet. The rest of Lee's army, on the south side of the Chickahominy, would feint an attack there to push McClellan further off balance.[23]

Only about a week after writing wistfully about the "big spree" he hoped for when he got home, Andrew Lewis was in a darker frame of mind. The embalmer's handbills, Stuart's raid, and the malaria cases from the Chickahominy swamps all probably influenced the Cambria Guards' captain to predict that the next battle would probably dwarf Fair Oaks. "I hop[e] that our friends in the North may not be disapointed in what they may expect of the reserv core [corps] when the time arrives for them to do their dutey," he noted, "but Maria if I am not mutch mistaken their will be one of the awfulest battles fought here that the world has ever wit-tnessed." Many would fall, he knew, "but who they may bee is hard to tell But if I should be so unfortinet as to be one of the number my onley wish is for you to show yourself capable of b[e]aring up against the loss. . . . for Maria recolect that maney [a] wife has the same or will hav the same thing to trouble them and how maney a mother will hav their sones to mourn for the lose of them." Perhaps trying to soften what he had just written, Lewis added that "even should I escap death from the bullits of the enimey at the most there is but a fiew short years for us to liv together in this world before one or the other of us must be called home B[e]aring this in mind I hop[e] you may try and do your duty as a mother and I will try and do mine as a soilder so that you shall not be asshamed of me."[24]

Independent Blues Pvt. James X. McIlwain was also thinking of home. Then about twenty-eight, McIlwain was a former saddle-maker from Apollo with dark eyes and black hair. His unusual middle initial may have stood for Xenophon, the name he gave his firstborn child. Detailed since mid-May as the brigade's saddler, he wrote regularly to his wife Emma, whom he had married in 1858. Others may have had to help Emma read her husband's letters, for (at least in later years) she signed her name by making an X. "You will hear of a big fight in these quarters between two Mighty Armies," McIlwain wrote Emma the same day Lewis penned his pessimistic missive. He described McClellan's force as so big that when "drawn up in line of battle you would not know how or where [so many men] come from."[25]

A week later, McIlwain sounded optimistic about Richmond's fall, but also frustrated with the slow pace of the campaign. "I Suppose long Enough before you get this letter the City of Richmond will be ours," he wrote, adding that "I think there will not be much danger in takeing it." But he wanted the "great Battle," which would be "the finishing Stroke of the war," to come soon.

> You wanted to know in your letter when I was coming home or if I had set any Time for coming home. I thought last fall that we would all get home again [by] Chrismas. Then when that time arrived I thought the 1st of April would certainly see me at home but when that failed I set the middle of May we all thought surely by that time we would be winding our way Towards home. And even then When we was disapointed I was positive that the

Glorious 4th of July would be spent at home but Alas There is no chance for Seeing Apollo my wife And little ones then but I Suspect if I have the Luck to be Spared to See The Capitol of the Rebel Confederacy by That Time, and if I do I will Then soon be on my way to Old Apollo.[26]

While the rest of the division watched Beaver Dam Creek, the Second Brigade encamped in woods along the Chickahominy. Gallagher's men saw their enemies digging fortifications and placing cannon. They were also close enough to hear bands playing in the Light Division's camps. McCall prohibited music, drums, and bugle calls unless warning of an attack.[27]

The Chickahominy at this point was narrow, but 800 yards of heavy swamp separated the opposing pickets. The latter rarely fired at each other, but Union batteries sometimes opened up at Confederates, a practice Meade thought frivolous. Rebel gunners returned the favor by chasing away Union fatigue details, and Meade ordered his men to stay away from the riverbank to avoid drawing fire. For some reason, they disregarded his command when shelling started on 20 June. Meade wrote home that some of his troops rushed "through the woods into the open ground beyond, to stare about like idiots. The enemy, seeing the crowd, soon ascertained our position, and moving one of their long-range guns, began throwing shot and shell right into our camp, scattering the curious gentlemen and giving them a pretty good scare." According to Lantzy, who took in the start of the action from atop a small tree, the Rebels had been shelling a bridge before they spotted the onlooking infantry and altered their aim. Kepler remembered that "shells were dropping in pretty lively. Their 'bomb whizzes' played us quite a tune." No soldiers were hurt, but a piece of shell hit Gallagher's horse, perhaps the same one accidentally shot at Camp Wright, in the neck. Meade rode amid the troops, cursing them for disobeying orders. "After letting them stand the fire till they were pretty well subdued," he wrote home, "I moved the camp to another position, and all has since been quiet."[28]

The new site, Kepler recalled, was near a large plantation, "with the old-fashioned typical buildings of the South, with beautiful surroundings, and every indication of wealth by its owner." It was occupied by "a very handsome, dignified middle-aged woman with two full-grown daughters and a few old negro servants." The menfolk were probably in the Confederate army, but Gallagher put a guard on the house. Kepler, who drew some of this duty, remembered the daughters as "splendid types of southern beauty with tall, graceful figures and coal-black flashing eyes." He was thrilled one morning to hear an "upper window slowly opening, and, glancing upward, I saw the girls with rosy cheeks, and roguish eyes looking down at me. Playfully I saluted them, with a demand for the countersign; they smiled at me in turn, then closed the window and vanished."[29]

On 21 June, a Rebel deserter reported that the Union lines would be attacked the next day. The alarm proved unfounded. More deserters kept coming, one being a Louisianan who brought tales of starvation in Richmond—and details of another impending attack. The Confederates kept to their positions across the Chickahominy, although several dozen North Carolinians deserted en masse to McCall's lines. Enough Rebel soldiers pursued them to spark a firefight which ultimately involved a full Union regiment supported by three cannon. The tension increased again on the 23rd, when one of Fitz-John Porter's aides informed McCall that five contrabands had reported "that the enemy intend making an attack on our right, crossing at Meadow Bridge." McCall kept his division under arms until nightfall, when Reynolds' brigade crossed Beaver Dam Creek, chasing off A. P. Hill's pickets outside Mechanicsville. Heavy rain fell during the same night, flooding the Chickahominy and, Meade thought, "probably preventing any attack."[30]

The respite was short-lived. On the 25th, the day before Lee's offensive was to start, Gallagher's regiment went to picket the far left of the line, where Beaver Dam Creek met the Chickahominy. Lewis dashed off a note home before leaving, closing with an ominous postscript: "I belive that we are a going to hav a fight ri[gh]t off so good by."[31] The Eleventh was to guard against a Rebel attempt to lay pontoons or otherwise effect a crossing. Kepler recalled that each captain dispersed his men "at short intervals along the bank in the grass, lying flat on the ground, so as to be completely hidden from the enemy." Near midnight, they saw Confederate pickets deploying on the opposite bank, "presumably for the same purpose that we were on. We could have shot them on sight in the bright moonlight, but as they did not interfere with us, we kept perfectly quiet until morning, when they filed out of our way, greatly to the relief of our high-strung nerves."[32]

Fortunately for the Federal troops, Stonewall Jackson's flank march and attack on Porter, which Lee so carefully planned, never came off. If Jackson's fame was based largely on his ability to move men quickly, this characteristic was absent here. His force spent 26 June crawling toward

Porter's right, while Gallagher's men sat tensely at the far end of McCall's left. Yet the enemy was stirring. As the sun came up, cavalry patrols found Rebel columns coming. While word was passed in the camp of the Fifth Reserves, then holding Mechanicsville itself, other alarming news filtered back from elements of the Thirteenth Reserves doing picket duty at Meadow Bridge.

Only a fraction of the Bucktails were represented in McCall's division at the time. Four of the picturesque regiment's ten companies had been detached to serve in the Shenandoah Valley along with Bayard's cavalry. What remained formed a six-company battalion under Major Roy Stone. The two companies he had placed at Meadow Bridge now found themselves receiving fire from Rebels trying to cross. One company, its captain intent on (as Seymour later phrased it) "holding ground too eagerly," was forced to surrender.[33]

Their captors belonged to A. P. Hill's Light Division, which was getting restless waiting for Stonewall Jackson to open the battle. At about noon, Hill's batteries tossed shells at the Eleventh Reserves' pickets, visible on the Chickahominy bank. No one was reported hurt, but the anxiety raised another notch. At about 3 P.M., with Jackson nowhere in sight, the 14,000-man Light Division advanced.[34]

An observer from the Rebel lines remembered that, before smoke settled across the field, the "flash of guns, and long lines of musketry fire could be seen in bright relief against the blue and cloudless sky." The assault forced the Fifth Reserves out of Mechanicsville and across the Beaver Dam Creek crossings. As gunfire picked up—by four o'clock the firing became general—Gallagher's men were still scattered in a series of picket outposts. James McGinley later noted in his diary that the regiment's position was "on the left of the line half a mile from the battle field." At about 6:30 P.M., while the Light Division battered against the Union left and center, a Confederate brigade under Roswell Ripley, loaned from D. H. Hill's neighboring division, started to advance against Seymour's left. This was held by the Twelfth and Ninth Reserves, the latter's front skirting the Eleventh's Chickahominy picket line. When one of Ripley's units, the First North Carolina, appeared in skirmish order slowly advancing, Seymour called on Meade for help.

Meade dispatched the Seventh Pennsylvania Reserves, which formed between the Twelfth and Ninth. Seymour wanted more troops, however. His aide-de-camp found Andrew Lewis and the rifle-equipped Cambria Guards, who as the right flank company would have been closest to the main battle line, and ordered them into action. Lewis, seeing his first real battlefield since Mexico, hurried his men into a skirmish line, bridging the gap between the Seventh and Ninth Reserves.[35]

Across Beaver Dam Creek, another Mexican War veteran was on his horse, surveying the front against which his First North Carolina was to charge. This was Montford S. Stokes, a dark-haired, youthful-looking colonel who wore a pince-nez when being photographed. Stokes dismounted and personally led his men forward, but Federal gunfire forced his troops to lie down shy of the creek's edge. Then, one of his soldiers recalled, Stokes ordered them to "rise up and charge." They responded, shrieking their high-pitched Rebel yell, and "proceed[ed] half way down the hill, halt[ed] and exchange[ed] shot for shot with the yankees, who had the very best of covering."[36]

Beaver Dam Creek proved an effective abatis, halting or at least delaying the attackers. Additional Union artillery "went into action, the men working the pieces with their coats off and sleeves rolled up." Most of the Rebels again lay down and sought shelter, but at least one made it into the creek near where the Cambria Guards were deployed. Sgt. John E. Scanlan captured him on the opposite bank.[37]

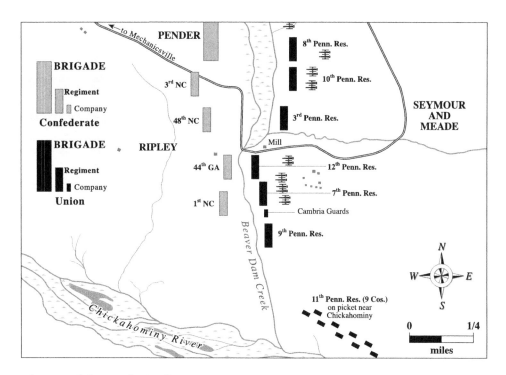

The Union left at Mechanicsville

None of the Cambria Guards seems to have left an account of what it was like to stand on a firing line for the first time. They were undoubtedly affected to varying degrees. Historian Bell Wiley, who spent his life studying Civil War soldier letters, assessed their accounts of battle fear as manifesting itself in "dryness of the throat and lips; a sense of heaviness in the area of vital organs, as if a stone were weighing on the chest, making breathing difficult; and excessive perspiration. Some soldiers noted a sharpening of recollective powers with the result that many long-latent memories of home and childhood passed in rapid succession across the canvas of consciousness." The call to battle usually brought on a stark silence from the men. The first shots might bring about reactions ranging from calm to the anger of blood lust, men weeping and cursing as they went through the motions of loading and firing. Tearing cartridges apart with their teeth, the men took on macabre appearances as loose gunpowder became smeared on sweaty faces. A Confederate spotted a comrade through the smoke of a battle line: "His face was cold and pallid and bloodless, but not from fear. Blackened with powder stain, through which the perspiration trickled in streams, his eyes flashed defiance with every flash from his gun, . . . he stood there a perfect demon of war, with no thought save to kill."[38]

Little thinking was done once a battle began, as the deafening noise of musketry joined the adrenaline of fear in taking over the senses. The sound of impacting artillery rounds could rupture eardrums. A survivor of Mechanicsville recalled that "The commands of officers at five paces distant, could not be heard." Sgt. John H. Miller of the Brady Guards later wrote of one battle (Fredericksburg) that "for hours the roaring of cannon, the crash of arms was the only sound that greeted your ear, unless you occasionally heard the dying scream of a companion who had fallen at your side." Those cries echoed in the heads of men well aware that the hot lead of bullets and shells could not only kill but mutilate while sadistically leaving the victim alive. After the Mexican War engagement at Palo Alto, Ulysses S. Grant wrote his wife, "a ball struck close by me killing one man instantly, it [k]nocked Capt Page's under jaw entirely off and broke in the roof of his mouth . . . Capt Page is still alive." When a Civil War shell fragment did the same to a New York private, surgeons sewed the skin together where his chin should have been, contracting what was left of his face into a perpetual moan. A British officer was similarly wounded at Waterloo. Missing his jaw and tongue, he slowly starved to death.[39]

If Lewis' men were conscious of such fates, they likely were desperate to be seen as brave—their regiment had, after all, styled itself the "Bloody Eleventh" as early as Camp Wright. Contemporary society understood little of human psychology and mocked "cowardly" soldiers. The historian of the Second Pennsylvania Reserves wrote of a man at South Mountain who was "always shirking, and neither the threats of his officers or ridicule of his comrades could induce him to go into danger, as he declared he had a presentiment when a boy that he would be killed the first fight he went into. Some of his comrades, however, determined he should go into this battle, and threatened to shoot him if he did not." Once under fire, he lay down behind a tree trunk, but in moving to a better spot behind a large rock "he fell dead with nine of the enemy's balls in him." The writer concluded that "Bravery is born in us and not acquired. . . . Courage, which is generally confounded with bravery, is not always united with it. . . . It is not inaccessible to fear; but it overcomes it."[40]

Because so many could not overcome fear, commanders and noncommissioned officers in battle became "file-closers," authorized and expected to use swords and pistols to threaten the privates into staying at their posts. Meade disgusted witnesses at Antietam when, having spied a frightened Eighth Reserves soldier cowering behind a tree, he beat him with the flat of his saber.[41] Yet he did what every man ranking above private was supposed to do.

Writing with almost four decades between himself and the war, Aaron Kepler maintained that "A true soldier makes up his mind that he may not get out of battle alive, and the mind, once decided, will overrule and conquer the body, so that there will be but little fear." Not all men could control themselves this way. Some who acknowledged their nervousness blamed it on causes other than fear of being hit. A member of the Seventh Reserves, writing about Mechanicsville, conceded: "I went out with an anxious heart, not that I feared the bullets of the enemy, but because I was afraid of myself. I did not know what effect the excitement of the battle-field would have up on me, because I had never tried it, so I looked forward with a sort of anxious curiosity to the time when I should become acquainted with myself in this respect." Once engaged, he found he could easily concentrate on the task at hand. "I felt more cool headed," he wrote, "and appeared to have a clearer conception of things around me, than I had before on one of our every day drills."[42]

If he and his comrades became focused during their baptism of fire at Mechanicsville, they also nearly shot some Cambria Guards. Smoke limited visibility—Union signalers found their flag stations useless—and men in the firing lines were easily confused. During the fight with the First North Carolina, a company from the Seventh Reserves shifted to its left to face what it thought were approaching Rebels. The new targets happened to be Lewis' men; the Seventh Reserves' volley fortunately went too high to do damage.

As officers sorted out the mixup, a different threat—a Confederate one this time—was developing on the Eleventh's right. Another of Ripley's units, the Forty-fourth Georgia, was advancing in support of Stokes' stalled regiment. Lewis ordered a retreat, and fire from other Union regiments halted the Georgians' attack. Ripley's brigade eventually drew back. The First North Carolina suffered 142 casualties on its advance to the edge of Beaver Dam Creek. Besides Stokes himself, the regiment's major, adjutant, and the captains of six companies were killed or mortally wounded. That unit got off lightly compared to the Forty-fourth Georgia, which suffered 335 killed, wounded and missing—a casualty rate of 65 percent. The losses reflected the intensity of the Federal gunfire all along the line. "In the woods beyond Mechanicsville," a Richmond newspaper correspondent wrote a few days later, "some of the trees, as thick around as a man's body, are shot through and through by round shot, and the bushes are everywhere cut and nipped by the bullets."[43]

For two more hours, the Cambria Guards held their position between the Seventh and Ninth Reserves, watching the battle slowly die down. As smoke cleared, eerie images appeared in the twilight. "Barns, houses and stacks of hay and straw were in a blaze," a Rebel observer wrote, "and by their light our men were plainly visible rushing across the open spaces through infernal showers of grape." As Kepler, whose company was still picketing the Chickahominy, remembered: "The artillery duel at night was especially grand, interesting and exciting. The sudden flash and roar of the deep-mouthed cannon sending solid shot with lightning speed screaming through the air, and shells with trailing fuse, like meteors in the sky, bursting and booming on their deadly mission was thrilling beyond description." A soldier in another Pennsylvania Reserves regiment wrote how the "long lines of flame, shining out of the darkness, together with the loud roar of artillery and musketry, formed a scene both grand and terrific."[44]

As nightfall came, Adjt. Robert McCoy brought two companies to the battle line and relieved the Cambria Guards. Elements of the Ninth Reserves later shifted to their right and relieved McCoy's force. The general action ended at about nine o'clock, when the Confederates withdrew under cover of darkness.[45]

Ebensburg's Company A had been part of a grim victory, for the battlefield was a gray slaughterhouse. "Through the night," Seymour wrote in his report, "the cries of wounded and suffering rebels came plainly to our ears and attested the vigor of our defense." One of the Bucktails wrote home that "after the firing had ceased, we could hear the wounded rebels cry for help and asking for some one to bring them a drink of water and calling on the Maker to help them. It seemed the most pityful of anything I ever heard or seen to hear the different sounds and moans over the ground.—Some seemed to be in awful agony; but they had to lay there without any one near to give them water or help in the least."[46]

The attack was a debacle on a level with any of the Civil War's disastrous frontal assaults. McCall's Pennsylvania Reserves, holding an enormous advantage of position, needed only to load and fire. A. P. Hill lost almost 1,500 men from his division, Fitz-John Porter less than 300 throughout his entire corps.[47]

Federal commanders expected the battle to be renewed the next morning. Given the successful repulse, Porter thought McClellan might even order the V Corps to advance on Richmond. Preparing for any eventuality, McCall sent the wounded to the rear, ordered weapons cleaned and ammunition issued. By 1 A.M. on 27 June all of his officers reported their commands ready. But while McClellan at first thought Porter had dealt with Stonewall Jackson's troops, new reports confirmed the latter's force, though too slow to join the fight on the 26th, was still out there and approaching the V Corps' right.[48] Given that threat, McClellan decided that it was time not only to stay on the defensive, but to call off the entire campaign and retreat from the Peninsula. It was a stunning strategic decision for a man who had just won a battle and marked one of his few quick, decisive moves as commander of the Army of the Potomac.

Although he told his immediate staff of the decision, he kept its substance from his corps and divisional commanders. First he had to complete the already-prepared shift of base from White House Landing to Harrison's Landing. Porter was told to withdraw to a new site further back on the Chickahominy line, though until White House Landing could be evacuated he was evidently to be kept on the Chickahominy's northern bank. The new defensive site was near Dr. Gaines' land and just beyond Powhite Creek, about four miles distant from Beaver Dam Creek. This was a plateau behind Boatswain's Swamp, another marshy bog curling north and east from the Chickahominy. Looking at the defense plans, which essentially put his corps' back against the latter river, Porter decided to place the divisions of Brig. Gens. George Morell and George Sykes on the high ground that arced directly behind the swamp. McCall was to be in reserve.[49]

The directive for a withdrawal reached McCall just before dawn, and he found it troubling. "Had it reached me at midnight," McCall wrote in his report, "the movement might have been accomplished without difficulty and without loss, but now it would be daylight before the movement—under fire, one of the most delicate and difficult in war, and now in presence of a superior force—could be commenced."[50] But he complied, with Meade's troops, along with a brigade from Morell's division (reinforcements for McCall commanded by Brig. Gen. Charles Griffin) among the first to be shifted. McCall's aide transmitted the order to Gallagher, telling him that the Eleventh Reserves was to forego breakfast and pull back to a peach orchard near which McCall had made his headquarters. From there, it was to march toward Gaines' Mill and the new defensive line. Gallagher's men were disgusted. "There was a good deal of dissatisfaction expressed at this order," Lt. James Burke of the Cambria Guards wrote later, "and we executed it with reluctance, it being . . . believed that we could thrash [the Rebels] easily by being reinforced."[51]

McCall's fears about the withdrawal soon came true. As soon as Meade's and Griffin's movement was spotted, Rebel batteries and sharpshooters opened up, assuming the Federals were attacking. Firing soon spread all over the line, and at one point Gallagher was told to rush back to the battlefield and place his regiment in reserve.

The Eleventh Reserves suffered its first battle death shortly after it reformed. A Confederate marksman had infiltrated the same plantation house the regiment had once guarded. At about 9 A.M., he aimed his rifle from an upper-story window—Kepler thought it was the same at which he had seen the owner's beautiful daughters. The minié bullet he fired killed Company H drummer John Loor, the young musician who had earlier written home that he would be "gay and happy still" no matter how long the war lasted. The regiment's position on the battlefield in relation to the house is unclear, but any plans to rout out the sniper faded when Gallagher received word to immediately resume the march. Kepler recalled bitterly that "as we were closely pressed by the enemy, we had no time to halt to avenge his [Loor's] death."[52]

Dead drummers did not figure into McCall's report of the division's withdrawal. He termed it a success, noting: "our killed had been buried, the wounded had been sent off, and not a man, nor a gun, nor a musket, nor a knapsack was left upon the field. The different regiments filed past as steadily as if marching from the parade ground, and it must have been some time before the enemy were aware that we were gone, as no attempt was made to follow immediately." But McCall, who wrote those words after a stay in a Richmond prison, was probably ill informed. Seymour's brigade, which followed Meade, did beat back a Rebel probe and withdrew in good order. But in Reynolds' command part of Major Stone's abbreviated Bucktails' battalion was flanked and overrun. The Thirteenth Reserves' color company became the second Bucktails company taken prisoner within twenty-four hours. Although its members hid the silk regimental standard in swampy ground near Beaver Dam Creek, Confederate troops found it. Jefferson Davis received it as a trophy of war. Other Union flags would follow.[53]

A modern historian has described the battle of Gaines' Mill, at which most of the Eleventh Reserves was surrounded and captured, as one "fought entirely without subtlety." What began as an effort to turn the V Corps' flank ended as simply another Confederate frontal assault. The Pennsylvania Reserves again played a key role, though not as a division. Their regiments were deployed piecemeal to plug gaps, launch counterthrusts, and relieve other exhausted units. As Seymour noted in his report, "No brigade went into action entire, and it is difficult to describe connectedly the movements of any one command." The confusion may be illustrated by the fact that Gallagher's regiment ended the day fighting alongside a New Jersey regiment from a different corps.[54]

By mid-morning on the 27th, Stonewall Jackson was still dragging his men toward the V Corps' right. A. P. Hill's and Longstreet's forces kept up fire on McCall's rear elements. The sounds of battle were well behind the Eleventh Reserves as its brigade withdrew toward positions behind Boatswain's Swamp. The march took Gallagher's men by the Gaines' Mill hamlet where they had camped after they first joined the V Corps. They also passed through New Cold Harbor, a place name which within two years gained its own infamy.

Fitz-John Porter's new lines extended about a mile and a half. Morell's division was placed on the left in heavy woods. Sykes' (whose command consisted almost entirely of Regular Army troops, as opposed to volunteers mustered into Federal service from their states) went into "comparatively open" ground on the right. Batteries bristled along the line. Destined for reserve use, McCall's men filed across rough bridges over the swamp and were stationed about a quarter-mile behind the front: Meade on the left, Reynolds on the right, Seymour further to the rear.[55]

Gallagher's regiment received some unofficial reinforcements at about this time. They came when seven slaves belonging to Sarah E. Watt, whose house and slave quarters were within the new Federal lines, joined up with the Eleventh Reserves as a group. "Contrabands" commonly found menial jobs with McClellan's army, though some officers and men may have considered them an impediment. Evans Brady considered ex-slaves poor army laborers. "They complained bitterly that they had to work in the heat of the day," he wrote his mother, "and say the Yankees are harder masters than the ones they left." Regardless, on the lines outside Boatswain's Swamp enough spare clothing was found to fit out one of Watt's slaves, a youth about fifteen, in full Federal uniform; five others got blue trousers. Their presence is undocumented in regimental records but Richmond newspapers detailing the aftermath of Gaines' Mill linked them with Gallagher's command.[56]

All across the Federal line, the tired men had little time to rest. As Jackson and his three divisions neared Fitz-John Porter's right, A. P. Hill and Longstreet came hard from Mechanicsville. By 11 A.M. Rebels were in sight behind the swamp, and shells began to drop into the Federal posi-

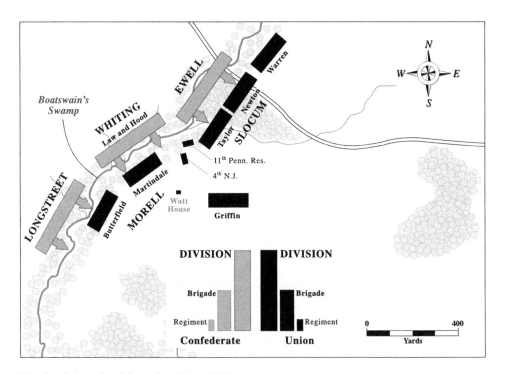

The Confederate breakthrough at Gaines' Mill

tion. Officers kept the men digging in, and some of Gallagher's soldiers collapsed from fatigue.[57]

At about 2:30 P.M. Longstreet and Hill attacked Morell's portion of the line in a series of charges that, as at Mechanicsville, failed in the face of massed artillery, rifle and musket fire. But Morell was hard-pressed and called upon Meade for reinforcements. By about 3:30 P.M., Meade had marched his command to just behind the Union center, at a position to the rear of Griffin's brigade. Sweating in their heavy wool uniforms, Gallagher's men were allowed to remove their knapsacks, then were ordered forward to screen a battery. Peering through the clouds of gunsmoke that hugged the field, the Eleventh could see Confederates advance toward the tree-cluttered Union positions.[58]

The regiment stayed near the battery until Meade withdrew it and told Gallagher to report to Brig. Gen. John H. Martindale, whose brigade held the center of Morell's line. At about this time another order filtered through; men were needed for an unusual bit of fatigue work. Fitz-John Porter had asked headquarters for tools to help the men entrench, and a supply of axe heads, though without handles, had been carted to a field hospital. Union troops must have still been trying to fell trees and create abatis, for one of Meade's staff officers went looking for men to make the tools usable. The task fell to Gallagher's Company B. As its captain, Daniel Porter, recalled in a letter home, "We were marching with the regiment right into battle, when an aid[e] came riding up and detailed us to put helves to 500 axes." The task spared the Indiana National Guards the eventual fate of the rest of the regiment, and the company commander deemed the orders "providential."[59]

It was now about 4 P.M. Meade had ordered the Third Pennsylvania Reserves, under Col. Horatio G. Sickel, previously screening a battery, closer to the front. Its new location was in the woods along Boatswain's Swamp, near Martindale's position. Meanwhile, reinforcements from outside Fitz-John Porter's corps were adding to the defense. Col. J. H. Simpson of the Fourth New Jersey Volunteers, from Brig. Gen. Henry Slocum's division of the VI Corps, was marching and countermarching his men in response to conflicting orders from his brigade adjutant and one of McClellan's staff officers. Eventually, the latter pair coordinated and sent Simpson to support Sickel. Meade stayed alongside Sickel's regiment for a while, presumably encouraging and steadying the men.[60]

Orders were on the way to bring Gallagher forward as well. Martindale, evidently worried about his flank, ordered the Eleventh Reserves to form behind the Fourteenth New York, part of Griffin's brigade, posted on the right of Morell's line. The regiment marched to the new position, two men from each company staying behind to guard the knapsacks. Gallagher went forward amid the deafening sounds of battle and found the New Yorkers' commander, Col. James McQuade, a veteran of the siege of Yorktown and at one time acting commander of the brigade. McQuade declined Gallagher's offer of relief for his men, explaining that his regiment had been in action for only a short time. Gallagher returned to his own ranks and ordered his men to lie down while he awaited word to move them into line. From here they watched as Confederate attacks splintered against the Federal front. Some Rebel gunfire reached the Eleventh's position, fire which the prone soldiers could not effectively return. It was probably at this point that Meade and Martindale spoke a few words of encouragement to Gallagher's men. Survivors would tell Samuel Bates after the war of the commanders telling them that "as they were going upon a part of the line which was weakest, they were expected to hold it at all hazards."[61]

The lull was relatively short. At about 4:30 P.M., more elements of Slocum's division were shifted into the Boatswain's Swamp positions to relieve Griffin's brigade, which was moved back into reserve having engaged part of A. P. Hill's division. Martindale sent an aide with fresh orders for Gallagher to shift his men closer to the center of the line. Their new position was diagonally behind and to the right of the Fourth New Jersey, part of Brig. Gen. George Taylor's brigade of Slocum's division. Gallagher formed his men there, again telling them to lie down. "The bullets and shell were flying like hail about us, but the boys stood it like veterans," Sgt. Daniel Jones of Company A wrote a few weeks later.[62]

In front of them, the Third Reserves was holding its own against A. P. Hill, now being reinforced by troops from Richard Ewell's division of Stonewall Jackson's force, which had finally arrived on the battlefield. "This regiment stood its ground well," Simpson wrote approvingly of Sickel's command, "and was incessant in its firing." At about 6 P.M., Simpson walked up to Sickel, reminded him of his regiment's presence, and said the Jerseymen would take over as soon as Sickel wished. The latter took up Simpson's offer about a quarter of an hour later when the Third Reserves had almost run out of ammunition. Sickel's troops filed back into the woods, through the Fourth New Jersey's battle line, which moved forward.[63]

By 7 P.M., Stonewall Jackson's three divisions were adding their combined weight against the Union center and right, and for the first time in two days Lee's entire attacking force was engaged on the battlefield.

Those hammering the center of the line, beyond the woods in front of Sickel's and Simpson's commands, may have included six Georgia regiments formed into a brigade headed by Confederate Brig. Gen. Alexander R. Lawton, part of what had once been Stonewall Jackson's own division (now headed by Brig. Gen. Charles S. Winder). Also moving up to this critical spot were two brigades—a total of nine regiments—from the division of Confederate Brig. Gen. William H. C. Whiting—with a pair of batteries attached. One brigade was led by Brig. Gen. Evander Law, whose battle-tested force included, besides his old Fourth Alabama, two regiments from Mississippi and one from North Carolina. The other's commander was a tall, blond-bearded brigadier named John Bell Hood. One of the war's most colorful and tragic figures, Hood had been born in Kentucky, attended West Point, fought on the frontier, then went with his adopted Lone Star State when war began. By war's end, he had lost a leg and the use of an arm. Yet he also received promotions; his final campaigns, leading the Army of Tennessee while strapped to his saddle, were marked by some of the war's most fruitless frontal assaults. The success of Hood's actions at Gaines' Mill probably spelled doom for his western army two years later, for here the frontal assault worked.[64]

Hood swung his "Texas Brigade," which despite its nickname included units from Georgia and South Carolina, into battle line, with Law's force deployed to his right. After issuing orders for the attack to the commanders of the First and Fifth Texas and to a South Carolina unit known as Hampton's Legion, he marched his Fourth Texas and Eighteenth Georgia into an open field opposite the Watt house and stationed them on the other side of Law's brigade. There, Hood later related, he "halted and dressed the line whilst under fire of the long-range guns, and gave positive instructions that no man should fire until I gave the order; for I knew full well that if the men were allowed to fire, they would halt to load, break the allignment [*sic*], and very likely, never reach the breastworks. I moreover ordered them not only to keep together, but also in line, and announced to them that I would lead them in the charge." At some point shortly after 7 P.M., the two brigades stepped off "at a rapid, but not at a double-quick pace" into the wooded swamp.[65]

The Federal troops put up a lethal resistance. On the right of the Hood-Law force, the smoothbore-equipped Georgians were unable to get close enough for their buck-and-ball ammunition to take effect. As they staggered to safety, comrades from the neighboring (and better armed) Fifth Texas, bearing British-made Enfield rifles, tried unsuccessfully to urge them back. In their wake, a survivor recounted, the Georgians had left a comrade "whom a shot in the head crazed, and who, standing upright, was making the wildest and oddest gesticulations imaginable, with his arms." A pair of Texans managed to haul him toward the rear. As the Texans continued on, a "cannon ball came rolling slowly down the hill. Nobody feared it—it was moving, apparently, with too little momentum to be at all dangerous." But when it struck one unfortunate man it "drew from him a scream of pain that was fearful to hear. Its movement arrested by impact with the poor fellow's body, it stopped within ten feet of him." The man died the next day, "his body having swollen to near the size of a flour barrel."[66]

Further to the Hood-Law left, the Fourth New Jersey was running low on ammunition. Intense firing left Simpson's men exhausted, their bodies bruised from their guns' recoil. Musket barrels clogged with powder residue or so overheated that they were dangerous to load. Gallagher recognized the situation because at some point before 7 P.M., he came forward through the grimy air to see if it was time to relieve Simpson. At first, Simpson said his line could hold a while longer. When Gallagher repeated the offer a few minutes later, Simpson agreed that it was time for the Eleventh to exchange places with the Jerseymen. The latter would stay behind and alongside the Pennsylvanians (on their left) to support them.[67]

Gallagher returned to his nine companies—averaging about 60 men each, for a total of about 540 men—and got them up and into a line of battle. Then, lighting a cigar, he led them into the smoking woods to relieve Simpson's force, stopping his men at the edge of a ravine. The Fourth New Jersey streamed through the Pennsylvanians, Simpson re-forming them behind and to the left of Gallagher's command.

Swarming after the New Jersey troops came Law's leftmost regiments, plus Hood's First and Fifth Texas. Accounts vary as to how the Eleventh met the oncoming enemy. Lieutenant Burke maintained that the Pennsylvanians "went with a yell and many a Rebel bit the dust when the 11th opened upon them with their minies." Sergeant Jones later recalled: "They did not see us . . . and we let them come to the edge of the ravine, when we poured a volley into them that sent them back reeling. They charged on us twice, but were driven back both times in confusion." He maintained that Lewis, leading the Cambria Guards sword in hand, told the troops "not to fire until they could do good execution."[68]

Either way, Kepler remembered that the troops the Eleventh met in this smoky, sweaty hell "came yelling like demons." Lt. Col. Samuel Jackson, Maj. Peter Johns, and Adjt. McCoy paced back and forth on the line, encouraging and steadying the ranks. McCoy was remembered as being "as cool as a cucumber—as much self-possessed as if the battle were nothing but a dress parade." But Confederate shots found targets. On the right flank, where Company A was positioned, about half an hour after the regiment became engaged Capt. Lewis took a musket ball in the right knee, shattering the bone. Command of the Cambria Guards passed to Burke.

Casualties quickly mounted. Sgt. John Scanlan received wounds in the left hip and below the left knee. Rebel marksmen hit Pvt. David James in the left shoulder. Pvt. Thompson Carney, the company's fiddler, doubled up with a wound in the left groin. Pvt. Thomas Dunn was wounded in his chest and both arms. Cpl. William Leavy was shot through the left breast. A spent musket ball thumped against Lantzy's back. It "did not hurt me enny, it just bounced of A gain," he wrote home later, noting in the next line, "My prayers was not for gotten before I went in the battle field and are not neglected since."[69]

Other companies also took casualties. Dark-haired Westmoreland Guards Pvt. Benjamin A. Job was struck by a musket ball at the edge of his left, brown eye. Where the other Westmoreland County unit stood—the Washington Blues of Company I—a piece of a shell hit Capt. Thomas Spires, a surgeon reported, "upon the posterior part of [the] Chest." A private in the same company, William A. Gray, received two leg wounds. Capt. James Speer, leading Armstrong County's Independent Blues, took musket balls through the right thigh and left shoulder. Dickson Guards Pvt. George Rothmire was shot in the lung.[70]

Because of either confusion or a lack of stretcher bearers, most of the wounded stayed on the battlefield. Civil War soldiers exhibited a great difference of opinion on what to do when wounded. A bleeding, injured man obviously wished to get to medical help as quickly as possible. Yet an attitude existed in the army that, as a soldier in another Pennsylvania Reserves regiment put it, a wounded man should avoid calling on comrades for transport as healthy men were needed on the firing line. This was in part a response to the inclination of "a certain class of skulkers" who might escort the wounded to the rear and stay there themselves. Hence, "The proper way, and the only way to rightly take care of the dead and wounded, is to gain the victory."[71]

Aaron Kepler's behavior after being wounded—as he remembered it in 1900—echoed this concept. As the Dickson Guards came under fire, a bullet drilled into the back of his right thigh. The wound, he later wrote, "completely disabled me. A couple of my comrades helped me a short distance to the rear and tied a bandage tightly around my leg above the wound, so as to keep me from bleeding to death." They gave him some water then returned (at his insistence, he wrote) to the firing line. One was killed, the other taken prisoner along with Kepler himself.

Although he sent his friends back to the ranks, Kepler did not wish to meet another bullet. He and a few more of the Eleventh's wounded crawled into a nearby hut for shelter, "but soon the stone chimney, and, even the top of the house was torn off by cannonballs, and we abandoned it." A high rail fence "too, was soon shot to the ground. We then gathered dead bodies, and piled them around us in heaps, which gave us a slight protection." Somehow, his comrade Thompson Carney was helped far enough to the rear to be transported to a field hospital near Savage's Station. It would be abandoned to the Confederates, along with Carney and the rest of its inmates, on 29 June.[72]

Back on the firing line, a short time after Lewis went down, Burke himself fell with a bullet wound just below his right knee. Lantzy estimated that nine of the company were killed and ten wounded in the woods. The chaos alternated with images of strange calm. In the sector held by Fayette County's Union Volunteers, comrades helped wounded Pvt. Joseph H. Fisher away from the line, and Maj. Johns saw him "sitting against a tree smoking his pipe perfectly composed."[73]

Meanwhile, the rest of Whiting's troops succeeded in breaking through to the left of Gallagher's and Simpson's commands. The lack of visibility caused by gunsmoke, coupled with the thick vegetation around the swamp, slowed Rebel movements. As a Texan wrote: "when we were within a hundred yards or so of the Enemies Lines every one Seemed to falter. Fireing almost ceased. An order was passed down the line to ceace fireing, that we were Shooting our own men. Our boys lay quiet for a few Minutes, when Some keen eyed fellow discovered and Said they are Yankees Shure I can See the Blue uniform and the U.S. Buckles on their Shoulder Straps. Then the order to Charge was given. You ought to have seen those Texans go forward over gulies, ditches, Through and over a dence Mass of fallen timber, Onward Now into the Enemies works."[74]

Simpson spotted these troops moving along his left. Their uniforms and flags were unclear in the haze, and the New Jersey colonel sent a lieutenant to investigate. He came back "pointing to the bullet-holes through his clothes as evidence that they were the rebels." Simpson wheeled his regiment's front around to the left, still connecting with the Eleventh Reserves on his right and probably making mental preparations to order a retreat. Soon the Rebels collided with the exhausted Jerseymen, firing volleys which Simpson described as "very destructive . . . , the hissing of the balls (I can compare them to nothing else) being like that of a myriad of serpents."[75]

Gallagher was also aware that the Rebels had broken through along the left side. Evans Brady, whose rifle-equipped Brady Guards held the far left of Gallagher's line, reported seeing the adjacent Union troops break. Brady and Maj. Johns wheeled Company K and its neighboring company—the company letter is unspecified—at an angle and "by a well directed oblique fire . . . the enemy were checked and did not at that time further advance." This action may have seen Brady Guards Pvt. Thomas Sallade's wounding. He was struck in the middle third of the left thigh, the musket ball tearing through muscle and coming out the back of his leg.[76]

The threat was not isolated to the left of Simpson's and Gallagher's commands. At about the same time their regiments had exchanged places on the front line, most of the units to their right had started to give way. Gallagher and Simpson were now unprotected; word that a withdrawal was under way was never transmitted to the Pennsylvania and New Jersey troops fighting side-by-side in the woods along the swamp.[77] This occurrence was later attributed to the smoke, noise, and confusion of battle. The fact that Simpson's and Gallagher's regiments were separated from their parent brigades further hampered efforts to recall them. As a result, the two Union regiments stood their ground as support around them disappeared. A shadowy force materialized behind Simpson's command: more Rebels. Simpson ordered his men to lie down, hoping to keep them from being spotted from the rear.[78]

At about this time, Gallagher and the Eleventh's other field officers were finding out the bad news about their situation for themselves. Off to the left, gunfire came from where Maj. Johns thought there were Union troops. Some enlisted men in Company F thought this was a Union regiment coming to relieve the Eleventh, which by now was low on ammunition. "Don't fire," one man cried at some of his Fayette County comrades, "they are our own men!" Johns went to investigate, hoping to halt what he assumed to be friendly fire and redirect it toward the breakthrough point. The Confederates he met took him prisoner.[79]

Back at the ravine, Gallagher sent McCoy to ask Meade to have the regiment relieved so it could replenish its cartridge supply. The adjutant, in Gallagher's words, "soon returned and reported that, having been as far out in the field as he could get he could see nothing of our forces, except the 4th N.J. in position as support to my regiment, that our line to the right and left of my regiment had been driven back, and that we were surrounded. This was quite surprising to me, as from our position in the woods and the smoke of battle, I could see but a short distance to the right or left." By a postwar account, McCoy reported seeing nine Confederate battle flags.[80]

Gallagher then tried to reconnoiter for himself but was unable to see even Simpson's command due to the smoke. As he pondered his next move, three of Hood's regiments—the First and Fifth Texas and the Hampton Legion—charged the ravine. The Eleventh gave ground, Gallagher staying with a rear guard as the rest of the regiment ran from the woods to the open field beyond. Gallagher kept enough men together covering the retreat to deliver at least one effective volley at the charging Rebels, enough "to cool their ardor, and completely check their fiery onset." He finally caught sight of Simpson and gestured in a way that made it clear. Simpson wrote "that the enemy was close upon him. This was soon evinced by the rebels appearing in full pursuit at a double-quick and passing immediately by our front."[81]

Intense fatigue by now had likely caught up with the Eleventh Reserves. The fight in the woods may have lasted less than an hour, but each minute dragged for those caught in it. Gallagher believed that his "regiment engaged the enemy for an hour and a half." Lantzy estimated "we was in the fight about 2 hours." Jones thought the Eleventh "fought two hours and forty minutes in the woods, when the Colonel ordered us to fall back into the field." At the moment Gallagher gave that last order, Company C Pvt. William A. McBride had just finished loading his gun. Before turning about, he decided to fire one last shot. As he raised his musket, a Rebel bullet struck him in the face and passed through to his brain, killing him instantly. A bullet also pierced the abdomen of Company D Sgt. Jacob Baiers at about this time. The missile penetrated his lungs.[82]

As the yelling Rebels crossed the swamp, the Jerseymen got off a volley in support of Gallagher's retreating men, then joined them in flight. As a Texan recalled the scene, "McClellans line is now broken and his troops are on the Skedaddle as fast as their Legs Could Carry them across a large rolling Open field, to be Shot down like Varmits." Doing much of the shooting was Law's brigade, which having followed Hood's through the break in the Union center had paused to re-form. Law recalled watching as "a large body of Federals rushed out upon the plateau on our left and rear, retreating rapidly and in great confusion. Part of them passed to our left, while the greater portion were running across our rear in the attempt to escape to the Chickahominy swamp in that direction." Law's rear rank about-faced, officers yelling for the onrushing Federals to surrender. "No attention was paid to the first summons," Law wrote, "and a few shots were fired into our ranks." His memory tallied with Sergeant Jones' account, published about two months after the battle: "When we reached the field, we found four rebel regiments drawn up in line all around us. The rebel officers ordered us to surrender, but the boys wouldn't do it." Confederates on every side now opened up, but Jones believed their fire killed "more of their own men in the operation than they did of ours." His account seems confirmed by a postwar memoir by a Texas soldier. "Desultory firing continued until it was so dark we could not distinguish friend from foe a few yards from us," he wrote, adding that his own army's bullets killed a lieutenant in his unit.[83]

Adding to the chaos, a Rebel battery began firing grape and canister shot into the confused mass. The gunners' aim was too high to have much effect, yet Gallagher knew the end was near. The companies split up to try to break through individually, evidently at Gallagher's orders, though with little success. At least a few enlisted men made it out from Fayette County's Union Volunteers; the Brady Guards' escapees included two sergeants. Nineteen of the Independent Blues ultimately presented themselves for duty with the skeleton command that rallied around Daniel Porter's Indiana National Guards.[84]

Whether or not Gallagher formally surrendered what remained of his command or if it merely disintegrated, Confederate troops secured the large silk regimental flag from the color guard. For their part, the Cambria Guards worked to deny the Rebels an equally important trophy. They swung their rifles against rocks and tree trunks, shattering the stocks and rendering the barrels unusable to their captors. Not far away, Sarah Watt's former slaves, now wearing bits of Federal blue, were taken prisoner along with the rest of Gallagher's men. They had stayed with the regiment long after the situation deteriorated.[85]

The Fourth New Jersey met an especially tragic fate. A Rebel remembered that the Jerseymen were "So anxious . . . to surrender, that they came running toward us. . . . [But] although offering every other evidence of surrender, they forgot, or at least, many of them did, to throw down their guns. As a consequence . . . many were fired on at close range by individual members of the Fifth Texas." Simpson wrote from prison that he looked "upon it as a great mercy [that] we all were not shot down."[86]

When the Rebels finally got the site under control, the worn-out Fifth Texas escorted the better part of the two Yankee regiments to the rear. Law remembered counting about 800 Federal prisoners. Casualty returns tallied the Fourth New Jersey's captured at more than 400; the

Eleventh Pennsylvania Reserves officially listed more than 600 captured, including many wounded men, but this figure seems high given Gallagher's estimate of leading about 540 men into battle. McCoy later unofficially listed 290 unhurt and 50 wounded prisoners from the Eleventh. The unwounded captives were sent to a holding area near Longstreet's headquarters. Many were soon put on the road to the Rebel capital, though some did not start the march to Richmond until the next day.[87]

The cries of wounded men broke through the dark. A Virginian wrote home just after the fight ended: "The groans of the wounded are truly distressing. I wish the poor fellows could be attended to tonight." In some parts an eerie quiet settled on the battlefield, or else the soldiers blocked out the sounds of the wounded. A Texan picketing near what had been Porter's headquarters remembered how "the loneliness of the night was increased by the wail of the whip-poor-wills that came to us from the swamps below us."[88]

In spite of their heavy losses, some of the victors mocked their opponents' performance as soldiers. One Rebel officer ungallantly observed that the Federal works would have been harder to take "had they been garrisoned by *men* (emphasis added)." Northern critics were capable of such remarks, but Union postscripts were fair to the Eleventh Reserves. A volunteer writing home to the *Pittsburgh Gazette* reported: "The 11th Pennsylvania Reserves . . . suffered more severely than any regiment in the fight. It was the most exposed all the time, and behaved bravely." The writer erred when he reported that Gallagher had been wounded, but he noted that when the men were surrounded, "they refused to surrender, and they charged on the rebel lines to cut their way out."[89]

In his report, Simpson wrote that his ill-fated Jerseymen and "the Eleventh Pennsylvania . . . had done our whole duty in keeping at bay the enemy for an hour after every other regiment on our right and left had fallen back, and attributing the mishap entirely to the fact that I received no orders from the brigadier general commanding or any other authority to retreat (being in the woods it was impossible for me to see what was going on on the flanks), I cannot reproach myself or my regiment with any fault on account of our capture."[90]

For his part, McCall praised "these two brave regiments, which had so nobly maintained their ground." He added: "No censure can possibly attach to either Colonel Gallagher or Colonel Simpson or the brave men of their respective regiments on account of this ill-turn of fortune, but, on the contrary, they are entitled to the credit of having held their ground until it was tenable no longer."[91] A darker view prevailed in Gallagher's ranks, thinned by seventy-one killed or mortally wounded, and with hundreds more imprisoned, many of them badly hurt. "It is the general belief," Burke wrote about a month after the fight, "that we were sacrificed to save the remainder of the Reserves."[92]

Chapter 5

Another Way to Take Richmond

Libby Prison, Belle Isle, and Glendale

As word of the battle of Gaines' Mill filtered back to western Pennsylvania, a pall descended on the counties that contributed men to the Eleventh Reserves. "A gloom has been cast over our town," one newspaper reported, "and sadness comes to the hearthstone of many families in this neighborhood."[1] More tangible misery lay on and near the swampy battlefield, where hundreds of wounded remained under what cover they could find. Himself badly hurt, Aaron Kepler recalled "their pitiful and heart-rending lamentations during the long night [after the battle], as they lay on that bloody field, praying, moaning, cursing, and crying for water; others in their delerium [sic] talking of loved ones in their far-distant homes, sending messages and last farewells, or entreating someone to mercifully kill them and end their misery and suffering. . . . What little sleep we had was broken by dream pictures of the bloody battle." A heavy rain fell near dawn; if it eased any thirst it also created a sea of cold mud. Kepler, who stripped off most of his bloody clothes as the day grew hot, watched the Confederates dig long trenches to bury the battle fatalities, and "almost envied the dead."[2]

Some of the wounded stayed near the battlefield for almost three weeks, receiving little attention from overburdened Rebel doctors or Federal surgeons captured or left behind to care for their own army's casualties. Nursing his torn leg, James Burke thought most of the injured got no attention for up to five days after the fight. He and eight other wounded men from the regiment "lay upon the battle-field twenty days, most of the time in a negro hut." Rebel authorities provided "flour mixed in water, a half cupful three times a day."[3]

Burke's captain, Andrew Lewis, was picked up by Confederates after the battle ended, his right leg soon amputated above its shattered knee. It is possible that the regiment's captured surgeon, J. S. DeBenneville, wielded the saw on Lewis. Despite Kepler's dislike of DeBenneville, the doctor "rendered noble service in the Richmond prisons" according to Josiah Sypher's 1865 history of the Pennsylvania Reserves division. The operation on Lewis may have been done at Dr. Gaines' house, which Kepler saw used as "a kind of headquarters and hospital combined, and was the place where the field surgery mostly took place after the battle. Stacks of amputated limbs were to be seen about the place. The busy surgeons were still at work when we got there, and I saw some heart-rending scenes that morning as they amputated limbs of Federal and Confederate alike, some of the poor fellows dying in the operation." Lewis hung on for a few days after the amputation, but died on 2 July. Fellow prisoners from the Eleventh Reserves buried him near the battlefield.[4]

Himself ill when repatriated later in the month, DeBenneville reported Lewis' death to Daniel Porter, whose Indiana National Guards constituted the sole remnant of the regiment still in active service. The captain sent a pained note to Lewis' wife, who evidently had already contacted him seeking news of her husband. Porter closed his note:

> Allow me to write the inscription of him who now lies in the grave, in a southern clime, surrounded by traitors & demons to

the best of governments. In memory of Capt. Andrew Lewis, who died from the effects of a wound received June 27th 1862 at the battle of Gaines Mill, fighting for the maintenance of law and order. No braver man ever lived—no braver man ever fell. No child of his need blush at the name of that patriotic, brave man. His character here was without a stain. In all intercourse he was most honest. He stood high in the regiment. Accept my heartfelt sympathy, and may God who pities the widow & orphan enable you to bear your load of grief & sorrow like the true christian who looks forward to a better & happier world.[5]

Confederate wounded who could be moved were transported to Richmond as soon as the battle died down. Wagons and train cars full of maimed and dying men started pouring into the city at first light on Saturday, 28 June. Most were collected at the central railroad depot. "The wounds of the majority of them were slight—in the limbs," a newspaper correspondent wrote, "but others were terribly mangled, apparently by the explosion of shell. One man whom we saw in the cars had both eyes shot out, and another had his jaw carried away by a round shot. . . . One of the wounded, as he was being carried from the cars on a 'stretcher,' implored those around him to send for his mother. That was all he could say. No name, no regiment, nothing—it was 'mother.' He was shot through the lungs with a Minie ball."[6]

Others—columns of Union prisoners—marched to, then through, the Rebel capital on their own legs, arriving at about 4 A.M. Most were from the Eleventh Pennsylvania Reserves and the Fourth New Jersey. There was a scattering of other volunteers—the Bucktails, the Eighth Reserves, and the Sixty-second Pennsylvania were among those represented—and some U.S. Regulars from Sykes' division.[7]

Colonel Gallagher did not accompany this contingent, perhaps being allowed to arrange some care for the wounded. But Lt. Col. Jackson, Adjt. McCoy, and Lt. Daniel Coder of Indiana County's Washington Blues arrived with this first stream of prisoners. The procession also included "several very fine Federal flags taken from the enemy on Saturday and Sunday," reported the *Richmond Examiner,* though the paper garbled the details: "One belongs to the 'Bucktail Rifles' of the Eleventh Pennsylvania Reserves, and two others to the Fourth New Jersey regiment." The competing *Richmond Enquirer* wrote: "They were all splendidly made flags, one being the 'stars and stripes,' and the others made of green silk, with State arms and mottoes emblazoned." The paper claimed that the Bucktails' "watch word was, 'We never Surrender.'"[8]

Two decades later Fayette County's Sgt. George Kremer recalled "hearing some women at a window shout to us as we went by: 'This is another way to take Richmond.'" Kepler, brought on a stretcher, remembered females spitting and cursing at the wounded, yelling that the Federal prisoners "should be thrown into the dock or to the dogs. I believe they would have done us bodily injury had they not been held back by the guards at the point of the bayonet."[9]

The captives' first destination was Libby Prison, a trio of loft-style tenement buildings at the corner of Cary and Twentieth Streets, which before the war housed a ship chandlery business. Libby was meant for officers only, but no segregation by rank was practiced on 28 June. Later, the enlisted men were culled out for shipment to a tented stockade on Belle Isle in the James River.

Prisoners at Libby were housed, fed, and tended in eight large unplastered rooms, each measuring 103 by 42 feet. Each floor had a water supply, Kepler recalling that it consisted of "a wooden water trough and a spigot." Each floor also had latrines, which quickly became filthy, and lice were rampant. The absence of buildings on the prison's south side, from where the prevailing winds came, aided warm weather ventilation. Only a few windows were glazed; in winter the rest were boarded up or screened off with canvas. Prison authorities eventually placed nine cooking stoves among the quarters, though little fuel was made available. Discipline was harsh. Slight offenses resulted in a prisoner's being forced to "mark time," but graver misdeeds might result in a captive being "bucked"—tied up. Hard cases went to "Castle Thunder," a converted tobacco warehouse located on Cary Street's northern face, between Eighteenth and Nineteenth Streets, used largely for civilian prisoners, including spies.[10]

Libby quickly filled the day after Gaines' Mill, and a nearby factory was pressed into prison service. A reporter described the captives' muster as "a much slower and more tedious process than might be supposed. They are first drawn up in column before the prison, and then by fours marched into the clerk's office, where their names and description and place of capture are taken down. They are then led off and turned into their quarters." Here, McGinley wrote in his diary, the prisoners' names, states, and regiments were recorded, then they were searched before being "Stowed away for Safe keeping" in what he described as "a larg Brick tobackow Factory near the River. Sour Bread and Soup is our fare."[11]

The ordeal exhausted Jackson, who once inside Libby Prison fell to the floor and slept. He spent only one night as the regiment's senior representative. The next day, Gallagher and Maj. Johns arrived, along with 6 captains, 11 lieutenants, and (by Jackson's count) 295 other ranks from the Eleventh Reserves.[12]

Within a few days, Confederate authorities separated the enlisted men. Sgt. Kremer recalled "standing near the guarded door of the prison, when a Rebel officer appeared, and said he wanted some 'Yanks'—I don't remember the number—to go to Belle Isle to assist in putting up tents, &c., and arrange the Island for the bulk of the prisoners, who would be transferred from Libby and the other prisons in Richmond the next day." Kremer volunteered, "only too glad to get out of that horrid hole."[13]

Rebel guards marched this contingent down Cary Street. In front of another warehouse-prison, Kremer remembered, they met up with "another squad (larger than our own) drawn up in front . . . I judge our number was over a hundred. Before starting for the Island we were given each a loaf of bread—small-sized baker's loaf—as extra rations for the labor which we were expected to perform." They then marched across the Richmond & Petersburg Railroad bridge that connected the city with Belle Isle. Here, Kremer "assisted in putting up one tent—a [circular] Sibley [tent]—and succeeded in capturing a part of another, which was too rotten to put up and assisted in occupying said Sibley while I remained on the Island." They were soon joined by the bulk of the enlisted men captured at Gaines' Mill, as well as those taken in the other Peninsula battles, who would be incarcerated here until their parole or exchange. By the time David Lavan made it to Belle Isle—the Brady Guards sergeant arrived there on 16 July—"there were several thousand prisoners" held at the site.[14]

A contemporary account described Belle Isle as "about one mile in length and a quarter of a mile in breadth, with two branches of the river that forms, clasping the shores on either side." As of early August 1862, the prison consisted of 400 or 500 closely spaced tents, housing then about 4,500 Federals, who named the stockade's main street "Broadway." A 300-man guard force was stationed on a hill overlooking the tent city, the latter enclosed by a railing beyond which prisoners were forbidden to tread. The camp's administration, headquartered in an old schoolhouse, allowed prisoners to dig wells; details took ten men at a time to bathe in the James River. Within another year, Belle Isle's prisoner population more than doubled.[15]

Diarrhea affected many of the Eleventh's inmates on Belle Isle, perhaps because the James River where they bathed was also their cesspool. "There was a kind of Platform and pole fixed out over the edge of the river for a closet," Levi Wise of the Brady Guards recalled in a statement accompanying the postwar pension request of his comrade Lemuel Dobbs, "and each prisoner had to form in line and take his turn to pass out by the guard." Early one morning, Dobbs, then twenty and suffering from intense diarrhea, could not wait. "The boys in our tent was waked up with an unusual nois[e] caused by Dobbs coming huriedly into the tent, followed closely by an Irishman who was kicking and swareing at him, and saying I'll larn yees what to be doin in front of our tent; Dobbs having ben pressed so hard by the moving of his bowels that he had not time to fall in line and wait his turn, had stoped near the other tent to eas his bowels." Another witness, a prisoner named Wilson R. Ramsay, heard Dobbs "Plead for mercy" from his assailant.[16]

Such anecdotes were probably included in the version of events John Roberts of the Cambria Guards later gave an *Alleghanian* writer of his Belle Isle stay. The correspondent attributed to Roberts "a highly interesting account of Rebel prison life, and although not charging any direct complaint of neglect or cruelty against them [the Confederate authorities], he still insists that he would prefer entering Richmond next time in the midst of a victorious Federal army." Philip Lantzy's only reference in his letters home was a laconic one about rations: "We all was used bad while we was prisinors for they did not give us a Nough to eat." His experiences might be divined from what returning prisoners from the Ninth Reserves told a comrade: "All they got to eat was one fourth ration of sour bread," the latter wrote home, "and a small piece of stinking fresh beef without salt each day."[17]

Food was already on the captives' minds as they marched into Richmond. On the way to Libby Prison on 28 June, Robert Holliday, a private in the Eleventh Reserves' Company F, spotted a little boy named James Ballou. Holliday asked the child to get him some bread and gave Ballou a ten-dollar Confederate note. An onlooker stopped the child and examined the bill, which was proclaimed a forgery. The *Richmond Examiner* spent some ink wondering how Holliday should be punished. Counterfeiting, it noted, carried the death penalty in the South.[18]

The newspaper also had suggestions regarding the fate of the contrabands captured alongside the Pennsylvanians. The former slaves marched in Richmond at the rear of the prisoners' column, their blue clothing inciting rage in the residents. "As regards the Virginia negroes taken in Yankee uniform," remarked the *Examiner,* "we think a most salutary effect would be produced by hanging them in a public manner. If every slave taken in the enemy's service were immediately shot or hung, Yankee newspaper correspondents would soon lose their most prolific source of information. Contrabands would 'cease to come in.'"[19]

Many injured or ill captives were segregated in a hospital set up in another Richmond warehouse. "There were eight-hundred and thirty-four sick and wounded men in one building," Cpl., later Sgt., William A. Leavy of the Cambria Guards wrote after being repatriated, "among whom were a large number who had undergone amputations . . . We were obliged to lie on the floor, which was coated to the depth of an inch and a half, with filth of every description. Our food was 8 ounces of bread per day." Kepler, whose cousin William Halderman had also been wounded and captured, remembered that the ration sometimes also contained a small piece of pork, or that in place of the bread the prisoners received "musty corn meal which we mixed in water and ate without cooking." Some prisoners managed to keep their morale in place. Cambria Guards Sgt. John Scanlan, wounded in the left hip and knee, was a particular example. "His wounds were extremely painful," Leavy wrote, "but I never heard a murmur escape his lips, and he appeared cheerful on all occasions, notwithstanding being a prisoner and subjected to all the insult, starvation and persecution of Jeff's myrmidons." A Confederate doctor treated Leavy, shot through the breast at Gaines' Mill, removing the ball from near his spine. But Leavy complained that "the rebel authorities were humane and magnanimous enough to assign one surgeon to attend all these [sick men], while forty of our own surgeons were prisoners in the city, and would gladly have cared for our wounded, had they been permitted."[20]

Some Federal surgeons proved inattentive. Burke criticized "Surgeon White, of Martindale's brigade" whose name, he wrote, "deserves to be cursed by every Northern man. His tyranny and barbarism were unparalleled. He allowed the men to lie four and five days without dressing their wounds, thus producing excruciating pain to the sufferers!" Burke finally found a helpful assistant surgeon—he did not state whether Union or Confederate—who gave him enough lint and bandages to bind some of his comrades' injuries.[21]

The Federal doctor about whom Burke railed, William H. White, attained the rank of major during a checkered career as an army surgeon. Although no evidence exists of his being callous to patients, he once remarked that "twenty months experience has taught me that soldiers need but little medicine."[22]

At Gaines' Mill, he set up a hospital which, he later wrote in his pension application, "became the center of a crossfire—our red flags afforded no protection. Shot & Shell came crashing in from artillery on one side, and showers of bullets from the other. When the smoke of battle was lifted an awful scene of Slaughter was displayed [,] at least two thousand dead & wounded lay around, and I was a prisoner."

What happened next, White wrote, was that, still as a captive, he took charge of all the Federal wounded "north of the Chickahominy and on this field amid the stench of decaying animals I labored night & Day with the most imperfect means, for our wounded, for nearly three weeks, when they were removed with a view to exchange, and I was sent to Richmond to report to [Richmond provost marshal Brig.] Genn'l [John Henry] Winder who threatened me with hanging because I was a Marylander by birth and from a Slave State."[23] In spite of Burke's scorn, there is no trace of professional criticism in White's government files at this time.

His military career, however, ended under a cloud. By early July 1863, after he was exchanged White was serving as surgeon of the III Corps artillery brigade. There he had an altercation with his clerk, Stephen T. Denny, whom White had ordered "arrested, detained and searched" on charges of stealing fifty to sixty dollars from White. Denny, by one account, confronted White with "great provocation," prompting White to strike him "with the face of an axe," and attempting to do so several more times. Hauled before the provost marshal, Denny responded with his own charges against White. Not only had he been arrested "upon a false and unfounded charge," but Denny alleged that his accuser/attacker had spent most of July drunk on stolen hospital liquors.

Of the case, an artillery captain wrote that "From what I can learn there is little foundation for the charge of drunkenness or misappropriation of Hospital Stores but there is some Evidence in the case that can only be brought out by a court martial." A senior III Corps surgeon added his own thoughts: "If guilty of the within named offenses I would recommend his [White's] dismissal from the service." By this time, however, White was on sick leave. Late in September he applied for a discharge on medical grounds, which was granted. He lived less than three more years, his 1867 death attributed to "Rheumatism & Heart Disease"—the same conditions he cited in his request for a discharge.[24]

The Pennsylvania officers in Libby Prison soon received some distinguished fellow guests. At Gaines' Mill, the Rebel breakthroughs on the left and right also cut off John Reynolds from the rest of the army. He spent a night hiding in the woods; the Confederates who found him the next morning brought him to Stonewall Jackson's headquarters. He was courteously treated, escorted on horseback to Lee's headquarters, then taken to Richmond with other captives in an army ambulance, passing over the Mechanicsville battlefield. Winder put Reynolds in the Spotswood House hotel, where the Pennsylvanian pledged to remain in quarters.[25]

McCall joined him a few days later. The division commander had been captured at New Market while leading troops forward to retake a battery. McCall actually had been lucky: during the fight a spent ball struck him in the chest, "the effects of which were but temporary." Earlier, he narrowly avoided capture at Gaines' Mill when he ran into unexpected Rebel pickets near a farmhouse that had earlier served as V Corps headquarters.[26]

The distinguished prisoners remained at the hotel until after the 1 July battle of Malvern Hill, the last of Lee's counteroffensives on the Peninsula. One evening Winder sent a squad to take Reynolds, McCall, and other officers to another warehouse set aside for officers, though not Libby. Field officers—those of regimental staff rank and above—were confined on the first floor; a space was closed off for McCall and Reynolds. The floor above them, Reynolds told an investigating commission in 1863, "was occupied by the captains and the floor above that by the subalterns." The officers received a daily bread-and-meat ration, but officers with money could buy provisions through prison officials; for $16 per week, McCall and Reynolds had their meals brought from Spotswood House. [27]

Such arrangements gave the Union captives a chance to learn about conditions in the Rebel capital. "Things look terrible in Richmond and prices are enormously high," wrote Burke, who seems to have had plenty of chances to patronize the local economy. "Coffee, poor article, $2.50 per lb; tobacco, $1.00 per lb; dried apples, $5.00 per bushel; shoes, $10 to $20; boots, $30 to $50. Rebel officers have to pay high for their uniforms—coat $100, pants $35 to $40!—They are very anxious to get gold and silver. Two dollars in specie brings a five dollar Confederate note. We experienced no difficulty in disposing of our Treasury notes. They passed the same as Confederate treasury notes."[28]

Perhaps the currency collapse prompted the *Richmond Examiner* to knock the delicate treatment afforded Union officers whose "antecedents . . . recommend them to but little consideration." Authorities began to rethink the relatively loose confinement awarded ranking Union commanders when a handful of McCall's and Reynolds' fellow captives escaped. On Saturday, 5 July, orders were issued to transfer the Pennsylvanian generals and their remaining companions to Libby Prison. They were first paraded down the Richmond streets as a kind of punishment. Reynolds believed this "was done because it was supposed that the remaining officers had connived at the escape of the others."

At Libby the food arrangements continued as before, and enlisted prisoners were detailed to cook for the officers. Peter Johns, the Eleventh Reserves' major, wrote his wife that "by buying some vegetables we can get up quite a nice table." Overall, he wrote, "Our captors have treated us extremely well; we have plenty of good fresh bread, fine beef, &c., furnished us." McCall and Reynolds shared the floor with thirteen field officers, but still enjoyed a section to themselves; Johns described it as measuring about 36 by 40 feet, equipped with five gas burners, light from which at night "gives our hall the appearance of a gay assembly of joyous gentlemen."[29]

To kill time, the prisoners adopted regular religious services. Samuel Jackson noted that the Fourth of July was marked with morning prayer, singing some national songs, and a "Short speech made by Col. Simpson." The captors held their own celebrations later in July to mark the first anniversary of the Bull Run victory. On Belle Isle, James McGinley looked across the James River on 21 July and wrote in his diary: "flags can Be Seen on almost every Hous there was two larg[e] flags on the State House and there was a grate display of Sky Rockets in the evening."[30]

The officers had plenty to read, Samuel Jackson noting that a preacher "brought us some books and tracts." He consumed several titles, including *The Scalp Hunters* and *Earnest Linwood*. Nor did the officers lack visitors, though most were of Confederate persuasion. Brig. Gen. John Bankhead Magruder was among several "secesh [who] came in to see us this day," Jackson noted in his entry for Sunday, 6 July. The next day, "Judge Gilham, author of *Gilham's Manual,* came in to see us." On a Saturday near the end of the month, James Longstreet visited old friends there from the prewar army. He also arranged to send copies of the New York and Philadelphia newspapers from the week before.[31]

Other old acquaintances were renewed. A week before Longstreet's visit, Maj. David M. Whaley of the Fifth Texas Regiment came to Libby Prison to visit Johns and Everard Bierer. Born in Fayette County, Whaley moved to Texas about 1850 and followed his state into the Civil War. Bierer detailed their conversation in a letter he later sent to McCall: "He told me he had been in all the battles of Richmond, and that he never saw better fighting than that of the Pennsylvania Reserves. He stated that at the battle of Mechanicsville the Confederate forces were repulsed at every point, and that their loss was very heavy—about 2,000 in killed and wounded. He was astonished when I told him our loss was only about 200. Though in the rebel army, Major Whaley is a gentleman of high integrity, and perfectly reliable, as I believe."[32]

In spite of the capture of nine companies, the death, wounding, or imprisonment of most of its officers, and the loss of its flag, the Eleventh Pennsylvania Reserves stayed on the Union rolls. A fragment of the regiment regrouped around Company B, the only element that remained intact. The confusion caused by movement and frequent Union withdrawals meant that some survivors from other companies did not find the skeleton regiment's whereabouts for days.[33] James McIlwain, who slipped the net at Boatswain's Swamp, wrote his wife Emma that he and his comrades had "to retreat at a rate that I have never moved before and hope I shall never have again. There was no blue streaks left behind that I Saw, for I did not look to see them. The Enemy were right at our heels, killing and taking prisoners all that could not crawl along."[34]

Company B fought on its own at Gaines' Mill. Detailed for fatigue duty when the fighting became general, Daniel Porter's men had been fixing handles to axes at a field hospital. "This we did," Porter later wrote, "and then moved back a few paces." The hospital had already started to fill with wounded men, scenes that Sgt. John Sutor recalled more vividly than the battle itself. "I will not cause you to shudder," he wrote home, "by telling you of the many horrible sights we were beheld." After they finished their task, Porter recalled, "the order came for a squad to go forward and pile axes away. . . . Shortly afterwards the rout commenced." At this stage, Porter "formed my company to stop the stragglers; but artillery, cavalry and men rushed headlong through." The Indiana National Guards came under heavy fire before withdrawing, Pvt. Moses B. Charles being killed.[35]

Because events moved swiftly, Porter was unable to tabulate his exact losses at Gaines' Mill. Besides Charles, the casualties included Sgt. Harvey Fair, who had led the squad ordered to pile the axes. Rebel troops found him after the battle, severely wounded in the leg, which a Confederate surgeon sawed off. Captured Cambria Guards Sgt. William Leavy came upon him later, feverish and near death, lying in a farmhouse shed connected to a stable. Leavy described what he saw in a letter to his comrade's father:

[Fair's] mind was wandering very much on the scenes he had gone through . . . of the battle, speaking several times of preventing the rebels from crossing some bridge at which, I presume, he had been stationed. I spoke to him and he recognized me. I talked to him for some time but he was too delirious to get anything more from him than a recognition. As I knew the poor fellow had not long to live, I said to him, "Harvey, there is a probability of some of us whose wounds will permit, being sent North, and, should I be among the number, I would be very happy to be the bearer of any message to your friends in Indiana, or if you wish I will write to Capt. Porter anything you desire." He replied that Capt. Porter was there not an hour ago. I did not know what course to pursue; but just as I was going, his reason returned, and he desired me to write to you and inform you of all. I told him to rest assured it should be done the first opportunity. . . . Harvey died in half an hour after I left him. I carved his name on a piece of board and placed it at his grave.[36]

After Gaines' Mill, McClellan's strategy was to withdraw from the Chickahominy positions to the Harrison's Landing base, where the army would be under the added protection of gun-laden Federal ships on the James River.[37] The night of the battle, Daniel Porter led his remaining men across the Chickahominy bridges. McIlwain, who before the battle evidently served as an aide to regimental quartermaster Hugh Torrance, seems to have traveled with a Company G contingent that escaped encirclement, though it is unclear when the group linked with Porter's. In his letter to Emma, McIlwain described exhaustion, hunger, and thirst. Luckily, he "had a few of unkle Sams crackers Stored away in the Quartermasters desk"—evidently one of the portable field desks today prized by collectors and reenactors. When those ran out, he subsisted for a while on blackberries and sassafras sprouts. "I paid one man twenty five cents for a drink of water which is the only time in my life that I knew the value of water," he added. "I have formerly thought that water was not to quench thirst but let any one be compelled to run for his life on an hot day . . . and he will find to his Satisfaction that water is for a more nobler purpose than washing dirty shirts [illegible] and running Canal Boats in."[38]

On Sunday 29 June Daniel Porter's small command was attached to the Seventh Pennsylvania Reserves, maneuvering into positions near a crossroads called Glendale, adjacent to another boggy watercourse known as White Oak Swamp. Poor roads and bridges—some of the latter had to be rebuilt—slowed their progress. Lee had only four-fifths of the Union strength, yet Army of the Potomac commanders from McClellan on down were sure they were outnumbered by their pursuers. Phantom assaults materialized out of the tension: the noise of a sutler's wagon sparked panic in McCall's division during the withdrawal.[39]

Lee's vanguards were indeed out there, pushing along the same York River Railroad axis on which the Yankees had come. A few miles from the Glendale position on 29 June, a Confederate division clashed with the Union rear guard along the rail line; the engagement would be known as Savage's Station. Daniel Porter's tiny force was far removed from this fighting, but Lee remained in pursuit. The Union army continued its withdrawal, but on the next day elements of the Army of Northern Virginia again bumped against McClellan's lines. The battle that occurred received many names, Glendale, Frayser's Farm, and White Oak Swamp among them. Pennsylvania Reserves survivors called it the battle of Charles City Cross Roads. By whatever title, it was one of the most terrible of the Seven Days.

Daniel Porter could call upon only 106 men in what remained of the Eleventh Reserves. Besides the Indiana National Guards' own lieutenants, the only uncaptured officer in the regiment was Dickson Guards Capt. Samuel Louden, who was still at home in Butler County recuperating from illness.[40] Porter divided his men into two "companies," retaining command of the right wing; the other he assigned to Lt. Hannibal Sloan. The unit as a whole formed the left of the Seventh Reserves and took orders from the latter's commander. By the time the fighting spread to its sector at about 5 P.M., this ad hoc force had formed about thirty yards behind the Fourth Pennsylvania Reserves, the latter positioned behind a six-gun battery.

The sector grew hot as the Rebels charged the Napoleons and the remnants of three Pennsylvania Reserves regiments defending them. With the heavy guns spitting canister and enlisted men letting volleys loose, a charge spearheaded by the Eleventh Alabama died out 100 yards in front of the battery. A second rush came half that distance closer before again wavering. Seeing the Alabamians falter, and with their own blood up, the Pennsylvania Reserves fixed bayonets and charged in for the kill.

Although bayonets were issued to virtually every soldier in the Civil War, the rifle's emergence virtually spelled the end of close-quarter combat. This hand-to-hand clash was, therefore, a rarity. A well-traveled Confederate officer later wrote that the fight here saw "more actual bayonet, & butt of gun, melee fighting than any other occasion I know of in the whole war." The Alabamians fiercely held their ground, and the shock of the repulse stunned the Pennsylvanians. In Daniel Porter's words, "The men became scattered and confused." They lost their presence of mind to the extent that in falling back, the Pennsylvanians ran directly toward the canister-loaded battery instead of around the sides. Yankee gunners, unable to fire without massacring their own men, gave way and the Rebels overran the position. The Eleventh Alabama's color-bearer was shot down after he jumped on a cannon, but the flag was quickly caught up again and the Confederates seemed to have won the day on this part of the line.

The Pennsylvanians fell back to nearby woods. Lacking a regimental flag of their own, Porter's troops rallied around the Seventh Reserves' colors. Meade rode his horse into the mass and was trying to sort out the men when a pair of musket balls struck him on his back and right forearm. He managed to stay in the saddle but turned his horse to the rear, and slowly rode in search of a surgeon.[41]

But other efforts at rallying the Federal troops succeeded, and as Porter described in his report: "The Seventh and Eleventh in a short time made another charge with better success." A pair of twenty-three-year-old corporals in his command, Henderson Howard and Prussian-born Charles Shambaugh, started toward the Rebel who had picked up the colors near the battery, having decided to avenge the loss of the regiment's flag at Gaines' Mill. The pair became separated, and six-foot-tall Howard was seen taking on four Confederates at once. He shot one, bayoneted two, and watched the fourth run off. Shambaugh, an inch taller than his comrade, got far enough into the Rebel mass to knock down his target and seize the flagstaff. He made it back to his lines, where he was quoted as breathlessly stammering that "I go-go-got the d-d-damned thing."

Both men earned the Congressional Medal of Honor for gallantry in a fight later remembered for its savagery. A Seventh Reserves captain targeted a Rebel lieutenant who had already been bayoneted, shooting him in the arm. The Federal then whipped his sword at the victim's head. Though mortally wounded, the Alabamian jabbed his own blade through his tormentor's body. A similarly resilient Alabama captain survived despite three bayonet wounds and having his leg shattered by a minié ball.[42]

Scenes like this made Sloan write home: "This battle, I do not think, can be exceeded for fierceness. The butternuts were piled up in perfect heaps." Lt. Archibald Stewart described the fight as one in which the regiment virtually "walked right into the Rebels" and fought them "on their own hook." Porter reported losing thirty-four men killed, wounded, or missing, more than a third of his force.

The mortally wounded included Henry Hazlett, about seventeen at the time ("badly wounded in three places" Sloan wrote home). A bullet or musket ball struck his older brother William in the left hip. Comrades carried the elder Hazlett off the field, but Pvt. James J. Oatman was less lucky. Knocked senseless by a shellburst, he was subsequently captured. More than 200 became casualties in the Fourth and Seventh Reserves, with every man in the latter's color company hit. The Eleventh Alabama lost 181 taking and then defending the battery.[43]

Although his units finally got the better of the Alabamians, Meade's shattered brigade pulled back as darkness fell. The remnant of the Eleventh marched five miles to a new position and was placed in reserve. The next day Shambaugh's prize "attracted great attention." He eventually sent it home to his family in Indiana County. A reporter there described it as "about 4 by 5 feet. It consists of a red ground, crossed diagonally by two strips of blue on which are sewed thirteen stars. It bears the inscription 'Seven Pines,' indicating that it was borne in that battle, and is much torn and riddled."[44]

Such trophies did little to reassure the Pennsylvanians. "If any one tells you that the Rebels will not fight," a private in the Seventh Reserves wrote home, "just tell them to come down to this neck of the country and try them on." A man in the Ninth Pennsylvania Reserves echoed his thoughts. "I am satisfied with fighting," he wrote after describing what he had seen at Glendale. "I wish the War was over."[45]

While men killed each other on the Peninsula, their leaders were trying to decide how to dispose of the prisoners both sides had collected. Discussions of exchanging and repatriating captives had begun following First Bull Run. A South Carolina congressman at one point proposed simply sending Federal prisoners back North. Nothing came of that suggestion, but the Confederate surrender of Fort Donelson stimulated further talk. Negotiations in early 1862 snagged over such issues as transport costs. But in July, with both sides' prison camps full, emissaries agreed on an exchange system. This included a liberal method whereby each side would "parole" prisoners "if it be practicable to transfer them to their own lines" within ten days. Parolees were not to perform military duties until formally exchanged.[46]

The protocol was signed at Haxall's Landing on the James River on 22 July. The news filtered through to Libby Prison within three days, and western Pennsylvania newspapers soon announced "an immediate and general exchange of prisoners."[47] Some wounded were paroled and transferred a few days before the signing. Benjamin Job arrived at City

Point on 19 July, and was sent to a Federal hospital for treatment of the wound near his eye. Though sightless, the eyeball was intact and looked normal. A scar near the edge of the socket later healed, but the musket ball could not be removed, and caused Job pain for the rest of his life. [48]

While the prisoner talks progressed, the Eleventh Reserves experienced several organizational changes. In July, the army decided to break up bands below brigade level. On 3 August, the regiment's band leader and six musicians went back to what remained of their original companies. Nine others, specially recruited the previous fall, were discharged from the military altogether. Factoring in returning stragglers and detailed men, Porter had about 150 troops. [49]

Other changes occurred at higher levels. Following McCall's capture, Seymour assumed temporary command of the Pennsylvania Reserves division. The Third Reserves' Colonel Sickel took command of the Second Brigade as Meade recuperated. Confederate papers at first reported Meade killed, and they were almost correct. After riding away from the lines near Glendale, Meade was forced by pain to dismount. Attendants placed him in his own mess cart, a two-wheeled rig, then took him on a bumping, jittery ride that ended after midnight at Haxall's Landing. The Army of the Potomac's adjutant general, Brig. Gen. Seth Williams, put Meade in his own tent. A surgeon found the gunshot areas badly swollen because of the ride, the pain so severe in Meade's back that the wound could not be probed. Doctors feared the bullet had passed through his right kidney, and there was blood in Meade's urine; the missile actually punctured his liver. The wounded brigadier was put on a hospital boat and sent to Fort Monroe, then Baltimore, then Philadelphia, where he would stay until 12 August. [50]

Sickel must have realized that Daniel Porter's much-bloodied command needed a rear-area posting. By late July, it was assigned to guard duty at the Federal hospital at Harrison's Landing. During this time the captain received offers to merge his troops with other splintered Reserves units. Archibald Stewart wrote home: "Some of the very kind Colonels of our Brigade would have liked very much to have had us fill up their thinned ranks, and very kindly offered to draw rations for us." But Porter refused these entreaties, and "By that means the 11th Regiment Pennsylvania Reserves is still in organization." [51]

Through his private secretary, Gov. Andrew Curtin contacted the captain for a status report on the regiment. Porter's response showed him determined to keep the Eleventh on the rolls but also desperate for more men. "You will remember, I asked privilege to take the regiment back to

Pennsylvania to recruit up," he wrote. "I most respectfully ask that this request be granted or some measures taken, by which we can be made sufficient & ready to do our duty in this hour of peril to our common country."[52]

The guard-duty posting came at about the same time that divisional commanders were ordered to standardize weaponry across regiments. Some Pennsylvania Reserves regiments found themselves with a miscellany of weaponry following the chaos of the Seven Days. A member of the Second Reserves recalled a long list of makes, including Confederate-made ordnance, "all mixed promiscuously together among the men, who having lost their own, appropriated their neighbors." This phenomenon presumably caused problems for quartermasters struggling with requests for ammunition.[53]

Seymour on 16 July issued the following order to Porter's command: "The fragments of the 11th Infantry will at once turn in to this Hd. Qrs. all its surplus arms and all arms of a caliber other than smoothbore muskets Cal. 69 and receive in Exchange the required number of Cal. 69."[54] This rule stayed in place after the Eleventh was rebuilt with returning prisoners, despite the fact that its flank companies originally bore rifles. Gallagher's regiment therefore became a Civil War rarity—an active combat unit that saw its overall weaponry quality diminish (although a few Enfields would be scattered in the regiment in 1864). Ordnance inventory forms made the transition clear. The .58-caliber Springfields were "First Class Arms"; the model .69-caliber smoothbore fell into the "Third Class" category.[55]

No accounts seem to exist of how the flank companies reacted to being de-rifled. Events likely moved too fast. At the end of August, Lantzy noted in a letter home, "Since [being released from prison] we have been moving all the time and are at this Present time."[56] The Eleventh Reserves was headed for Manassas.

Chapter 6

Shot Down Like Sheep

Second Bull Run

The story of the Second Bull Run campaign began the same day Lee attacked the V Corps at Mechanicsville. On that date, President Lincoln issued orders consolidating the scattered Union elements in the Shenandoah Valley and at Fredericksburg into a roughly 50,000-man force called the Army of Virginia. To command it, he selected one of his successful western generals, John Pope, a man whose unfortunate sense of bombast has clouded most accounts of his service in the east.[1] With

McClellan on the defensive on the Peninsula, the initial role of the Army of Virginia was to threaten Richmond from a direct, northern approach. It was hoped that Pope's presence would draw Confederate troops away from McClellan's front. At this stage at least, Pope's mission did not include a march on Richmond.

This passive assignment was ironic given Pope's oft-stated love for attacking, although it added the opportunity to harass the railroad center at Gordonsville, which controlled the flow of Confederate supplies from the fertile Shenandoah Valley to Richmond. The picture changed, however, after the Seven Days, when McClellan, who felt Lee outnumbered him, made it clear that he was staying on the defensive pending heavy reinforcement. As early as 8 July, Pope told the Committee on the Conduct of the War that he felt McClellan's troops should be withdrawn and combined with his own for a grand thrust on the direct Washington-Fredericksburg-Richmond axis. On 4 August, with McClellan's army still huddled in its lines around Harrison's Landing, Maj. Gen. Henry Halleck—Lincoln's new general-in-chief—put such a plan into motion.[2]

A modern historian, John J. Hennessy, spelled out the implications of this strategic change in his 1993 study of the Second Bull Run campaign. In spite of demoralizing days at First Bull Run, Ball's Bluff, and during the Seven Days' battles, Washington had hitherto retained the initiative in Virginia. The new plan effectively eliminated any threat to Richmond until the armies could be combined, reorganized, and redirected. It handed control of the situation to Lee, who had shown he could hit hard and fast. Meanwhile, McClellan, whom Halleck hinted would command the combined force, continued to drag his feet. He delayed starting the withdrawal for more than a week, a decision that left Pope to face Lee alone.[3]

Once the withdrawal began, some of McClellan's contemporaries were so unhappy at the thought of serving with Pope that they took their time joining him. The Pennsylvania Reserves division was a notable exception; John Reynolds swiftly marched it seventy miles to link with Pope. As Samuel Bates noted after the war, "Had Generals [William B.] Franklin and [Fitz-John] Porter, who had a much shorter distance to march, shown the same enterprise and earnestness in moving their commands as was exhibited by the gallant Reynolds, a grievous defeat might have been averted." And although Second Bull Run was a disastrous Union defeat, the Pennsylvania Reserves, the Eleventh included, again performed capably under the circumstances.[4]

In early August the captives from Libby, Belle Isle, and other prisons were returning. They traveled by boat from Richmond up the James River, alighting first at the exchange point at Aiken's Landing, then proceeding to the Army of the Potomac's base at Harrison's Landing. Both sides recorded for whom each officer was handed over. Reynolds and McCall had formally been exchanged respectively for Confederate generals Lloyd Tilghman and Simon Buckner. Gallagher was exchanged for the colonel of the Forty-ninth Tennessee, while Lt. Col. Samuel Jackson was traded for his counterpart in rank from the Twenty-sixth Mississippi. An elaborate formula allowed exchanges across ranks: Hence, James Burke and two other Union lieutenants were judged the equivalent of the lieutenant colonel of the Fifty-third Tennessee.[5]

Shortly after he arrived at Harrison's Landing, Philip Lantzy wrote home to tell his family he was well, remarking that one of the army's observation balloons was "up at A bout a thousand feet this morning within A bout 2 hundred yards of our camp." Of the regiment, he wrote, "Now I supose we wont be poot on duty for a good while yet for we will hafta get Clothes and guns an Cartriges." He added, "I cant give much news at this time . . . paper is carse [scarce] and just coming in to camp I have not got much money yet." The Eleventh also acquired a new regimental standard to replace the colors lost at Gaines' Mill, although no description of it exists. It may have simply been a large United States flag.[6]

More than a lack of guns and uniforms incapacitated the Eleventh. Many men were physically unable to return to combat duty. As Lantzy put it, "there are many sick ones in the army but I hope My health will keep Like it has been." Gangrene had set in around the thigh wound Pvt. Thomas Sallade had suffered. Somehow, he survived without needing amputation. The divisional commander, McCall, came back feverish and suffering from liver trouble and did not see active service again. The Pennsylvania Reserves' interim commander, Truman Seymour, returned to his brigade as the divisional helm passed to senior brigadier John Reynolds.[7]

Gallagher's stay in Libby Prison was marked by illness in addition to his increasingly painful kidney ailment. Samuel Jackson earlier described his colonel's condition as "dumb ague." Lewis A. Johnston, an officer in the Westmoreland Guards of Company H, destined to lose a leg at Fredericksburg and endure a second stay in Libby Prison, later wrote Gallagher's widow: "While we were in prison, [Gallagher] failed very rapidly in health, and became so reduced that we feared he would not survive. At the time we were exchanged . . . he was transported with a few others to the landing, in an ambulance, while the rest of us were marched." At Harrison's Landing, Gallagher received twenty days' sick leave, "not to go beyond Fort Monroe" because of the campaign then in progress.[8]

Capt. Thomas Spires of Westmoreland County's Washington Blues was also in bad shape. At Gaines' Mill he suffered a shell wound in his chest. Picked up by Confederate soldiers, the Company I captain contracted pneumonia in Libby Prison. Gallagher later recalled that Spires "was unable to walk without assistance." Spires' first lieutenant, Eli Waugaman, remembered that the captain had to be "hauled" to the boats taking the exchanged captives to Aiken's Landing. Spires hung on with his unit until about the time of Antietam, the day after which he was granted a thirty-day leave of absence. His orders noted that upon his return "he will, if still unfit for duty, be examined with a view to his discharge." He did not return, his resignation taking effect 17 October 1862. He eventually qualified for a half-disability pension—$10 per month—retroactive to his date of resignation. The regiment's chaplain, the Reverend William Dickson, was another broken by military service and Libby Prison. He tendered his resignation as soon as he reached Harrison's Landing on 7 August. Company C's veterans presumably kept their moniker as the Dickson Guards.[9] Some prisoners were too sick to be exchanged right away. Shortly after Thomas Litzinger was transferred to Belle Isle from Libby Prison, he developed a case of chronic diarrhea. He was so debilitated that he had to be left behind when most of the Eleventh Reserves were exchanged in early August.[10]

The enlisted men started marching from Belle Isle at noon on a steamy 5 August. "Hundreds of our men gave out," James McGinley wrote in his diary, "and Som died on the road." The next morning, the survivors filed onto six transports waiting to take them back to the North. McGinley noted, "we met the Rebel prisoners who wer exchanged for us on our way to the Boats." McGinley became a passenger on a transport whose name he wrote as the *Richenbocher,* which had "plenty of provisions on board which we mad[e] scarse in a short time." Weeks of poor rations at Belle Isle kept McGinley and his comrades acutely aware of their hunger on their trip. On 13 August, McGinley wrote in his diary that he "Robed a sutler of all he had and then took the cars for Fredericksburg."[11]

By mid-August, the Pennsylvania Reserves division was near Fredericksburg, having sailed from Harrison's Landing on the Peninsula to Aquia Landing. Evidently seeking some sort of minor break from the war, Lt. Col. Jackson, Maj. Johns, Adjt. McCoy, and seventeen other exchanged officers signed a 14 August letter to the Army of the Potomac's adjutant general asking for permission to visit Washington on their way back to duty. The request was granted. Jackson noted in his diary the same day that he "Received orders for all the officers to join our Regiment at Aquia Creek by way of Baltimore and Washington."[12]

Accompanied by Gallagher, the group embarked from Harrison's Landing at 9 A.M. on 15 August. Seven hours later, they arrived at Fort Monroe, where Gallagher stopped off. An hour later, they took a boat across the Chesapeake Bay bound for Baltimore, which they reached at 7 A.M. the next morning. Here the officers bought new clothing, probably on credit, then stopped at Brown's Hotel for supper. Jackson visited old friends, leaving captains Nathaniel Nesbit and Spires, both ill, at the hotel. On 18 August, a Monday, the officers went to the War Department where they all drew four months' pay. By 4 P.M. on 20 August, having traveled all day, they reported to General Meade near Fredericksburg. The soldiers of the Eleventh, Jackson noted, were "wild with joy on seeing their old officers."[13]

A new theater of conflict loomed along the Rappahannock. The Eleventh was re-forming near Fredericksburg because the Pennsylvania Reserves division was being returned to Irvin McDowell's command, now the III Corps of Pope's Army of Virginia. The latter had, just a few days earlier, been concentrated around Cedar Mountain, located between the Rapidan and Rappahannock, a position Pope had "won" at tremendous cost in a fight earlier in the month. Recognizing the river-bordered triangle was a trap, Pope had sensibly withdrawn northeast across the Rappahannock. He was now waiting for reinforcements to arrive from the Peninsula, via Aquia Landing: the re-forming Pennsylvania Reserves division was soon expected to march and join Pope's main body. It is hard to assess the Eleventh's strength on the eve of this movement. The regimental papers do, however, contain an 18 August list of men reported absent. It yields the following chart:[14]

Co.	Sick	Wounded	Prisoner	Detached*	Missing	Without leave
A	10	13	5	24	3	
B	5	10		16	1	2
C	8	21	7	18		
D	15	15	2	21		
E	10	12	2	17		2
F	11		11	18	6	
G	12	1		18	26	
H	18	8	4	19	1	
I	19	4		20		
K	15	6	1	13		1

*"Detached" includes men detailed for provost duty, hospital guard, gunboat service, teamster work, and recruiting.

Battle deaths aside, the equivalent of more than two full companies of the Eleventh Pennsylvania Reserves—213 men—were recuperating from illness or wounds. According to the list, 113 of the 184 detached men were still guarding the hospital at Harrison's Landing. The Peninsula was now being evacuated, but the detached guard force—later put at 130 privates and noncommissioned officers—was transferred to guarding the Federal hospital on Craney Island, adjacent to Fort Monroe, where the wounded from Harrison's Landing had been moved starting 30 July. Gallagher, who stayed on sick leave until early September, was unable to get the detail released back to the regiment until November.[15]

John Reynolds bore many of the attitudes of the pre–Civil War Regular Army. As his biographer noted, in an era when ideas of total war were forming and would be pressed home by such figures as Ulysses S. Grant and William T. Sherman, Reynolds "could be classed as a kid-glove general." Like McClellan, he loved parade ground pageantry, once organizing a massive review of the entire division when the wives of McCall and Meade visited camp. Like Meade (and most other Regular Army officers) he felt uneasy with nonprofessional soldiers. "I begin to agree with somebody who, writing in one of the papers said: 'You cannot make soldiers of volunteers,'" he wrote home late in 1861 when his brigade was encamped near Langley. "I thought in Mexico that I would never have anything to do with them under any circumstances, and nothing but this state of things in the country would have induced me to take command of any body of them."[16]

Also like Meade, he had been disgusted at the excesses that manifested when the units received orders to raid Dranesville farms for forage. "They plundered and marauded most outrageously and disgracefully," he wrote of his men. "Of course it was stopped but not until great damage had been done. I see by the papers that great praise had been given Genl. McCall's division for being exempt from this stain upon our Army, our Country, and our character. Do not believe one word of the accounts, which must be written from here by some of the very scoundrels who were the leading characters of it." At one point, he considered seeking a transfer.[17]

The Peninsula changed that, and the Pennsylvania Reserves rose in Reynolds' estimation. "I am to have the Division of the Reserves," Reynolds wrote his sisters from on board the steam tug *Delaware* on his way to the Rappahannock bases, "now sadly diminished in numbers yet in good condition, and I hope as able as ever to do efficient service."[18]

At the same time, Reynolds began to reorganize the division. An immediate consequence for the re-forming Eleventh regiment, being led by Samuel Jackson in Gallagher's absence, was that it would not return to Meade's brigade. It was instead placed in the reorganized Third Brigade, now headed by the former colonel of the Ninth Pennsylvania Reserves, Brig. Gen. Conrad Feger Jackson.[19] Conscious that the position was considered the place of honor in the line of battle, Samuel Jackson noted in his diary, "We are to occupy the right of the 3rd Brigade." He added that "General Meade [is] dissatisfied with the arrangement" that cost Meade having the Eleventh in his brigade.[20]

There seem to have been no complaints, however, about the new brigade commander. Alsace, Pennsylvania-born Conrad Jackson was a forty-nine-year-old Mexican War veteran and former railroad administrator. One of his directives during this interlude on the Rappahannock was evidently given to Philip Lantzy. "I was detailed by the General to Guard a house in the county about two miles [away]," he wrote home, "and they was to let me [k]now when the Regiment would start So I could come in."[21]

But on 21 August, orders arrived for the Pennsylvania Reserves to start marching towards Pope's lines. The suddenness of the command—the brigade broke camp at 8 P.M. to make an unusual night march—meant that Lantzy was overlooked. As he expressed it, "the Rebel General Stonewall Jackson had attacked General Pope of our army and So I am left behind . . . hear with the sick and So I am detailed to cook for [the] sick and tend to them Till we Leave this Camp which I think will be in a few days." Other men from the Eleventh Reserves—at least a portion of the Brady Guards—also drew field hospital duty.[22]

Lantzy, who evidently missed Second Bull Run, made it clear he was uneasy being away from the Eleventh, especially as "the Regiment has Been Engaged in a Nother Battle but I hope if they have had a chance to take Revenge for what they done to us when they took us prisoners and I all so hope they could whip them bad and Make them Run. I could hear the cannonading for 8 days in that Direction of Gordonsville and by all we can hear now our army is Retreating again and are falling back towards Monassus Junction."[23]

If Lantzy garbled the details, sporadic artillery fire and skirmishes created the feeling of constant fighting, and withdrawals were indeed taking place along Pope's front. The Pennsylvania Reserves had been on the march during the preceding days while Lee conducted several probes of Pope's Rappahannock lines. "Heavy cannonading up the river," wrote

Samuel Jackson in his diary for 23 August. On the same date, McGinley wrote that when the regiment passed by Rappahannock Station that night, they found "the R.R. Bridge, Depot and other buildings on fire and our Army in retreat. [W]e had to follow them[,] the Rebels Sheling our rear." By 3 P.M. the next day, the day on which Lantzy penned the letter quoted above, Reynolds' division was just coming into Warrenton, pitching tents a half-mile from town.[24]

Confusion marked the withdrawal. Pope's whereabouts were unknown for part of the day. The telegraph operator at Warrenton Junction, pestered with messages for him, pleaded with his superiors for help in finding the Army of Virginia's commander. "Please send an orderly out with message to General Pope," he wrote delicately to Union Maj. Gen. Philip Kearny. "It is very important and must be sent out to him at once. We have no orderlies here." The army also suffered from supply problems. At 11:30 A.M., Reynolds was complaining about the laggard pace of an ammunition train, noting, "I found teamsters halting along the road for no other purpose than to roast corn, and have started them on, but they have halted again." Reynolds kept up the pace despite the fact that he had misgivings about the whole campaign. "I do not approve of the operation of leaving the line of the James River," he wrote home earlier in the month, adding that "to be sure I do not take political projects into consideration and I suppose they will have, as they have heretofore, overruled all military ones."[25]

The line of march put the Reserves, with the rest of McDowell's corps far behind, following Maj. Gen. Franz Sigel's corps up the Manassas-Sudley Road headed for Manassas. It was an unfortunate pairing, for Sigel intensely disliked McDowell, whom he considered incompetent, and let his feelings extend to the troops under McDowell's command. Although positioned next to each other at Second Bull Run, each corps would essentially fight on its own.[26]

The August weather turned strangely cool overnight, and, Samuel Jackson noted, "Our men suffer for want of blankets." Yet the morning of the 25th turned hot as the men marched along dusty roads toward Fauquier White Sulphur Springs, weighed down by four days' rations distributed the day before and which, it developed, they were lucky to have. By 8 A.M. on the 26th, Samuel Jackson heard "Very heavy cannonading" in the distance. A day later, he wrote that Stonewall Jackson was "reported at Manassas. Expect a fight with him this night or tomorrow."[27]

Two days earlier, Lee had embarked on one of the grandest gambles of the war. He left Longstreet's "wing" (still not yet a formal corps) of his army facing Pope across the Rappahannock, while sending the rest of his troops—Stonewall Jackson's "wing"—on a wide flanking march. Jackson first stopped at Salem, well to Pope's northwest, then marched due east to Manassas Junction, cutting Pope's direct rail and telegraph link to Washington. Several days later, Lee sent Longstreet along the same route, leaving only a 5,000-man division under Maj. Gen. Richard H. Anderson in place along the Rappahannock.

Events showed Pope vulnerable to battlefield stress, but at this point he sensed opportunity. His cavalry and scouts told him Longstreet was still near Salem Court House. If Pope moved fast enough—along with the reinforcements arriving from the Peninsula—he had a shot at overwhelming Jackson while Lee's army was still divided. Jackson, however, was content to sit and be attacked while waiting for Longstreet to join him. He had chosen a good defensive position, an arc-shaped, unfinished railroad grade cut into Stony Ridge, a curved outcropping running about two and a half miles long, its northeastern flank covered by Bull Run itself. The site was a few thousand yards from the Henry House Hill position where Jackson earned his "Stonewall" nickname in mid-1861.

The first clash on this field came late on 28 August well in front of the railroad bed, on the Brawner Farm adjacent to the Warrenton Pike. Union Brig. Gen. Rufus King's division, part of McDowell's corps, had been marching eastward along the pike, which roughly paralleled the unfinished grade. Stonewall Jackson's batteries placed along the ridge opened fire, surprising King's command but also signaling the Rebels' whereabouts. At this time, Sigel had arrived at the First Bull Run battlefield, and his command was deployed with Henry House Hill at its approximate center. Meanwhile, Reynolds had been on the march since 4 A.M. and was now advancing his division northward along the Manassas-Sudley Road, which bisected the Warrenton Turnpike near a stone house that was a landmark of First Bull Run. Reynolds halted his division well before the junction, and received 150 Confederate prisoners rounded up by King's and Sigel's men. Samuel Jackson noted in his diary that they were "Placed in a church for safe keeping," likely a reference to the Bethlehem Church on the Manassas-Gainesville Road, well to the division's rear.[28]

The division lay on its arms during the uneasy night of 28–29 August. In his diary Samuel Jackson noted, "Great alarm last night, caused by a horse running among our men." The Eleventh, having finished off the last of its marching rations at suppertime, foraged for food. Evans Brady wrote that he "had two green apples for . . . supper, and the next morning a roasting-ear."[29]

At daylight the Reserves got orders to march west to be deployed along the army's left flank. The Bucktails, now in Meade's brigade, were thrown out as skirmishers along the Warrenton Turnpike, in roughly the same spot where King's troops had earlier come under fire. Behind them, Meade advanced the rest of his brigade in two lines. To the left and rear of this force, the First Pennsylvania Reserves were deployed as skirmishers, with the rest of the division—Seymour's and Conrad Jackson's brigades—in reserve behind them. The division of Union Brig. Gen. Robert C. Schenck from Sigel's corps followed Meade's brigade. At about 8 A.M. firing started on the right, where Sigel was launching unsuccessful attacks against Stonewall Jackson's lines.[30]

More help was coming for the Federals. From Centreville, across Bull Run to the northeast, the Army of the Potomac's IX Corps under Jesse Reno and the III Corps under Samuel Heintzelman were marching west on the Warrenton Turnpike to link up with Pope's rapidly coalescing army. Heintzelman arrived on the field at about noon, but nobody seems to have told Reynolds, holding the far left of the front. At 3:30 P.M., he was in the dark as to the location of the rest of the combined army, outside of Sigel's troops. "General Sigel is moving on Gainesville down the pike, with my right near Groveton, my left toward the railroad," he wrote to an officer on Pope's staff. "I do not know where anybody is but Sigel. Please let me hear from you."[31]

Frosty relations with the uncooperative Sigel aside, Reynolds' anxiety was probably arising from the fact that by about 2 P.M., his brigades started to exchange fire with Rebel skirmishers. Their opponents were from the Confederate brigades of Micah Jenkins (pushing up against the Twelfth Pennsylvania Reserves) and Eppa Hunton (which met with the First Pennsylvania Reserves to the right of the Twelfth). The battlefield here was a wooded patch near a watercourse called Young's Branch running south of the Warrenton Turnpike. Late in the afternoon, Pope arrived on the battlefield from Centreville and wanted new attacks on Stony Ridge. On the left, he ordered Reynolds to advance, in order to (as Reynolds described it in his official report) "threaten the enemy's right and rear." With Meade staying in his advanced position, Seymour and Conrad Jackson led their brigades into action, despite what Reynolds termed "a heavy fire of artillery from the ridge to the left of the pike"— likely a reference to guns on the Brawner farm commanded by Confederate artillerist Stephen D. Lee. Captain Brady described this as a "masked battery not three hundred yards in front of us."[32]

The attack failed. "Notwithstanding all the steadiness and courage shown by the men," Reynolds later reported, "they were compelled to fall back before the heavy fire of artillery and musketry which met them both on the front and left flank, and the division resumed its original position." George Trimble of the Indiana National Guards (one of two Trimbles in the company) remembered marching "up a narrow ravine, the place being so narrow that the whole four regiments were crowded close together, and not even a scout in front. The first thing we knew was a cloud of grape, round-shot, and canister in our faces." A piece of shell struck William H. "Harry" Empfield on the head. The wound was at first thought mortal, but Empfield clung to life and was later discharged by a surgeon's certificate. Shortly after Empfield's wounding, another piece of shell skimmed across Trimble's chest, "just hard enough to graze the skin and sicken me," he wrote home. "I feel some slight pains about the heart yet." By the time orders to withdraw came, the situation came near to being a rout. "Two whole companies surged down against us to avoid the fire," Evans Brady wrote home, "yet my men stood firm and by their example saved the whole brigade." McGinley was possibly referring to the whole regiment when he wrote of the action: "Retreated without firing a gun." Samuel Jackson estimated that thus far there had been "One man killed and six or eight wounded in my Regiment."[33]

The Rebels they had met were part of a division temporarily commanded by Brig. Gen. James L. Kemper, and their appearance signaled that Longstreet's wing of the Army of Northern Virginia had arrived. As early as 11 A.M. that morning, Union cavalry Brig. Gen. John Buford informed McDowell, who was bringing the rest of the Army of Virginia's III Corps to the field alongside Reynolds, that Longstreet had pushed through Union resistance at Thoroughfare Gap. By 9 A.M., Buford reported, Longstreet was within a mile or so of the battlefield. McDowell, for whatever reason, failed to communicate to Pope the news that the Rebel army's wings had joined.[34]

As night fell on the 29th, Reynolds withdrew the bruised division eastward. The famished, exhausted men slept on their arms. Some soldiers tried to brew what remained of their coffee ration—survivors told Samuel Bates the culprits were "stragglers"—but Rebel gunners shot at the flames. No reports exist of losses in this "coffee brigade" action, but it probably further sapped the strength of the Eleventh's soldiers and their officers' patience.[35]

Firing also kept up on the right and left of the Pennsylvania Reserves as McDowell and Fitz-John Porter maneuvered their respective corps into position. The latter's V Corps had marched along the Manassas-Gainesville Road until Jeb Stuart's pickets stopped it at an offshoot of another stream, Broad Run. Meanwhile, McDowell brought the rest of his corps into position to Reynolds' right, astride the Warrenton Turnpike. Both had received unclear, "discretionary" orders from Pope, who evidently wanted the two to push westward in hopes of turning Stonewall Jackson's left flank on Stony Ridge. In Porter's case, he halted at the creek, called Dawkin's Branch, where he ran into Stuart's skirmishers. The V Corps' presence here indeed worried Longstreet, who feared being flanked. But Porter, the extent of whose knowledge of the forces in front of him has been a subject of controversy, was in a quandary as to how to proceed. His failure to continue the advance formed part of the charges Pope brought against him at a later court-martial.[36]

McDowell meanwhile ran into a Confederate counterattack by a division led by John Bell Hood, which contained both his "Texas Brigade" and Evander Law's brigade. The attack, involving the same troops who broke the Federal line at Gaines' Mill, was intended to alleviate Federal pressure on Jackson. Advancing east along the Warrenton Turnpike just as the sun began to set, Hood lacked enough daylight and support to make great headway. Before dawn broke on Saturday, Hood withdrew into line with the rest of Longstreet's portion of the Army of Northern Virginia.[37]

The Federal line of battle also shifted as the sun came up on the 30th. Porter withdrew his V Corps from Dawkin's Branch and marched several miles to link up with Pope's main body on the First Bull Run battlefield. There were key changes within the Eleventh Pennsylvania Reserves' brigade as well. The stress of the battlefield proved too much for Conrad Jackson, who, by an 1865 account, "ruptured a blood vessel and became severely ill" and removed himself from command. The ailment must have been debilitating, for Reynolds had only praise for him in his report. The ill officer's replacement was Lt. Col. Martin D. Hardin, commander of the Twelfth Pennsylvania Reserves.[38]

As its parent brigade was changing hands, Samuel Jackson's regiment was shifted to the far right of the line at 3 A.M., just as dawn was breaking. They saw evidence, as Samuel Jackson wrote in his diary, that "the fighting at this point was very severe last night." The Eleventh, although armed with only smoothbores, went into a skirmish line in front of the brigade. The Pennsylvania Reserves were still famished. Brady had only some raw corn found along the way to eat for breakfast.[39]

Hood's tactical withdrawal had led Pope (who still insisted he was fighting only Stonewall Jackson) to the erroneous conclusion that the Confederates were retreating and using the Warrenton Turnpike as the logical route. As Longstreet wrote in his official report: "The enemy seized that opportunity to claim a victory, and the Federal commander was so imprudent as to dispatch his Government by telegraph tidings to that effect." Pope compounded his misinterpretation by issuing new orders for attacks on the morning of the 30th. While the relatively fresh V Corps would provide the main thrust, Pope told Reynolds the Pennsylvania Reserves would, as their commander expressed it, "be the pivot in the attack which Porter's corps was to make on the enemy's right, then supposed to be on the pike and in retreat." Reynolds was to form his division on the left of the Warrenton Turnpike, on Chinn Ridge opposite Henry House Hill, "in column by company at full distance, with the whole of my artillery on the left."[40]

After getting the brigades into formation, Reynolds ordered his batteries of rifled artillery to push the Rebels off a small rise directly in front of the division. With the sounds of Fitz-John Porter's attack on their right filling the air, the Bucktails moved forward as skirmishers. But once they again approached the woods opposite Groveton, they met heavy fire from Rebel skirmishers, probably from the command of Brig. Gen. Lewis Armistead. Reynolds sent the First and Seventh Reserves to aid the Bucktails and managed to push the Sixth Reserves into the woods on the left.[41]

The resistance in his front convinced Reynolds that the Confederates were not fleeing. Going forward to reconnoiter, he later reported, "I found a line of skirmishers of the enemy nearly parallel to the line of skirmishers covering my left flank, with cavalry formed behind them, perfectly stationary, evidently masking a column of the enemy formed for attack on my left flank when our line should be sufficiently advanced." Rifle fire wounded one of Reynolds' orderlies during this mission, and he hurried his party back to safety. Once within his own lines, Reynolds either sent a message to McDowell, who hurried forward, or himself went looking for the III Corps commander. Either way, the two had a quick deliberation, and McDowell told Reynolds to prepare for defense and to be ready to receive reinforcements. By some accounts, Reynolds also brought his information directly to Pope—the intimation is that he shared Sigel's lack of confidence in McDowell.[42]

But Pope's chief concern at this time lay not with Reynolds' immediate front, but rather with Fitz-John Porter's V Corps. Its attack on Stonewall Jackson's lines had failed like those before it, and Porter's divisions were under fire from Longstreet's batteries along the Federal left. Pope ordered Reynolds to assist Porter, and to "form a line behind which the troops might be rallied." The new position would be astride the Warren-ton Turnpike, under the protection of a row of batteries along high ground known as Dogan Ridge. An element of the V Corps—Gouverneur War-ren's slender, two-regiment brigade of volunteers from Sykes' otherwise all-Regulars division—was to be left in place holding the Reserves' for-mer position along the left flank.[43]

Reynolds complied and put his division into marching order but found moving difficult. Not only was the ground very broken, but sur-vivors of the V Corps' attack fell back in great confusion. Before his troops had gone far, the looming Rebel attack across the weakened Fed-eral left started. A screaming horde of Confederates under John Bell Hood charged, again, up the Warrenton Turnpike, punching their way through Warren's thousand-man command.

Elsewhere amid the Union lines, Hardin's brigade, containing the Eleventh Pennsylvania Reserves, had not yet formed on the new front. Reynolds seized this opportunity to swing it and three batteries—includ-ing some rifled guns commanded by Capt. Mark Kerns—into line to support Warren. Hardin, survivors told Samuel Bates after the war, "advanced [the regiment] to the top of a small ridge, in an open field"— a bit of raised, cleared ground between Chinn Ridge and Groveton. Here he set up a double line of his four regiments, the Eleventh and Twelfth Reserves in front. In front of them, Hood's men were chasing panicked Zouaves from the Fifth New York—one of Warren's now-shattered regi-ments—toward the position.[44]

Although the likelihood of a Gaines' Mill reunion probably went unnoted at the time within the Eleventh Reserves, the oncoming battle line—as Hardin's brigade faced it—from left to right was composed of the Fifth Texas, Hampton's Legion, the Eighteenth Georgia, and the Fourth Texas. The Eleventh's officers dressed the lines and the men stood ready with buck and ball charges. Kerns' gunners loaded canister—a des-perate thing to do with rifled guns, as such charges ate away the grooves inside the barrels. Their first shots went high—they had aimed cautiously out of fear of hitting the fleeing Zouaves—yet the fire persuaded Hamp-ton's Legion and the Eighteenth Georgia to pause for cover at one of the fingers of Young's Branch, which embraced both the front and rear of the Federal position. But the flank regiments—the Fifth and Fourth Texas— continued on impulsively, a move that spurred their hesitant comrades stopping at Young's Branch to follow.[45]

Heading for the Eleventh Pennsylvania Reserves' position, the Fifth Texas charged up the hill through the smoke and the broiling August

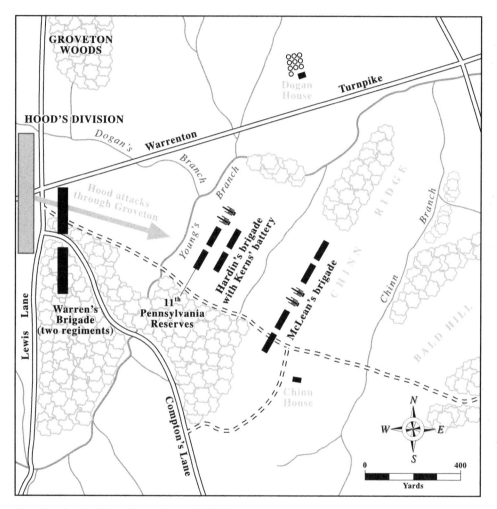

Hood breaks the Union line at Second Bull Run

sun. Samuel Jackson's men lay prone, and when the Rebels got close enough, a hail of buckshot mixed with .69-caliber musket balls ripped holes in the gray line. A Fifth Texas captain named W. T. Hill remembered that "a line of Federals sprang up from the ground where they had been lying so flat we could not see them, and poured a volley into our ranks that was terribly destructive—many of our men falling dead or wounded." At the same time, Kerns' gunners continued to fire canister rounds. Hoping to dodge the fire, the Texans eyed some woods that flanked the Eleventh's left. One of the Union regiments to the Eleventh's rear seems to have started to shift troops to the woods even before the Texans' charge reached the hill. In his report of the battle, Col. Jerome B. Robertson of the Fifth Texas—who interpreted Hardin's deployment as "three lines of battle"—saw through the smoke that "the rear line . . . was moving by the left flank at a run, for a point of timber on my right, some 400 yards distant." The movement spurred Robertson into urging his men on to the trees: "Seeing no support on my right, it was evident that I must gain this point of timber before him to prevent my right from being turned." Somehow, the Texans won the race, Robertson writing that "We gained the woods, the head of my column leading the enemy's by some fifty yards, when we fired into them and drove them from the woods." Samuel Jackson changed the front of his leftmost companies, trying to counter the enemy fire. Luck must have been with Evans Brady's company, which if still on the far left of the regiment when in battle line would have been directly adjacent to the trees. "I did not have a man injured," Brady wrote his mother afterward, though he allowed that "several have been sent to the hospital completely prostrated by fatigue."[46]

By now Hood's own cannoneers had unlimbered and found the Pennsylvanians' range. In the Cambria Guards, a piece of shell wounded Sgt. Daniel D. Jones, while Lt. Rowland Jones was struck in the genitals by a musket ball. The ball, a medical report later noted, entered "the penis about one and one half inches from the end[,] passing through lengthwise, striking the chord of the right testicle . . . tearing the muscles and nerves of the groin, injuring the tendon and large nerve inside, grazing the femur and making its exit on the outside of the right hip near the joint." Adjt. Robert McCoy witnessed the officer's wounding and gave orders that he be carried off the field. McCoy was then himself struck by a shell fragment which bruised his abdomen, then by a musket ball which lodged in his hip. A piece of shell hit Indiana National Guards corporal Constantine Morton, but its force was deadened by his haversack and bayonet scabbard, leaving him with only a bruise. Pvt. J. M. "Mac" Laughery of the same company was also evidently hit by shell fragments but was less lucky. His leg was perforated with eleven wounds. Although he was mortally wounded, his comrades arranged to carry him with them when word was passed that the brigade would withdraw toward Chinn Ridge. There, a brigade consisting of four Ohio regiments commanded by Nathaniel McLean, along with a battery, had established another make-shift defensive line.[47]

Amid this scene, a musket ball struck Hardin on the left side, piercing the thorax and the pectoral muscle. Fortunately for the brigade commander, the shot was deflected around the outside of his rib cage and missed his lungs. He was helped off the field and command of what had started the day as Conrad Jackson's brigade now fell to Lt. Col. Robert Anderson of the Ninth Pennsylvania Reserves. A Mexican War veteran, Allegheny County's Anderson was about forty-four years old at the time of Second Bull Run, and this would mark the first of several occasions during the following months in which he would assume command of the brigade.[48]

The withdrawal toward Chinn Ridge seems to have been orderly at first, though Kerns' cannon and caissons were lost. The regiments held together, as Reynolds later put it, "taking up new positions wherever the advantages of ground permitted." On Reynolds' part, although he still had two brigades and a battery under his own control, his force found "ourselves perfectly out of place" at this time and unable to do anything to stem the chaos that had developed on the left.[49]

In the swirling, smoky mass between Groveton and Chinn Ridge the Eleventh's regimental organization dissolved further with each new Confederate attack. A minié ball passed through both hips of Indiana National Guards Sgt. Henderson Howard. He was also nicked by bullets on the left knee and on the right side of his face, just above his mouth. Left behind to be taken prisoner, he was evidently exchanged a few days later, for a doctor cut out the bullet at an Alexandria hospital in early September. Cpl. Charles Shambaugh was wounded in the left leg. His injuries were at first thought mortal, but he survived an amputation to be discharged in October. Brothers Frank and William "Billy" Harbison were both hit, though not mortally. Cpl. Garvin A. "John" McLain suffered a relatively minor wound on the end of a finger. Pvt. James W. Davis took a musket ball on his inner thigh—"a very tender part" George Trimble noted in a letter home.[50]

Butler County's Dickson Guards were relatively unscathed, losing only Pvt. James R. Porter to wounds that would, within a month, prove mortal. Less fortunate were those in the regiment's other Butler County unit, the Connoquenessing Rangers, which bore the brunt of the day's fatalities. Its captain, William Stewart, was hit, though not disabled, by Rebel ordnance. Five of his privates were killed outright, however, while a sixth would die of his wounds. It was said that privates Jesse Fry, underage but later to make corporal, and M. F. "Boss" McCullough, destined to die in the Wilderness, "were the only men of the company on their feet and unhurt at the close of the battle." In Company E, 1st Lt. Daniel R. Coder took a Rebel bullet or musket ball in his mouth. It struck him on his upper lip on the left side but was halted by his upper teeth; the impact splintered his left eye tooth and the incisors on either side. Color sergeant James L. Hazlett "fell severely wounded" while carrying the regiment's replacement flag. The Eleventh ultimately listed fourteen killed or mortally wounded in this battle.[51]

Hood lost men as well. One wounded Texan told a comrade of laying "on that field as the sun was slowly sinking behind the hills, and as the shadows of night came on, the feelings that came over him were beyond his powers of expression; midway between two lines of battle with shot and shell from friend and foe falling thick, and every few moments some poor unfortunate would cry out in anguish, 'Oh, God, I am hit again.' His mother from his infancy had taught him to pray, but on this day the thought of prayers never entered [h]is mind, and yet, he says, he could embrace every act of his life in a single thought."[52]

The Eleventh Reserves was in pieces by the time its survivors reached McLean's line at Chinn Ridge. James McGinley wrote in his diary that "our men wer Shot down lik Sheap." Evans Brady considered the rout's aftermath almost as nightmarish as the battle. "When the left broke, the rush was for Centreville," he wrote home of the situation as Anderson's brigade fell apart, "and such a time no one can describe: regiments and companies were divided and mixed up." While they struggled in the morass and confusion on the Federal flank, one of Pope's staff officers was placing the other two brigades of the Pennsylvania Reserves division on and around Henry House Hill, their lines about a half-mile from Chinn Ridge. By about 5:15 P.M. Sykes' division of U.S. Regulars had extended this defensive line along the Manassas-Sudley Road. An hour and a half later, Confederate attacks pushed the Rebels beyond part of Chinn Ridge to the Henry Hill perimeter. The Union line there held, thanks to elements of Jesse Reno's IX Corps. But shortly afterward, the rest of Pope's army, Reynolds' shattered division included, started retreating toward Centreville along the same Warrenton Turnpike it once advanced. The exhausted, famished Pennsylvanians made what camp they could alongside Sykes' division once both had crossed to the east bank of Cub Run.[53]

Before regrouping with the rest of the division, the Eleventh Pennsylvania Reserves made its way toward Centreville in splintered battle groups, which tagged along with other, often equally bloodied regiments. Evans Brady had only thirteen men from Company K rallied around him, and this squad joined the line of march of the Sixteenth Maine. They "proceeded a mile or two when Capt. Porter and a few of his men from our regiment joined me." In the dark, the Porter-Brady force lost track of the Maine regiment, and for a time linked with the Third Michigan. "This regiment we left as soon as we found water, and some of the boys having coffee, we kindled a fire and made a cup of warm coffee." Army wagons were scattered around, and from one the troops "took a box of crackers, which were soon stored away in our empty haversacks. It was fortunate we done so, as we got nothing till Sunday night."[54]

The next day, the remnants of the Pennsylvania Reserves division staggered into Centreville. They were on the same route as McDowell's army in its retreat from the same field a little over a year earlier. There were some differences however. "When the army reached Centreville," Brady wrote home, "the new troops had a strong guard along the fortifications, and stopped all who came up. Had it not been for this the whole army would have rushed together to Washington as they did a year ago."[55]

Huddled in what must have been a miserable bivouac, Samuel Jackson again counted the cost of Pope's misadventures. "The loss of our Regiment in yesterday's fight, about 50 killed and wounded," he noted in his diary entry for Sunday, 31 August, adding, "The 11th Regiment down to 100 fighting men." The same night, his small force went on picket about two miles west of Centreville. There they heard and saw the muzzle flashes of Rebel skirmishers testing the Federal lines. Recalled at 3 A.M., as dawn was breaking, the men were allowed a few hours' rest. By 2 P.M., they were again headed northeast toward Fairfax Court House, about fifteen miles west of Alexandria. Along the way, they heard the gunfire from the battle of Chantilly, where two of Stonewall Jackson's divisions attacked a strong Federal position and were repulsed.[56]

The dead of the Eleventh lay, mixed with those of dozens of other units, between Groveton and Henry House Hill. A volunteer nurse, captured by the Rebels on 30 August, glimpsed the area when he was sent to the rear via the Warrenton Turnpike. After being repatriated, he found himself unable to describe the scene. "It was," he wrote, "a sight only to be felt."[57]

Chapter 7

Brave Comrades Falling

South Mountain and Antietam

After Second Bull Run, Lee decided to carry the war north. But rather than challenge the Washington fortifications, where Pope's army regrouped, he chose to veer into Maryland. The border state would provide food and fodder; moving there also relieved Virginia from some of the pressures of war. On 4 September, the Confederate army started crossing the Potomac at a point about thirty miles from Chantilly.[1]

To meet the threat, Lincoln turned to George McClellan to reorganize and revitalize the Union army in the eastern theater.

The weeks that followed saw the siege and Confederate capture of Harpers Ferry along with two battles, South Mountain and Antietam, the latter still literally "America's bloodiest day." The Eleventh Pennsylvania Reserves was heavily involved in the campaign, despite barely functioning as a regiment. With more than a hundred of its able-bodied men still guarding the Craney Island hospital, Second Bull Run had reduced the Eleventh, again, to company size. George Meade wrote home that the Pennsylvania Reserves division as a whole "is pretty well used up, and ought, strictly speaking, to be withdrawn, reorganized, filled up with recruits, and put in efficient condition."[2]

At the same time, the Union army's method of allocating replacements guaranteed the decline of veteran units. Most of the 300,000 men Lincoln now sought were to be used in creating new units, instead of filling battle-tested ones. As a consequence, existing regiments had to keep their own recruiting details active in their member companies' home areas.

Back on 7 August, with exchanged men just returning from Richmond, Capt. Daniel Porter had detailed two lieutenants, two sergeants, and eight privates to go back to Pennsylvania on recruiting duty. Nine days later, Maj. Gen. Ambrose Burnside, commanding at Fredericksburg, authorized each company in the regiment to send another man home for the same purpose. In the case of Company A, recently exchanged Pvt. John Roberts went to Ebensburg as the Cambria Guards' sole recruiter, his name listed on both orders cited above.[3]

Roberts' mission earned mention in one of Philip Lantzy's letters. In it the young Carrolltown volunteer struck a note of urgency.

> [If] we do not wa[t]ch the Rebels they will have there Confederacy in Spite of us for our army is very weak now and the Rebels [k]now it and they are lashing on us Every where but if we can hold them in check for a week or So we will be Reinforced[.] [T]hat will [re]turn the compliment and Run them in to Richmond and take there old Capitol and hang Jeff Davis and then we will soon gain the great day when we will all go home but we will hafta have a good Many More Men then We now have[.] I think if we get them three Hundred thousand that the President has called for we can crush this Rebellion in a short time
>
> [I]if there is Eny of the boys wants to Join a Company to be Soldiers there is a chance in our Company[.] There is one Man

in Ebensburg from our Company Recruiting for it and so they can juist Put there names down on his Roll and he will Bring them to our company free of all Passage[.] It would be much easier in our Regt That has been in Service[. T]hey will not need to drill half as Much as they will in a New Regiment And I would like to see Some of our Boys Pick up heart to come out as a Volenteer and help to defend our country for it [i.e., the war] wont last long if they come out and help us whip the Rebels.[4]

Lantzy's worries may have been fueled by a crisis of confidence in the army itself. The question of abolition polarized many units, and discussion drew in men from the Eleventh Reserves. Writing his brother after Second Bull Run, George Trimble of the Indiana National Guards attributed Federal failures to the tolerance of slavery: "I think my prophecy will come true," the Company B private wrote, "that so long as our government lets slavery exist, we will meet defeat in its rudest and most heart-sickening forms. We cannot expect to get rid of an evil until its cause is removed. This war is a pestilence; rising from the loathsome, stinking carcass of slavery. Who can ask God's blessing, and at the same time 'roll sin as a sweet morsel under the tongue?' How can our nation cry to Him for peace, and at the same time cling to the stinking, damning sin of human bondage?"[5]

Captain Evans Brady indicated less enthusiasm for abolition, but felt that military pragmatism defined the issue. "I see that they keep up the negro question in the North and talk of breaking the rebellion by freeing the slaves," he wrote his mother about a week after Second Bull Run. "There is one thing to talk and another to act. How are the[y] going to free the slaves before the army reaches them. Wherever the army has gone the negroes have run away; but we cannot reach the slaves in the far South." Brady felt agitation on the issue did more harm than good. It stiffened Southern resolve and caused bickering in an army already worn by constant marching. "If it was fight all the time, we would be better satisfied," wrote Brady, who confessed being close to resigning his commission. "I could write much about the conduct of the war, which if known would open the eyes of the people in the North; but I refrain, because I would not be believed, and my motives would be attributed to other than the real cause." He ended with a note of fatalism: "Do not grieve or feel anxious for me—if any accident befalls me, you will hear of it soon enough."[6]

The lull following Chantilly saw the Eleventh Reserves moving to different Alexandria-area camps almost every day as the army reorganized.

Although he could walk only with a cane, Lieutenant James Burke returned to the Cambria Guards during this time from Convalescent Camp Alexandria, the Rebel bullet from Gaines' Mill still in his leg. The regiment also received an influx of men released from hospitals, beginning on Wednesday, 3 September. A few days later, it drew new issues of clothing and blankets to replace those lost during the Manassas campaign. "Mustered for pay," James McGinley wrote in his diary on 6 September, adding the regiment "got a new flag" to replace whichever saw service at Second Bull Run. Lt. Col. Samuel Jackson spent that date making out muster rolls and preparing the men for an inspection. Late in the day, Gallagher returned from sick leave, resuming command of the regiment and providing a significant morale boost. "Boys all jubilant on his return," Jackson noted in his diary. The evening also brought a set of marching orders, and midnight found the Pennsylvania Reserves division on the road to Maryland.[7]

The army was regaining its confidence as the march started. Pope had been transferred northwest, and most soldiers were delighted when McClellan took the helm of the united armies of Virginia and the Potomac. Just as important, on 6 September McDowell was relieved of command of the Pennsylvania Reserves' parent corps, which also included the divisions of Rufus King and James Ricketts. "The army is down on Pope and McDowell," Brady wrote home, "and the restoration of McClellan to the command has inspired our men more than anything I have witnessed for a long time. The people at the North seem to be opposed to him, but I assure you the army has every confidence in his abilities. During the retreat on the Peninsula, the soldiers cheered and waved their hats for him while they lay in the mud and swamps—while McDowell might ride along his whole line and fail to elicit a single sign of approbation."[8]

George Trimble shared most of those sentiments: "There is not a man in the army who has the least confidence in General McDowell, and they never will fight with any success under him," he wrote his brother. "But McClellan has the confidence of every soldier." Unlike later observers, Trimble rated Banks and Sigel highly and even allowed that "Pope is a good general among second rate ones, but is far behind McClellan." He shared darker suspicions about the unlucky McDowell: "There is just one of two things about McDowel—he is either a traitor, or else his military talent has been immensely overrated. One thing makes me think he is a traitor, and that is, in a fight he wears a cap that is not the shape or color of any other in either army. At any other time he has a regular army cap. He goes out in the direction of the enemy without an aid or an orderly attending him, and in the midst or rear of his army he is attended by four or six hundred men. These things I have witnessed with my own eyes, and I know that the things I am telling you are literally true."[9]

These comments might be dismissed as nonsense. But as historian John J. Hennessy notes, much of the rank and file believed that McDowell's strange battle hat—one man described it as looking like a capsized canoe—somehow signaled treason. Three decades later, a veteran alleged: "On August 30 [1862], wherever the 'Hat' appeared, defeat and disaster followed in quick succession."[10]

The attitude was so prevalent—and so damaging—at the time the Maryland campaign started that McDowell requested a court of inquiry to clear his reputation. As he wrote to Lincoln in early September:

> I have been informed by a Senator that he had seen a note, in pencil, written by a colonel of cavalry mortally wounded in the recent battle, stating, among other causes, that he was dying a victim "to McDowell's treachery," and that his last request was that this note might be shown to you.
>
> That the colonel believed this charge, and felt his last act on earth was a great public service, there can be, I think, no question.
>
> This solemn accusation from the grave of a gallant officer, who died for his country, is entitled to great consideration; and I feel called on to endeavor to meet it as well so general a charge, from one now no longer able to support it, can be met.[11]

After sixty-seven days of testimony, the court cleared McDowell. It added: "It is to be hoped that the public misfortunes entailed by such calumnies will in future lead to greater circumspection and secure for patriotic and meritorious soldiers more considerate treatment from the American press and people."[12]

McDowell's replacement at the head of the Army of Virginia's III Corps was Maj. Gen. Joseph Hooker. Within a week of his 6 September appointment, Hooker's command received a new designation as the I Corps, Army of the Potomac.[13] Hooker's promotion to the Pennsylvania Reserves' parent corps was ironic because the general known as "Fighting Joe" had criticized the division's performance. During the fight near Glendale on the Peninsula, Confederate attacks overran the Twelfth Pennsylvania Reserves of Truman Seymour's brigade. The rout also affected the Second Pennsylvania Reserves, as well as two New York batteries and part of a cavalry regiment. Order was eventually restored, but Hooker's report took the Reserves to task. He wrote: "after an ineffectual effort to resist [the Rebel attack] the whole of McCall's division was completely routed, and many of the fugitives rushed down the road on which my right was resting, while others took to the cleared fields and broke through my lines from one end of them to the other, and actually fired on and killed some of my men as they passed. At first I was apprehensive that the effect would be disastrous on my command and was no little relieved when they had passed my lines. Following closely upon the footsteps of these demoralized people were the broken masses of the enemy."[14]

After the criticism found its way into New York papers, McCall sought a retraction from Hooker. Fighting Joe held his ground. "I reported that your command was routed," he wrote McCall, "and if it was not I shall be rejoiced to be convinced to the contrary . . . I simply announced what I believed, and still believe, to be a fact, without reflecting upon the conduct of your men while engaged with the enemy or expressing an opinion of his force which required your command to give way before him." McCall felt obligated to publish a small book defending his division's performance.[15]

Lee's appearance on the western Potomac spurred Pennsylvania's Governor Curtin into action. Besides readying the state militia—he eventually sought 50,000 men—on 4 September he urged the formation of new companies and asked business owners to close early each day to facilitate militia training. Two days later, he sent the first of several cables to Secretary of War Edwin Stanton warning of Rebel concentrations nearing his state's long southern border. It read in part: "Parties who left Frederick City at 4 o'clock this afternoon, who have just arrived, say that 6,000 rebels arrived to-day there. Report main body on the way to Baltimore. . . . Only three companies Pennsylvania Twenty-ninth here [Harrisburg]. People greatly alarmed here. . . . Troops in large numbers necessary in Cumberland Valley."[16]

By 8 September, a Curtin aide was asking Stanton if it were possible "to send a brigade of disciplined troops to this point [Harrisburg], as a nucleus for an army . . . and then concentrate new regiments here until a large army is organized, to stop movements of enemy into Pennsylvania. The people need something to restore confidence, in order to get them to step forward in support of the Government. If no organization is made, they will leave en masse as the enemy approaches." Curtin's requests also included: "an officer [who could] be sent at once to take command of the line of the State. We could at least hold the rebels in check until the forces which you have now in motion reach the Upper Potomac, which must soon become the theater of active hostilities."[17] To this and other messages Stanton replied that "We have no troops in Washington or Baltimore to send to Harrisburg, it being supposed that the best defense of Harrisburg is to strengthen the force now marching against the enemy under General McClellan."[18]

During these tense days, more changes affected the Eleventh Reserves' parent brigade. Its commander at the time Second Bull Run began, Conrad Jackson, was still recovering from the burst blood vessel that took him out of that battle. His immediate replacement, Martin Hardin, remained incapacitated, his left arm and shoulder swollen from the wound suffered during the battle's second day. The returning Gallagher became the brigade's ranking officer. On Tuesday, 9 September, with the Eleventh marching to Brookville, Maryland, orders came placing him in brigade command, Hardin's successor Robert Anderson returning to the Ninth Reserves.[19]

Gallagher was still very sick. Despite treatment from various doctors, including regimental surgeon DeBenneville, he was in agony from his kidney stones. Pvt. Christopher Herbert, suffering with a similar complaint, recalled Gallagher being "so afflicted with his kidneys that he could scarcely sit on his horse."[20]

Although his own illness took him out of action early in the year, old friend Robert Litzinger was one of the first to answer Curtin's call for new militia. The former Eleventh Reserves major assembled a new Ebensburg unit, likely with help from A. A. Barker, for it was called the "Barker Guards." Sent to Harrisburg along with a company formed in Carrolltown, the small force went into a regiment drawn from Mifflin, Lycoming, Schuylkill, Delaware, and Dauphin Counties. Litzinger was elected colonel of this regiment, which had a six-gun battery attached, but it saw no action. Its men spent only about a week away from home before Antietam ended the Rebel threat to Pennsylvania in 1862. (When Lee invaded the state the next year, Litzinger formed and led an independent 400-man infantry battalion, which served for about a month on the fringes of the Gettysburg campaign.)[21]

Curtin did not get the seasoned troops he wanted, but he at least gleaned a veteran general. His office continued to sound out Stanton on "an active, energetic officer to command forces in the field . . . one that could rally Pennsylvanians around him." The governor wanted John Reynolds. On the morning of 11 September, Henry Halleck wired McClellan asking if the

Pennsylvania Reserves' commander could be released. McClellan was reluctant. "General Reynolds is now engaged on important service," he telegraphed Washington. "He has one of the best divisions, and is well acquainted with it. I cannot see how his services can be spared at the present time." But Halleck informed McClellan that "General Reynolds' division can be commanded by some one else. He has been designated for other duty, and must report here immediately."[22]

Hooker especially was unhappy at losing Reynolds. The I Corps commander sent a remarkable note to Seth Williams of McClellan's staff, requesting "that the major-general commanding will not heed this order." Dismissing fears of a Rebel attack on Harrisburg, Hooker argued that "a scared Governor ought not to be permitted to destroy the usefulness of an entire division of the army, on the eve of important operations." But part of his concern came from his prejudices about the Reserves. "General Reynolds," he wrote, "commands a division of Pennsylvania troops of not the best character; is well known to them, and I have no officer to fill his place."[23]

Halleck's order stuck. On Friday, 12 September, while the Pennsylvania Reserves marched toward Frederick, Maryland, Reynolds and his staff took the road for Harrisburg. Meade, next in seniority, assumed Reynolds' place, writing home that Reynolds "obeyed the order with alacrity, though very much against his will." Taking charge of the division, command of his brigade passing to Col. Albert L. Magilton of the Fourth Reserves, Meade reported to McClellan. Meade found him "very civil and polite. I only saw him for a few minutes, surrounded by a great crowd." Afterward Meade ran into Williams, to whom Hooker had addressed the protest over Reynolds' loss. By Meade's account, Williams "seemed quite surprised that Reynolds had left so soon. I told Williams very plainly that I saw no occasion for [Hooker's] making such an outcry against Reynolds's removal; that I considered it a reflection on my competency to command the division, and that if he [Reynolds] came back on any such grounds, I should insist on being relieved." Meade added that "I should have been delighted to have gone to Harrisburg in Reynolds's place, as I have no doubt he will get a large command there."[24]

Reynolds was destined to be disappointed with his new job. After the Maryland campaign ended, he volunteered privately: "if the militia of Pennsylvania is to be depended upon to defend the state from invasion, they had better all stay at home, [because] they can be of no use in any military point of view if they are to act as they did here, every man to decide for himself whether he will obey the orders given or not and take his time at that to do it or no."[25] The militia reciprocated in their assessment of Reynolds. "West Point notions will not accord with the opinions and education of a newly organized militia," one Pennsylvania newspaper editorialized, adding that "The distinction between them and regulars did not seem to have occurred to him [Reynolds], and his treatment of the former has been very severely commented upon." One private reportedly told Reynolds off during a stop in Chambersburg, "which so startled this magnificent officer that, at the moment of the company's leaving, he had not yet recovered from it." Another newspaper account noted that "at one time a revolt was actually threatened by some of the men," though it provided no further details.[26]

Lesser discipline problems affected the Eleventh Reserves. On 8 September, while the brigade was encamped at Leesborough, Maryland, a Regular Army artillery captain, for whatever reason, arrested a man from the Eleventh who had been detailed as a hospital steward. This was Connoquenessing Ranger John Elliott, a twenty-year-old laborer when he joined the company in April 1861. Some of his friends in the regiment evidently tried to force his release and were arrested as well. Burnside, commanding a "wing" (the I and IX Corps) of McClellan's army, ordered the arrested men drummed out of the service. With the regiment set to march for Brookville, Maryland, the next day, Samuel Jackson persuaded Burnside to countermand the order, though Elliott and one of his would-be rescuers, John McMillan of the Brady Guards, remained under arrest. Their absence may have been noticeable given that the regiment was so understrength. Everard Bierer's Union Volunteers from Fayette County, for example, pursued Lee with only eighteen men.[27]

Besides foraging in Maryland and hoping to lure McClellan into a battle on preferential ground, Lee's plans included retaking Harpers Ferry. The town had changed hands several times and was now a Federal supply base, but its unusual geography presented a strategic problem affecting the campaign itself. Located at the confluence of the Potomac and Shenandoah Rivers, Harpers Ferry was covered by dramatic heights from which any attacker could lob shot and shell. A defender needed a big enough garrison to hold that high ground. Yet because the rivers' courses split the area into three parts, any attacker had to assault each separately, sending troops on roundabout courses to conduct essentially independent operations.

To accomplish all of his goals in Maryland, Lee decided to divide his army into several parts. Three were to maneuver around the Harpers Ferry terrain and besiege it. The rest of the infantry concentrated near

Hagerstown, a railhead along Antietam Creek. Meanwhile, Jeb Stuart's cavalry kept watch on the Federal army's progress while guarding passes through South Mountain, a series of ridges through which McClellan would have to come to intercept Lee directly from Washington.

In splitting his army, Lee counted on McClellan remaining cautious. But on the morning of Sunday, 13 September, Union soldiers found a stray dispatch intended for D. H. Hill, revealing Lee's plans, showing how he had divided his army and detailing a line of march that showed that each segment was relatively isolated. The discovery of this dispatch drove McClellan to a short-lived burst of energy.[28]

Late on 12 September, a few hours before the "Lost Order" was found, elements of Maj. Gen. Jesse Lee Reno's IX Corps drove in Rebel pickets—probably Stuart's—outside Frederick, west of the Monocacy River. The Eleventh Reserves camped near the river's eastern bank that night, and by 9 A.M. the next day Gallagher's brigade and the rest of the I Corps were following Reno by 9 A.M. The Eleventh crossed the Monocacy and after marching until 4 P.M. set up camp.[29]

Reno was still forcing his way through the Catoctin Mountains, about two miles west; beyond them and across the Catoctin Creek lay South Mountain. Once it got to the latter, Burnside's wing was to push through a pass in the ridge known as Turner's Gap. An advance on Crampton's Gap to the south—a manageable march away from Harpers Ferry—was earmarked for William Franklin's VI Corps, which ultimately pushed through, although not in time to save the Union garrison.[30]

As Reno's IX Corps started its assault early on Sunday, 14 September, the Pennsylvania Reserves were still in camp near Frederick. In a letter he wrote that morning, James McIlwain described Maryland as "a beautiful Country and it is a great pity that the troops of either Army Should invade and destroy the beautiful farms which are full of every kind of fruits most of which are ripe or nearly So." Blaming the Confederate invasion on "the Secessionists of Maryland," he nonetheless noted that "It is pitiful to See the women and children leaving their homes and fleeing for the Union Army to protect them. The Rebels where ever they find Union people they take evry thing they have—rob their Orchards destroy their Corn and Kill their Cattle. They Say that we done in this way when over in Virginia [and] they intend to do the Same in Maryland and Penna."[31]

But as the sound of firing came from South Mountain, Hooker's divisions—about 9,000 fighting men—broke camp and marched onto the road toward South Mountain. Soon the Eleventh Reserves was marching through Frederick proper. Joseph Miller of the Brady Guards later described it as "a beautiful city and its location delightful as it is situated near the base of the Blue Mountains." Residents waved flags and proffered water. At one point, McClellan passed the marching Eleventh Reserves on his way up the National Road, which led to the brewing battlefield. He stopped his black horse on a hill and pointed toward South Mountain, where smoke from Rebel guns hung like thunderclouds, and the soldiers cheered.[32]

Gallagher's brigade passed through the Catoctin range at about noon, then through the village of Middletown. They halted for an hour by Catoctin Creek, making coffee with its water while Hooker rode toward the sounds of battle. He learned that Reno's attack had stalled. To break the stalemate, Hooker was to expand the Union's right front and attack the Confederate left.

As he prepared his corps for combat, Hooker made an unusual administrative move, sparked evidently by concerns about the health of division commander Rufus King, who had recently experienced problems with epilepsy. Hooker now relieved King and turned his troops over to Brig. Gen. John P. Hatch. For the coming attack, Hooker planned to deploy Hatch's and Meade's divisions from left to right, with Ricketts in reserve. All three would be fed into the area via a byway known as the Old Hagerstown Road. Several adjacent farm trails offered additional paths for flanking effect.[33]

By about 2 P.M. Gallagher had his regiments back on the road. One of Reno's soldiers looked back at the I Corps advance, and saw in it "a monstrous, crawling, blue-back snake, miles long, quilled with the silver slant of muskets at a 'shoulder,' its sluggish tail writhing slowly up over the distant eastern ridge, its bruised head weltering in the road and smoke upon the crest above."[34] The picture was less enticing in the ranks. Although he chronicled the day's events in his diary, James McGinley was among many men taken ill on the march. Diarrhea was prevalent among both armies during the Maryland campaign, due in part to roadside foraging of unripe fruit and corn. McGinley's sickness was real enough for him to be excused from having to form in line of battle.[35]

Meade began his approach to the battlefield about a mile west of Catoctin Creek. At a crossroads called Bolivar, he sent his brigades to the right, off the main turnpike of the National Road and onto the Old Hagerstown Road. This led to a hamlet called Frosttown, surrounded by open fields and commanded by South Mountain's cannon-studded, crescent-shaped "north ridge." By 4 P.M. the division was roughly in position—Magilton on the left, Gallagher in the center, and Seymour on the right, the last deployed in front of a forest.[36]

Waiting for the signal to advance on South Mountain itself, the soldiers had company. Civilians had followed the Pennsylvanians hoping, as one veteran recalled, "to see the fun." As Gallagher's brigade deployed through the pastures, Rebel guns on the high ground began firing, and the onlookers panicked. "The children lay down upon the ground, the women shrieked," a soldier recalled, "and the men displayed wondrous agility in leaping the fences, which caused considerable amusement among us." A Federal battery on a hill to Gallagher's left fired back a few shots, which seem to have silenced the Confederate gunners temporarily. Gallagher used the lull to finish arranging his line of battle. From left to right it comprised the Twelfth, Eleventh, and Ninth Reserves, the Tenth Reserves fifty to seventy-five yards to the rear.[37]

Gallagher's brigade was thus formed when Meade ordered a general advance, his division's assault taking the form of a gradual wheel from right to left. Its objective, the crest of the "north ridge" of South Mountain, was about a mile away from the starting point. Reaching it would be hard going. Although the ground was mostly open (save for the woods in front of Seymour), Meade called it "the most rugged country I almost ever saw." But his troops dutifully set off across what another Union officer described as "a succession of parallel ridges, alternating with deep irregular valleys and broken ravines."

In Gallagher's brigade, the Eleventh Reserves started out marching downhill and crossed several slopes until the men were nearing a cornfield bordering a ravine. Over them, stationed on prominences that loomed out from the north ridge, Rebel guns became active again. Beyond the ravine, the arc of which ran roughly perpendicular to the Eleventh's line of advance, was a stone wall being used as a Rebel breastwork. A log cabin before the ravine provided cover for waiting Confederate snipers.[38]

In front of Meade's troops were Alabamians from a veteran and correspondingly understrength brigade commanded by Confederate Brig. Gen. Robert Rodes, holding a broad front and hoping for reinforcements. The first Rebels the Eleventh Reserves met likely were elements of the Fifth Alabama, a company of which formed a skirmish line in woods directly in the path of Gallagher's brigade. While this firefight was ongoing, Seymour's brigade drove off the Sixth Alabama from its front, then helped Gallagher's men clear the other Rebels from the woods. The Confederate survivors fled to the stone wall.[39]

With relatively few casualties suffered thus far, Gallagher's brigade advanced again. Although in intense pain from his kidney stones, Gallagher appears to have led from the front. The Ninth Reserves surrounded the sniper-filled cabin at this point—its men eventually took fifteen prisoners from within its walls.

Reports of the rest of the brigade's movements are confusing and conflicting. Gallagher evidently intended to halt in the ravine, which would provide some cover. From there, with the cabin taken, he could use volley fire against the Confederates behind the stone wall, prior to another advance. Either way, he was still out in front of his men, who had apparently just gotten in the ravine, when a musket-equipped Alabamian fired at him. Struck in the arm, the colonel collapsed, and for the second time in two weeks, Robert Anderson of the Ninth Reserves found himself an acting brigadier.

The shot that knocked Gallagher out of the fight either just preceded or came simultaneously with a much-larger-scale blast from Rebel guns. Samuel Jackson remembered this as a "single volley [which] brought down more than the half of my commissioned officers present," all of them evidently following Gallagher's example and at the heads of their units. One musket ball struck Quartermaster Hugh Torrance in the left cheek, fracturing the lower jaw and lodging in his neck. The missile's entry at a downward angle (as noted on an anatomical chart in Torrance's pension file) hints that the volley came while the regiment was in the ravine, rather than approaching it.

Other wounded officers included Lt. J. S. Kennedy of the Connoquenessing Rangers and Everard Bierer, who took a musket ball through his left arm. Rebel gunfire killed Lt. Walter F. Jackson, leading the Independent Blues while Capt. James Speer recovered from his Gaines' Mill wounds at home. A Rebel marksman found Brady, a minié bullet entering "under his right arm and [which] came out at his sword Belt at the right side." He was so badly wounded that he could not speak, but a comrade recalled that the former newspaperman's "eye glanced upon the rugged hill up which [we] were charging, and driving the enemy and seemed to say, 'go on and do your duty for I am done with mine and earth.'"[40]

At this point, not only was the Eleventh left with few officers to direct it but the rest of the brigade was bogged down in confusion. Anderson by now also lacked the Tenth Reserves, detached by Meade from the rear of the battle line to watch one flank. Perhaps prodded by Meade, who later faulted several subordinates' performance here, Anderson renewed the attack with the Ninth, Eleventh, and Twelfth Reserves.

In spite of what must have been a hail of Rebel gunfire, the battered blue regiments this time surged to the stone wall. In the Eleventh Reserves, the charge was preceded by an episode that, while unusual to modern ears, was remembered as important. A corporal "who was possessed of great powers of mimicry, crowed lustily, like a cock uttering the note of triumph." The sound of a fighting rooster, survivors told Samuel Bates for his postwar history of Pennsylvania volunteers, "heard amid the pauses of the battle, so inspirited the men that they went forward with renewed zeal to assured victory." Bates gave the man's name as "Koons," adding that he was "afterwards killed at Fredericksburg." This probably meant Sgt. William D. Kuhns of the Indiana National Guards, wounded a few days later at Antietam and indeed a fatality at Fredericksburg.[41]

There were other episodes of gallantry. The regiment was still using a replacement for its state-issued flag, and it is unclear who bore the colors at the start of the battle. Whoever it was, by one account he went down mortally wounded early in the fight, the first of five or six color bearers. One of these—perhaps the day's last—was Pvt. Henry C. Stone, a Cincinnati-born teenager who gave his prewar occupation as sailor. But at the time the Eleventh re-formed to charge the stone wall, buttressed by Kuhns' cock-crow, Nathaniel Nesbit, the twenty-eight-year-old captain of Indiana County's Washington Blues, had grabbed up the colors. When the command to advance came, the Company E commander led the regiment forward flag in hand. His gallantry was short-lived as a Confederate musket ball found his right breast. He was carried severely wounded from the field.[42]

Once they vaulted the stone wall, Samuel Jackson's men and their counterparts on the other wings of the battle line gradually forced Rodes' troops out of their positions. "The firing was incessant on both sides," wrote a captain in the Twelfth Pennsylvania Reserves, stationed on the Eleventh's left, "the rebels yielding the ground only when routed out of their hidden positions by the balls and bayonets of our men." The Independent Blues were especially heavily engaged, with six killed and five wounded. Bierer's Company F had two privates, John Wilson and Philip Sutton, wounded. The Cambria Guards, who likely still served on the right flank, also lost two wounded: Cpl. George W. Books and Pvt. Henry G. Krise.[43]

The surviving Alabamians fled up the hill, many stopping for short spells to blast harassing fire at their slowly advancing pursuers. Rebel casualties were heavy—Rodes later reported 61 killed, 157 wounded, and 204 missing. McGinley, who being ill did not make the charge, wrote in his diary that the regiment "drove the jonies off the Mountain with grate Slotter."[44]

Federal commanders watched Meade's progress from a distance. The *Alleghanian* later reported an alleged exchange between McClellan and Hooker discussing this attack:

McClellan: "Look! See those noble men climb that dangerous mountain! Think you they can reach the summit, in the face of that destructive fire."

Hooker: "If there are any men on the face of God's earth who can do it, the Reserves are those men!"

McClellan: "I know it, General Hooker? I *believe* and trust they will do it."[45]

The dialogue is unlikely given Hooker's misgivings about the quality of the Pennsylvania Reserves, yet the drama was there. Darkness by now was falling over the smoking ridges, and one of the Brady Guards recalled that "the sun set in the western horizon as if shuddering at the dreadful slaughter of that day." The regiment was short of ammunition by the time its companies reached the summit, and Samuel Jackson sent word for support. Meade had already requested reinforcements from Hooker, who sent a brigade from Brig. Gen. James Ricketts' division. These troops arrived after most of the Confederates had retreated, Meade noting, "only one regiment had an opportunity to open fire before the enemy retired and darkness intervened." They stayed, however, holding the crest of the ridge, and Anderson's brigade withdrew.[46]

Ammunition wagons came up, and each man secured a fresh supply of cartridges. At the same time the tired soldiers searched in the gloom for wounded men. Survivors of Company K gathered around Brady's now-dead form amid several other corpses. One recalled how some survivors of Brady's command gently, "as if afraid of awakening [their] dead chieftain, . . . carefully raised him from the earth and pillowed his head in the long row of the fallen heroes of that day." McClellan, by one account, spotted Gallagher being taken away on a stretcher, asked an aide for the injured officer's name, then rode over to meet him. "Col. Gallagher," McClellan reportedly said, "this is neither the first nor the second time the Reserves have saved the army. You have reason to be proud of the wound received while leading your men to victory. God bless you and them!"[47] It is unclear how the Reserves "saved" McClellan's army, relatively little of which was engaged in clearing Turner's Gap. Yet the dialogue sounds like something the oft-theatrical McClellan could have said.

Nesbit, also transported to an army ambulance, was a graver case. Taken to a hospital in Middletown, he hung on for several days. Doctors evidently told him his wound was mortal for Nesbit reportedly was "fully aware of his condition and remarked to one who was with him that he had nothing to regret. He continued to give directions concerning his personal affairs, until his eyelids closed in death" at about midnight on Saturday, 22 September.

Five days later, his body arrived in Blairsville, lying in state in the hall of Evans' Hotel. His family brought the casket to a cemetery near the homestead in Livermore for burial. The company flag the ladies of Blairsville gave him upon the unit's departure in June 1861, now "torn, ragged and faded," was placed in his coffin.[48]

The Eleventh Reserves settled into an uneasy bivouac at South Mountain's base. The men slept on their arms. Many expected orders to renew the attack at dawn. But daylight brought a heavy mist, and as Meade reported, "it was not till 7 A.M. that it was ascertained the enemy had retired entirely from the mountain." Such news may have been welcome in Samuel Jackson's command, the previous day's losses being 15 killed and 28 wounded. "Our Regiment nearly annihilated," the lieutenant colonel wrote in his diary. South Mountain had reduced his regiment to fewer than 200 men.[49]

Not all of the Rebel army had withdrawn, and some Confederates were close enough to make mistakes. The fog disoriented the adjutant of the Fifth Alabama, who rode into the camp of the Second Pennsylvania Reserves, part of Seymour's brigade. He started rousing the sleeping Federals, warning that the "Yanks" were close by. The Rebel was pummeling some Union soldiers awake when, a Pennsylvanian later wrote, "one of them got up and knocked him down, and took him prisoner."[50]

But the "Yanks" were on the move themselves. Once Federal skirmishers reported that the Rebels had fallen back toward Boonsborough, Hooker sent one of his relatively fresh brigades after them, accompanied by elements of Edwin Sumner's II Corps and Alfred Pleasanton's cavalry. Hooker ordered the rest of his exhausted I Corps troops "to make a little coffee and eat their breakfasts, which they had not been able to do since the beginning of their march from the Monocacy, the morning previous." After this hasty breakfast, Hooker got the I Corps, Meade's division included, on the road again.[51]

In spite of orders to move rapidly, Samuel Jackson may have detailed men to stay behind and intern their comrades' bodies. Such activity would have been a new experience for many in the regiment. At

Mechanicsville, where the Union army retained possession of the field, the Eleventh Reserves had not lost a man. Every other engagement— Gaines' Mill, Glendale, Second Bull Run—had been followed by rout or withdrawal, forcing the Pennsylvanians to leave their dead as they fell.

In April the War Department had issued orders to Federal commanders instructing them to reserve burial sites near each battlefield, and to be sure to mark and register every grave. At South Mountain, the Union troops buried the dead in shallow trenches, usually about two feet deep. Identification tags had not yet come into general use, but when possible, papers were pinned to the dead men's uniforms giving their names, state, regiment, and company. With the Confederates retreating toward Sharpsburg, where Lee would set up a new defensive line, some Union dead were buried with their feet pointing toward the town—facing the enemy.

This bit of defiance aside, handling and burying the dead was emotionally difficult and physically repulsive. In addition to the reek of blood and entrails, gases building up in corpses left unburied for a day or so forced out the bowels' contents. Rather than touch the bloated, stinking bodies themselves, men in burial details often used picks or bayonets bent into hooks to drag the corpses into the graves. Canteens of whiskey were sometimes issued to burial squads to help deaden their senses.[52]

Besides their own comrades, detailed men from the Second Pennsylvania Reserves buried the colonel of the Twelfth Alabama, "a very gentlemanly looking fellow." They also found a young Rebel still alive despite having a musket ball through his forehead. He was unconscious and insensate, yet when the Pennsylvanians put a canteen to his lips he "swallowed water freely."[53]

While the bodies were being interred near South Mountain, Hooker's I Corps followed the Rebels through Boonsborough and Keedysville. Historians have criticized McClellan for maintaining a laggard pace behind Lee, yet Samuel Jackson felt the army kept up a hot pursuit on 15 September. "Our Cavalry brings in long lines of prisoners," he wrote. "Press the enemy closely."[54]

About a mile west of Keedysville stood a stone bridge over Antietam Creek—known to history as the Upper Bridge—across which the Confederates retreated, taking positions on high ground beyond. "The rebels," Hooker wrote in his report, "appeared to be ostentatiously deployed in two lines, perpendicular to the road leading to Sharpsburg, with [their] batteries posted to resist the passage of our forces over the bridge which crosses that stream." The Potomac curled around to the rear and sides of this position, protecting Lee's flanks, but also blocking an easy retreat should McClellan be able to force the Confederates from their lines. Hooker was unwilling to advance with just the forces at hand, but within a few hours he saw the Rebel left—facing his own right—"break into column and march to the rear, behind a forest." Union engineers now secured the bridge and also found two usable fords. It was getting late, however, and Hooker declined to order Meade and his other divisions on "a night march through a country of which we were profoundly ignorant."

Early on the 16th, McClellan told Hooker to cross the Antietam that day and strike Lee's left flank. Meade's and Ricketts' divisions were to traverse the Upper Bridge. Hooker's other division, now led by Brig. Gen. Abner Doubleday following Hatch's wounding at South Mountain, was to use the ford at Pry's Mill about a quarter mile to the south. Once the crossing was accomplished, the I Corps' objective was to occupy high ground about two miles northwest of the Upper Bridge. The territory was astride the Hagerstown Pike, and the idea was for Hooker to advance up this road, following the elevation until the I Corps met the Confederate front. With that done, his troops were to wait while McClellan prepared a general assault meant to drive Lee's troops from the field.[55]

Before his regiment marched that morning, McIlwain scribbled a note home about the fight at South Mountain.

> Kellysville [Keedysville], Md.   Sept. 16th 1862
>
> Dear Emma
>   I write in haste to let you know I am well and has just went through a hard fight and Thank God I have this far escaped unhurt. Lieut. Jackson[,] Saml Stewart[,] Thomas James[,] Benj. F. Whitlinger, Labanna[h] Sarver, and James Johnston were killed.
>   John W. Scott[,] Absolem Withington[,] D. W. Scott[,] George Fry and Henry Fulton were wounded.
>   Absolem Withington was slightly wounded in the arm and John Scott in the toe. Both will be able for duty in a few days.
>
>   Your Husband
>   Jim X. McIlwain[56]

Crossing the Antietam took hours, and it was not until 4 P.M. on the 16th that Hooker's divisions were assembled on the other side. The Pennsylvania Reserves now formed the advance of the march to the new position near the Hagerstown Pike, from which they were to assault Lee's left the next morning. The I Corps' destination for this evening was a ridge situated on a farm owned by Joseph Poffenberger. Meade sent the Bucktails and four companies of the Third Reserves forward as skirmishers, supported by three companies of the Third Pennsylvania Cavalry. The cavalrymen pushed Rebel pickets off the sprawling farm owned by a local man named Miller. By the next morning, his forty-acre cornfield, which lay to the south, would become a terrible landmark.[57]

Anderson's brigade was on the right during this march from the Upper Bridge to the Hagerstown Pike, farthest from Rebel guns which opened on the column. "Heavy cannonading in front," Samuel Jackson noted in his diary. Sounds of musketry later filtered back as the cavalry met Rebels in a cluster of trees along the road to Smoketown—the terrain would be called the East Woods. The Confederates were from Evander Law's brigade of John Bell Hood's division. The breechloader-armed Bucktails helped the horsemen push them back, but Hood's old Texas Brigade was close by, positioned in a field adjacent to a simple church built by the local Dunker sect. As Hooker understated in his report, "the resistance became formidable" as Texas regiments entered the forest, Rebel fire claiming the Bucktails' colonel.[58]

Helped by the rest of Seymour's brigade, the Bucktails held their ground. With the sounds of heavy fighting emanating from the East Woods, Anderson ordered his regiments into a line of battle alongside a separate forest which bordered Poffenberger's farm and which would be known as the North Woods. Meade's remaining brigade, Magilton's, was on Anderson's left, with Doubleday's division lined up on Magilton's own left, behind the smoking East Woods. Expecting the Confederates to attack, Anderson ordered Samuel Jackson to send out a skirmish line and be prepared "to hold our position here at any cost."

The feared assault never materialized. As night fell, Anderson's brigade lay down in a low field, its pickets covering much of the North Woods, stopping at the Hagerstown Pike where the cavalrymen were stationed. The Eleventh Reserves regiment slept on its arms. Campfires were prohibited, but Rebel shells found the brigade's position anyway. Samuel Jackson reported losing one man wounded to the Confederate artillery. "The enemy shell us all night," he wrote in his diary. The sentries were close enough to hear orders given by enemy officers. A cold drizzle fell, and what little sleep the Eleventh Reserves got was interrupted by occasional gunfire. There were no picket-line truces here.[59]

What unfolded in the Eleventh Reserves' front the next day remains challenging to describe. The battle of Antietam began with a piecemeal assault on Lee's left by three Union corps—the I, II, and XII—attacking over parts of the same ground between dawn (about 6:30 A.M.) and 10 A.M. Confederate counterattacks created enough chaos that by mid-morning any given Union regiment might find itself alongside one from another corps. As officers' reports disagree on the timing of events—by hours in some cases—it is difficult to establish when or where certain units became engaged. The stress of combat, coupled with the disorientation caused by thick gunsmoke and deafening noise, echoes in the confused accounts survivors left.

Hooker's objective on this foggy morning was, he later estimated, about three-quarters of a mile away from his starting point. The I Corps aimed for a patch of high ground on the Rebel left. If taken, Union guns could enfilade Confederate positions between there and Sharpsburg. At its apex stood the Dunker church, set on the edge of another forest that would become a landmark, the West Woods. Once Anderson's and Magilton's troops cleared the North Woods, their objective stood beyond plowed fields between which lay Miller's cornfield, bordered by rail fences.

Although he knew he would receive support from the II and XII Corps, which began the day encamped behind him, Hooker started 17 September on his own. He planned a line of battle with Doubleday on the right, Ricketts on the left, and Meade's Pennsylvania Reserves stationed behind as a reserve. Meade's division probably earned reserve status because it started the day disjointed, with Seymour's brigade still posted in the East Woods. As dawn broke, Doubleday's division assembled behind Anderson's and Magilton's brigades. Hooker gave the order to start the advance, and Doubleday's men began to maneuver through the Pennsylvanians' lines.[60]

Even in the fog, a Confederate battery, posted on a crest just off the Hagerstown Pike, could sense blue ranks forming. As the advance started, a trio of shells burst amid troops commanded by Brig. Gen. John Gibbon, four crack midwestern regiments collectively called the "Iron Brigade." One shell caused thirteen casualties. More Rebel gunners opened as the light gathered on what would be a humid day.[61]

But Doubleday's advance continued, and by about 6:30 A.M., Anderson started to move his brigade forward. He knew that his regiments could end up anywhere, Hooker having told Meade "to spring to the assistance" of Doubleday or Ricketts "as circumstances might require." Ahead and to the left, Seymour's brigade kept its picket posts in the East Woods as Doubleday's and Ricketts' lines passed on their right. Then the

Bucktails and the other Pennsylvanians formed up and moved deeper into the scene of the previous evening's firefights. They soon ran into opposition, now from a brigade led by Confederate Col. James Walker, whose men also came under fire from Union cannon stationed across Antietam Creek.

Once Anderson's regiments cleared the North Woods behind the Iron Brigade, their commander received new orders. Meade again wanted the Tenth Reserves for duty on the flanks. He ordered the regiment to veer off about 700 yards to the west, toward Nicodemus Hill, to relieve a unit in Brig. Gen. Marsena Patrick's brigade. The location was perilously in range of Jeb Stuart's batteries there, but it was feared a Rebel flank attack might come from this area. Anderson's other regiments—the Ninth closest to the Hagerstown Pike, then the Eleventh in the center, and the Twelfth on the other flank—marched in line into Miller's plowed field.[62]

The area ahead had already become an abattoir. As Gibbon's skirmishers advanced to the edge of the cornfield, Hooker, leading from up front, spotted sun glinting off bayonets amid the stalks—skirmishers from a division now led by Confederate Brig. Gen. Alexander R. Lawton, sent forward to contest the Federal advance. The field, Hooker later wrote in his report, "was filled with the enemy, with arms in their hands, standing apparently at 'support arms.'" Hooker directed nearby Union gunners to fire canister toward the field, and in a few minutes, "every stalk of corn in the northern and greater part of the field was cut as closely as could have been done with a knife, and the slain lay in rows precisely as they had stood in their ranks a few moments before." The survivors fled back to Lawton's main line in front of the Dunker church, near which four Rebel batteries lent support.[63]

To the rear of this line lay Hood's division. Following the struggle in the East Woods the previous evening, Hood obtained Stonewall Jackson's permission to pull his men back for rations. As he wrote in his report, "The officers and men of my command having been without food for three days, except a half ration of beef for one day, and green corn, General Lawton, with two brigades, was directed to take my position, to enable my men to cook." Lawton's men contested Gibbon's advance across Miller's farm, but the Union force pressed the Confederates back. Lawton called for help, and Hood accordingly marched into what he later described as "the most terrible clash of arms, by far, that has occurred during the war."[64]

Meanwhile, elements of Doubleday's and Ricketts' divisions forced their way through the cornfield, over the severed bodies of the Rebels killed or wounded by the earlier cannonade. Behind them, Anderson's and Magilton's brigades also stumbled across casualties in the fog and sulphur clouds until they halted at the cornfield's edge. From behind breastworks they made by knocking down fence rails, Samuel Jackson's men peered into the smoking cornfield. Inside it they could hear—but not see—the assaults, counterattacks, and flanking efforts which commanders attempted inside the inferno.

On the Confederate side, the bulk of the fighting directly in the Eleventh Reserves' front was being done by the Texas Brigade, which Hood had already launched into the cornfield. Anderson and Magilton stayed at the edge trying to sense what was happening inside. Their first indication of Hood's success came when a flock of broken Union troops came running toward their breastworks, shouting that the Rebels were in pursuit.

The Eleventh Reserves still lay behind the rails. If the approaching enemy used the Rebel yell, nobody could hear it above the gunfire. The regiment's first glimpse of the oncoming battle line was misleading—the Confederates had picked up a stand of Federal colors, which to the Pennsylvanians seemed to be waved aloft. As a result, Samuel Jackson wrote in his report, the Rebel charge "advanced to within a few paces of our lines before we discovered them to be foes."

Ragged gray or butternut uniforms now became visible through the smoke about twenty yards away. Officers gave the orders to fire; the first volley, Samuel Jackson reported, took "signal effect" and was followed by several more. Dozens of .69-caliber musket balls—and three times as many buckshot—tore new holes in the Confederate line. Between the Eleventh's position and the Hagerstown Pike, the Ninth Reserves also opened up on the Rebels.[65]

Their victims seem to have been the First Texas, whose commander reported that "we had advanced to within some thirty steps of his [the enemy's] second line, secreted behind a breastwork of fence rails thrown up in heaps upon the ground, when a battery of artillery some 150 or 200 yards in our front was opened upon us. My men continued firing, a portion of them at the enemy's men and others at the artillerists." Evidently, a portion of the Pennsylvanians' line at this point was breached, for the same officer maintained that this line behind the breastwork "broke and fled" at the same time the artillerists began to limber up their guns. If the Eleventh or Ninth Reserves did fall back, a second line was pushed into place, and the First Texas retreated, leaving its colors behind.[66]

The Eleventh Reserves' new colors survived the day, though several color bearers were shot down. The last to carry them was Sergeant William H. Timblin of the Dickson Guards, who ultimately carried them off the field; he repeated the service a few months later at Fredericksburg. In Timblin's company, Lt. John C. Kuhn and Cpl. Hiram Black were mortally wounded. Westmoreland Guards Capt. Daniel Kistler also received a mortal wound during this exchange. The Company H commander hung on for eight more days and survived what must have been an agonizing trip home to Greensburg before dying.[67]

Thomas S. Moore of the Indiana National Guards was shot through his right lung. His captain, Daniel Porter, helped pull the wounded man away from the line, yanking off Moore's cartridge box and belt while trying to staunch the blood, which was flowing "most profusely." After doing what he could, Porter told Cpl. Henry Prothero and Pvt. James Trimble to carry Moore off the field. Moore apparently lost consciousness at this point, for Porter subsequently countermanded the order, having decided that Moore was dying. "We laid him on his back and went back to the line," Porter wrote the soldier's father. "I had not been back long before I heard Tom calling me. I went back to him. He was sitting up and seemed revived. He said if he was not carried away he would bleed to death." Porter again called Prothero and Trimble, as well as Cpl. Constantine Morton, and they all put Moore onto a blanket and lugged him to an ambulance. Prothero stayed with the wounded man; the others returned to the line.[68]

Shortly afterward, Anderson's brigade was relieved by elements of the XII Corps. Samuel Jackson's command, along with the exhausted men of the Ninth and Twelfth Reserves, fell back to the North Woods, where the Tenth Reserves rejoined the brigade. While Maj. Gen. John Sedgwick's division of the II Corps rallied near the same spot, Anderson led his brigade back to its starting point on Joseph Poffenberger's farm.[69]

At about this time, Daniel Porter detached himself from the regiment and searched for Moore among the surgeons' tents. He found him in the afternoon in a field hospital being tended by another, less seriously wounded Company B soldier, Garvin McLain. The surgeon, Porter wrote, "had dressed [Moore's] wounds, but expressed no hope for his recovery. He promised me to do everything in his power. I asked it as a special favor." Porter left Moore in pain but alert and thinking clearly. When the captain returned the next morning, Moore was dead. "His eyes were closed, and he seemed to have slept life sweetly away." He had Moore's body put in another ambulance and taken to Keedysville. Four members of Company B stayed there at Porter's direction "and had him interred in a coffin, suitably marking his grave, so that should you desire to lift it, it can easily be found."

Their captain assured Moore's father: "Your son's wild, generous nature made him a favorite with the company. On the day he fell, he fought most heroically, and I am sure from the steady aim he drew, more than one rebel was made to bite the dust. . . . Everything was done for his comfort and proper interment that possibly could be done." After commenting that Antietam "was a terrible battle and the slaughter was awful" and acknowledging "It was sickening to pass over that bloody field," Porter let his mask of command slip. "I feel lost," he wrote. "My brave comrades are falling around me."[70]

Most of 18 September was spent collecting and transporting the wounded. The next day, after it became clear that McClellan would not pursue Lee, whole regiments, rather than just a few detailed men, were tasked with burial duties. Samuel Jackson rode over the battlefield and wrote in his diary that he found "the sight beyond description. The field covered with dead horses and men co-mingled."[71]

An engineer attached to McClellan's staff described the scene around the cornfield and East Woods, where the Pennsylvania Reserves had fought: "In every direction around men were digging graves and burying the dead. Ten or twelve bodies lay at the different pits and had already become offensive. In front of this wood was the bloody cornfield where lay two or three hundred festering bodies, nearly all of them rebels, the most hideous exhibition I had yet seen. Many were black as Negroes, heads and faces hideously swelled, covered with dust until they looked like clods."[72]

When several Ebensburg residents, *Alleghanian* editor Abraham Barker among them, visited the Antietam battlefield, they found Lieutenant Burke's company "dwindled down almost to a 'Corporal's Guard,'" though the members who had survived seemed in good health. The Cambria Guards in fact had twenty men present for duty, fifteen sick, eighteen wounded, six paroled prisoners awaiting exchange at Annapolis, Maryland, and eleven detailed at Craney Island. In addition, one man was still detached on gunboat service, one was detailed to the Ambulance Corps, and John Roberts remained in Ebensburg recruiting.

Barker, who walked the field with a *New York Tribune* correspondent, found it covered with "mounds [which] marked the last resting place of those who had passed away in the bitter struggle. The country for miles around presents the appearance of a vast city of the dead—the mausoleum of high hopes and ardent aspirations." One such mound would have contained the remains of Philip Lantzy, who may have fallen as the line crossed the North Woods or been hit near the cornfield when Hood's men met the Eleventh Reserves at close quarters.[73]

He was probably set aside for burial near where he fell, along with five other comrades evidently killed outright on the field: Sgt. George S. Gourley and Pvt. James Beobut of the Independent Blues, and Brady Guards privates Albert L. Brown, William Clark, and Perry Welsh. As coffins were unavailable, the bodies were likely wrapped in blankets and buried with their remaining possessions. If their comrades marked the burial spots with headboards, they fell or faded by war's end. Farmers intent on reclaiming their land were also known to pull up the boards and plow over the graves. By the time plans were made to reinter Union dead in what would become Antietam National Cemetery, almost 1,800 could not be identified. Aside from Clark (grave 3,691) and Moore (3,730), the latter moved from Keedysville, the bodies of the men of the Eleventh Reserves killed at Antietam presumably lie beneath headstones marked "Unknown."[74]

Hooker came away from the battlefield with a changed perception of the Pennsylvania Reserves. About a month after Antietam, Hooker informed Seth Williams that he felt the division George Meade had led into battle had "nobly redeemed" its reputation during the Maryland campaign. "The language of my report [of the Peninsula fighting] was just and called for when made," Hooker wrote, "but I do not think that it was so much the fault of the men as of other causes. I am now of the opinion that the men were all right."[75]

Chapter 8

Butchered Like So Many Animals

Fredericksburg

After reading Antietam's casualty reports at Harrisburg, Gov. Andrew Curtin proposed that his battered Pennsylvania Reserves be sent home to rest and recruit. Although McClellan believed the idea had merit, he kept the veteran division with the Army of the Potomac. Lincoln desperately wanted Lee pursued, and though he was reluctant to start the chase, McClellan was not ready to part with any of his forces.[1]

While the army waited for marching orders, several administrative changes affected the Eleventh's parent corps and division.

Joseph Hooker had been slightly wounded at Antietam, and George Meade was elevated during the battle to temporary I Corps command, with Truman Seymour succeeding him at divisional level. Burnside later assigned Hooker to the V Corps when Fitz-John Porter was removed to answer John Pope's charges from Second Bull Run. Meade did not get to keep Hooker's old job. The I Corps went instead to John Reynolds, back from his stint with the Pennsylvania militia and newly promoted to major general. With Meade resuming command of the Pennsylvania Reserves division, Seymour returned to his old brigade for a time, then was given another command in a Union-occupied part of North Carolina. He was succeeded by Col. William Sinclair of the Sixth Reserves.[2]

The picture at the top of the Eleventh Reserves' own brigade was also fluid. Thomas Gallagher's wound at South Mountain earned him a twenty-day certificate of disability—a standard time frame issued to wounded men—but his prospects for recovery were unclear. If Gallagher returned, it would be to his old regiment; Conrad Jackson, who outranked him, was due back from his own medical leave.[3]

Until Conrad Jackson returned in mid-October, administrative issues forced the brigade through several command changes. Lt. Col. Robert Anderson, although he seems to have led the unit capably at Antietam, earned Meade's wrath at South Mountain. Meade placed both him and Twelfth Reserves Capt. Richard Gustin under arrest, charged with abandoning their posts during the fight at Turner's Gap. Gustin earned an additional count of disobedience of orders. Despite Meade's testimony, a court-martial acquitted both officers, and they returned to their commands.[4]

By this time Anderson was no longer the brigade's ranking officer. A full colonel, James T. Kirk of the Tenth Reserves had returned to duty after a few weeks at home. Originally mustered in as captain of his regiment's Company D in April 1861, Kirk had struggled with various ailments since the Seven Days' battles. He was felled by sunstroke and fatigue on the evening of Glendale. He served at Malvern Hill, but spent the rest of July sick at Harrison's Landing with diarrhea and "nervous debility." When Kirk submitted an application for medical leave, Seymour endorsed it with the words "approved strongly." He added that "the Service must Soon lose the Experience of an Excellent officer unless some change takes place in Col. K's condition."[5]

Kirk returned to the regiment in time to be shot in the right hip at Second Bull Run, the ball passing near his spine. An army doctor patched him up enough for Kirk to ride into Maryland in an ambulance, and although he was on the field at South Mountain, he was not well enough to succeed Gallagher after the latter's wounding. During the hiatus following Antietam, the regimental surgeon wrote that Kirk needed another medical leave, without which the colonel "could not live thirty days."[6] Returning from a stay at home, Kirk continued to struggle with illness and exhaustion. He tendered his resignation a few days before Conrad Jackson's return, "Owing to ill health which entirely unfits me for Service in the field."[7]

Anderson's and Kirk's problems made Samuel Jackson the brigade's chief administrator on at least one occasion. The lieutenant colonel himself was sick, although he was well enough in late September to take dinner with a Maryland farmer and a few days later shared a turkey with another regiment's adjutant. He led the Eleventh on 3 October when it paraded for President Lincoln but found the review a grueling affair. "The President did not arrive until 2½ P.M.," he wrote in his diary. "All tired waiting."[8]

Samuel Jackson's duties included replacing his regiment's officer casualties. His late-September recommendations included promoting Company A 1st Lt. James Burke to captain, to replace Andrew Lewis. 2d Lt. Rowland Jones was to fill Burke's old slot, while Sgt. John E. Scanlan assumed a second lieutenant's rank. In Company C, Capt. Samuel Louden's resignation—probably linked to his earlier illness—was coupled with the death of wounded 2d Lt. John Kuhn. With the Dickson Guards now officerless, Jackson elevated three sergeants to fill the gaps: William Timblin, one of the heroes of Miller's cornfield, became captain; George W. Fleeger became first lieutenant, replacing Newton Redic, killed at Gaines' Mill; and John Sutton entered into Kuhn's slot as second lieutenant.[9]

As the promotions took months to become official, other officers stepped in to do some paperwork for the Dickson Guards. Three days before Christmas, Daniel Porter signed a discharge for Aaron Kepler, who returned from Richmond disabled by the gunshot wound at Gaines' Mill and spent time in army hospitals before his release.[10]

In Company E, 1st Lt. Daniel Coder assumed the late Nathaniel Nesbit's captaincy, while 2d Lt. Richard Birkman took Coder's place, his spot being filled by Sgt. Theodore Marshall. In his old unit, Jackson named Company G Pvt. Andrew Ivory to replace 2d Lt. Walter Jackson. A Company K private, Harvey Clover, was similarly elevated, former 2d Lt. Cyrus Butler being promoted after 1st Lt. James George replaced Evans Brady as captain.[11]

A conspicuous new face arrived on Monday, 29 September, in Rev. Adam Torrance. Then about fifty-eight, the Westmoreland County clergyman had presided over Gallagher's wedding, and the latter likely asked him to join the unit when Rev. William Dickson resigned the chaplaincy in August. Two days after turning up in camp, Presbyterian minister Torrance toured the Antietam battlefield in company with Samuel Jackson. The grim scenery made an impression on the new chaplain, who held his first morning and evening services the following Sunday.[12]

His flock was due to expand. Although only 150 men answered roll call on Tuesday, 7 October, two days later 54 recruits joined. With them came warm weather and orders to draw ammunition. Expecting orders to move, Jackson started a new round of regimental drilling. At this time, however, he was still fighting with illness, and he soon had company as the weather turned rainy. Reverend Torrance was among those taken sick in the Eleventh Reserves, and the swelling number of hospital cases inspired the divisional surgeon to order "a careful policing of all the camps." As hopes faded that McClellan would finally move, it appeared that the army would stay here until spring. Jackson spent a few days on a survey board reviewing army greatcoats and noted in his diary: "Our men fix up their quarters as if they designed staying all winter."[13]

At this time Q.M. Hugh Torrance was suffering intensely from the wound he received at South Mountain. After being carried off the field, the lieutenant was taken to Washington's United States Hotel, now converted into a hospital. His face was so swollen that doctors could not find the musket ball that pierced his left cheek and lodged in his neck. A surgeon in early October reported Torrance unable to chew and living on fluids and soft foods. During this time, the ball lay near "the inner side of the serno-clido-mastoid muscle" and had apparently injured "the great sympathetic nerve[,] leaving the parts very sensitive and [Lt. Torrance] in a very nervous condition."[14]

The injury seems to have compounded an already serious condition, for earlier Torrance began suffering from what sounds like epilepsy. At Camp Tennally, surgeon James DeBenneville sent Torrance home for ten days after finding the quartermaster "suffering from disorder of the brain and stomach accompanied with much depression and frequent attacks of fainting."[15] Whereas those attacks may have subsided enough for him to rejoin the regiment, the wound from South Mountain aggravated an existing problem. Granted medical leave, Torrance had a Pittsburgh surgeon extract the musket ball, but soon after he became increasingly "nervous and excitable" and endured excruciating headaches. The entry wound, an inch to the left of his mouth, healed into a small, acutely sensitive scar. Nearby muscles atrophied to the point where he had trouble opening his mouth.

Yet Torrance did not resign. In mid-November he would report that "I have improved very fast but am unable to Masticate. The jaw is still sore & stiff. But am in hopes that at the expiration of this [medical disability] certificate I will be able to rejoin my regt. & give my aid to the crushing out of this unholy & cursed rebellion brought upon our nation by the Jefferson Davis clan." He returned to the Eleventh Reserves the next year.[16]

Robert McCoy came back sooner. He was in Washington being treated for the shell wound from Second Bull Run when news arrived of the fight at Turner's Gap. With permission to return to the regiment, he boarded a train that took him near Monocacy Junction, although he did not arrive at Sharpsburg until three days after Antietam. His return caused some confusion at headquarters, for he penned a report to Seymour meant to "definitively explain my absence on the 18th and presence on the 22d inst."[17]

Thomas Spires still suffered from illness contracted in Libby Prison. The day after Antietam, evidently when it became clear that the battle would not be renewed, the Westmoreland County captain received a thirty-day leave, "at the expiration of which he will, if still unfit for duty, be examined with a view to his discharge." He did not return to duty, his resignation taking effect 17 October. The new commander of Company I was 1st Lt. Eli Waugaman, later promoted to captain.[18]

Red-haired, gray-eyed Irish immigrant Robert McElhaney also remained in a Union hospital long after his exchange. The former Butler blacksmith had been twenty-four in June 1861 when he joined the Dickson Guards. At Gaines' Mill he had been crippled for life by a gunshot wound in the right knee. In a late September letter to his sister, he noted that he knew of only nine of his original company still fit for duty. He observed that the colonel "in place of commanding 1000 men has only ninty. Alas where is all this to end."

Apparently referring to the effect talk of the pending Emancipation Proclamation was having on the army, McElhaney acknowledged feeling "discouraged about our National affairs." He added: "Were it alone for the just purpose of restoring the union, we would have been victorious long, ere the soldiers are discouraged and disgusted. All join [?] in crying out against abolition interference and all now think tis solely [for?] the Negroes they now fight. What wonder then we are defeated."

McElhaney was discharged early in 1863. He died thirty-four years later in Cherry township, having suffered intense pain from his wound throughout the rest of his life.[19]

By late fall 1862 some members of the Eleventh Reserves captured at Gaines Mill had been paroled to the Northern lines but not yet formally exchanged. Until that happened, they were barred from performing military duties. They waited out part of this limbo at "Camp Parole" in Annapolis, a site notable for poor facilities. Their lot improved when they were moved to a new camp at Alexandria. "We have been uniformed anew, washed, combed, and cleaned up generally, and the effect is astonishing," observed a writer to the *Alleghanian* who signed his letter T.D. This was probably Thomas D. Litzinger, whose severe diarrhea had abated enough for him to be paroled to Aiken's Landing.[20]

His new home was formally known as Camp Banks. It was overseen by Lt. Col. Gabriel De Korponay, who had led the Twenty-eighth Pennsylvania before taking charge of paroled prisoners for the Military District of Alexandria. His efforts, which earned praise, included setting up a camp theater and organizing team sports. "Although we are not allowed by the provisions of our parole to drill, stand guard, or follow the enemy, we still have prospects of putting in the winter charmingly," maintained "T.D.," adding, "I am free to say that the last one of us would much rather be with our respective regiments."[21]

That restless feeling also prevailed in the Eleventh Reserves' contingent at Craney Island. On a late September afternoon, thirteen enlisted men—they represented seven of the regiment's ten companies—scuffled with a sentry. The surgeon in charge, Dr. Anthony E. Stocker, sought help from the provost marshal, reporting, "Insubordination having manifested itself in the guard at this hospital, you will oblige me by sending a Company to this Island and arresting the disobedient." The detachment remained at Craney Island for another month and a half before rejoining the regiment.[22]

Company F Capt. Everard Bierer finally secured a colonelcy in October after a long effort to get noticed at high levels. From the onset of his Federal service, Bierer—surely like many other soldiers—showed an inclination for taking matters over his immediate commanders' heads. As noted earlier, he ignored Gallagher's presence late in 1861, writing to Meade for instructions on handling underage recruits. But months earlier, he wrote to none other than Secretary of War Simon Cameron asking him to clarify a procedural issue arising from the promotion of his company's first lieutenant, Peter Johns, to adjutant. Ignoring every officer between himself and the cabinet member, Bierer asked Cameron to "please inform me whether or not he [Johns] retains his Lieutenancy in my Company, & if So whether he is required when not attending to his duties as Adjutant to assist in Company drills, or other duties, or not. If not, can my Company Elect, or yourself appoint, a first Lieutenant. Will you please inform me as soon as Convenient."[23] If Gallagher explained how the chain of command worked, Bierer forgot the lessons by the next spring. Guarding a railroad bridge over the Rappahannock in May 1862, Bierer again addressed Meade directly, asking that his company be allowed to remain on picket "in preference to laying about camp."[24]

From an early stage, Bierer wanted to lead more than an infantry company. At one point while at Camp Pierpont he wrote Curtin, with whom he evidently had some prewar political dealings, asking: "Will you give me a Commission and Authority to raise a battery of Artillery in Fayette Co.? If so I will resign and go home and get up one in 3 weeks, as many Persons there wish me to do so. From my Experience of military life I very much prefer the Artillery Service to the Infantry." He credited this insight to Sen. James Henry Lane, a major general in the prewar Kansas militia and a close Lincoln supporter. "Before he left Washington City for Kansas," Bierer wrote, Lane "Spoke to me on the Subject and wished me to raise an Artillery company and join his Division in his contemplated Expedition into Arkansas and Texas. . . . I am heartily tired of inaction on the Potomac and would like to be with Lane by whom I believe Something will be done."[25]

When that venture fell through, Bierer aimed for a more senior infantry posting. Returning from Libby Prison with hard service on his résumé, he used his surgeon's certificate of disability to get a ten-day leave. No less a figure than the new secretary of war, Edwin Stanton, authorized an extension, proving that the Fayette County captain had powerful friends. Bierer seems to have spent some of this period contacting other politicians, Pennsylvania Congressman John Covode and Senator Edgar Cowan among them.[26]

On the same day his regiment was routed at Second Bull Run, Bierer was hobnobbing at the War Department, where he learned about a new unit forming in western Pennsylvania. He prevailed upon an official in the Federal attorney general's office to remind Stanton of his availability.[27] The next day, Bierer informed Curtin that he had "written permission from [the] War Department to accept a Field Office in a new Pa. Regt." He added: "I would like to have a colonelcy. If you can not give me that, give me a Lieut. Colonelcy." Lest he be seen as busy politicking, Bierer stressed he was in Washington against his will: "I tried to get up to Manassas Yesterday Evening but after being out all night and all day could get no further than Fairfax and had to Return here this Evening." He closed by noting, "So far as I can learn and see everything seems to be going on well at Manassas."[28]

Curtin does appear to have promised a field-grade post to Bierer, but the latter hedged his bets. On 4 September, he wrote to "His Excellency A. Lincoln."

> Sir. I have been in the Service of my Country nearly Sixteen Months, one & a half months of which I have lately passed as a prisoner of war in Richmond. I was Taken Prisoner at the Battle of Gaine's Mill June 28.
>
> I know all about the Defences on the North & East of Richmond. It may Seem to you sir a Ridiculous presumption in me to say so: but I do say it. Give me *now* 50,000 men and Richmond with all its Southern Railroad Connections shall be yours and ours in *two weeks*. I would move via Fredericksburg. I have never sought Promotion. I do not ask it now, but Richmond can be taken now. For the sake of my country I write you. God preserve it in this hour of Peril. I am not a Great man, but men who have accomplished Great Events were once humble. I can Refer you to Messrs. Covode and Senator Cowan of P[a] who Know me intimately, but hope if you take no note of this you will consider it confidential.[29]

How this "confidential" note found its way into Bierer's personnel file in the Eleventh Reserves' regimental papers is unrecorded. Also unstated is how a captain could be allowed to command 50,000 men—a force roughly the size of Pope's ill-fated Army of Virginia—without a corresponding promotion.

Bierer did indeed rejoin the Eleventh Reserves, and publicity resulting from his South Mountain wound likely enhanced his reputation as a fighting officer. Recuperating at home in early October, he asked the Pennsylvania secretary of state to pitch a new idea to Curtin. The missive, which has survived, shows that the infantry captain who once eyed an artillery commission now wanted to join the cavalry.

> Dear Sir.
>
> As there are a great many vacancies in Field Offices of old Regts as well as appointments in new, which will have to be made by the Gov. Soon, will you please attend to my interest & Remind the Gov. of his promise to me. He asked me [on] one

occasion if I would accept the Colonelcy of a Cavalry Regt as he said he was going to raise several new ones. I see there is a Regt called the Stanton Cavalry about organizing at Camp Howe near Pittsburgh. Perhaps the Gov could give me a position in it.

Perhaps I am troubling you too much about my case but what you do for me shall not be forgotten. Were I able I should go to Harrisburg myself.[30]

Such efforts paid off. While the Eleventh regrouped after Antietam, Bierer got his colonelcy, and with it command of Camp Curtin. Yet Bierer did not simply want the new rank if it meant sitting at a desk. He wanted action and his own regiment. In November, he again reminded the governor about the War Department's permission slip "to accept a position from You in some New P^a Regt. Perhaps the Secy of War had best be reminded of that fact."[31]

His eventual command was a new, nine-month regiment, the 171st Pennsylvania, comprising mostly drafted men from Bradford, Juniata, Lycoming, Somerset, and Tioga Counties. The 171st Pennsylvania served in North Carolina, then later in Virginia and Maryland on the fringes of the Gettysburg campaign. Bierer did his new job credibly enough to ultimately lead its parent brigade. Yet some of his hardest fights after he left the Eleventh Reserves were not to be decided on the battlefield.[32]

McClellan delayed moving back into Virginia until October's clear weather slipped away. On the 26th of the month, his troops finally began crossing the Potomac. Cold weather marked the plodding trek south, and there was little wood left for campfires. The sick in the Eleventh Reserves still included James McGinley, who spent some time riding in an ambulance. On 6 November, the regiment pulled into Warrenton, where advance parties captured a few Rebel stragglers before the main body encamped a mile from town. A blizzard on the 7th halted further progress, though the snow began to melt the next day.[33]

This crawling pace did not satisfy Lincoln. On Sunday, 9 November, the president transferred command of the Army of the Potomac to Ambrose Burnside. The next day, soldiers in the Pennsylvania Reserves stood silent as officers read McClellan's farewell address. When McClellan later appeared before them, the emotional Pennsylvanians sent up a series of cheers. "The air was black with hundreds of caps," a Seventh Reserves veteran wrote his sister, "which men tore off, and threw high in the air, so great was the excitement." In the Eleventh Reserves, Lt. Col. Samuel

Jackson was among those who deemed McClellan's removal a mistake.[34]

For all McClellan's delays, Burnside found the Army of the Potomac in a good strategic position. At the time of the change in Union command, Robert E. Lee's force was divided again, both halves beyond supporting distance of the other. Stonewall Jackson's wing was back in the Shenandoah Valley behind the Blue Ridge, based between Winchester and Front Royal. The Army of Northern Virginia's other half, under James Longstreet, was at Culpeper, about forty miles to the south by a direct line. The situation invited the kind of separate assaults John Pope once envisioned. Yet strategy targeting Lee's army, rather than Richmond, had not yet taken hold among Union commanders. Rather, Burnside opted to move straight for then-undefended Fredericksburg, lying to the southeast, and directly from there toward Richmond.

Whatever merit the plan had ebbed through bad luck and inefficiency. Elements of the Army of the Potomac arrived on the Rappahannock opposite Fredericksburg in mid-November, but they were stymied by the lack of bridging equipment. Burnside stood still while Longstreet marched to Fredericksburg, arriving a few days later, and by early December the rest of Lee's army had gathered.[35]

But Burnside did not abandon the idea of taking Fredericksburg, despite knowing how difficult it was to coordinate and lead the unwieldy Army of the Potomac. Meade, who was not ill-disposed to his new commander, wrote home of "a very general opinion among officers and men, brought about by his [Burnside's] own assertions, that the command was too much for him." Burnside had in fact told Lincoln of his self-doubts, but the president laid the command on him anyway. With political stresses in mind—the Republicans had been punished in the 1862 elections—Lincoln also urged him to undertake the winter campaign. Such pressure from Washington likely dissuaded Burnside from abandoning a plan already obsolete.[36]

Pontoons finally in hand, Burnside first considered crossing the Rappahannock at Skinker's Neck, about ten miles east of Fredericksburg. The arrival of a Confederate division on the opposite shore nixed that plan, and Burnside rerouted the army back to Falmouth. As a result, the Eleventh did some heavy marching as the early December weather turned frosty. The regiment's bivouac site, known as Camp Brooke, was poorly equipped. James Fulton of Company H, starting to feel the pangs of rheumatism, recalled that while "the weather was extremely cold and several inches of snow [were] on the ground, . . . we had no tents or shelter of any kind."[37]

The Eleventh Reserves spent the afternoon and early evening of 3 December on picket duty. After returning to camp, officers learned that the brigade was to move at daylight. But the next morning the orders were countermanded, and the Eleventh instead drew new clothes and shelter tents, which were especially appreciated when wet snow fell the next day.

Two dozen men were detailed on Saturday, 6 December, to build roads, and on a frozen dawn two days later, Meade's division started toward King George Court House. After marching about ten miles the Eleventh Reserves made camp in mid-afternoon in a pine forest near White Oak Church. The men felled trees with an eye to building cabins, but Samuel Jackson noted "many indications of an advance movement." One was the issuance of three days' cooked rations. Another was an order for the men to draw twenty cartridges in addition to the standard forty-round supply. After midnight on 10 December, the regiment was on the road to the Rappahannock and before dawn gazed again on the strategic Virginia river.[38]

Burnside had selected several crossing sites to accommodate the army, which was organized in "Grand Divisions." The Pennsylvania Reserves' I Corps fell into the Grand Division of Maj. Gen. William Franklin who also had the VI Corps under his wing. In his front, about three miles east of Fredericksburg, engineers set to work assembling the pontoons. Elements of Conrad Jackson's brigade, along with several batteries, covered them; the Twelfth Reserves and two companies of the Tenth Reserves were placed around the work area, the Eleventh in reserve. By midmorning the engineers had finished two bridges despite fire from Rebel snipers concealed in farmhouses. The sharpshooters wounded half a dozen bridge-builders before Union batteries drove them off with shells. The artillerists also used canister to break up an attack by a roughly two-regiment force that had massed in nearby woods. On Conrad Jackson's orders, the gun crews tried to destroy the farmhouses with a combination of shells and case shot. The sturdy little buildings, at least one of which was made of stone, "resisted our efforts." The stone house would later become a Federal hospital.[39]

Things went less smoothly for bridging teams in front of the city, and Union cannon responded to sniper fire there by bombarding Fredericksburg itself, a fact Samuel Jackson noted in his diary. He also noted that at about 5 P.M. Franklin started a few regiments across the bridges in his sector. More followed the next morning, the VI Corps assembling within Fredericksburg itself. By 3 P.M. on 12 December the Pennsylvania Reserves and the rest of the I Corps had crossed, skirmishers pushing back Rebel pickets but the whole stopping well short of Lee's trenches. Conrad Jackson's troops, Robert Anderson later reported, "crossed the river in rear of the Second Brigade, and, moving down the river, bivouacked for the remainder of the day and the following night about 1 mile below the place of crossing, the left resting upon the river."[40]

On the Confederate right—where Stonewall Jackson had established his lines on and around Prospect Hill—observers watched from cannon-studded breastworks concealed by heavy woods. The position, perhaps a mile from where the Pennsylvania Reserves tried to sleep, overlooked a mostly clear field of fire. An attacking force would find only slight cover—a ditch, and beyond it a raised railroad bed, roughly paralleling the high ground. When Reynolds rode forward to reconnoiter, "All that could be seen of the enemy's position was that he occupied the crests of these heights with his artillery and infantry," with skirmishers posted behind the railroad cut.[41]

During the tense, cold night near the Rappahannock, Samuel Jackson counted his forces and tallied 392 men, the most the regiment had mustered since Gaines' Mill. The evening had its share of the bizarre. Somehow, Maj. Peter Johns fell off a fence, sustaining injuries reported as serious, but which the rank and file came to suspect were a ruse to avoid combat. Whether the hurts were genuine or not, Johns went to the rear. Given the reception prepared for the Union army, the major may have considered himself the luckiest man in the Eleventh, though the episode caught up with him later.[42]

Others were conspicuous by their absence. Company H privates John L. Avery, Adam Huff, and John E. Steinberg may have had a premonition of what was to happen, for all were absent without leave for three days, missing the battle. When tried, each was described as having "good character" and got off relatively leniently. Avery, who had "fought well at Antietam and Gaines Mill," was fined $10 a month for four months and confined ten days on bread and water. Huff and Steinberg—the latter "did his duty at Gaines Mill"—were fined $10 a month for six months and sentenced to 40 days on bread and water, the confinement spread out in monthly, ten-day installments.[43]

The morning of the 13th was unseasonably warm. Mist draped over the field, which began to turn muddy. The battle formation on the Union left, which Reynolds had devised, had the Pennsylvania Reserves in the center of the coming attack, while Abner Doubleday's division guarded the left and John Gibbon's brought up the right. When Meade's men were drawn up in battle line, Conrad Jackson's brigade stood on the far left, its front from left to right consisting of the Tenth, Twelfth, Fifth, and Eleventh Reserves. Before them, the Ninth Reserves were deployed as skirmishers. On the right, William Sinclair's and Albert Magilton's brigades—each reinforced by a single regiment from outside the Reserves organization—formed a double line, Sinclair's old Sixth Reserves in front as skirmishers. There was little talking within the Eleventh Reserves. Chaplain Adam Torrance, about to witness his first battle, remarked on the "peculiar silence in the ranks."[44]

To get to their jumping-off point, Conrad Jackson's men crossed a ravine near the charred remains of a mill, passed through a wide field, then advanced over a turnpike known as either the Old Richmond Stage Road or the Bowling Green Road. To their front and left, artillery commanded by John Pelham, of Jeb Stuart's cavalry, kept up a harassing fire. Meade in response called up three batteries to counter the Confederate guns, placing one in front of Conrad Jackson's brigade. A Rebel solid shot soon splintered the axle of one of the newly deployed Federal pieces. Another destroyed much of the same gun's caisson limber. The remaining guns kept up enough fire to force the Rebel batteries to change position, but within fifteen minutes a new barrage killed or wounded about a dozen Union artillerists, along with many battery horses. The Union gun crews shifted their pieces by hand until new horses arrived.[45]

Cannon fire also found targets in the Eleventh Reserves. A solid shot struck Company D's Capt. William Stewart, by one account striking him in the breast. The wound was mortal, but he remained conscious as he was taken off the field. His Connoquenessing Rangers had no other commissioned officers present, so command passed to Cpl. John O'Harra Woods (or Wood). Remembered as being "a beardless youth," Woods had given his age as twenty, his hometown as Petersville, and his occupation as farmer when he joined the Rangers in mid-1861. His dying captain reportedly asked the men "to go into the impending struggle as bravely as if he were with them." Stewart died within two hours. His replacement was destined to die at Gettysburg as a lieutenant.[46]

Artillery also killed Cambria Guards Pvt. John Camp, who Meade "through some queer fancy," ordered buried on the spot. He gave the task to a party from the Second Reserves. "A grave was dug with bayonets and hands," recalled that regiment's historian, "and wrapping the soldier in his blanket he was laid in his honorable grave, while the shells were singing his requiem over his head." Camp's effects included almost eighty dollars, which were turned over to his company commander, James Burke.[47]

Finally, at about noon, Conrad Jackson received orders to advance. Meade's goal was to break deep enough into the Confederate lines on Prospect Hill to sever the military road that ran behind the enemy works. His immediate target was a marshy finger of woods, held by two brigades separated by a 600-yard gap but backed by artillery. To reach this point, Conrad Jackson's troops would have to deal with several companies of Tennessee skirmishers blocking their progress in the open field. Once they pushed past those riflemen, the Pennsylvanians might find cover in, first, the muddy ditch, and then the bed of the Richmond, Fredericksburg, and Potomac Railroad. But Pelham's agile artillery, screened by a brigade of cavalry under Fitzhugh Lee, remained in position to enfilade oncoming Union troops.[48]

The Union assault on this part of the line stepped off at about noon. But as soon as the blue troops got within 800 yards of the enemy's artillery (a distance Rebel gunners paced off earlier) the Confederate cannon opened. Their fire stalled Meade's and Gibbon's men. The latter ordered his men to lie down. Meade hustled Sinclair's and Jackson's brigades back about a hundred yards and into a small gully then rode off to order up more guns.[49]

Within an hour, the Union artillery had seemingly bested their Rebel counterparts. Meade prepared to renew the advance. How the Eleventh Reserves felt about the situation went unrecorded, but at about 1 P.M., orders came for the division to resume the march. The Pennsylvanians' lines were closely packed as the men began their charge. They found enemy skirmishers only about 200 yards in front, and enough Rebel artillery continued to fire for one Union veteran to maintain that the rain of lead here was worse than that experienced in front of Miller's cornfield at Antietam. The shelling caused the blue troops to press still closer together, an instinctive move that hindered mobility while transforming their lines into increasingly broad targets.[50]

The Eleventh Reserves moved forward at the same slow pace as the rest of the division. By the time the confused Union mass had pushed back the skirmishers, crossed the ditch, and struck the railroad tracks, the Confederate fire hit a new intensity. One Rebel sergeant recalled how the blue troops melted away like mist at sunrise. The Pennsylvanians remained at the rail bed for perhaps ten minutes, units colliding and intermingling. Although his brigade commander was urging the units on, Samuel Jackson did not like the look of the ground ahead. By the account survivors gave Samuel Bates after the war, the lieutenant colonel "saw that to attempt to scale the hill in his immediate front, and to carry the works by direct assault, would cause the utter annihilation of his command." Instead, he advanced the regiment toward a patch of woods to the right, allowing the Eleventh to threaten the flank of the closest Confederate defenders—likely men from Brig. Gen. James Archer's brigade—who retreated. The maneuver was made possible at least in part by the Bucktails, whose commander positioned his regiment, on his own initiative, to fill a gap between Samuel Jackson's unit and its neighboring Fifth Reserves.[51]

But a new line of Confederate infantry—possibly troops from a brigade commanded by Edmund Nathan Atkinson—was coming hard toward this part of the line even as Pelham's artillery was finding more targets to the regiment's rear and flank. Conrad Jackson was atop the railroad bed receiving a report from one of Meade's aides when both were killed, the brigadier with a bullet through his skull. His body would be left on the field. Command of the Third Brigade again fell to Robert Anderson.[52]

It seems likely that Anderson had little chance to influence the engagement; his regiments were scattered and soon amid thick woods. Poor visibility added an extra hellish quality to the stress of battle. An Indiana County soldier in the Twelfth Reserves was surprised to see the forage cap fly off a comrade, and suddenly realized the man had been shot through the head. But the Pennsylvanians cleared out the first line of trenches. At one point officers started two sets of Rebel colors and hundreds of prisoners headed for the Union lines.[53]

Confederate counterattacks, however, soon forced the Union regiments to simply hang on. Men struggling in the woods lost track of time. Meade, watching from a distance, thought his Pennsylvanians stayed there twenty minutes. To Anderson, amid the chaos itself, the period seemed like an hour. Expecting to see support coming, he was convinced "that had we been promptly supported, that portion of the field gained by the valor of our troops could and would have been held against any force that the enemy would have been able to have thrown against us."[54]

But Gibbon's division never got its attack coordinated, despite personal attention from Reynolds, who gave its commander two of his own aides to help deliver orders. Instead, Gibbon's assault bogged down, hindered by mud and Confederate fire. Meade galloped back and found Brig. Gen. David Bell Birney, whose III Corps division had taken the Pennsylvania Reserves' starting positions near the battery line. Although Meade wore only a brigadier's single star, he had his major general's commission in his pocket, and he cited it in ordering Birney to advance to the Pennsylvania Reserves' aid. Birney complied, but as his troops reached the rail bed they were swept back by retreating Union soldiers.[55]

Like Anderson, Company E Capt. Daniel Coder kept looking anxiously back for support but found none. "We lost color bearer after color bearer, I know not how many," he wrote afterward. "I picked up the colors at three different times myself. The flag staff was shot off and the flag perforated in nineteen different places by rebel bullets." Thirty of the thirty-one men of his Indiana County company became casualties at Fredericksburg. The wounded included James Oatman, back in the ranks after being disabled and captured near Glendale the previous summer. Casualties in Company F included twenty-year-old Sgt. James A. Hayden, a onetime Uniontown printer, hit on the right hand and ankle. A Rebel bullet sliced through the tunic of Brady Guards Pvt. William W. "Osse" Oswandle, giving him "a slight though painful gash across the abdomen." Company G Capt. James Speer, still living with the effects of thigh and shoulder wounds suffered at Gaines' Mill, took a minié ball in the right wrist. His company emerged with only four men unhurt.[56]

As the division tumbled back, Meade and Reynolds tried unsuccessfully to rally and reorganize the men near their original start line. One scared Pennsylvanian whom Meade confronted aimed his rifle at the general. Meade promptly broke his sword over the man and sent him back toward the firing.[57]

The Federal assault on the other end of the Rebel lines, centered on a ridge beyond Fredericksburg known as Marye's Heights, also failed disastrously, closing the action on one of the Union's—and the Pennsylvania Reserves'—most terrible days. Unable to see the extent of the carnage from his headquarters across the Rappahannock, Burnside initially planned to renew the attack the next day, but his subordinate commanders talked him out of it. On the 15th, the Army of the Potomac began to withdraw. The broken Pennsylvania Reserves recrossed the pontoon bridge below Fredericksburg that night.[58]

The army's contemporary returns cited 10 killed, 147 wounded, and about 50 missing in the Eleventh Reserves, but many of the wounded and captives died, so that a later tally dramatically upped the number of Fredericksburg deaths to 49.[59] In an emotional letter home, Daniel Porter wrote of how the regiment had helped break the enemy's line, "but no support came to our assistance, and we were driven back." About half of his 45-man Indiana National Guards were casualties; 1st Sgt. William Kuhns of South Mountain heroism and privates James Trimble and John Lewis were among the dead.

Several of the regiment's wounded had been left behind to become prisoners. They included Company E's Andrew R. Mitchell, wounded in the leg; Company C's Eli Hillard, struck in the hip; and Company K's William Chamberlain, who lost his shattered arm to a Confederate surgeon's saw. All three died in Richmond prisons in January.[60]

Another prisoner was twenty-seven-year-old Lt. Lewis A. Johnston, of Company H. The Pleasant Unity resident had been leading the company forward until a Confederate bullet broke his right leg. Johnston remained on the field, unable to follow the regiment in the race back to the Rappahannock.[61]

Those casualties helped off the field included Lt. Andrew Ivory, struck in the right leg below the knee by a musket ball, which shattered the fibula. Doctors saved the leg but Ivory was never able to put his weight on it again. He was discharged and pensioned early the next year.[62]

Surgeons had less luck with Pvt. William Conner, one of a pair of identically named men in the Eleventh Reserves, one in each of its Indiana County companies. Company B's Conner had joined the unit in June 1861, was taken prisoner at Glendale and later exchanged. At Fredericksburg, a Confederate bullet struck the back of his left thigh, three inches above the knee, fracturing the femur. He was carried to a field hospital, where doctors put splints on the leg, which was not bleeding heavily but was so swollen that the bullet could not immediately be found. Four days later, a surgeon reported, "The patient was put under the influence of chloroform and a thorough examination made. Amputation being found necessary, it was done in the lower third of the thigh by the flap operation."

The same doctor found the wound unusual and wrote up his postoperative examination of the amputated leg. The bullet had "passed along the back of the femur against the bone into the notch between the condyles and had broken through the articular surface of the inner one, infringing against the patella but not entering the joint." Conner's doctor would have continued his study of the limb, but "The attention of the surgeon being required at other duties the part was laid away for further examination and became lost."

Regarding the patient himself, the doctor noted, "The usual dressings for an amputated thigh were applied," and five days after the operation Conner was sent, in good condition, to a Washington hospital. There, the wounded man took a turn for the worse. He died on 21 January.[63]

Incensed by the lack of support his men received on the battlefield, Meade's fury found several targets as he rode back to the sad Rappahannock bivouac. He ripped into Birney while still on the field, then located Reynolds, asking incredulously whether the army's commanders thought "my division could whip Lee's whole army?" Special wrath was saved for a *New York Herald* correspondent who reported, Meade wrote home, "that we ran scandalously at the first fire of the enemy. This is the harder, because I saw the *Herald* correspondent on the field, and he might have known and indeed did know better. What his object in thus falsifying facts was I cannot imagine, but I would advise him not to show himself in our camp if he values his skin, for the men could not be restrained from tarring and feathering him."[64]

The Pennsylvania Reserves fared better in their native state's press, but in Ebensburg the *Democrat & Sentinel* charged that the state's sons had been "sacrificed again." Interestingly, it held general-in-chief Henry Halleck responsible for Fredericksburg, charging: "If General Lee himself had dictated the dispatches of Gen. Halleck they would not have been different." As for the Army of the Potomac's unfortunate commander: "We have no words of unkindness for Gen. Burnside. He is a very different man from the braggart Pope, and deserves commiseration rather than censure in his heavy misfortune." Underscoring its sentiments, the paper ran a poem on the front page of its Christmas Eve edition calling for Lincoln's resignation.[65]

The next day passed quietly within the Eleventh Reserves. Its men likely agreed with Daniel Porter's summary of the ordeal on the Rappahannock. "The boys fought like heroes," he had written home. "They were too brave. . . . We were butchered like so many animals."[66]

Chapter 9

A Regiment Worth Its Weight in Gold

Gettysburg

After recrossing the Rappahannock following Fredericksburg, George Meade brought his Pennsylvania Reserves division—less 1,853 casualties—into camp at Belle Plain Landing. Meade's report of 19 December showed 14 officers and 274 enlisted men present for duty in the Eleventh Reserves, slightly more than a quarter of the unit's original strength. Six days later, Samuel Jackson noted in his diary that the year had brought "a very dull Christmas to the soldiers" despite orders canceling all drills.

Jackson's correspondence that week included a letter from Thomas Gallagher, who was still recuperating at home. The former colonel had submitted his resignation the day before Fredericksburg. Accompanying it was a note from Gallagher's physician noting that the "wound is not yet fit—nor will it be for three or four months—to permit him to resume his duties in the field. And further he has been for some time troubled with a species of the Gravel which renders him unfit for Camp life with any degree of Comfort. These things would be much against him in the Summer Season but much more so in a Winter campaign." Gallagher's resignation was accepted effective 17 December.[1] But as with James Porter, Robert Litzinger, and other former members of the unit, Gallagher's war service did not end with the Eleventh Pennsylvania Reserves. At the time of Gettysburg, he was named colonel of the Fifty-fourth Pennsylvania Militia, an emergency unit that would be mustered out in mid-August. He later participated in the pursuit and capture of Confederate raider John Hunt Morgan and earned a brigadier general's brevet.[2]

In December 1862, Gallagher's resignation touched off a round of command changes. Samuel Jackson was formally commissioned colonel of the Eleventh Reserves, Daniel Porter replacing him as lieutenant colonel. Porter's elevation came at the expense of the regiment's major, Peter Johns. Although he had bested Porter in the election to replace Robert Litzinger, Johns slipped from favor after his inglorious injury the night before Fredericksburg. His most serious hurt suffered there, according to an army doctor, was a dislocated shoulder; on New Year's Day he came down with "chronic laryngitis." The result of these afflictions was that he spent only 15 of the next 170 days with his regiment.[3]

The enlisted men took a dim view of Johns' absence. When the lieutenant colonelcy opened, each company sent an identical petition to Governor Curtin, hoping to forestall any thought of elevating the major: "We the undersigned . . . would respectfully request that you will not promote Maj. P. A. Johns to any higher position in this Regiment, as we believe him to be totally unfit even for the position he now holds. That he has absented himself from his Regiment on the most frivolous pretense for the last five and a half months, drawing pay from the Government for which he has rendered no service whatever, and that he has done nothing at any time to entitle him to promotion. And as in duty bound, we will ever pray, &c."[4]

Johns' response has not survived in government records, but on 30 March, Fifth Reserves Col. Joseph Fisher, who now commanded the Third Brigade, requested that a court of inquiry look into Johns' protracted absence. The issue was moot, for on the same date an army board honorably discharged Johns due to injuries and illness rendering him "incapable of performing the duties of an officer." His discharge mentions that he exited the army "on account of injury received at the battle of Fredericksburg, Va., Dec. 13, 1862," rather than the fall from a fence reported the evening before. His post went to James Speer, captain of the Independent Blues.

If he went out awkwardly Johns retained an admiration for the military heroes of the day. When his wife gave birth to another son in summer 1864, Johns named him after the intrepid cavalryman Philip Sheridan. And the former major later led efforts to erect a soldiers' monument—a "Massilion sandstone shaft"—in a Fayette County cemetery.[5]

Although battered at Fredericksburg, the Pennsylvania Reserves sustained the will to keep fighting. A report by a captain from the inspector general's department, dated four days before Christmas, found the Third Brigade in remarkably good shape considering what it had been through. The arms in each regiment, including the Eleventh Reserves, were dirty and without bayonets but still serviceable. "The command is in a good fighting condition," despite morale problems arising from a lack of pay— some of the Eleventh's veterans had yet to receive money due from before Gaines' Mill. Discipline was lax "owing much to the scarcity of company officers, many companies being without a commissioned officer." The report concluded: "In regards to the regiments becoming demoralized I can see nothing which tends in the least that way, except that the men think it harder that they are not paid and the officers join in with them in their complaints; farther than this the command is ready and willing to go into an engagement."[6]

Two days before Christmas, Burnside gave Meade command of the V Corps, and Third Reserves Col. Horatio Sickel was pegged to temporarily succeed him as head of the Pennsylvania Reserves. Just before he left, Meade wrote to Franklin, commanding the army's left wing, urging that his old division be sent home to refit and recruit. The organization, which once totaled over 11,000 men, was down to 5,000 present for duty. Most of the 4,000 absent with authority were wounded, many "so maimed and disabled that no expectation need be formed of their returning to active duty." Meade estimated that 200 officers and 7,000 enlisted men would have to be found to bring the division back to strength, so many that individual recruiting parties could never accomplish the job. Yet he counseled against consolidating "the existing force into a number of regiments equal to the officers and men for duty," which would destroy "the organization, and the prestige which the good conduct of the corps has acquired for it." Instead, Meade recommended that the division return to Pennsylvania for a few months, "where, it is believed, from the great reputation the corps has acquired, the pride the State takes in it, and the enthusiasm its return would create, that in a short time its ranks would be filled, after pruning them of all useless members." I Corps commander John Reynolds, acknowledging the division's "uselessness in its present state," supported the idea, at the same time urging that the practice of electing officers be dropped.[7]

Meade's suggestions found favor with Franklin. The latter agreed that "it will be well to send the regiments home for a month, provided the Governor of the State will engage to send them back to their old corps at the end of that time, filled up."[8] Rumors that the Reserves "are to be withdrawn to Pennsylvania" reached Samuel Jackson's ears by the day after Christmas. Burnside, however, put the transfer on hold—he needed the troops, for he hoped to redeem Fredericksburg with a new campaign. He had already begun planning for another Rappahannock crossing, this one downstream from the site of the disastrous 13 December assault. On 30 December, Jackson "received orders to be ready to move at short notice with sixty rounds ammunition. Boys complain much on the prospects of leaving their comfortable quarters."[9]

But Washington put the move on hold after Burnside's subordinates, fearing another tragedy, secretly took their misgivings to Lincoln. A second plan, to move via Banks' Ford, received more support, and the new campaign was scheduled to begin 20 January. Unfortunately for Burnside and his soldiers, the march coincided with the start of an icy, 48-hour deluge. Weighed down with the extra ammunition and four days' rations, the Eleventh Reserves struggled over impassable roads. "We marched all day only stopping about 15 minutes during the whole day," a soldier in another Pennsylvania Reserves regiment wrote home. "We crossed hills and hollows and marched through pine woods so thick we could not see a foot before us." The exhausted soldiers dropped into a muddy bivouac late that night and woke up in several inches of water. The next day's march ended after only about three miles.[10]

On 23 January, Burnside called off the movement, subsequently known even in official reports as the "Mud March." For the enlisted men, the way back to their former camps proved even harder. The roads were full of wagons and artillery pieces buried in the mud, the mules hitched to them sinking so deep, one man noted, that "we could see nothing but their head and ears." The Rebels taunted them from across the river using signs announcing "Burnsides stuck in the mud." The affair killed what morale remained. As one of the Bucktails wrote home: "If it had not been for the rain perhaps we would [have] whiped the secesh very bad but through the luck we whiped our selfs."[11]

Three days after the Mud March ended, Joseph Hooker succeeded Burnside as commander of the Army of the Potomac. By the end of the month, Hooker and Halleck were conferring with Samuel Heintzelman, who now commanded Washington's defenses, about how to rest the Pennsylvania Reserves. Rather than send the crippled division home, the plan now was to send it to the capital garrison in exchange "for new regiments of the same State, from in and around Washington." Heintzelman was unenthusiastic at the idea. "Some of the [Pennsylvania Reserves'] companies are commanded by sergeants and corporals," he observed. "As most of the regiments are doing provost duty in the city, this is a most serious objection."

But Halleck and Hooker prevailed, and on 5 February, Reynolds was told to send his three brigades of Pennsylvania Reserves to Alexandria. He dispatched them with a special order noting his "deep regrets" that they were being separated. But he hoped "that soon their thin ranks will be filled, and they, once more restored and organized, will be returned to the field prepared to add new lustre to a name already endeared to our patriotic state."[12]

Bad weather delayed the transfer, and new controversy arose once their replacements reached the I Corps. One of its generals, Abner Doubleday, who incidentally spent a short stint heading the Pennsylvania Reserves during its transfer to Washington, reported to Hooker: "The Pennsylvania regiments given in place of the Reserves do not contain as many men as the latter brought here. There is a deficiency of about 250 men. I think they ought to give another regiment from some other State to make up the deficiency." Hooker subsequently asked Halleck to order Heintzelman to make good, but Halleck wrote on the memorandum, "Regiments cannot be broken up in order to exactly equalize." Hooker testily replied that "no further exchange will be made with my consent" and vented his wrath on Doubleday, who had originally arranged the swap's details.[13]

By early February, the Pennsylvania Reserves' new parent organization was the recently created XXII Corps of Samuel Heintzelman's Department of Washington. Stationed at Miner's Hill, Virginia, the rank and file had little time to actually rest, a fact documented by Jesse Fry's diary. Born circa 1846, Fry would therefore have been only about fifteen when he signed on with the Connoquenessing Rangers at Camp Wright on 5 July 1861. Though young, he was a good soldier and was promoted to corporal during the Eleventh's stay in Washington, a post that involved extensive fatigue duty in harsh weather. "Snowed until noon, Then rained in the afternoon," he observed on Wednesday, 18 February, the same day that "We fixed our tent To day and got a stove. It cost 325 [$3.25]." Fry spent the next day chopping wood in rain, which washed away the snow. He got to Washington two days later, where he visited some of his comrades wounded at Fredericksburg. He also "stopped at the avenue house," which could of course refer to any legitimate establishment. It is worth noting, however, that when the XXII Corps provost marshal later tallied up the city's dozens of houses of prostitution, the list included at least four each on Pennsylvania and New Jersey Avenues, and one each on Maine and Virginia Avenues. After one more snowy day the weather improved, and Fry's company and others were detailed for picket duty. At about the same time, James McGinley, who returned from a convalescent camp on 20 February, observed in his own diary that the regiment was having a hard time drawing rations.[14]

Many resented the new routine. "We go on picket duty every fifth day and remain twenty-four hours," Pvt. Joseph Miller of the Brady Guards observed in a letter to the *Brookville Republican*. "When not on picket there is camp guard and fatigue duty to be performed. If fatigue duty is scarce in camp it will be found in the neighborhood some place, and it is of little matter whether the labor of the soldier is of any benefit to Uncle Sam or not, so that he performs his task. Some of the boys are of the opinion that the officers (i.e. some of them,) branch out among the neighbors and seek employment for some of the men who may be fortunate enough to have a few hours or a day of leisure time." But Samuel Jackson kept the officers busy with Monday and Thursday evenings set aside for "recitation of tactics and Army Regulations." Like his predecessor he sent attendance and progress reports to brigade headquarters.[15]

He also kept the machinery of discipline running. Henry C. Stone, who had picked up the flag at South Mountain after five color bearers had been shot down, was among those missing at Fredericksburg and, to top the court-martial charges subsequently brought against him, missed the "Mud March" as well. There was testimony in his favor, however. At Fredericksburg, he had been fresh out of the hospital. Before the Mud March, he had complained of sore feet and had also suffered through a recent tooth-pulling. The sergeant who did the latter operation at first testified that "There was some hemmorhage [sic], but not enough to unfit him for duty." Yet after the sergeant conceded that his patient "was vomiting during the Mud March" period, Stone, who ended the war as Company H's first sergeant and reenlisted for another tour of duty, got off with a $10 fine and a reprimand.[16]

Recruitment for the Eleventh Reserves continued. A picture of the post-Fredericksburg regiment and its pre-Gettysburg rebuilding emerges from the records of the army's chief of ordnance. Captains (or those of other ranks filling their role) submitted quarterly reports listing the number and type of serviceable weapons and accoutrements present. The numbers therefore may not indicate the actual numbers of men present for duty. An added caveat is that some reports came in late; the fourth quarter 1862 inventory figure furnished by Company K was not received until the following August. That said, the reports yield the following musket-strength chart.[17]

Company	31 December 1862	31 March 1863
A (Cambria Guards)	23	35
B (Indiana National Guards)	25	39
C (Dickson Guards)	22	30
D (Connoquenessing Rangers)	23	33
E (Washington Blues [I])	16	23
F (Union Volunteers)	21	32
G (Independent Blues)	17	25
H (Westmoreland Guards)	30	35
I (Washington Blues [II])	16	20
K (Brady Guards)	32	43
TOTAL	225	315

By 4 April, when Miller wrote the letter cited above, his Company K had 49 officers and men present for duty and 18 "absent, sick and wounded." A total of 118 men had served in the unit during almost two years of service, and of them 18 had been discharged, 29 had been killed or had died from illness, and two had deserted. Taking the first quarter 1863 return at face value, the Eleventh regiment was in better shape than others. By Miller's account "there is scarcely a regiment in the Reserve Corps that numbers over 300 men."[18]

The Eleventh Reserves' posting to Washington kept it out of the Chancellorsville campaign. Accordingly, except for a few scares caused by reports of Rebel cavalry raids under Jeb Stuart or the equally dangerous John S. Mosby, the regiment had little war-related excitement in the spring.[19]

But fatigue details had their own dangers. With the regiment camped near Vienna, Virginia—about two dozen miles south of the capital—Capt. James P. George suffered a severe hernia while helping free a wood-laden wagon from a mire. Sgt. Edward Scofield got a look at the intestinal rupture, which he later described as "about as large as a childs head, looking a dark blue, and [which] settled into his [George's] testicles, making it very hard for [George] to move round." The suffering captain was barely able to walk and spent at least some time riding a borrowed horse. The wound tortured him during the marches of the upcoming summer campaign, and the unlucky officer sought a discharge in August.[20]

If George's injury was painful, darker forces tormented Sgt. Eugenius Tibbs. Five-feet, eleven-inches tall, with fair complexion, brown hair, and eyes which were either blue or gray, he gave his occupation as "laborer" when he joined Everard Bierer's company in May 1861. Born about 1827 in Hoopswood, Pennsylvania, Tibbs left behind his wife, the former Ruth Tailor, whom he had married in 1853, and daughters born in 1854 and 1858.

James Hayden, who succeeded Bierer as captain of the Union Volunteers, remembered Tibbs as "a good and meritorious Soldier." Yet two years of war started to unhinge things inside Tibbs, who had been captured at Gaines' Mill, exchanged, and saw further action at Second Bull Run, South Mountain, Antietam, and Fredericksburg. Hayden thought battle stress—the "excitement and other unavoidable causes incident to the life of a soldier"—sparked whatever problems became visible in the Company F sergeant's behavior. On 1 June, in camp at Vienna, something happened to convince Hayden that Tibbs needed help. He sent the troubled man to the Government Hospital for the Insane at Washington.[21]

Two days after Tibbs was dispatched to the asylum, the Pennsylvania Reserves got a new, permanent commander, Brig. Gen. Samuel Crawford, and Sickel stepped down to head the Second Brigade. Born in Franklin County, Pennsylvania, in 1829, Crawford studied medicine at the University of Pennsylvania and served as an army surgeon for a decade before the war. Like Truman Seymour, Crawford was at Fort Sumter when it fell, and a month later the then-major got a promotion and a career change, becoming a field officer with the rank of brigadier. One of his soldiers described him as "a tall, chesty, glowering man, with heavy eyes, a big nose and bushy whiskers," who "wore habitually a turn-out-the-guard expression." He served at Winchester and Cedar Mountain; at Antietam, he led a brigade in the XII Corps then succeeded his wounded division commander. Crawford himself took a musket ball in his right thigh that day, an injury that laid him up for months. The ball had brought bits of uniform and accoutrement material into the wound, which discharged over the course of time. Even before this injury, Crawford proved to be as cantankerous as Meade. On the Maryland campaign, he bawled out one regiment so effectively—he called them "Pennsylvania cattle"—that a sergeant told comrades he would happily fire should the general "accidentally" get between him and a Rebel.[22]

At the time Crawford took over the division, the Army of the Potomac was trying to recover from Chancellorsville. It had again regrouped behind the Rappahannock, its corps spread out near Falmouth. But the front did not remain quiet as Lee sought to follow up on his victory. His first move was to carefully maneuver his army, now reorganized into three large corps, behind the Blue Ridge Mountains. With the mountains screening the Army of Northern Virginia from Hooker, Lee moved north again into Maryland. Meeting no serious resistance there, he proceeded into Pennsylvania itself.[23]

News that Lee was threatening their home state caused the officers of the Pennsylvania Reserves to petition to be reattached to the Army of the Potomac. Their request was granted in part; Sickel's Second Brigade would be kept in Washington, but the bulk of the division would join the V Corps, to be reunited with Meade. Crawford accordingly readied the First and Third Brigades for movement, and on Tuesday, 23 June, Jesse Fry noted that his regiment received "orders this Evening to be ready to march at a moment's notice and to send off all Extra clothing." Sergeant Tibbs' pension files indicate that he served at Gettysburg; his mind must have cleared enough for him to rejoin the Eleventh Reserves at about this time.

On a cloudy 24 June, the regiment left its bivouac near Fairfax Station, passing Upton's Hill. With the same haze overhead the next day, the Eleventh marched up the Leesburg-Alexandria Pike to the Third Brigade's campsite near Vienna, where the men spent a rainy night. After breaking camp at 6 A.M. on 26 June, Crawford's two brigades traveled to the banks of Broad Run. The roads were muddy and, Miller wrote home, "having marched a distance of twenty miles . . . many of the boys had 'played out.'" The next day, while the regiment crossed the Potomac on a pontoon bridge near Edwards Ferry, some men in the ranks ruefully noted the anniversary of Gaines' Mill. A few days later they passed another reminder of hard service—the campsite where they slept before South Mountain.[24]

Meade was glad to receive his old division—Hooker was free to offer it to him as its place in the I Corps was still occupied by the "exchange" troops from the Washington garrison. The V Corps commander wanted all the reinforcements he could get. "I understand the Reserves are seven thousand strong, which will be a very decided addition to my present weak corps," he wrote home. The division's aggregate as of the end of February, was, in fact, slightly higher than Meade's estimate—7,625, up almost 3,000 from the month before. Most of the difference consisted of extra-duty men returning to their regiments. But with Heintzelman opting to keep the Second Brigade, Crawford had only 3,515 infantry.[25]

But by the time Crawford's division linked up with the V Corps at Ballinger's Creek, Maryland, Meade was no longer its commander. Hooker's temperament had previously irked Lincoln and Halleck, and the pressure of Lee's invasion had made Fighting Joe start to sound like George McClellan. Demanding more troops—in this case the garrison at Harpers Ferry—Hooker offered to quit when they were not forthcoming. Lincoln accepted his resignation, and on 27 June Meade was ordered to take command of the Army of the Potomac. In the reshuffling, Crawford learned that George Sykes, who had led the corps' all-Regular division, succeeded Meade as corps commander. Command changes also affected the Eleventh Reserves on the march to confront Lee in Pennsylvania. Company K Sgt. Edward Scofield suddenly learned that he had been promoted to first lieutenant, "and that in future he should act accordingly."[26]

The Eleventh Reserves learned of Meade's promotion just as it reached the V Corps' perimeter on 28 June. Samuel Jackson recalled that the men "shouted themselves hoarse over the welcome news" that their old brigade commander—irritable as he may have been when they first met—now led the largest army in the hemisphere. Headquarters apparently hoped the Pennsylvania Reserves' enthusiasm would be contagious, for the division, by Samuel Jackson's later account, paraded through the rest of the V Corps. However this was managed, Jackson came away convinced that the division's cheers "created a feeling of confidence among the officers and men of the army, in the ability of the new commander."[27]

Meade's name was forgotten in an instant a few days later when a new rumor spread. Captain Hannibal Sloan, commanding the Indiana National

Guards after Daniel Porter's promotion, took his company and the Cambria Guards on a detail to guard the division's wagon trains on 30 June. Near midnight, he later recalled: "cheering was heard on the road upon which we were marching, in advance of us, on other roads running parallel to our road, and the boys wondered what those fools were yelling for. The cheering came nearer and nearer, increasing in volume, and finally some one at the side of the road called out 'Boys, General McClellan is in command,' and then for the time being, empty stomachs, sleep and fatigue were all forgotten, and we joined madly in the cheers."[28]

The rumor was, of course, untrue, but whatever their thoughts about the command situation the men marveled at the scenery, as they had on a similar march the year before. Seeing farms untouched by war again convinced Private Miller of the Brady Guards that "we had in fact got back into the Union once more." James McGinley noted similar scenes near Frederick. "A plesant vale," he wrote in his diary on 29 June. The next day the regiment marched twenty miles, camping alongside elements of the II Corps. "This is a beautiful valley," he wrote of the site. "Grain Reddy to cut."[29]

That day the Pennsylvania Reserves' field officers rode to Meade's headquarters. Their mission, Jackson later recalled, was to "pay our respects to our old commander, and to congratulate him on his distinguished position." They found the grizzled general "in close conference with Generals Reynolds, Hancock, Sedgwick and others. He seemed delighted in welcoming us back to the army." Meade professed confidence but looked stressed and acknowledged "that he did not know whether he was a subject of congratulation or commiseration." Morale was on his mind. One of his first orders directed that once the army crossed into Pennsylvania, commanders from regimental to corps level were to "address their troops on the importance of every man performing his whole duty in the coming conflict."[30]

The speeches were among the only breaks in the heavy marching on steamy 1 July. The trek so wore down the men that they started leaving items along the road. When the V Corps crossed the Pennsylvania line, Crawford ordered a brief halt, and he and Fisher both made short speeches to the Third Brigade. Jackson recalled Crawford urging the men "to exert their every effort in the protection of their homes and firesides, since they were now on the soil of their native State." Fisher, "always anxious for an opportunity to make a speech . . . gave us a most excellent and eloquent talk, which seemed to arouse the men very much at the time."

The First Brigade also got a speech from its commander, William "Buck" McCandless. Its substance may have been echoed in a parody performed by a Sixth Reserves picket during a lull in the subsequent fighting at Gettysburg. Having found a horse, the soldier rode it down the picket line impersonating McCandless. "He appealed in the most pathetic tones to the boys to remember their 'daddies' and 'mammies' and 'best gal,' and never to desert the old flag as long as there was a ration left." The performance ended when the horse threw the actor, then galloped over to the Confederate lines, to both sides' amusement. Regardless, both brigade commanders were good enough at public speaking to be later elected to the Pennsylvania state senate. McCandless went on to become Pennsylvania's secretary of internal affairs. Fisher moved to Wyoming and became chief justice.[31]

Once over the border, the men heard cannon booming, indicating heavy fighting ahead. Having marched about fourteen miles, the regiment stopped for a short break, during which rations and sixty rounds of ammunition were issued. Back on the road, the Eleventh Reserves continued through Hanover, where they saw the aftermath of a recent cavalry fight. The area bore "all the marks of a well-contested battle," Jackson remembered, "being strewn over with dead horses, broken caissons and sabers, and the accompanying debris of a battle-field."

Eight miles later, the exhausted regiment collapsed into bivouac at about 2 A.M., along with the rest of the V Corps, near a village called McSherrystown. The speed of the advance left the regimental wagons many miles behind. The regimental chaplain, Rev. Adam Torrance, had stored all of his writing paper and envelopes on them. He later started a letter to his wife using pages torn from a notebook.[32]

The cannon fire heard earlier came from the guns of Reynolds' I Corps and Maj. Gen. O. O. Howard's XI Corps, holding back two Confederate corps—led by Richard Ewell and A. P. Hill—on ridges north and northwest of Gettysburg.[33] The day's action saw Reynolds' death. The onetime Pennsylvania Reserves commander was urging some of his men forward into woods on McPherson's Ridge, trying to stem a Confederate advance. He looked back toward the road from where he hoped to see reinforcements arrive, then suddenly fell to the ground. His orderly rushed to him and turned the general on his back. A Confederate bullet had struck him behind the right ear. Word of his death reached Crawford by the next morning. He told Jackson the news on the condition that he not yet inform his men, "saying it was a hard blow on the army and country just at this particular crisis."[34]

Lee's army eventually pushed through Reynolds' and Howard's lines, but the rapidly concentrating Army of the Potomac rallied on choice high ground south of Gettysburg. As a result, Meade ended 1 July holding an excellent defensive position. Yet Lee's veterans were capable of overwhelming it the next day if the remaining Union troops did not hurry to the scene.

The exhausted Eleventh Reserves got only three and a half hours of uneasy sleep on the morning of 2 July. At about dawn—the Reverend Torrance's watch read 5:30 A.M.—Crawford got the men back on the road in response to an order from Sykes. By noon, the Pennsylvania Reserves and the other two divisions of the V Corps had assembled along the Baltimore Pike.[35]

Here Fisher's brigade rested, the men settling in a field about a mile from the battlefield. In front of them, the rest of Meade's army lay stretched in roughly horseshoe shape. On the Pennsylvania Reserves' left were two round hills not yet occupied, but which would become centers of attention within hours: the tree-encrusted Round Top and the adjacent Little Round Top with its slightly bald crest covered with rocks. From there, the Army of the Potomac extended along a slight ridge to Cemetery Hill, which took its name from peaceful Evergreen Cemetery, marked by a distinctive gatehouse. Continuing to the right, the Union line ended atop heavily fortified Culp's Hill.

Jackson ordered his men to examine and clean their guns, and more ammunition seems to have been issued on top of the sixty rounds doled out earlier. Jesse Fry took time to note in his diary that it was a "Pleasant Day." He and his comrades tried to get some rest, broken by sounds of battle.[36]

The sounds grew closer by 3 P.M., when Meade was trying to forestall a crisis in his line. Maj. Gen. Daniel Sickles had advanced his relatively small III Corps from positions along Cemetery Ridge, where he had previously formed an even front with the II Corps, led by Winfield Scott Hancock. Sickles had no specific orders to stay put, and from a distance the new ground looked higher than Cemetery Ridge. He also feared the consequences should the Rebels advance artillery there and undertook his advance at least in part to deny the position to the enemy. Unfortunately, the rise offered little cover and was in easy range of existing Confederate artillery placements. Worst of all, the salient was directly in line with an oncoming Rebel assault, which swept Sickles' two divisions back before his men had time to entrench.[37]

The controversy over Sickles' move would come later. For now, Meade dispatched Sykes' divisions to hold the threatened part of the line, upon which the III Corps had all but disintegrated. Col. Strong Vincent's brigade of Brig. Gen. James Barnes' First Division was sent to the summit of Little Round Top, the importance of which had only just been noticed by Meade's chief engineer, Gouverneur K. Warren. The V Corps' Second Division, the all-Regular formation now led by Brig. Gen. Romeyn Ayres, meanwhile moved onto the hill's northeast slope, then advanced across a small watercourse called Plum Run, which formed a small valley between Little Round Top and, to its west, another rocky hill later known as Devil's Den. It formed on the eastern edge of a wheatfield, sandwiched by woods to its north and south, through which part of the III Corps had fallen back. As Ayres' men moved forward to the wheatfield, they encountered the brigade of Confederate Brig. Gen. William Wofford. Behind Wofford came the rest of Lafayette McLaws' division of Longstreet's corps, entering the woods west of Plum Run. The Regulars' fight here lasted under an hour and ended with Ayres' men making a more-or-less orderly withdrawal.

At the time Ayres' advance was getting under way, the destination of the Pennsylvania Reserves was still vague. Crawford later reported that he was told "to form my command at once, and proceed toward the left flank of our line, when my position would be indicated by a staff officer." The Eleventh got its marching orders, by its chaplain's watch, at 3:30 P.M. "The order was given to fall in," Adam Torrance wrote his wife. "Hundreds of the men piled their knapsacks together & left them. The order to load was given. That peculiar silence in the ranks which I remarked on the morning of the 13th of Dec. was equally manifest & impressive."[38]

Fisher's brigade had the advance but battlefield confusion delayed the Pennsylvania Reserves' progress. When Ayres' Regulars turned off unexpectedly to the left at a fork in the road, Crawford suspected they had taken the wrong turn. With no staff officers available to direct him, Crawford halted his troops. While he sought out someone who could clarify the situation, the Regulars continued their march to the north slope of Little Round Top, from where their advance to the wheatfield began.

Crawford soon determined the left fork was indeed correct and brought his two brigades down the narrow lane that Ayres had taken. Ambulances and walking wounded from the III Corps were heading the other way, and the Eleventh Reserves and the rest of Fisher's brigade kept to the sides of the road to let them pass. When the Pennsylvanians made it to the right of where Ayres' men had previously assembled, Sykes told Crawford to take up the Regulars' old position. The red sun was starting to set, one survivor remembering it as "wrapped in drifts of lurid smoke." A battery was already in position to the division's left and a second was setting up on the right. Chaplain Torrance thought the regiment had reached this point at about 4:30 P.M. and recalled how "our artillery was playing upon the enemy & was receiving a terrific fire from their batteries."[39]

As at Gaines' Mill, the Pennsylvania Reserves would not fight this battle as an intact unit. With Vincent's men hard-pressed on Little Round Top's summit, Sykes ordered Crawford to send one of his brigades—half his division—there as reinforcement. Crawford responded by sending Fisher's brigade, but first he detached the Eleventh Reserves and left it in place with McCandless' brigade. The decision to keep the Eleventh there was motivated, according to Joseph Miller, by the fact that its smoothbores would be especially effective against the looming Rebel assault: "At this moment a regiment was wanted that used buck and ball and the 11th being in the position was ordered to remain where it was." At the same time he dispatched Fisher, Crawford asked Sykes for orders concerning the remaining half of his division. The busy V Corps commander told him to use his initiative.[40]

Accordingly Crawford ordered McCandless to form a double line here on Little Round Top's northern slopes. The Eleventh was in the center of the first line, the First and Sixth Reserves on either side; the Bucktails and Second Reserves formed the rear rank. "Our position gave us a complete view of much of the day's battle-field," Jackson later wrote, "including the wheat-field and part of the peach orchard beyond, together with the woods on the right and left of the wheat-field and the greater portion of Devil's Den, that stronghold so tenaciously held by the foe." To their right was the VI Corps brigade of Brig. Gen. Frank Wheaton, containing three regiments from Pennsylvania and one from New York. The view of the battlefield was so good that the hill attracted a number of generals, with Meade, Warren, and cavalry general Alfred Pleasanton spending time alongside Sykes.

The men were in this new formation only a short time—Chaplain Torrance felt it was only about twenty minutes—before they spotted the remnants of Ayres' division falling back through the wheat. They were pursued by screaming Rebels from the brigades of Joseph Kershaw, Paul Semmes, and William Wofford of McLaws' division. Crawford remembered how "fragments of regiments came running back without arms, and behind them in solid column over the wheat field and through the woods came the masses of the enemy." Adjacent Federal batteries shot double canister on the Rebels, who reined up along Plum Run, about

150 yards in front of McCandless' line, and fired at the blue troops in front of them.[41]

A Union artillerist of German extraction—Jackson remembered the battery as the First Ohio—exhorted the nearby Pennsylvania Reserves to protect his guns. "Dunder and blixen don't let dem repels took my batteries," he allegedly said. The veteran who recorded his words recalled that the man was an officer, but a modern scholar, Harry W. Pfanz, has demonstrated that the nearest artillery officers were named Gibbs and Guthrie, surnames that "do not suggest that either would have had a German accent." Whoever the man was, Jackson reportedly told him the infantry would protect him, and someone in the Eleventh's ranks shouted, "Stand by your guns, Dutchy, and we will stand by you." At about this time, a major on Crawford's staff rode up and stressed the seriousness of the task to Jackson, telling him to "remain in position and hold this hill at all hazards."[42]

Holding the position would come at a price. "We looked down over the field of carnage, and could hear the victorious shouts of the enemy," wrote a survivor of the First Reserves, "and when the smoke of battle lifted momentarily, we caught glimpses of fleeing friends and hotly pursuing foes, the general outlook being anything but assuring." In the Brady Guards, Miller wrote home about how "the lead was coming thick and fast, patting against the rocks like large hail stones." Rebel bullets dropped several men in the Eleventh's ranks. Jackson asked Crawford for permission to return the fire. "Not yet Col.," Jackson later quoted Crawford as saying. "The way is not clear of our own troops." Federals still bounding up the slope toward safety would be in especial peril from a volley from the Eleventh, whose buck-and-ball-filled smoothbores would do an indiscriminate swath of damage. The situation left Jackson's troops frustrated— the enemy fire "was telling severely upon my men," he later wrote.

After several tense minutes, the last of the fleeing Regulars "passed pell-mell through our ranks," in the words of one veteran, while the Rebels had charged across Plum Run and were at the base of Little Round Top. His view obscured by gun smoke, Jackson stopped a pair of fleeing blue-coats and asked them if the troops behind them were Confederates. "Yes," they replied, "those fellows are Johnnies." At about the same time, Crawford finally gave the order Jackson's men had waited for, telling the entire front rank to stand and open fire. The line fired at least two volleys—Jackson described them as "withering" in their effect on the Rebels.

Crawford, mounted on a "blood bay" horse, then ordered the brigade to fix bayonets. Crawford rode to the left of the line and grabbed the

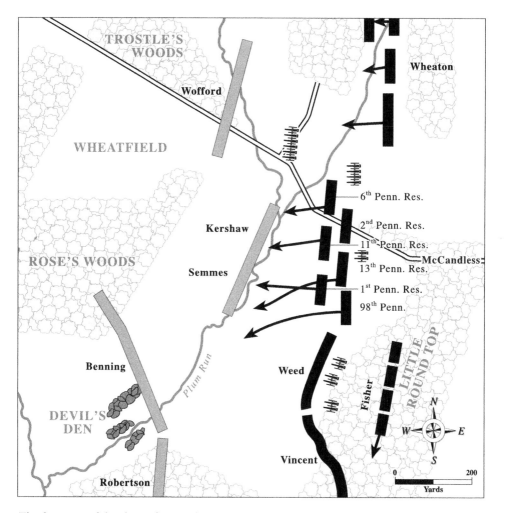

The first stage of the charge from Little Round Top toward the Wheatfield

First Reserves regimental flag from its color bearer, so reluctant to part with it that after giving it up he took hold of Crawford's pant leg and refused to let go. "Forward, Reserves" shouted Crawford. A member of the Second Reserves, on the right of the front rank, recalled how the troops fired a volley and then charged "with a simultaneous shriek from every throat, that sounded as if coming from a thousand demons, who had burst their lungs in uttering it." They also remembered the cheer, "peculiarly our own," in the First Reserves. And Private Miller wrote home about "a yell that echoed far and wide." Crawford himself, a few months later, wrote of a "terrific shout," one that "exceeded anything I ever heard as they dashed upon the Rebel hosts and drove them back."[43]

McCandless' brigade had help from another quarter. In the confusion along Little Round Top, a Union regiment from Wheaton's brigade, the Ninety-eighth Pennsylvania, had become separated from its parent unit by perhaps 400 yards—an enormous distance given the smoke and chaos in front of them. Using his own initiative, its commander lined up his 400 men behind and to the left of McCandless' double line. Although accounts differ as to the circumstances under which they joined the Pennsylvania Reserves' charge, the Ninety-eighth Pennsylvania was certainly part of the attack, racing down the hill with a cheer of its own, drawing fire from the Devil's Den but otherwise landing along boggy Plum Run in good shape. The Confederates were overwhelmed and fell back before the Pennsylvania units' combined counterattack. As Josiah Sypher wrote in his 1865 history of the Pennsylvania Reserves division, the Rebels were tough soldiers and victors of many battles, but their attackers here "were fighting on their own soil, with their back to their homes. . . . No foe could withstand a charge impelled by hearts thus nerved to the combat."

But this charge—joined on the right by the rest of Wheaton's brigade—did not stop at the base of Little Round Top. With Crawford leading the way, the men advanced across what would later be called "the Valley of Death." McCandless ordered his rear rank to fan out to the left; he shifted elements of the Bucktails into the advance on that flank, and they dueled with Rebel snipers in the Devil's Den. At the Wheatfield's eastern edge, there was a short struggle with Georgians and South Carolinians by a stone wall, the fighting being hand to hand and involving "the bayonet and butt of musket."[44]

McCandless called the action "a desperate struggle," but according to Miller it was short-lived, a "a feeble stance . . . of short duration, for our boys quickly dislodged the enemy and took possession themselves." Crawford, for his part, termed the battle here a "short but fearful struggle." The

Rebels retreated to positions in nearby woods, but Crawford had already directed McCandless to halt by the stone wall, which McCandless estimated was about 700 yards from the brigade's starting point on Little Round Top.[45]

As night fell, Crawford "directed Colonel McCandless to hold the line of the stone wall and the woods [Trostle's Woods] on the right. Heavy lines of skirmishers were thrown out, and the ground firmly and permanently held." Chaplain Torrance, who saw most of the action, noted afterward, "This successful charge has been highly commended by all the troops on this part of the line." Buoyed by the action, Crawford rode over to the Wheatfield, dismounted in the rear of the Eleventh's line, and sought out its commander. Decades later, Crawford was reported to have told Jackson, hat in hand, that "you have saved the day, your regiment is worth its weight in gold; its weight in gold, sir."[46]

The successful charge to the Wheatfield came at significant cost. The bill included the wounding of Company H Lt. James Fulton. The former Westmoreland County physician was left behind on the field after a Rebel bullet struck him in the right leg, passed through, and embedded in his left. Company I Pvt. Rob Roy McNulty came away with what was described as a slight head wound. Miller wrote home that in the Brady Guards, Perry A. Foster was "severely wounded in shoulder, by a minnie ball; R. Wilson Ramsey, slightly on knee by shell, and A. W. Perrin, on leg by spent ball."

Some casualties followed the taking of the stone wall, and Rebel gunners sent a few rounds at the new Union line. They had no effect according to McCandless' report, but a shell explosion partly deafened Company H Sgt. Benjamin Job, already half blind from the gunshot wound at Gaines' Mill. And at some point during the day's fighting, Company B Pvt. James Oatman suffered his third wound of the war.[47]

While McCandless' men dug in, Crawford spent some time tending to Fisher's brigade, which was involved in a complicated and frustrating series of nighttime maneuvers. The brigade, along with Col. Joshua Lawrence Chamberlain's Twentieth Maine, heroes of the day's fighting at the summit of Little Round Top, pushed Confederate skirmishers off nearby Round Top and secured the hill, along with thirty prisoners.[48] The climactic second day at Gettysburg was over. The battle's third, final day was about to begin.

During the night Brig. Gen. Joseph J. Bartlett's division from the VI Corps came to Crawford's support. Dawn broke "cloudy but warm," Jesse Fry noted. "We lay in front until a bout 5 o'clock all was quiet Except picket firing." Only the division's batteries played a part in the repulse, later in the day, of Longstreet's assault on the center of Meade's line. The doomed attack led by Maj. Gen. George Pickett came to dominate most contemporary and historical accounts of the battle, but there was other activity that day. At some point in the last moments Pickett's Charge, Sykes ordered Crawford, with Bartlett's assistance, to resume the advance into Trostle's Woods.[49] There the Pennsylvania Reserves ran into a surprise. "It was supposed," Crawford wrote in his report, "that the enemy had evacuated the position." But a Rebel battery was visible nearby and McCandless threw skirmishers toward it—including Companies H, I, and K of the Eleventh Reserves—as his brigade advanced through the trees.[50]

The Rebel guns started firing canister but fled as soon as the skirmishers approached. With the cannons gone, McCandless recalled his skirmishers and re-formed a solid battle line, then ordered a charge through the woods. Ahead lay another stone wall, behind which lay Georgians commanded by Confederate Brig. Gen. George T. Anderson. Their presence in the Eleventh's front signaled that it was again fighting troops in John Bell Hood's division, though Hood himself had been wounded in the 2 July fighting.

The Georgians had added rails and logs to their stone wall, and not far behind them lay the remnants of the Texas Brigade. But the Rebels were exhausted and McCandless' charge overwhelmed the breastworks. His men took 200 prisoners; a Bucktails sergeant came away with the Fifteenth Georgia's colors. The Texas Brigade, weakened by the previous day's fighting, withdrew (Crawford reported) "without firing a shot" and fell back toward Seminary Ridge.

The field the Pennsylvanians had taken was strewn with the previous day's dead. Besides one smoothbore Napoleon and three caissons, Crawford's men picked up thousands of abandoned arms. The Confederates had evidently planned to destroy some of the weapons, for McCandless reported finding many arms "piled on brush heaps, ready to be burned."[51]

More important, the charge's success restored dozens of Union wounded, who had lain unattended overnight, to their own lines. "Not one of our wounded had received the least assistance, and the groans of suffering and dying men were terrible," a newspaper correspondent recounted. A member of the Second Reserves recalled, "The poor fellows had suffered terribly for water, and had been robbed of all their money and valuables, and some of them of their clothing." Crawford had them transferred to the rear, where Doctor L. W. Read, the Pennsylvania Reserves division's chief surgeon, had set up a hospital in a barn. The images there, Chaplain Torrance wrote his wife, "were similar to those I wrote you about from Fredericksburg. I did not lie down till 2½ o'clock Saturday morning, & was up at 4 & again among the sufferers." Crawford's total losses were 20 officers and 190 men, with 3 missing. Of the Pennsylvania Reserves units engaged at Gettysburg, the Eleventh Reserves had been among the heaviest engaged, suffering 3 killed and 38 wounded from all ranks.[52]

The regiment had performed superbly at Gettysburg's most desperate moments. A few months later, Crawford wrote: "But for that charge on Thursday evening . . . the Key of our position would have been taken by the enemy."[53]

Chapter 10

Duty in the Context of the Cartridge Box

Falling Waters, Bristoe Station, and Mine Run

The Gettysburg campaign did not end with the repulse of Pickett's Charge. As at Antietam, Lee kept his army in place for a day after the fight ended, staring down the equally exhausted Federals. After Lee started to withdraw toward the Potomac and Virginia on a rainy 5 July, Lincoln prodded Meade to follow and finish off the Confederates. Meade, conscious of his own losses, enacted a cautious pursuit. The Pennsylvania Reserves figured in the chase after, as Jesse Fry wrote in his diary, being "relieved by the regulars of gen Sickles['] corps." Marching orders subsequently led the Eleventh Reserves (left in McCandless' First Brigade for a time) back into Maryland, through places like Emmitsburg, Utica, and Middletown to Fox's Gap.[1]

Nearing the Antietam battlefield on 9 July, Crawford's men heard heavy firing from the direction of Williamsport, Maryland, where Lee had dug in to fight a delaying action. Samuel Jackson's regiment encamped near Keedysville, where new shoes and stockings were issued. The next morning, the Eleventh crossed Antietam Creek, and at Delamont Mills they found fires still smouldering where the Rebels had cooked breakfast. Crawford sent the Bucktails out as skirmishers; they joined Union cavalry patrols in exchanging a few shots with Lee's rear guard. The Pennsylvanians kept up a slow advance along the Sharpsburg-Hagerstown Turnpike. It started to rain on the afternoon of 12 July, and although the Eleventh Reserves formed a line of battle at one point Jesse Fry noted in his diary that night that there had been "no fight yet."[2]

The rain continued the next day, the men digging rifle pits in the mud. As night fell, they formed in a field in front of their trenches, ready to move at dawn in an assault meant to bag the tail end of Lee's army before it crossed the upper Potomac at Falling Waters, Maryland. First light, however, found the Confederates gone, perhaps fortunately for the Pennsylvanians. "As we advanced," the historian of the Second Reserves wrote, "we found three long lines of most formidable rifle pits advantageously posted which the enemy had abandoned leaving many of their tools behind them. We also found a number of arms, and many prisoners were brought in, who proved to be the dirtiest set of mortals we had yet seen." By early afternoon, McCandless' brigade reached Falling Waters and witnessed the aftermath of a Union cavalry attack, which netted two cannon, three flags, and many prisoners. The latter included some exhausted stragglers who Maj. James Speer, riding in advance of the Eleventh Reserves, brought in.[3]

Late that afternoon the brigade set up camp and orders arrived that effectively ended the campaign. Meade was sending the Army of the Potomac back into Virginia, but by a different route. At Berlin on 17 July, the Eleventh Reserves crossed the Potomac, and six days later the regiment had marched as far south as Manassas Gap. By the end of July Crawford's division was encamped at Fayetteville, the rest of Sykes' V Corps spread between there and Warrenton, with the Eleventh Reserves back in the Third Brigade. The men rested, but there would be mud and hard marches to spare before snow closed the campaigning season.[4]

The rapid maneuvers strained the supply lines, and even in the good weather of late July the commissary wagons had trouble keeping up. James McGinley noted a complete lack of rations on 24–26 July. Crawford was incensed when some soldiers greeted him by chanting "Crackers." When he complained to Meade, the general known for using his sword on his own men allegedly told Crawford to dismiss the incident. "One night at White Plains where I marched the boys a couple of miles out of the road they actually called me a 'four-eyed son of a bitch,'" Meade is reported to have said, "and upon my soul I could not get mad at them."[5]

If the Brady Guards of Company K took war seriously, they also spent plenty of time coming up with nicknames for each other. "In every company you can find names strangely dissimilar to that you would know the persons by," Pvt. Joseph Miller noted at one point in a pre-Gettysburg letter to the *Brookville Republican*. "As for instance in our own company we have Plankhead, Cutting-box, Chaff, Tick, Rush, American Tadpole, Union Jim, Copperhead, Bad Bill, Long Agony, White Eye, Innocence, Earnest, Sea Horse, Paste Bob, Bald Headed Carpenter, Bummer, Flying Dutchman, and Japanese. There are a number of others but I have given enough for samples."[6]

A man nicknamed "Copperhead" seems out of place in a fighting regiment. The Copperheads were Northern Democrats who favored working out a peace arrangement with the South. They took their name from their habit of wearing the head of Liberty, cut off a copper penny, as a kind of badge. Their critics noted that the name also belonged to a poisonous snake. Lincoln's efforts to suppress them included closing down printing presses and suspending habeas corpus.[7]

Perhaps a member of the Eleventh earned the nickname out of irony, but it seems unlikely the moniker could have been given or taken lightly. The word drew only pariah status in letters home. A Westmoreland County soldier writing to the *Greensburgh Herald* referred to the "vile, cowardly traitor serpents [that] hiss at our backs" and vowed to fight "until the last armed foe shall breathe his last, and the last hiss of the last detested damnable Copperhead has ceased to sound in our ear as he sank down, down to the lowest, darkest, blackest corner of hell, there to dwell through ceaseless ages with demons and lost spirits."[8]

Such intense feelings brought some soldiers' politics under suspicion, even Jackson's. "I regret to learn that my policy concerning the great question which is now rocking this nation from State to State has been grossly misrepresented to my old friends and neighbors at home," the colonel wrote to the *Greensburgh Herald* earlier in the year. He continued:

> I am told that I have been there represented as being a strong advocate of unconditional peace, opposed to the policy carried out by the present Administration, and utterly disgusted with the proceedings of the Government both in its civil and military departments. This is false and without foundation. True, I am for peace, God knows. I have seen blood and suffering enough to satisfy my desires. . . . [But] I am not for peace as promulgated by [Copperhead-aligned politician Clement L.] Vallandingham or his style of peace men. I am not willing to shake hands with rebels over the graves of my murdered comrades, and beg their pardon; nor am I willing to patch up a temporary peace upon the grief-stricken hearts of twenty thousand mourning widows, whose homes are made lonely and desolate, with rebels whose hands are still red with the blood of those fallen martyrs.

Jackson allowed that "things have been done both in the Cabinet and field that I cannot subscribe to" and acknowledged having initially objected to McClellan's removal. "But would I (or any other loyal man who loves his country,) be justifiable in denouncing the legal representatives of the Government, merely because we differ upon some of the minor details included in the great machinery of this Government."[9]

Discussion about loyalty grew more heated as Pennsylvania's 1863 gubernatorial election drew near. Republican Andrew Curtin had a Democratic challenger, George W. Woodward, and after Gettysburg letters started appearing in newspapers claiming that Woodward had supporters in the Pennsylvania Reserves.

One July missive in the *Brookville Jeffersonian* signed by Brady Guards Sgt. James Elliott claimed that "every member" of his unit was with the Democratic candidate. But Cpl. Lemuel D. Dobbs of the same company took the unusual step, in his own letter to the crosstown *Brookville Republican,* of challenging his sergeant's statement. In mid-September, Dobbs underscored his views in another note to the editor, citing the Curtin campaign slogan that depicted the governor as "the Soldier's Friend." He added: "It is as necessary to defeat Woodward as it is to defeat Lee." Richmond, he wrote, would see Curtin's defeat as a sign that Northern resolve was weakening. He vowed that the soldiers of the Eleventh "will do our duty in the context of the cartridge box, and make traitors curs[e] the day and place in which treason was originated—Only help us."[10]

Curtin prevailed in the election. "Isn't it glorious to hear of the copperhead being defeated and old Andy reelected," a sergeant in another Pennsylvania Reserves regiment wrote home after the vote. "Wont he make the boys tremble the next draft."[11]

Any hard feelings between Elliott and Dobbs were moot by the time Dobbs sent his September letter. At the start of the month, Elliott was among the first of the Eleventh's soldiers transferred to the newly formed Invalid Corps—later given the better-sounding name of Veteran Reserve Corps. This was a repository for men disabled by illness or wounds who still wished to serve in military capacities, often acting as guards. In December, Dobbs arranged his own transfer, with a second lieutenant's commission, to the Nineteenth United States Colored Troops.[12]

Few details survive in government files about Elliott. After the war, he settled in Montgomery County, Iowa, with his wife, Margaret, whom he married in 1866 and who bore several children. By 1879 the former sergeant's health was poor. In early March, he set out from home, Margaret recalled, "for the purpose (as he said) of collecting monies due to him." He was never seen or heard from again.[13]

Dobbs' pension file shows that he was born in April 1842, in Buffalo township, Armstrong County, and worked as both a farmer and schoolteacher at the time he enlisted in the Brady Guards. Besides chronic diarrhea contracted at Belle Isle he had problems with sunstroke throughout his army career. He was shot in the breast and captured when his new regiment took part in the Petersburg mine assault—the Battle of the Crater—on 30 July 1864. The wound did not stop him from tunneling out of prison in November and making his way back North. A captain with Dobbs in the Nineteenth USCT described him as a man who "had no conception of fear," but he privately acknowledged to a pension examiner that Dobbs had a reputation for "dissolute habits," such as excessive smoking and drinking, once allegedly tampering with post funds to the sum of $50 or $100.

Dobbs brought his wife, the former Catharine Myers, along as the regiment took up different posts prior to being mustered out in 1867. Catharine bore five children, but her husband increasingly roamed, leaving her for months and returning only for short visits. They finally divorced in the district court at Marion, Kansas, in 1885. Two years later, Dobbs married again, in Holton, Kansas, and his new wife, Rhode, bore three children before her death in 1905. The old soldier was living in the National

Home for Disabled Volunteer Soldiers, in Chanute, Kansas, when he succumbed to heart disease late in 1918.[14]

While much of the Union army was basking in the optimistic glow of Gettysburg, former Company F captain Everard Bierer was fighting some personal battles within the service. Having risen to command his new regiment's brigade in mid-1863, he was disappointed at not being promoted to brigadier. Feeling he deserved a general's star, Bierer wrote in late July to Maj. Gen. John G. Foster, whom Bierer knew as commander of the Department of North Carolina, asking for "a Letter from you Recommending my promotion to be Brig. Genl. of Vols." As his regiments were soon to be discharged, he also asked "for authority to raise a Brigade of Vols."[15]

Bierer's chronic disregard for his superiors was coupled with an ability to make enemies among subordinates. At about the same time he wrote to Foster, a Union lieutenant serving as a provost marshal in occupied North Carolina filed charges against Bierer for stealing a mirror.[16] The episode is suspicious because the investigation and charges appear to have been brought without Bierer's knowledge. Plans were even made to dishonorably dismiss the colonel, evidently without benefit of a hearing. The order dated 8 August 1863 read: "Everard Bierer is reported a Colonel not mustered out by order of War Department—dishonorably discharged the Service of the United States."[17]

Bierer related the story to the Commissioner of Pensions in 1864:

> After I left North Carolina in June 1863, a combination of Scoundrels endeavored to fasten upon me the charge of pillaging a Looking Glass from Washington N.C. and entirely unknown to me until discovered by mere accident when nearly Consummated an Effort was Made to have me dismissed [from] the Service. Upon the Eve of publication of the order I discovered the attempt—got the proceedings Suspended—the Case referred to Judge [Advocate General Joseph] Holt, and the Result was upon a thorough Examination of the case, my dismissal was revoked and I was honorably discharged, my regiment having been mustered out on the 8th of August previously, its time having Expired.[18]

The result was indeed spelled out in an extract from Special Orders No. 431 from the adjutant general's office, dated 26 September 1863. "13. The dishonorable discharge at Expiration of Service in the case of Colonel

Everard Bierer 171 Pa drafted militia is hereby Revoked and under the Special Circumstances of the case he is hereby mustered out and honorably discharged the Service of the United States as of the date his Regiment was mustered out."[19]

But Bierer's bad luck held. Late in October, he finally heard back from Foster. By now, the ambitious officer-awaiting-orders was residing in his Uniontown home. What he received by post was his original letter, bearing a scribbled endorsement.

> Ft. Monroe, Va., Oct. 17/63.
>
> Under the present circumstances I must decline to make the Recommendations desired by Col. Bierer,
>
> J.G. Foster, Maj. Genl Commdg.

Bierer shot back a missive trying to clarify the situation. The claim of his improper conduct was, he wrote, "falsely made by some enemies of mine. . . . The Glass was given me under circumstances which I honestly believed and yet believe made it perfectly right for me to take it." Accordingly, Bierer argued, "Under these circumstances, having done me as I think unintentional injustice, and knowing Something of my Qualifications for a Brigade Commander, I think you ought to give me the Recommendation asked for."[20] Bierer never got his promotion.

Other men from the Eleventh Reserves were also being slowly destroyed, in body if not in reputation. Two years of war had almost broken Speer. Wounded three times—in the right thigh, right wrist, and left shoulder—the major was living with increasing pain and weakness. Late in August a surgeon found him unable to perform military service "without much suffering," and Speer summarily tendered his resignation. Adjutant Robert McCoy became the regiment's new major, his commission taking effect in late October.[21]

The next month, surgeon James DeBenneville, still weakened from his own illnesses, resigned from the regiment to become medical director of the Philadelphia recruiting board. DeBenneville, who had gotten married while on leave in early 1863, never regained his health. He died in Philadelphia September 1866, aged forty-three, at his 1716 Pine Street home. Assistant Surgeon William Lyons took his place within the Eleventh Reserves.[22]

Many stayed in the ranks despite their sufferings. Company I Capt. Eli Waugaman's rheumatism was so bad by December that, Pvt. William C.

Kyle later recalled, "at times . . . he was unable to get his coat on & off himself and required the assistance of some of his comrades. Heard him say at that time if he did not get better he would have to resign and go home. I know these facts from being with him almost every day in his tent and seeing him and hearing him complaining."[23]

Later in the year, James Burke of the Cambria Guards finally had the Rebel musket ball from Gaines' Mill extracted from his leg. Besides the lead, doctors removed seven pieces of bone from the wound. He remained on duty with the regiment.[24]

At about the time Burke was on the operating table, the war was ending for Lewis Johnston, hit in the leg at Fredericksburg. Rebel troops had picked the officer off the muddy field after Meade's retreat, transporting him to what he would later describe as "Libby Hospital at Richmond, Va." Someone here sawed off his shattered limb but did a poor job. "His right leg is amputated at junction of lowest and middle thirds," a Federal doctor reported after Johnston was paroled early in 1863. "The flap was insufficient, so that the skin is adherent to the bone. The two bones are cut of unequal length, hence he has not a good stump." Johnston remained in Federal hospitals until his discharge in November. The government gave him an artificial leg, made by a Pittsburgh firm, and a disability pension until his death in 1901.[25]

August was quiet for the Eleventh Reserves, with only occasional movement between camps near the Rappahannock. The weather was hot and sunstroke cases were reported during marches, but thunderstorms cooled the air. The sutler's wagons caught up to the regiment. The men also received an issue of tobacco—something they had run out of at the end of July—and camp rations were supplemented with apples, beans, and soft bread. James McGinley noted in his diary: "Got a Lot of comm[issary] Whiskey and Som[e] of the boys Got tite felt it myself prety freely." A few days later, he noted there was "a good deal of Gambling in the camp." The problem must have come to Samuel Jackson's attention, for McGinley soon recorded that Chaplain Torrance "preached this evening on the vice of Swearing and Gambling."

McGinley also recounted how "the Regt. Formed on the color line to hear the Order read for the Execution of five deserters from the 118th Penna [illegible] they are to be Shot to death with Musketry[.] Regt. Formed in line for to gow [*sic*] and See the sentence carried into effect when ther was an order came to postpone it until Saturday." At 7 A.M. on

the appointed day, the five were shot. McGinley wrote that the condemned men "took it well but one who became very much Excited."[26]

A deserter from McGinley's own regiment came back under army
jurisdiction that August but was dealt with leniently. Connoquenessing
Rangers Sgt. John Gansz had been wounded in the right shoulder before
being captured at Gaines' Mill. Released to the Union lines, he made a
direct, unsuccessful appeal to Governor Curtin for a medical discharge.
After that failed, while at Camp Parole in September he and several others sought leave from the post commander who, Gansz later claimed,
"sayed he could not Grant it but gave us to understand that we could go
provided we payed our passage ourselves." Gansz went home to Butler
County and did not return.

Seven months later, Samuel Jackson added the sergeant's name to a list
of deserters. The note, addressed to the provost marshal, stated that Gansz
was "Supposed to be at Evansburg Butler Co. Penna." The provost marshal found Gansz there shortly afterward, arrested him, and sent him back
to his regiment via a series of army prisons.

Facing desertion charges and a possible death sentence, Gansz sent
another appeal to Curtin. He acknowledged taking "rather a long stop" at
home without formal leave, "but I would not have stayed as long as I did if I
had considered myself fit for active service. I still have a secesh Ball in my
right shoulder and my left Arm is stiff. . . . Please intercede for me if they go
to extremes and keep an honest Soldier from being humbled in the dust."

Curtin duly informed Crawford that he had "no desire to interfere
with the course of military justice, but in case of Gansz's conviction, viz
consideration of his wounds and services, would earnestly commend him
to the clemency of the officers by whom his sentence is to be reviewed."
The governor's letter went to Jackson, who returned it to Crawford noting that despite the prisoner's long hiatus, "prior to his Desertion [Gansz]
was an obedient and brave soldier." The sergeant's life was spared, though
his rank was reduced to private.[27]

As the summer waned, the two armies again faced each other across the
Rappahannock. Both were weakened by detachments being sent to the
western theater. In mid-September, Meade was emboldened when he
learned of the extent of Lee's depletion—Longstreet's corps, a third of
the Army of Northern Virginia, had gone west. The Union commander
subsequently forced a crossing over the Rappahannock and Lee drew
back across the Rapidan. Within weeks, Meade had gathered more troops

and was set to continue moving south. But his adversary had gained reinforcements as well and planned a strike he hoped would at least wound the Federal army and force it north.

Lee's plan involved another wide-ranging maneuver. His two remaining corps would swing north of the Rappahannock and try to turn the right flank of part of Meade's army—a segment that included the Pennsylvania Reserves and its parent V Corps. Lee reasoned that Meade would retreat, and his columns strung out along narrow roads would be ripe for defeat in detail.[28]

The effort indeed sparked a Union withdrawal toward Centreville, starting on 9 October. While cavalry skirmishing took place in the gaps between the armies, the Pennsylvania Reserves served for several days as the V Corps' rear guard. Meade was, however, still unsure as to Lee's line of march, and kept shifting forces back and forth across the Rappahannock, trying to deduce where to meet the thrust.

This was another period of fluid leadership in the Pennsylvania Reserves division. Both Crawford (ill since the end of August) and Third Brigade commander Fisher were temporarily absent, their respective places being taken by McCandless and Martin Hardin. Perhaps because of this, relatively few documents detailing the Pennsylvania Reserves' service here found their way into the *Official Records.* But the diary entries of Pvt. Charles Minnemyer of Company D illustrate the period's hard marching. Minnemyer, whose name was rendered with several variant spellings, was a twenty-two-year-old wagonmaker from Evansburg, Butler County, when he signed on as a fifer with the original Connoquenessing Rangers in mid-1861. In autumn 1862 the provost guard for some reason arrested him and sent him to the Harpers Ferry stockade. Late in 1863 he became the regiment's principal musician.[29]

Of 12 October, Minnemyer wrote in his diary: "We marcht from ouar old camp at Rappahanock at day brak and recrosed the Rappahannock[.] Their we lay till 2 o'clock P.M. when the first devichiun [division] of our corps crosed Every thing appears to be on the move and a battel in progress." Later in the day, Minnemyer noted, "the [w]hole army advanced towards Culpepper and drove the rebel Cavelry back." Despite that local success, the Pennsylvania Reserves withdrew to the Rappahannock. The Third Brigade, now led by Martin Hardin, started at midnight on the 13th, crossing the river about two hours later. Near there, the Eleventh Reserves found its old campsite and got a few hours sleep.

Later in the morning, McCandless started the men moving toward Manassas Junction, halting for a brief rest about four miles from the Rappahannock, Minnemyer using the break to jot more notes in his diary. After encamping near Catlett's Station, on the morning of the 14th they heard cannonading coming from the direction of Warrenton. A Third Bull Run seemed in the offing.[30]

On this retreat for Manassas Sykes' divisions marched in tandem with the II Corps, now commanded by Gouverneur Warren. Both generals headed for Broad Run, which they planned to cross about a third of a mile from Bristoe Station. The latter was a point on the Orange and Alexandria Railroad, which ran parallel to the road leading across the river. After arriving on the creek's north side the Pennsylvania Reserves, bringing up the rear of Sykes' column, stopped to rest for a while in a field.

Knowing the Rebels were near, campfires were prohibited, but the hard-charging vanguards of Rebel Lt. Gen. A. P. Hill's corps had already spotted the withdrawal across Broad Run. What they had not seen was the II Corps, still on the southern bank, hidden from view behind the railroad embankment. As Hill's men became visible, preparing to attack across the Broad Run crossing and nip at the tail of Sykes's corps, Warren's troops cooly took up positions covering the road down which Hill's Confederates would come.

Across the creek, the V Corps followed orders and continued for Manassas. Sykes' first two divisions had already started off on the road, along with the corps batteries, when the Confederates began shelling the Pennsylvania Reserves, still adjacent to Broad Run. Hardin on his own initiative sent word for some guns to return, and after a quick consultation with McCandless "it was decided to remain where we were for the present." The men formed a battle line straddling the road. Rebel shells continued to fall, and in the Eleventh Reserves two Indiana National Guards privates were hit: Henry Powell was killed and George W. Lowman lost an arm. Minnemyer thought there were fifteen casualties in the whole division.

But the Pennsylvania Reserves did not meet Hill's advancing men; Warren's II Corps dramatically delivered a surprise volley at the flank of the approaching Rebels. It is unclear if McCandless' men understood how bloodily the Confederates had been repulsed, but orders came from Sykes at about 4 P.M. for the Pennsylvania Reserves and the cannon that had joined them to resume the move to Manassas. After they had marched about four miles, these latest orders were countermanded. Now the entire V Corps was to return to Broad Run, probably in response to Warren's earlier messages. The Pennsylvanians arrived to finally learn that Warren had, as Minnemyer put it, "rouded the rebels and capchard five peases of artilary and a lot of prisners."

The campaign did not end with that news. The Pennsylvania Reserves marched yet again for Manassas, getting a few hours of sleep after fording Bull Run early the next morning. The groggy troops then marched to Centreville, arriving at about 11 A.M. They finally got some rest after staggering into camp at Fairfax Court House.[31]

The Pennsylvania Reserves spent only two nights near Fairfax Court House. On 19 October, the division moved back toward Centreville, crossing Bull Run and bivouacing on the Second Bull Run battlefield. The place was still littered with Federal corpses. "Saw the Skeletons of men all over the fields," McGinley wrote in his diary, "the little dirt that was thrown over them had had [*sic*] been washed away by the rains." By the end of the month, the division was at Warrenton. It remained here for a week until assigned a reserve role in a relatively small fight at Rappahannock Station. Only 200 men from the Pennsylvania Reserves—the division's picket force on this particular day and time—were involved here. They were grouped into a 900-man skirmish line that forced back Rebel pickets and established a line along the Rappahannock. The leader of the skirmishing force did not specify which regiments contributed men to his command—at least 70 men from the Second Reserves drew picket duty later in the day at Fordman's Ford—but no casualties were reported among the Pennsylvania Reserves' contingent.

The next day, the Pennsylvania Reserves crossed the Rappahannock and found cabins built by A. P. Hill's men in anticipation of winter. They later found another such site at Mountain Run. Crawford, who had returned by now, started periods of drill. These had their own hazards— John Gansz "fell while drilling on the double quick" and was excused duty for several weeks—but it looked like the war was over for a while. The men were paid off, and had time to reflect on the fact that all the marching and fighting had left the strategic situation essentially unchanged since late September.[32]

Samuel Jackson's men may also have noted that they were still lugging .69-caliber smoothbores, this despite the gold mine of weaponry collected at Gettysburg. After that fight, Crawford had sent headquarters a list itemizing about half of the 3,672 arms his two brigades had picked up from the battlefield. The haul included hundreds of .577 Enfield rifles and .58 Springfield rifles, plus an assortment of lesser-quality pieces, such as .54-caliber Austrian rifles, more .69-caliber smoothbores, and even a pair of fowling pieces. Some Union Army regiments happily reequipped themselves from such captures. But quarterly returns show that Samuel Jackson's men kept their old muskets.[33]

The division remained in its new Rappahannock position only two weeks, for Meade envisioned one final offensive that year, a swing south across the Rapidan River to threaten Lee's left. On 24 November, Sykes started his divisions for the Rapidan, but heavy rain halted the movement and Crawford marched his men back to camp. Drier weather two days later brought a resumption of marching orders. After crossing at Germanna Ford, the Pennsylvania Reserves' two brigades marched for Parker's Store, a crossroads deep in the tangle of woods south of the Rapidan known locally as the Wilderness. The division supported Union cavalry during a small skirmish near there the next day, a shell at one point bursting beneath a horse ridden by Martin Hardin, knocking over both though failing to wound either. On 28 November, the Pennsylvania Reserves advanced in line of battle to Robertson's Tavern. The next day's march brought them to Mine Run, a creek that flowed south, perpendicularly, from the Rapidan.

Lee was expecting them. Eyeing Meade's movements, he had ordered his army to dig in on steep ridges on the Confederate-held side of the creek. One of Crawford's soldiers wrote home: "the rebels had a strong position and were strongly fortified." Any effort to take their works would involve a charge across a mile of open ground, fragmented by Mine Run's cold water. Meade directed corps commanders to scout out avenues of possible assault. Some data—though probably not optimistic conclusions— came from a lieutenant in the Twelfth Reserves, who led a scouting party out into no-man's-land to determine Mine Run's depth and probable fords. On the 29th, Meade issued orders for an attack the next morning.[34]

A cold rain drenched Samuel Jackson's men early on the last day of November. Prohibitions against fires meant that the soldiers suffered overnight, and some men in the division, though evidently none in the Eleventh Reserves, died from exposure. As dawn broke, orders came in the Eleventh Reserves to pile knapsacks preparatory to a charge on the Rebel works at 8 A.M. Occasional artillery fire punctured the morning air. A VI Corps surgeon considered the terrain in his front "the hardest I ever beheld. All along the heights could be seen battery upon battery . . . ready to belch their iron contents of grape and canister into the stiffened, freezing flesh of the best blood of America." Mine Run's cold water was itself intimidating. "Our orders were to charge right through Mine Run," one of Crawford's soldiers wrote home. "The Run the evening before was about four and a half feet deep and eight or ten feet wide. The morning was bitter cold and I knew if I did escape the bullets I would freeze to death after going through the Run."[35]

But as the same soldier later phrased it, "Providence ordered it otherwise." Warren, whose II Corps was to lead the assault, got another look at the enemy positions and decided an attack would be suicidal. He reported this to his hot-tempered commander, who likely railed inside but dutifully called off the attack.

In the Pennsylvania Reserves' ranks, the unbearable tension of waiting to charge was finally broken by orders to stand down. The men greeted the news with relief and smiles. The Eleventh Reserves' soldiers picked up their knapsacks and headed back to the old quarters across the Rapidan and Rappahannock. McGinley first heard the attack was canceled because Mine Run had been "found to be to[o] deep to waid," but when the fuller picture emerged the men had nothing but praise for their commanders' prudence. One of the few casualties the regiment suffered came by accident, when Lt. David Berry fell into a ditch during a night march. The mishap, he later maintained, precipitated a long-running problem with swelling in his groin and legs.

But he and his comrades were alive. By listening to Warren, Meade had avoided a second Fredericksburg. The men of the Eleventh Reserves went into winter quarters with relief and confidence, their onetime brigade commander looming large in the army's estimate.[36]

Chapter 11

Winter 1863–1864

After Mine Run, the Pennsylvania Reserves withdrew north of the Rapidan to Brandy Station, later crossing the Rappahannock and stopping at Bristoe Station. Here Crawford's men were to await the next campaigning season—the last of their three years of service—spread out along the Orange and Alexandria railroad line.[1] Writing to a Butler, Pennsylvania, newspaper, a soldier-correspondent left a picture of the Eleventh Reserves during this final winter in the field. "We have a very pleasant camp," he wrote, "our shanties (as we call them) are very comfortable indeed; they are built of logs about six feet high, and covered with shelter tents; we have good fire places and chimneys, and we cannot complain for the want of wood, as we have been well supplied with it this winter." Fresh bread, often still warm from the ovens, came from commissary bakeries at Alexandria. As a result, "we have not known what it is to eat hard tack this winter."[2]

Many men visited their families over the holidays. Samuel Jackson had not been home for fifteen months when he, on 11 December, penned a note to the V Corps' adjutant general asking for a furlough. "My home is in the western portion of the State near To The Ohio border," he wrote, explaining why he was seeking fifteen days' leave. "As much of the road will have to be Traveled by Stage, it would consume a great portion of that time in going and returning." He ultimately received permission to be away from 22 December to New Year's Day.[3]

The winter of 1863–64 saw something of a revival in the Army of the Potomac, thanks largely to the efforts of the U.S. Christian Commission, a civilian organization that, among other things, constructed brigade chapels and distributed religious literature. But Rev. Adam Torrance's mid-November resignation owing to disability—the V Corps' medical director approved it "as the applicant is 62 years of age"—meant that, for a while, men in the Eleventh Reserves had to get spiritual guidance outside the regiment.

Jackson found a replacement chaplain in his hometown of Apollo, and in mid-January Rev. John A. Delo, thirty-four at the time, took the oath from a mustering officer. Ten years earlier he had married then-sixteen-year-old Charlotte A. Buffum in a ceremony held in Jenks township, Forest County. By the time the minister marched off to war, the couple had three children.

Delo's efforts to spread the gospel in the Eleventh Reserves culminated in a mid-April mass-baptismal ceremony. On that day, musician Charles Minnemyer recorded in his diary, 130 men were "Baptised all soldiers of the Cros god grant that they may all be faith full to the end." Delo's religious conviction existed alongside a wry sense of humor. Once, when Capt. Daniel Coder, leading Company E since Nathaniel Nesbit's death at South Mountain, asked Delo to take care of a troublesome horse, the chaplain offered to lead it to a skirmish line in order to get it killed.

As with his predecessors, camp life impacted Delo's health. The Lutheran minister contracted chronic diarrhea, a severe cough, and what his doctor described as "great prostration of the whole system." He would die on 1 November 1864, less than five months after being mustered out.[4]

Dangers other than disease lurked in the winter, and worse things than a bad horse plagued Coder. At some point after snow started falling, a soldier dropped a bayonet on the outskirts of camp. The snowdrift into which it disappeared froze over, encasing the weapon point up. Coder found it while returning to quarters early in January after a visit to the latrine, stepping on the blade, he later wrote, "with force enough to send it through my leg." Assistant Regimental Surgeon William Lyons dressed the wound, which, Quartermaster Hugh Torrance later deposed, "gave him [Coder] a good deal of suffering . . . , and relieved him from duty for a time."[5]

The accident befell Coder at a period when, war notwithstanding, he should have been happy. Any disfigurement caused by his Second Bull Run wound had not dissuaded Ellen Ingersoll, the sister of one of Coder's longtime friends, from accepting the captain's marriage proposal. Back in Indiana County, Rev. Alexander McElwain married the couple in the bride's brother's home four days before Christmas 1863.[6]

Others in the regiment also had the opposite sex on their mind. Minnemyer wrote a poem in his diary about "My Emma Louise," but she, at this time at least, was uninterested. Former sergeant, now captain, Jacob Baiers conveyed that message following holiday leave, and Minnemyer noted receipt of a letter from "Miss E. . . . stading that all was trew that J. Baier told me tho i strive to think that she does not mean what she says my heart appears dull and cold towards her sinc[e] that."

Their mutual confidant, Baiers, had been a twenty-year-old shoemaker when he joined the Connoquenessing Rangers in June 1861. By now, he was suffering from the effects of wounds and would be discharged in April. His replacement leading Company D was James P. Boggs, a former Evansburg blacksmith, twenty-two at the time he became one of the fledgling unit's original corporals.[7]

Readers of the *Brookville Republican* learned of another soldier wanting a reason to survive the coming campaign: "A young man who has served in the Army of the Potomac since its original organization would be pleased to open a correspondence with some of the fair young ladies of the Wild Cat district, with a view to mutual improvement. Address Charles S. Brown, Co. K, 11th Regt. P.R.V.C., Washington D.C." This note was accompanied by the editorial comment: "Write to him Girls." Mysteriously, the Brady Guards had no soldier by that name.[8]

Marauders interrupted thoughts about romance. A mile and a half from Catlett's Station in mid-December, mounted guerrillas ambushed

Twelfth Reserves officers surveying the depot's defenses. Col. Martin Hardin, Lt. Col. Richard Gustin, and several others were riding the picket line, seeking sites for block houses, when five riders came up, approaching the Pennsylvanians on their left. They wore cavalry boots, black hats, and blue overcoats, and Hardin took them for a Federal patrol.

When he asked where they were headed, they opened fire with drawn revolvers they had concealed behind their right legs. One bullet hit Hardin in his left arm, already partially paralyzed from Second Bull Run; another wounded Gustin in the hand. Bullets also struck both officers' horses; Gustin's bolted and carried the rider toward a picket post before it fell dead. Hardin's arm had to be amputated, although he was not ready to quit the service. Their assailants escaped. By Hardin's account, besides a secessionist-minded preacher the guerrilla band included Lewis Paine, later to join John Wilkes Booth's conspirators.[9]

Another episode occurred in mid-February, when Crawford ordered the division's provost marshal, Capt. James Carle, to go scouting with a detachment from the Thirteenth Pennsylvania Cavalry. According to the report Carle later sent Maj. Robert McCoy, now attached to Crawford's staff as his assistant adjutant general, his riders chased guerrillas into a pine thicket opposite Cedar Run. The column dismounted to cross the stream via a narrow bridge. While the horsemen moved in single file, leading their horses, the Rebels opened fire with carbines. A subsequent, unsuccessful charge ended with seven Union casualties, one of the killed being the Thirteenth Pennsylvania Cavalry's major. The demoralized riders refused to attack again, and after forcing a few to recover the officer's body, Carle returned to Brentsville and reported to an enraged Crawford. A second force failed to locate the Rebels, though it discovered evidence that the Confederates had suffered a few casualties. The men reported finding "one dead body on the ground and traces (by pools of blood) of some two others having lain and being carried off."[10]

The hard luck of the Thirteenth Pennsylvania Cavalry continued into early March. On the 9th, a 40-man detachment was scouting around Greenwich when a Rebel force, estimated at about 200 men, captured it nearly intact.[11]

The Eleventh Reserves went into its final campaign without Daniel Porter. He had never abandoned his interest in a legal career, and at Camp Pierpont once sought leave from Meade stating, "I desire to be admitted to the bar." In January 1864, the lieutenant colonel applied for leave to care for his sick wife, Sarah, whom he had married just before leaving for war, and to attend to issues of personal finance. His visit convinced him that he was needed more in Indiana County than in Virginia. A few weeks after coming back, Porter resigned his commission, effective in early March.

McCoy, still on Crawford's staff, was commissioned the new lieutenant colonel. Cambria Guards commander James Burke succeeded him as major, with onetime sergeant Daniel D. Jones, by now a lieutenant, eventually assuming the captaincy of Company A.[12]

Archibald Stewart, first lieutenant of the Indiana National Guards, was also thinking about professional life. Three days before Porter resigned, Stewart wrote V Corps headquarters asking for leave to visit his brother in Chicago. "He and I are about to become partners in the Mercantile business," he wrote, "and wish to make some arrangements preparatory to commencing business." Stewart would die in the upcoming fighting.[13]

Some wanted to get back to Pennsylvania just to call Copperheads and others to account. One soldier in the Eleventh sent a warning to a stay-at-home critic. "Now I have a few words to say to a certain gentleman living in the neighborhood of Muddy Creek bottom, Butler county, Pa, who, we understand, has asserted that the 11th Reg. P.R.V.C. lost its colors, and with its colors its honor, at the battle of Gaine's Hill [*sic*] . . . and from that time it could not be trusted. . . . But one thing is for certain. If you live until this Reg. is disbanded, you will have to acknowledge that what you asserted was a big lie, and that you were the father of it, or else abide by the consequence."[14]

The same county's Copperheads tried but failed to dissuade underage blue-eyed, light-haired Robert E. McBride from signing up with the Eleventh Reserves, a decision made more poignant by his older brother William's death at Gaines' Mill while with the Dickson Guards. In early December 1863, on his seventeenth birthday, the younger McBride left Prospect—"a dreamy village of the olden time"—via the stagecoach for Pittsburgh. Upon arrival, he found the provost marshal's office and signed on as a replacement in the Connoquenessing Rangers. He lied about his age; his 15 December enlistment form, which gives his height as five-feet, seven-and-a-half inches, lists him as eighteen. Along with several other recruits, McBride spent a while at Camp Copeland, "then about the dreariest, most uncomfortable place I ever saw; shelter and provisions insufficient, bad whisky and blacklegs abundant." In late January he and a few others bound for the Eleventh Reserves entrained for Harrisburg, Baltimore, Washington, and finally Bristoe Station. After reaching his unit, McBride joined a mess with onetime guardhouse occupant John Elliott, the brother of one of McBride's childhood friends. McBride soon came down with measles and spent much of his early army career in the surgeon's tent.[15]

The regiment was gaining men, but the trickle of replacements was slow. Enlistment officers and recruiting parties found only indifferent success. Four joined from Allegheny during February, and on the fifth of that month the provost marshal responsible for Greensburg reported that six men signed up for the regiment but only five ultimately showed up to be mustered-in. Two more joined the next month.[16]

Some men found bad luck before they even reached the regiment. In Baltimore, on his way to join the Brady Guards, new recruit Pvt. David R. Hurst was accidentally shot and had to be hospitalized.[17] Other replacements were clearly not the men of '61. Mid-December special orders took John Silby, drafted from Cambria County in 1863 and a deserter from his original regiment, out of Georgetown's Forest Hall Prison and placed him into the Eleventh Reserves. His tenure there could not have been long, for his name does not appear on the rolls of any company.[18]

With Lincoln's recently appointed general-in-chief Ulysses S. Grant readying Meade's army for another try at Richmond, a problem emerged regarding the Pennsylvania Reserves. Some companies in the division had been mustered into state service within a few weeks of Fort Sumter's fall on 14 April 1861. Now their officers and men wanted assurance they would be released when their agreed-upon three years ended. The problem involved how the army was computing time in service. "The three years for which the men enlisted count from the date of their entry into the service of the State," Curtin wrote Lincoln. "They are now told, I understand, that they will be held for three years from the date of their being mustered into the service of the United States." Hanging on to the men for a short term would only create hard feelings, wrote Curtin, all at a time when the government was trying hard to get veteran soldiers to sign up for another enlistment.[19]

The issue predictably affected discipline. On 20 April, several men in Company G of the Sixth Reserves, citing their three-year anniversary, refused to report for duty. McCandless arrested them and threatened to try them for mutiny. Meade issued an order warning recalcitrant soldiers "of the consequences of refusing to do duty" but also told McCandless to let it be known that he was seeking a decision on the subject of muster-out date from Washington. He told McCandless: "Say to the men I expect every man will now return to duty and serve cheerfully till the time to be designated from the Department."

But at the same time Meade wrote to the War Department that "it is inexpedient and impolitic to retain men beyond the period which they honestly believe they are entitled to a discharge, and I would therefore recommend the Reserves be discharged from the date of enrollment or muster into the State service." He added: "It is of the utmost importance that a speedy decision thereon be made, as there are symptoms of disorder and mutiny appearing in this command." Meade did not get a response until mid-May, when the division was in the thick of heavy fighting.[20]

Nothing approaching mutiny emerged in the Eleventh Reserves, but there were signs of disorder in what was normally a well-disciplined regiment. On 23 April, the division's officer of the day inspected each regiment's camps and reported finding "them all well policed with the exception of the 11th Regt. P.R.V.C. which did not meet my approbation. The picket guard I found dilatory in the discharge of their duties and poorly instructed—some of them having no instructions." He also found the regimental guardhouse unmanned. Jackson received crisp instructions to "prevent the repetition of such reports."[21]

The discharge date was on the minds of many Pennsylvania Reserves soldiers through the upcoming campaign. Although losses indicate that the division often fought desperately, there may have been questions about the Reserves' commitment to the constant attacks of May 1864. As historian Bruce Catton put it a century later: "Who wanted to get shot, so near the end of his time as a soldier?"[22]

Another issue was that of reattaching the Second Brigade, still in Washington, to the parent division. "Can you not let me have the brigade of the Pennsylvania Reserves left at Alexandria?" Meade telegraphed Halleck at one point the previous summer. "It seems a pity to break up an organization which has gained so much prestige, and they are very anxious to be reunited." But the capital's garrison commander, Samuel Heintzelman, was reluctant to part with the remaining Pennsylvania Reserves: "The number of troops in this department has been so much reduced that it is impossible for me to spare even a single regiment unless immediately replaced by another," he replied, though he offered to "exchange this brigade for two full regiments." As two full regiments could not be spared from elsewhere, Sickel's understrength brigade remained with the XXII Corps.[23] Grant and his aides eventually entered the discussion, trying to find a way to release the brigade, perhaps to have it replaced by Veteran Reserve Corps troops. They ultimately succeeded in having two of the wayward regiments permitted to rejoin the division in time to take part in the next campaign.[24]

In the Eleventh Reserves, a member of the Westmoreland Guards stayed on the rolls despite his father's best efforts to get him back home. One by one, between June 1861 and December 1862, Henry, George, and James Dunn left their aged parents' farm to join Company H. After James, the youngest of the three, died from typhoid in camp near Bristoe Station in January 1864, his father decided to act. Then about seventy and almost blind and burdened with "a Sickly daughter," Dunn *père* enlisted a local judge and several attorneys to ask Governor Curtin to try to get George, his second son, released from the service. George Dunn was twenty-two when he signed up late in August 1862, and his father wrote Curtin that he was his "only support." The governor eventually sent his "regrets that a due regard for the interests of the service will not admit of the request of Mr. Dunn being favorably considered." The two remaining brothers survived their service, George finishing out his three years in the 190th Pennsylvania.[25]

A sense of the Eleventh Reserves' battle strength on the eve of the coming campaign can be drawn from its first quarter 1864 ordnance inventories. These figures serve only as an approximate measure. As about 400 names were on the regiment's final rolls, many seem to have been detailed or detached elsewhere at this time, evidently taking along their weapons and accoutrements. Additionally, no return was received from Company I. Interestingly, the same returns show that though the regiment remained smoothbore-equipped, a few men now had Enfield rifles—one or two each in companies A, B, C, D, and G.

Company	Rifles/Muskets
A (Cambria Guards)	35
B (Indiana National Guards)	33
C (Dickson Guards)	26
D (Connoquenessing Rangers)	24
E (Washington Blues [I])	25
F (Union Volunteers)	36
G (Independent Blues)	26
H (Westmoreland Guards)	30
I (Washington Blues [II])	—
K (Brady Guards)	39
TOTAL	274

Next to the word "colonel," the return also lists 18 Enfields and 31 smoothbores—perhaps this figure includes Company I's holdings—giving the regiment a total of 323 shoulder arms.

The rifles (in .577 caliber) reappeared in the Eleventh Reserves on ordnance returns for late 1863. Then, Company F reported having 20 Enfields; the rest of the regiment was listed as having only smoothbores. But by the time of the 1864 accounting detailed above, Capt. James Hayden's company was back to lugging the same .69-caliber muskets it had following Gettysburg and Falling Waters. Barring a clerical error, perhaps Hayden had been allowed to reequip his men from captured stores, then faced a new effort at standardizing arms across regiments. But if so, it would not explain the later presence of individual rifles in the other companies.[26]

Better weather brought more excitement guarding the railroad against partisans. Early one mid-April morning, a Ninth Reserves picket spotted some Rebels "creeping toward him." They ran off after he fired and raised the alarm. Later that day, three Rebel horsemen skirted another picket line and fired into a squad from the Tenth Reserves guarding a wood-gathering detail. They killed a pair of Federal soldiers—one was shot five times—before heading toward Milford. There they crossed Broad Run and surprised four Thirteenth Pennsylvania cavalrymen picketing a road a mile and a half from Bristoe. "These vedettes . . . behaved shamefully," reported McCandless, disgusted at the cavalrymen "abandoning one of their comrades, who was killed, and losing their horses. I have placed them in arrest and had charges preferred against them for misbehavior before the enemy."[27]

Such guerrilla incidents, and the tensions that must have greeted preparations for the spring campaign, likely had an effect on Eugenius Tibbs. Released from the Government Hospital for the Insane in time to serve at Gettysburg, he appears to have had a relapse during the march to Mine Run. It is unclear what treatment, if any, he received then, but his mental health was again in decline in April 1864. On the 22nd, he was readmitted to the asylum suffering from "acute suicidal dementia." His situation improved by early May, but doctors recommended his discharge from the army, stating that he was "not likely to become able to return to the service." On 5 May while the Army of the Potomac was locked in battle in the Wilderness, the hospital staff turned Tibbs over to his wife's care.[28] His war was not yet over.

Chapter 12

An Awful Sight of Men Cut Up

The Wilderness to Bethesda Church

The soldiers of the Eleventh Reserves marked the beginning of
the 1864 campaign with a small celebration. At supper time on
25 April the men formed a hollow square in front of Samuel
Jackson's quarters, and Capt. William Timblin of the Dickson
Guards presented the colonel with an engraved, jeweled sword.
It had cost $500, raised by the men. The scabbard bore portraits
of Reynolds and Meade, together with the names of the regiment's battles up to then.

Sword presentations were common during the Civil War. The Pennsylvania Reserves division as a whole gave one to George Meade after Gettysburg, and the Indiana National Guards had presented one to Daniel Porter a month before the Bristoe Station campaign. Now, in receiving the gift from Timblin, Jackson remarked that he accepted it not because he "merited it at your hands, but because in it I recognize another symptom of your devotion to that glorious cause in which you have been so manfully struggling. . . . You have stood by me, and with me, where none but hearts of steel could stand; and have ever willingly, and cheerfully, obeyed my harshest mandates. I am proud here to say . . . that no regiment in the Federal service has made a brighter record than that made by the officers and men of the Eleventh Pennsylvania Reserves." The men gave him three cheers at the end of the speech.[1]

The 25th of April was also the third anniversary of Connoquenessing Ranger John Elliott's enlistment, although he had not been sworn into Federal service until 5 July 1861. He drew picket duty that morning, and his messmate Robert McBride relieved him at breakfast time. When Elliot returned, McBride recalled, he was "in a more than usually cheerful spirit." Elliot told McBride he had decided that even though it was uncertain "whether the government has a right to hold me any longer or not . . . I will stay till it sees fit to discharge me. The country needs soldiers this Spring. . . . God has kept me safely through all these battles, and I can trust him for time to come." Ten days later Elliott was missing in action in the Wilderness. By McBride's account, his friend died in a Rebel prison.[2]

Meade fought what some historians have called the Overland Campaign with Ulysses S. Grant by his side. Now Lincoln's chief general, Grant was ostensibly there as an observer, but he was in fact directing most of the Army of the Potomac's operations. It had been reorganized into three consolidated corps—the II, V (in which the Pennsylvania Reserves remained), and VI—and accompanying it was the IX Corps under Ambrose Burnside. The IX Corps was nominally an independent entity, tactfully reflecting Burnside's brief tenure leading the Army of the Potomac, but it nonetheless factored very much into Grant's plans.

With Lee's Army of Northern Virginia too strongly entrenched to allow a direct assault, Grant envisioned a flanking movement involving what he hoped would be a quick march through the Wilderness. It was the same ground where Hooker came to grief a year earlier at Chancellorsville and through which Meade marched the army on the way to Mine Run in late 1863.

Before crossing the Rapidan, the V Corps, now commanded by Gouverneur Warren, was to form near Grant's headquarters at Culpeper Court House. The Pennsylvania Reserves' movement there effectively started on 18 April when the long-detached Seventh and Eighth Reserves arrived from Washington. By themselves, they represented the division's Second Brigade, but orders from V Corps headquarters soon dissolved that formation. The Seventh Reserves went to William McCandless' First Brigade, based at Bristoe Station; the Eighth Reserves went to the Third Brigade, now led again by Joseph Fisher and camped at Manassas. On 29 April IX Corps troops relieved the rest of the Pennsylvania Reserves from guard duty along the railroad, and the division marched to Culpeper, arriving the next day.[3]

The men had a few days before the next march. On 1 May, which dawned cloudy and cold but grew warm as the skies cleared, Chaplain Delo preached at 2 P.M. Afterwards, Charles Minnemyer wrote in his diary, the men heard a rumor they would be discharged "from the day of our muster into the stade serves [state service]." The news "gave the boys much pleasur to hear it," he reported. The division's returns for that day counted 3,460 officers and men present within its ten regiments.[4]

Samuel Crawford had been ill with fever at the time of the march to Culpeper Court House. He was back in command on the afternoon of Tuesday, 3 May, when Warren told his division commanders that the army would move before dawn. The V Corps, followed by the VI Corps, was to cross the Rapidan at Germanna Ford. If the roads were in good shape, the force was expected to proceed to the Old Wilderness Tavern by nightfall.[5]

At Crawford's headquarters, Robert McCoy drafted a circular that went to the two brigade commanders. Its points stipulated a midnight march, with each man carrying fifty rounds and the equivalent of six days' rations; a herd of beef was also to accompany the division. Fires were prohibited, and wagons kept to four for each brigade: one each for hospital equipment, medicine, headquarters stores, and "sales to officers." The rifle-equipped marksmen of the Bucktails regiment were to "habitually lead the column on the march."[6]

These orders arrived at the Eleventh Reserves' campsite late on a day which included company drill at 10 A.M. and battalion drill at 3:25 P.M. The men presumably tried to get some rest before starting to break camp late that night.[7]

Ahead lay an almost constant series of fights, and the often-rainy lulls between them saw heavy marching. The pattern exhausted and numbed the men on both sides, who saw firsthand that the war in Virginia was now a campaign of attrition. McBride acknowledged many of his memories of the period as simply "fragments of a half-forgotten dream, distinct in themselves, but without any definite connection as to time or place."[8]

At 1 A.M. on 4 May, the Eleventh Reserves got under way along with the rest of the V Corps. Warren's chief artillerist noted "a kind of weird excitement" in starting the new campaign with a night march. "The senses seemed doubly awake to every impression—the batteries gathering around my quarters in the darkness; the moving of lanterns, and the hailing of the men; then the distant sound of the hoofs of the aide's horse who brings the final order to start. Sleepy as I always am at such times, I have a certain amount of enjoyment in it all."[9]

In McCandless' First Brigade were the Bucktails, the First, Second, Sixth, Seventh, and Eleventh Reserves; Fisher's brigade consisted of the Fifth, Eighth, Tenth, and Twelfth Reserves. Moving without bonfires or torches, the units groped from their camps near Culpeper Court House through Stevensburg, Shepherd's Grove, then toward Germanna Ford, which the entire corps crossed by about 9 A.M. Warren's divisions then followed the Germanna Plank Road for about four miles until they reached the tavern, located at the intersection with the east-west Orange Turnpike. At about 3 P.M., Minnemyer wrote in his diary that "we have jest left the planck road." While the Pennsylvania Reserves encamped in fields, Warren and his staff took over "Ellwood," the stately home of Confederate Maj. J. Horace Lacy, in whose family cemetery Stonewall Jackson's arm—amputated following his mortal wounding at Chancellorsville—was buried.[10] Earlier in the day, Grant telegraphed Washington from Germanna Ford to announce the Rapidan crossing. He added: "Forty-eight hours now will demonstrate whether the enemy intends giving battle this side of Richmond."[11]

Crawford's orders on the morning of 5 May were to take the advance of the V Corps to a point about two miles south: Parker's Store, on the Orange Plank Road. The Bucktails led the division down a rough, thickly overgrown trail. At about 7:30 A.M., they broke through into a twenty- or thirty-acre clearing surrounding a house owned by a farmer named Chewning. The ground was elevated here, and the men could see Parker's Store and the Orange Plank Road about a mile away. They could also see that a force of Union cavalry—the Fifth New York—had preceded them to their destination.

As they watched, a brigade of North Carolina troops—the vanguard of Lee's effort to intercept Grant before he cleared the Wilderness—attacked up the Orange Plank Road and drove the horsemen along it. While the Eleventh Reserves listened to the action, and possibly got close enough to see some of it, Crawford readied for a fight.[12]

On the small plateau where his men halted, Crawford crafted a battle line of five regiments facing toward the scene of the fighting. His formation ignored the brigades' organization: the Bucktails covered the trail on which the division had come; the Sixth, Tenth, and Twelfth Reserves were on their left; the First Reserves was deployed at a sharp angle on the right. Samuel Jackson's command was part of a five-regiment reserve.[13]

Crawford's presence was unknown to the Rebels who continued to push the New Yorkers back. At one point, several of the Army of Northern Virginia's most senior generals—Lee, A. P. Hill, Jeb Stuart, and others—stopped in a field a short distance from the action. While they rested and conferred, two companies from the First Reserves came through nearby woods to the edge of the clearing. The startled Rebel officers, including Lee who was reading a map at the time, beat a hasty retreat from the equally taken-aback Federals, who were only about 200 yards away. A force of North Carolinians was promptly shifted to watch the trees; Crawford held his position and awaited orders.[14]

Warren had already begun to worry about the unexpected Confederate presence. At 7:30 A.M., about the same time the Pennsylvania Reserves arrived at the Chewning farm, Warren sent orders to halt Crawford's advance; he was instead to connect with the left flank of a V Corps division commanded by Brig. Gen. James Wadsworth. Crawford received the order at 8 A.M.; Warren's headquarters received Crawford's response, which included word of Rebels in his front, at 9 A.M. Crawford, however, was unclear as to his new orders, for at 11:15 he queried Warren: "Shall I abandon the position I now hold to connect with General Wadsworth, who is about a half a mile on my right?" There was confusion at V Corps headquarters as to the wisdom of Crawford leaving his position. Nonetheless, by 11:50 A.M., Warren wrote to Crawford: "You must connect with General Wadsworth, and cover and protect his left as he advances." Doing this meant the Pennsylvania Reserves would have to march back up the trail, then veer northwest, and find Wadsworth's flank.[15] But Wadsworth had already been attacked, and the Georgia troops who had broken through his lines began to show up in Crawford's rear. McCandless, in charge of the reserve that lay behind Crawford's front line, advanced the Second, Seventh, and Eleventh Reserves toward where he believed Wadsworth's front to be. As this force got under way, with Samuel Jackson leading, a signal officer galloped up to Crawford and told him that his division was now in danger of being isolated from the rest of the army.

Crawford's first reaction seems to have been to follow McCandless' vanguard with the rest of his force. He detached the Sixth Reserves from his battle line near the Chewning Farm and started it off in McCandless' path. But the situation between the two segments of his division had become fluid. A surgeon who volunteered to take a message from Crawford was captured on his way to find McCandless. Realizing that his force was effectively split, the Pennsylvania Reserves commander called the Sixth back to the division's main body. The halves would have to break out on their own.[16]

Those cut off with McCandless included Pvt. Elijah Bish of the Eleventh Reserves. Born circa 1844, five-foot-nine-inch-tall Bish was living in Knox township when he signed up with the Brady Guards in Brookville on 22 July 1861. He went into the Wilderness missing part of his second and third toes on his left foot, the result of a woodcutting accident at Fairfax Court House two years before.[17] Writing in 1890, Bish recalled that McCandless' three-regiment task force suddenly found plenty of Rebels blocking its path. Bish wrote: "We drove the line of the enemy back through the woods into the farther clearing, and were beginning to attack their main line, when Gen. McCandless came along and threw out our company on the right as skirmishers, as the enemy seemed to be coming in our right, which showed that Wadsworth's Division was falling back." A few minutes later, the Brady Guards met Rebel skirmishers from the Sixty-first Georgia by a fence. There was some confusion within the company as to whether they had actually come upon the enemy. Bish's captain, Edward Scofield, thought he spotted blue uniforms and may indeed have seen Rebels wearing captured Union items. Incoming bullets probably convinced Scofield that he had stumbled upon Confederates, and he gave orders to fire.[18]

By now, more Rebels appeared on the right and rear, and some of the Gaines' Mill's survivors may have had a sense of déjà vu. Samuel Jackson, likely acting under orders from McCandless, formed the Eleventh and Second Reserves in a new line of battle and ordered a charge through the clearing. It was a wild, reckless maneuver, and it carried them through the enemy. As Josiah Sypher described it a year later in his history of the division, "the men brought down their muskets and dashed into the hostile line with an impetus that broke and scattered the Rebel regiment and

—

opened the way of escape." The attackers' Union "hurrah" came out as a desperate scream.[19]

Connoquenessing Ranger Robert McBride recalled that the Eleventh Reserves met a particularly effective Confederate volley on this charge. One casualty was Pvt. M. F. "Boss" McCullough, a Prospect resident like McBride, who had joined the Rangers in June 1861 as a musician. When he joined, he gave his age as nineteen and his occupation as shoemaker. Now, McBride remembered, McCullough fell dead with a bullet in his forehead, "a portion of his shattered brain lodging on the arm of John Stanley, a boy of seventeen, who had come to us during the Spring. John shuddered, shook it from the sleeve of his blouse, raised his gun and began firing." Survivors agreed on the desperation of the action. Three separate accounts of the fight—Minnemyer in his diary the next day, Samuel Bates writing a few years after the war, and Bish writing two-and-a-half decades later—described it as one in which the regiment "cut" its way out.[20]

With the road back to Ellwood temporarily reopened, the Pennsylvanians retreated through the smoking bramble. On the way toward their own lines a new disaster was narrowly averted, according to Bish. "When we came back out of the woods in front of where the [Union] batteries were on the knoll the other side of the little creek," he recalled, "they were going to fire on us, thinking we were the enemy. So Col. Jackson's Orderly went up and told them who we were, and they did not fire." Crawford's division now re-formed with Wadsworth's remnants on its right. The Pennsylvania Reserves' left hung in the air for about a mile of shattered woods, back to where Winfield Scott Hancock's II Corps stood. The latter force slowly closed the gap over the next few hours until a ragged front was in place. At 5 P.M., Minnemyer wrote in his diary of hearing heavy musketry off to the regiment's left. In spite of the presence of many cannon, the congested terrain prevented their use, a fact Minnemyer noted.[21]

Writing years later of the episode at the clearing, Hardin noted: "The gallantry of the Eleventh Regiment saved it from capture. It charged right through the Confederate intercepting force." Not all of McCandless's units were so lucky. Left to form the rear guard, the Seventh Reserves found its path blocked by a small but determined force—two companies of the Sixty-first Georgia, just about forty men. With Rebel officers and men yelling orders to nonexistent regiments, this small battalion tricked the Seventh Reserves soldiers into believing they were surrounded. The unit subsequently surrendered.[22]

The price of the Eleventh Reserves' escape was high; the first day of the Wilderness ranks as one of the regiment's costliest engagements. Samuel Jackson's initial tally listed one officer and three enlisted men killed; three officers and thirty-four men wounded (some later dying); and four officers and fifty-four men missing or captured. From the entire division, only the unfortunate Seventh Reserves suffered more casualties than the Eleventh's total of ninety-nine. Minnemyer, who may have been slightly wounded in the scramble through the clearing, remarked in his diary that "there is an aufal site [awful sight] of men cut up."[23]

Losses in the regiment included Capt. James Hayden of the Union Volunteers, taken prisoner along with Cambria Guards Lt. Charles Fagan. The latter's captain, Daniel Jones, was killed by the volley that met the Eleventh's charge, as was Dickson Guards Pvt. Allen White. Indiana National Guards Pvt. William Hazlett was hit on his left leg. A surgeon dressed the wound, and Hazlett returned to the regiment rather than going to a hospital. Hazlett's lieutenant, Archibald Stewart, was struck in the arm by a bullet but was able to make his way to the Union lines. "Mortification"—gangrene—set into the wound, and Stewart died on 20 May. His father, John Stewart of Mahonney, Indiana County, sent friends to retrieve the body for burial back home.[24]

Company F Pvt. Isaac Miller was also among those captured during the desperate charge. About thirty-five at the time, "Ike" Miller was described as being of medium height, with sandy brown hair, gray eyes, and a fair complexion. He was presumably a good soldier, though he came across as unsavory even to the rough-edged folk of his native Fayette County. A postwar pension examiner, after interviewing people who had known Miller and his family, summed him up as "well known as a man of little principle and less industry" and noted that one of the soldier's brothers had been known as "Devil Fred."[25]

In 1860, Miller wed Rachel Lindsey, the illegitimate daughter of George Lindsey of Salt Lick township; her mother—known in later life as "Mrs. Hall"—lived on a mountain near Mill Run. The couple's married life was interrupted in July 1861, when Isaac joined the company Everard Bierer was forming. He was among those to get leave late in 1863, for a pass book stub in his name is preserved in the regimental files.[26]

After learning of his capture in the Wilderness, Rachel feared with cause for her husband's health in a Rebel prison. (He later identified his place of confinement as Andersonville.) Late in 1864, she sent a missive to the man she addressed as "abrem linceln." Although her letter lacked punctuation, spelling, and grammar, its anguished tone was clear: "I want you to get him acros the lin[e] and Send him home," she wrote the president, "for i have got 2 litel childern and no home of my one [own] and no mon[e]y and i am a Sickly all the time now." She begged Lincoln "for god Sake to hav mursy on him for the eny may [enemy] is Starven him what a wicked wurld this is to liv[e] in."[27]

A War Department clerk responded with advice on how to draw Isaac's accumulating salary. Although the once-fluid prisoner exchange system was now strained, he added that "the subject of exchanges is receiving every possible attention the state of the country will permit, and it is hoped that the release of your husband may be soon effected."[28] The words were not hollow. Miller's exchange was finalized the same day the letter was dated—13 December 1864. Six days later he was repatriated, discharged, and sent home to what must have been a grateful Rachel.[29]

While Confederates marched Isaac Miller and other unlucky Federals to the rear, the bloodied Army of the Potomac was still grappling with Lee's troops. Shortly after the Eleventh Reserves rejoined the main Union lines, Surgeon William Lyons detailed McBride to serve at hospital tents set up east of the Wilderness Tavern. The seventeen-year-old found the road there crowded with stretcher-bearers and walking wounded. He took charge of a tent with twenty-seven injured men, several of whom had undergone amputations. "They lay with their heads toward the canvas, a narrow path being left between their feet," he later wrote. "All that could be done for them was to give them food and water, bathe their wounds, and render any little service by which their sufferings might be mitigated." McBride was "astonished" by their reluctance to cry out, "except sometimes when sleep or delirium found the overmastering will off guard."[30]

But wounded men left on the battlefield who could did raise their voices. They were seeking not only medical aid, but rescue from fires sparked during the fight. Many could not be recovered—both sides' pickets were edgy and fired at anything that moved—and morning found them burned alive.[31]

The fighting on 6 May remained indecisive—Minnemyer described the morning as quiet and noted that the hospitals were being shifted farther to the rear. The wounded arriving in McBride's hospital included two men from his own company. One was Capt. James Boggs, who received a rifle bullet in his thigh on the previous day. The other was Sgt. David Steen, bruised by a piece of shell. Steen confided to McBride that he had started to dread battle; he would, in fact, not survive the war. Others also had muster-out in mind, for Minnemyer wrote in his diary of a rumor that "we will be discharged as soon as this move is over."[32]

Many Union troops counted the Wilderness to be a defeat and expected to be withdrawn, the usual pattern thus far in the war. But Grant still hoped to maneuver Lee into another fight in which the Army of the Potomac could crush or at least severely wound its skilled opponent. Orders came to shift each Union corps methodically to the left—Lee's right—heading southeast toward Richmond. If he wanted to block the Union advance, Lee would have to move fast, and get the most in battle from his numerically smaller force.

When Meade got the troops in motion at 9 A.M. on 7 May, the V Corps was to head southeast through the Wilderness on the Brock Road, its destination Spotsylvania Court House. Meade's cavalry escort got in the way of the Pennsylvania Reserves, who spent an hour and a half waiting for the road to clear. They stopped again about two miles beyond Todd's Tavern, at the intersection of the Catharpin Road, as Federal cavalry tried unsuccessfully to clear out Confederate horsemen, who put up a heavy fire from behind timber felled across the roadway.[33]

By nightfall the Yankee riders gave up the struggle, and Warren decided to try again the next morning using infantry. This, the first of several 8 May actions, did not involve Crawford's men. The blue-clad attackers succeeded in moving the scattered Rebels some distance along the Brock Road toward Spotsylvania. But near the fork where the Brock Road joined the Old Court House Road, they ran into the hard-marching vanguard of James Longstreet's Confederate corps (now commanded by Richard Anderson, Longstreet having been wounded in the Wilderness). The Rebels had taken up positions that straddled the junction and awaited the Yankees on high, broken farmland owned by a local family named Spindle. Union veterans later mistakenly called the site "Laurel Hill"—that title belonged to another ridge, a farm which served as a Union hospital after the fight—but the soon-to-be-bloody landmark kept that name. Warren now deployed Crawford to the left of the rest of his divisions. He started his next advance at about 10:15 A.M.[34]

This mid-morning attack failed. At one point, apparently just as the assault was about to get under way, Crawford was struck by a tree limb sheared off by a Rebel shell. Dazed, he turned the morning attack's leadership over to McCandless, who was also unlucky, as were the soldiers under his command. Preceded as usual by the Bucktails, his regiments and those of the Third Brigade (temporarily led by Eighth Reserves colonel Silas M.

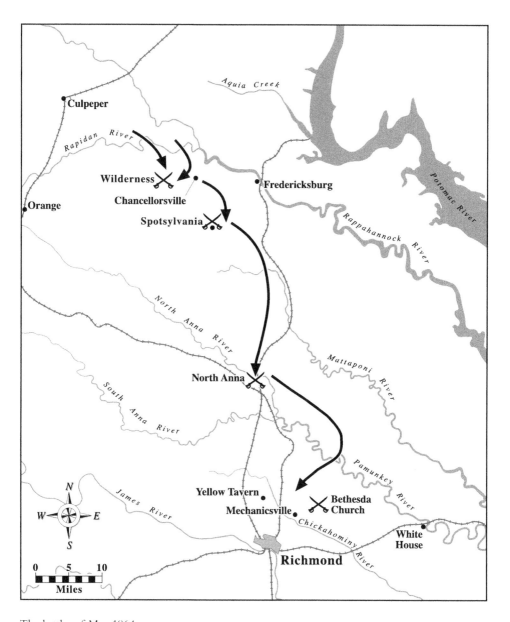

The battles of May 1864

Baily, Fisher being ill) slogged through a muddy, knee-deep swamp under heavy Rebel artillery fire. The Pennsylvanians overcame the first line of Confederate trenches but while approaching the second McCandless was wounded in the arm. Command of his brigade devolved to William C. Talley of the First Reserves. By now the division had become scattered and demoralized—"more or less disorganized through the distance they had advanced" was how the Bucktails' historians expressed it—and tumbled back. With Crawford still affected by his injury, Robert McCoy tried to sort out the division before resuming the offensive. Among his first orders was one commanding the men to fall back and rest. The men took out their marching rations and a few even tried to get some sleep.[35]

Meanwhile, with Meade pressuring him to renew the attack as soon as possible, Warren reinforced Crawford with elements of another V Corps division, that of Brig. Gen. Charles Griffin. With John Sedgwick's VI Corps on the way to bolster his lines, Warren still believed he faced only Anderson's Confederate corps. At about 1:30 P.M., Crawford (now back in commission) spotted Rebels moving to the left, extending Anderson's right flank. These were likely two brigades from a Confederate division led by Brig. Gen. Joseph B. Kershaw, earlier detained by Federal cavalry action. Crawford reported the news to Warren. The latter remained optimistic about the situation. "When Sedgwick comes," he informed Crawford, "we'll smash him up."[36]

The plan to "smash him up" called for Warren's and Sedgwick's linked forces to angle slightly to the left of Warren's mid-morning's target—further to the east of the Brock Road—turning or breaking what Meade hoped was Anderson's still-thinly-held right flank. If they could push through that bit of marshy, forested ground and reach the next farm, the two Union corps might end the day roughly a mile-and-a-quarter distant in Spotsylvania.[37]

But not only had the rest of Kershaw's division filed into the Confederate left, more reinforcements were due: Confederate Lt. Gen. Richard Ewell's corps was marching hard, like Anderson's had before it, from the old Wilderness lines. Its elements began to arrive behind Anderson's position at about 5 P.M.—just as the new Union assault was getting under way. And as the Pennsylvania Reserves advanced with parts of Sedgwick's corps on either flank, Ewell's battle-tested regiments began to deepen the Confederate right.

McCoy's orders placed Talley's troops in front and Baily's behind them. Again the blue line forded muddy waters, and Rebel skirmishers started a harassing fire as the attackers closed. The Federals got within a short distance of the main Confederate line before a volley halted the advance. McCoy seems to have ordered two more charges, both unsuccessful, and then the Confederates counterattacked. Darkness, thick woods, and gunsmoke limited visibility so that each side saw their opponents only after closing within a few yards. Talley was among the Union soldiers taken prisoner in this often hand-to-hand part of the struggle. At some point after Talley's capture, McCoy gave the First Brigade to Col. Wellington Ent of the Sixth Reserves. Ent subsequently turned command over to Samuel Jackson, whose commission date Ent knew to be senior to his own. Acting brigadier or not, by the end of the fight, the Eleventh's colonel joined his division and its VI Corps supports in their former trenches. Spotsylvania remained in Confederate hands.[38]

As casualty reports for Spotsylvania reflect losses over several days, it is unclear how many men in the Eleventh Reserves were lost on 8 May alone. At least two officers were wounded by shrapnel: Maj. James Burke on the head and abdomen, and Company I Capt. Eli Waugaman on the right knee and right foot. Both eventually returned to duty, although headaches tortured Burke and Waugaman came back lame. Both Burke and Waugaman also told old friend James George in Georgetown after the battle that they understood Brady Guards Capt. Edward Scofield to have been fatally shot through the neck, though neither saw his body on the field. Their story made its way into newspapers back home, but the information was false, for Scofield survived the battle and the war. His later pension claims make no mention of a wound at Spotsylvania.[39]

As night fell, Crawford's division held the battle-flag of the Twelfth Alabama and about 70 prisoners, if little else. For their part, Griffin's men reported taking 200 prisoners, including the colors of the Sixth Alabama. Before midnight, Crawford sent along some intelligence provided by a Confederate deserter. The man, a New Yorker forced into joining an Alabama regiment, told Crawford that the Rebels were strengthening their works and bringing up artillery.[40]

Rations were issued at midnight, and the V Corps stayed in place early on 9 May while the rest of the army inched closer to the enemy. Warren was now at the center of the Army of the Potomac's line, with Hancock on his right, Sedgwick on his left. Burnside's IX Corps had been sent off to the east and was angling toward Lee's right flank. Within Crawford's division, Samuel Jackson still headed the First Brigade. Given Major Burke's wounding, the Eleventh Reserves were at this point commanded by Capt. Daniel Coder of Company E.[41]

Hancock made the day's principal movement, crossing the Po River in his own front and edging closer to Lee's left. Some of Crawford's troops were engaged in another probe against the Laurel Hill position, but the Eleventh Reserves does not seem to have been involved. Minnemyer noted that the morning saw "but littal fiering dun But towards Evening there was som pretty heavy fiering on our left" where the VI Corps was stationed. That formation lost its commander, Sedgwick, to a Confederate sharpshooter that day.

John Gansz was a casualty in the Eleventh on 9 May; his left hand was so badly injured that he was sent all the way back to Fredericksburg. Minnemyer was also seeing the inside of a hospital at this time; an army doctor detailed the musician for medical service at some point during the Wilderness fighting. Accordingly, the fifer lost track of his regiment when it began the 7 May side-step to the left. He and other detailed members of the Eleventh followed a wagon train and on 9 May appear to have found their unit. Its parent division was clearly marked for coming action, with Crawford's force temporarily augmented by a brigade from another V Corps division. This unit, commanded by Col. Richard Coulter, included among its regiments the Eleventh Reserves' "non-Reserves" counterpart, the Eleventh Pennsylvania Volunteers.[42]

The 10th of May broke with the sounds of skirmishing to the Pennsylvania Reserves' left. Grant's plan for the day involved a series of late afternoon assaults all along the front which, if they could be coordinated, he hoped would break Lee's lines. Crawford's division would be part of an all-out attack by the V Corps, reinforced by Birney's and Gibbon's divisions from the II Corps, on the Laurel Hill trenches.

The problem was that while the action was largely a V Corps attack, Grant and Meade wanted Hancock to lead it. As historian Gordon C. Rhea has argued, this was a slight to Warren, who had been seen as more timid than prudent since Mine Run. The decision, and Warren's reaction to the snub, set a strange chain of events into motion. They began shortly before 2 P.M., when Hancock was rushed away from headquarters to deal with a threat caused by a Confederate counterattack. His absence now made Warren the senior officer on the Brock Road front. Even though the attacks were not scheduled until 5 P.M., the V Corps commander seized the moment. Evidently hoping to redeem his reputation on the offensive, Warren told Meade he felt the enemy-held ridge in front of them was vulnerable to immediate attack. He asked for permission to advance now. It was granted.

Warren was enthusiastic as he prepared his men, but those in the ranks sensed what was in store. A survivor of the attack described the enemy position—which Anderson still held in strength—as "a densely wooded crest, crowned by earthworks, and additionally protected by a dense thicket of low cedars." Crawford's men were told to give a Union "hurrah" when they attacked; they dutifully raised what one remembered as a "mournful cheer" when they moved forward at 4 P.M. Each charge—there seem to have been at least four made—failed, though some of Crawford's and Gibbon's men claimed to have reached the enemy's trenches before being forced back. Minnemyer acknowledged that evening only that "the Battel has bin very heavy all allong the line there was som pret heavy canonading on our left." As the Eleventh Reserves' reported losses were comparatively light for the entire series of battles near Spotsylvania, either the regiment was lucky during this attack, or else its officers and men declined to present themselves as easy targets in an effort few felt could succeed.[43]

The 11th of May was relatively quiet for the Pennsylvania Reserves, Minnemyer recording "som stray shots fiard allong the line." One of them, however, was an artillery round that cost Lewis Grossman of Company C, then deployed as a skirmisher in front of the regiment, an arm and leg. "He was a young man of great physical endurance, or he would never have rallied from the shock," recalled McBride, still serving as a hospital orderly. "He was as pale as a corpse when first brought into the tent, but rallied in a little while, and was able to take some refreshment. When left to himself his mind wandered, and he would talk as if he were engaged in the quiet pursuits of peace. Unless prevented, he would remove the bandages from the stumps of his amputated limbs." He died 3 August and was buried in Arlington National Cemetery.[44]

On the day Grossman was wounded, the rest of the division held its place while Hancock shifted to the left. His troops marched behind Warren's lines to position themselves for an assault the next day on the Rebel salient formed by Ewell's corps, a position known to history as the "Mule Shoe" because of its shape.

Warren readied his own corps for a supporting attack. His chief of staff went with Crawford to the right of the Pennsylvania Reserves division's lines, braving sniper fire to scout the Rebel position. Crawford reported to Warren: "The enemy are throwing up a line of breast-works in a parallel direction to my line." At 3 P.M., Warren responded with an admonition to continue fortifying and to clear trees as far out in front of his works as possible. Four hours later, he cautioned Crawford to be ready to extend his lines to the left, in order to cover space then occupied by part of Gibbon's command, scheduled to be withdrawn for maneuvers elsewhere.[45]

Soon after receiving this order, Crawford sent word that the Rebels were placing cannon "which will enfilade my line from the right." Warren told him to go ahead and extend the line, "even if they are in but one rank. I want this line thin, because of the enfilading battery you speak of. . . . If your men are attacked on the outer line, let them hold on as stubbornly as possible. General Gibbon will communicate with you when he wishes to withdraw, and you must replace his line as quickly as possible." The day closed, according to Minnemyer's diary, with "very heavy cannonading in the frunt."[46]

The situation changed little between then and about 9:15 A.M. the next morning, 12 May, when Crawford received the anticipated orders to attack. Before he moved, however, his men had to defend against a dawn assault, which carried all the way to the Pennsylvanians' breastworks. Having repelled the Rebels, Crawford advanced his battle line into a strip of woods which, to judge by his reports, separated his men from the Rebel entrenchments. But once his men cleared these trees, Rebel canister and rifle fire threw the Pennsylvanians back. Soldiers hugged the ground along the tree line while Crawford sent word back to Warren that the attack had failed. His note promised, however, to resume the offensive when the neighboring division, now commanded by Brig. Gen. Lysander Cutler (its former commander, Wadsworth, having been killed), advanced.

Pressured by Meade to keep attacking, Warren sent a terse response to Crawford at 9:30 A.M. "The orders are peremptory to charge the enemy's intrenchments at once with all your force," he wrote. "Do it. It is but a repetition of my orders." Warren apparently rethought his hastily written command and sent several new ones. The first seems to have been transmitted verbally by courier, and it gave Crawford a measure of discretion: If he could not assault, he was to send back Coulter's brigade for use elsewhere.

Yet the situation again changed because Cutler reported that "the right of his line [was] passing over [Crawford's] troops." Warren dashed off a new note to Crawford: "Do not fail to advance with General Cutler, if he does." But this new attack had already failed, driven back in part by the enfilading Rebel cannon.

Warren still hoped for progress. At 12:30 P.M., he informed Crawford: "The enemy is falling back on our right. Watch him closely in your front, and if you see the battery withdraw, or any indications of having left a weak force in the breast-works, try again to take them. Press them with skirmishers." Twenty minutes later, Crawford reported having "taken personal charge of the picket-line." The enemy battery had "been withdrawn down a little ridge, so that it can be loaded and run into battery out of fire of my sharpshooters. The muzzles are plainly visible. The enemy's sharpshooters fire at any one who shows his head. I can see their men occasionally above their breast-works."[47]

By about 2 P.M., Rebel counterattacks were being felt on other parts of the Union line. Reasoning that Crawford's sector was quiet for the moment, Warren ordered him to leave only a skeleton force in his trenches; the rest of the division would be plugged into other threatened areas. The tension broke long enough for Minnemyer, at 3 P.M., to note in his diary, "this morning the fight opened very Early and has bin teribell all day till this houar." Wounded were pouring into the rear areas; "the Bras bands are playing at the hospital to chear the woundet." As night fell, Warren reinforced Crawford with a heavy artillery battalion and a few regimental detachments set up as skirmishers. Picket firing started during the night, and at one point the Rebels exerted enough pressure on Crawford's left to push it back. On the right, the obstinate Rebel battery lobbed some shells into the division's rifle pits.[48]

Dawn broke on the 13th of May with Confederate artillery still covering the road to Spotsylvania Court House. Some of Crawford's rifle-equipped regiments were low on ammunition. Regardless, Crawford ordered his picket line "to be relieved with some show" of aggression. The probe revealed Rebels still thickly settled in front. The issue of whether Warren should renew the advance here went all the way up to Grant. "I do not desire a battle brought on with the enemy in their position of yesterday," the Union commander wrote. "We must get by the right flank of the enemy for the next fight." Subsequent orders put Warren and the Pennsylvania Reserves on the move at dark, and this night march leapfrogged the V Corps over Hancock and Burnside. By dawn on the 14th they faced a different wing of Lee's army.[49]

Minnemyer spent most of the 14th helping the doctors. At 10 P.M., orders came for the field hospital personnel to follow the V Corps in its arcing march around to the other side of Lee's trenches. Minnemyer and his comrades got lost in the dark and only caught up with the Pennsylvania

Reserves division near the new front at about 4 P.M. on 17 May. Martin Hardin had by now returned to service, having recuperated from the amputation stemming from the wound he received in the guerrilla attack. He was given command of the First Brigade of Crawford's Division, paving the way for Samuel Jackson's return to the Eleventh Reserves' command.

Hardin arrived just as Grant ordered another movement by his left flank, which as always began by shifting the rightmost unit around the rest of the army. As the units to his right withdrew, and his troops became the right flank outside Spotsylvania, Warren's division commanders sensed an increase in the number of local counterattacks. One landed in Crawford's sector late on 18 May, when Confederates attacked the remnants of the Bucktails, holding the crest of a ridge in front of the division's actual picket line. This advanced position was important because from here the riflemen could draw a bead on a nearby Rebel battery. This rare night attack, which started at about 9 P.M., ended with the Bucktails forced to withdraw. The threat of pressure on Warren's right may have sparked orders, given earlier in the day, for Minnemyer to move the hospital tents to the division's left.[50]

Minnemyer was soon back at the front line. The hospital staffs were ordered to report to their regiments on the morning of the 19th. Here they heard special orders which, as Minnemyer put it, stated "that all musician should stay with there Regt hear after and that no doctor had any right hear after to detail any musician." The order was issued in time for Minnemyer to take part in the response to an attack by Ewell later in the day. The Confederate corps commander's 6,000 men wheeled northeast out of positions near Spotsylvania and tested Warren's right flank near a farm owned by a family named Harris. The battle began about 4 P.M. and continued until dark. The Eleventh Reserves was dispatched four or five miles, at a fast march, as reinforcements to the Union line. The front held, however, and Jackson's regiment did not join the fight. Ewell's troops withdrew during the night, having been deprived of their goal— the Fredericksburg Road that ran behind Grant's army. Federal losses were 900; Ewell lost 1,250 killed and wounded, plus 500 taken prisoner.[51]

Seen in terms of prisoners taken, the Pennsylvania Reserves' role in the fight at the Harris farm was relatively small, accounting for only 12 of the 116 captives sent to army headquarters. But Warren, in ordering Crawford to forward a list of the previous day's casualties "without delay," also noted that "Orders complimenting the troops for their conduct yesterday are sent." The next morning, the Eleventh Reserves moved about a half mile toward the Rebels, apparently to ensure the front was clear, then turned about and marched back to its former campsite. Although picket-line truces and trade resumed on the 20th, when the Eleventh Reserves went on picket the next day its men found no sign of the enemy. "The report is that the rebels are retreating," Minnemyer wrote. "We starded after them about 11 o clock and marcht hard all day." During this pursuit, the Pennsylvania Reserves came under artillery fire after crossing a stream south of Guiney's Station. The division took cover behind a ridge, and after two more hours of ineffective shelling the enemy gunners withdrew. Crawford's division took the high ground they left behind.

From history's vantage point the Battle of Spotsylvania was over, and a new phase of the Overland Campaign was beginning. Lee was withdrawing to a new defensive line about twenty miles south, behind the North Anna River near Hanover Junction, a stop on the Richmond, Fredericksburg, and Potomac Railroad. Those coherent enough to keep count after days of fighting and marching may have noted that the Eleventh Reserves' losses had been relatively light between 8 and 21 May: one killed, seven wounded, and one missing.

Samuel Jackson's veterans bagged eight more prisoners during the eight-mile march on 22 May in pursuit of Lee; their division as a whole collected several hundred. That evening, the Eleventh Reserves camped near an old mill. But even with scores of worn-out Rebel stragglers willingly surrendering, the next day promised another fight.[52]

A week earlier, the War Department announced an amended decision on computing the release date for the Pennsylvania Reserves. Seth Williams, the army's assistant adjutant general, wrote Warren that the division was now authorized to be removed as a whole from the front on the last day of the month. This was subject to one condition: that those men "entitled to their discharge before the 31st of May [e.g., whose third anniversary of state service fell before then] shall agree to serve with this army until that date." The 31st of May marked an approximate median exit date for regiments that would otherwise "be discharged between now and the 20th of June."

The compromise was probably cheered around many campfires, but it did no good for the Eighth Reserves, whose three years of state service finished the day before the message came. Warren and Crawford respectfully hinted to Meade that the unit, down to only about seventy-five men, might be sent home without affecting operations. Meade consented, and the skeletal Eighth left the front. Some of the units left behind seem to have misunderstood the new timeline; the Bucktails' historians, for instance, thought their regiment was entitled to leave on 29 May.[53]

At 5 A.M. on 23 May, the Pennsylvania Reserves division, now including Col. J. Howard Kitching's brigade of two untested heavy artillery-turned-infantry regiments, joined the V Corps in marching due south. Warren's divisions crossed the North Anna River at Jericho Mills, and by 3 P.M. Crawford's men halted along Beaver Dam Creek. The namesake of the Chickahominy offshoot of Mechanicsville fame—the latter lying about thirty miles southeast—Beaver Dam Creek also lent its name to a station on the Virginia Central Railroad. "There is som fighting on our left," Minnemyer wrote in his diary at this time. The regiment soon got orders to form a line of battle, and then the men were told to lie down. In a while, the firing on the left grew more intense, and the regiment marched to the top of a nearby hill. About a mile away were the entrenchments of A. P. Hill's Confederate corps.

At about 6 P.M., Hill launched the attack he hoped would drive Warren's divisions back across, or into, the North Anna. Minnemyer felt the artillery fire that preceded the infantry assault was "the grates fier on us that ever i exspearanst." Others classified it less grand, remembering the barrage that preceded Pickett's Charge. The Rebel gunners targeted, among other things, an ice house that served as First Brigade headquarters. A shell unhorsed Hardin.

But Hill's attacks were poorly coordinated—Lee was ill at the time and unable to personally oversee the fight. Minnemyer wrote, "our men stad firm and our batteris silenst them after som hard fighting." The Rebel charges were repulsed, and the Pennsylvania Reserves division took 400 prisoners, many from South Carolina units. Once the Confederates withdrew, the V Corps spent the rest of the night improving its trenches to prepare to resist another attack. Men were detailed from the Eleventh Reserves to get rations, but it took Minnemyer and others all night to distribute them.[54]

Facing Lee's always-formidable defenses, Grant decided again to shift by his left flank and sidestep the Army of Northern Virginia. While the Army of the Potomac maneuvered, the 24th saw action by the First Reserves at Ox Ford; the 25th passed with just "a littal scrimishen" by Minnemyer's account as the Pennsylvania Reserves advanced alongside a division from the IX Corps. At 7 P.M. on the 26th, Jackson received word of a night march to the southeast, and the men were ordered to avoid unnecessary noise. At 10 P.M., the Pennsylvania Reserves disengaged from the front. After marching about a mile and crossing the North Anna River with the rest of the brigade, the Eleventh Reserves drew rations as dawn broke. The regiment marched another eight miles southeast, stopped for lunch, then marched for the rest of the day with just a short break for coffee. Samuel Jackson's men camped for the night of the 26th in a thick pine forest.[55]

The next two days were spent edging toward Richmond. At about noon on Saturday, 28 May, Hardin's brigade crossed the Pamunkey River at Hanovertown, some two dozen miles upstream from the old White House Landing base. The Eleventh Reserves dug rifle pits and stayed there overnight. The regiment learned early next morning that it was to resume movement at 5 A.M., but it was 9 A.M. before Jackson's men took up the march, and then for only a mile before halting. They were still lying at the roadside by noon, when Minnemyer finished his diary entry.[56]

There were several reasons for the stalled movement of the Army of the Potomac on the 29th. Meade was having trouble sorting out corps movements; with the IX Corps being interposed between Hancock and Warren, Burnside's men frequently blocked roads needed by the V Corps. Another factor was the inability to locate Lee's army. Philip Sheridan's Union cavalry was recuperating from clashes on the previous two days. In the interim, Grant used infantry to reconnoiter, Meade ordering each corps commander to send a division forward to scout. Warren complied using Griffin's division, the force later supplanted with one of Crawford's regiments on either flank, and he went forward personally to inspect the front along Totopotomoy Creek. Griffin had found enough Rebels to make Warren conclude that an advance across the Totopotomoy would require coordination and support among several corps, which would have difficult terrain between them.[57]

The 30th of May also broke with early orders to march, and another four-hour delay. Samuel Jackson's men started their short advance to the Totopotomoy at 11 A.M. After crossing along with the rest of the V Corps, Warren found Lee in his front in strength. The Eleventh formed a line of battle here, and a plan for attack developed. Warren sent Griffin's division on the Shady Grove Road, which led directly to Richmond, a pike brimming with expected opposition. To their left, Crawford's Penn-sylvania Reserves were to keep in touch with Griffin's flank and advance about a mile down the rough Walnut Grove Road to the Old Church or

Mechanicsville Road. In front of Crawford was a strip of woods, beyond it a force of Rebel cavalry, and behind them stood Ewell's old corps, now being led by Confederate Maj. Gen. Jubal Early.[58] The fight that was about to commence would be named for Bethesda Church, which lay southeast of the crossroads. Hours earlier—at 5 A.M.—Warren had reminded Burnside to have men of the IX Corps ready to replace the Pennsylvania Reserves division, "who have to be relieved to-day on account of the expiration of their term of service."[59]

The air punctuated with Rebel artillery shots, the men of the Eleventh Reserves lay on their arms in battle formation for about an hour before another order came to advance. Elements of Fisher's Third Brigade—the Fifth and Tenth Reserves—failed in separate attempts to clear the Rebels from the trees. Now all of Hardin's First Brigade formed into battle line to do the job right, though by Hardin's account the breechloader-equipped Bucktails did most of the fighting. Their success brought the Eleventh Reserves and the rest of its parent brigade to the Old Church/Mechanicsville Road. Men conscious of this being their last day of service observed that it was only about six miles to Mechanicsville itself, where the first of the Seven Days' battles took place.

This reconnaissance-in-force put the men into position a half-mile forward of the rest of the division. Hardin later recounted that he sent back word that his unit "having accomplished the object of its reconnaissance, should be withdrawn. The answer was to hold on where the brigade was, but no reinforcements came up." Robert McCoy rode up to inspect the scene himself, then left to help fetch Kitching's brigade. Meanwhile, Hardin's men dug in, as experience had taught them, tearing down fences and piling the rails into breastworks. They worked quickly, sensing a Rebel attack brewing in their front.[60]

Put very briefly, the coming Confederate counterattack was a direct result of the lack of coordination among the Union units crossing the Totopotomoy. At this point, the Federal V Corps was essentially alone on the creek's south side; its commander was sending out aides trying to locate Hancock or Burnside, either of whose corps Warren had expected to have on his left. Informed of Warren's exposed position, Lee told Early that he had the freedom to attack at his discretion. The grizzled Confederate corps commander opted to use it.[61]

As McCoy tried to get Kitching's brigade on the move, gunfire from Early's skirmishers heralded an attacking column headed straight for Hardin. In his front, the Bucktails bought some time for his regiments to improve their rifle pits. Although well-armed with breechloading repeaters, the

Bucktails could not hold the Confederates back forever, and the screaming Rebels soon approached the half-built Union breastworks, which Minnemyer described as "of a pour Contriving." The Pennsylvanians' defensive
fire was ineffective, Hardin recalling, "The volley or two delivered by our
feeble force made no impression on the enemy; he ran over and around the
piles of rails, and his division headquarters arrived amidst the headquarters
of the First Brigade before the latter could extricate itself."

With no support on either flank, Hardin's brigade appears to have
been nearly routed, beating a hasty retreat across a field and back into the
woods. A Second Reserves officer, echoing a contemporary newspaper
account nearly word-for-word, later wrote, "We retired slowly for three-
quarters of a mile, delivering so steady and heavy a skirmish fire that the
enemy did not follow us vigorously." An officer in the First Reserves
remembered it differently: "Such skedadling to the rear was never seen
before, 'every man for himself, the de'il take the hindmost.'"[62]

The casualties left behind included Benjamin Job. Although previous
fights had left Job half-blind and partly deaf, early in the year Samuel
Jackson recommended the then-sergeant for promotion to captain of
Company H, a post he took in March. In the fight here near the Mechanicsville Road, a piece of shell struck the twenty-two-year-old officer on
the pelvis. Left on the field, Confederate troops took him prisoner for
the second time in the war. In the Connoquenessing Rangers, Cpl.
David S. Parks was mortally wounded and Cpl. Daniel Graham captured.
Pvt. John Stanley, splattered by brains in the Wilderness, was wounded in
the arm and side—two of his comrades carried him, pale but calm, back
to safety.[63]

Hardin's regiments were in an open field, trying to regroup, by the
time McCoy appeared. He brought Kitching's "Independent Brigade" in
tow on what, once Hardin's disorganized men faced about, would be
their left. Fisher's Third Brigade was not far behind them, coming up
behind Hardin's other flank and taking up positions in a ravine. A battery
was also to hand, and a pair of cannon was set on high ground on either
side of Hardin's section.

There must have been a significant pause in the action because here,
Minnemyer wrote, the Eleventh Reserves had enough time to put up
new rifle pits, "better on[e]s then those before," fence rails and logs with
dirt thrown over them. When Early's skirmishers finally appeared in their
front, some of the new men in Kitching's brigade showed their inexperi-
ence by refusing Hardin's entreaties to lie down. They preferred to stand
and fight, and would soon become targets. Hardin solved the problem by

suggesting to their commander a new configuration for the spot where the brigades' lines met. Those preparations made by about 5 P.M., the Pennsylvania Reserves—about 2,500 men, perhaps a fifth of the division's original complement—awaited the last attack they were to face in the war.[64]

It was about an hour later, at roughly 6 P.M., that Early's assault column stepped off into one of the most disastrous offensive actions of the war. Hardin overestimated the attacking force's size as about 5,000 men. It was in fact a single, much-depleted brigade of 1,000 men.

The Rebels quickly sensed the odds before them. Confederate survivor C. B. Christian later wrote that once the brigade approached the Pennsylvanians' lines, "the enemy opened with the heaviest and most murderous fire I had ever seen with grape, canister and musketry. Our veterans of a hundred fights knew at a glance that they were marching up to die, rather than to waver. Our line melted away as if by magic—every brigade, staff and field officer was cut down, (mostly killed outright) in an incredibly short time." Confederate officer casualties were ultimately figured at about 90 percent.

Still, the Rebels charged courageously, firing volleys, closing up gore-filled gaps in the ranks caused by the four Union cannon. Rebel gunners made their presence felt in the Eleventh Reserves. Shell fragments struck and severed the flagstaff held by Company D Cpl. James B. Shafer; earlier in the day the same Connoquenessing Ranger just missed being hit by a minié bullet. Shrapnel also tore the forage cap of Company E Pvt. Michael Coleman, and McBride remembered a shell splinter that tore the arm off a man named Culp, though that name does not appear in the regimental rolls. Another shell set fire to a house behind the line. Soldiers helped its occupants—a woman, a baby, and a small child—to safety.

Then the gray mass neared the trenches. Christian remembered how "men who usually charged with the 'rebel yell' rushed on in silence." When the attackers were 150 yards from the Union breastworks, the Eleventh Reserves joined in on a volley that tore the enemy apart. The shattered Rebels somehow managed to re-form and repeat the effort twice, each time their color-bearers being among the first to fall. After the third charge evaporated, Union officers stood up on the firing line and called on the surviving Confederates to surrender. Many were helped into the Union trenches, where their captors—for most of whom the war was all but over—praised them for their courage.[65] As the prisoners passed into the Union lines, Crawford jumped on the breastworks and ordered a charge. Shortened by the pending darkness, this advance cleared the immediate front and bagged more exhausted Confederates, then fell back to the Union trenches as night came.

Crawford's final battle report as commander of the Pennsylvania Reserves included a litany of Confederate officers killed and wounded; cited the capture of 6 commissioned officers and 70 enlisted men; and noted that 60 Rebels had already been buried. About 240 more men reportedly lay dead in front of the Pennsylvanians' position. Recounting the action at a reunion years later, a Pennsylvania Reserves veteran told his comrades that at Bethesda Church "you probably killed more rebels in one hour than you killed in any one battle in which you were engaged." Crawford's losses were relatively light; the Eleventh Reserves' parent brigade suffered 134 casualties, including 7 killed. For the Eleventh on the eve of discharge, both phases of the day's fight resulted in 3 officers and 6 enlisted men wounded; 2 officers and 14 enlisted men were captured or missing.[66]

In the lull after he returned to the trenches, Minnemyer jotted a succinct description of what he had seen: "After a hard fight [the Rebel army] was repulsed and drove back it is now getting dark and all appears quiet in front of us but there is som fighting on our right this is up to 8 o'clock." His regiment's three years of service had ended.[67]

Chapter 13

A Remnant Returns

Muster-Out

As midnight approached on the day of the Bethesda Church fight, Meade's headquarters reminded Warren that the Pennsylvania Reserves needed to be relieved. Those men whose enlistments were expiring were to "go in a body and take their arms with them and escort a train of empty wagons" to White House Landing, McClellan's old Pamunkey River base. Transport ships would take them to Washington, from where they would entrain for their home state. But picket-line firing kept the Pennsylvania Reserves division in place on its last night of front-line service. Warren, who informed Meade of that fact while he watched for signs of a renewed Rebel attack, also reported that Crawford's men would prefer to stay put "until all their dead and wounded had been cared for."[1]

At some point after daybreak on 31 May, Warren judged those tasks nearly finished. With IX Corps troops on the way to relieve Crawford's division, he sent its commander a note, addressed to the soldiers: "With this is the order for the return of the Pennsylvania Reserves, whose term of service expires today. The General commanding begs leave to express to them his great satisfaction at their heroic conduct in this arduous campaign. As their commander, he thanks them for their willing and effective efforts, and congratulates them that their successful engagement of yesterday, closing their term of service, and being the last of many battles bravely fought, is one they can ever remember with satisfaction and pride."

Crawford later issued his own farewell orders, over Robert McCoy's signature (as assistant adjutant general). He praised the division's "unwavering fidelity," and the general, whose service would continue with another command, noted that the Pennsylvania Reserves' record "terminates gloriously."

> Go home to the great State that sent you forth three years ago to battle for her honor and to strike for her in the great cause of the country.
>
> Take back your soiled and war-worn banners, your thinned and shattered ranks, and let them tell how you performed your trust.
>
> Take back those banners sacred from the glorious associations that surround them, sacred with the memory of our fallen comrades who gave their lives to defend them, and give them again into the keeping of the State forever.[2]

At about 4 P.M., units from the IX Corps relieved Crawford's men and crawled into the Pennsylvanians' trenches. After giving three cheers for the Union, the division now, as Minnemyer put it, "stardet back on the roads home." The new objective was about three miles from the front. A brass band greeted the approaching regiments with "Home Sweet Home," then shifted to boisterous, patriotic airs. After reaching the new campsite and stacking arms, Minnemyer noted that "the boys are all in good glea[.] I regread the lose [loss] of the rest of our Compney."

Men with time left on their hitch in the Eleventh or who had opted to reenlist were to form part of the new 190th Pennsylvania Volunteers, one of two high-numbered units formed from the old Pennsylvania Reserves. The men destined for the 190th were allowed to spend the rest of the day with their old unit.[3]

On 1 June the men were up early and the farewells started. "It was one of the saddest and most trying hours of our lives," a soldier in the Second Reserves remembered, and his experiences probably echoed within the Eleventh. "We . . . could not realize the strong attachment that had grown up between us, until the hour of separation came. It was the parting of those who had shared their last cracker, who had slept under the same blanket, who had picketed together through many weary hours of the night, and who had stood by side when the storm of death was sweeping by—it was the parting of brothers." Samuel Jackson was among those overtaken by emotion, McBride recalling how he "saw tears in a certain brave colonel's eyes."[4]

The regiments had a two-hour march ahead of them to rendezvous with the wagon train they were to bring to the Pamunkey River base. The morning route evoked memories. A few miles southeast lay the battlefields of the Seven Days: Mechanicsville and Gaines' Mill, and beyond them Glendale. After linking up with the wagons, the Pennsylvanians deployed as an escort and the convoy started for White House Landing. This last trek of the war lasted all night, with a three-hour break commencing at about 6 A.M. on 2 June. The men finally reached their destination in midafternoon. They set up camp and looked forward to embarking for Washington, and home, the next day.

Back at the front, the Army of the Potomac prepared for an all-out assault to take place at dawn on Lee's works near Cold Harbor. It got under way on 3 June at about the time the sleepy veterans of the Pennsylvania Reserves fell in for their last roll call in Virginia. The attack, which did not involve the V Corps, was repulsed in minutes at the cost of 7,000 Union soldiers.[5]

At noon on 3 June, while a new contingent of Union casualties spent its first hours on the Cold Harbor battlefield, the Eleventh Reserves and other returning regiments boarded a transport ship from White House Landing. An hour into the trip down the Pamunkey a Twelfth Reserves corporal fell overboard and drowned. The man fought the waves for a time, Minnemyer recording how "the pour fellar tryde hard to get to shore." He noted no other incidents on the ride, which lasted into the next day and took the men through Chesapeake Bay and up the Potomac to Washington. They disembarked late in the afternoon, and were fed and accommodated overnight at the "Soldiers Rest." In the morning they boarded a train to Baltimore, marching crosstown to switch cars. The city, which in 1861 rioted when Federal troops moved through, cheered the Pennsylvanians on every street.

The Northern Central Railroad took the men to Harrisburg, the returning soldiers arriving at midmorning on 6 June. They were a few hours ahead of schedule, but the local fathers who had planned a noon reception quickly set up a repast for them at the Volunteer Refreshment Saloon. Shops closed so that every citizen could greet the guests, and church bells, cannon on Capitol Hill, and furnace and factory whistles created a din of salutes. When noontime came, brass bands, politicians, clergy, civic organizations and the fire department escorted the Reserves to Capitol Hill. Apologizing for the improvised feel of the morning's proceedings, the mayor told the veterans that "you are as sudden with your friends as with your enemies; you took us unawares and by surprise. You outflanked us."

Andrew Curtin followed. The governor, surveying the remnants of the military organization he had created, acknowledged an inability to express his feelings. He observed at one point that "when I say, as we all say, 'You have done your whole duty,' I but faintly convey to you the universal verdict of the whole people of this commonwealth."[6]

The Pennsylvania Reserves regiments spent that night at Camp Curtin, then began moving to different locations to be formally discharged. Pittsburgh was the destination for the roughly 200 Eleventh Reserves, who detrained there on Wednesday, 8 June, and remained until the formal muster-out date five days later. A Westmoreland County paper, readying the populace for the return of just a few Westmoreland Guards and Washington Blues, listed the battles in which the Reserves division had taken part and observed, "When the division reached Harrisburg on its return, it numbered less than 2,000." Crawford actually sent home 124 officers and 2,038 enlisted men, although they may not have arrived together.[7]

Friends and relatives came to visit the Eleventh's survivors in Pittsburgh, and preparations began to honor the units once they returned home. The Ebensburg *Alleghanian* took note of the Cambria Guards' return, observing: "compared with what went out, they are a mere handful." Editor Abraham Barker took time to shake hands with Samuel Jackson, ready to return to Armstrong County with the Independent Blues. He "found him what we had so often heard him described, to wit, not only a thorough soldier, but a genial and accomplished gentleman. His record, from first to last, is bright and untarnished, and it may be said of him, what can be said of but few military commanders, that he leaves the regiment with the ill will of no one man in it."[8]

The Cambria Guards—seventeen were present at muster-out—made it home on Wednesday, 15 June. A brass band and "at least three-fourths of all the people of town" met them at Wilmore station. They were taken to Town Hall for a banquet followed by speeches, which included tears "dropped to the memory of the dead."[9] Other counties scheduled similar welcomes for their contingents. The Indiana National Guards, led home by Hannibal Sloan, had twenty-eight men left. About two dozen men accompanied Daniel Coder in the Washington Blues.[10] In Butler County, William Timblin led home a similar number of Dickson Guards. James Boggs, captured once and wounded twice, brought back fifteen other Connoquenessing Rangers, fifer Charles Minnemyer among them. Leading citizens arranged for a soldiers' picnic in Hazlett's Grove, outside the town of Evansburg, to mark the Fourth of July. "The members of Co. D, 11th P.R.V.C. [Pennsylvania Reserve Volunteer Corps] and all other Discharged Soldiers are cordially and especially invited to attend," the organizers wrote in the local paper. More than 400 people turned out for the event, at which a speaker (not a member of the unit) recounted "the brave deeds of the 11th Pa. Reserves, a number of whom were present, giving a short history of the noble part which they performed on many a bloody battle field."[11]

Company K made it home to Jefferson County on or about 16 June. The unit which the *Brookville Jeffersonian*'s Evans Brady led to war came back at about a third of its authorized strength. Brady's old crosstown rival, the *Brookville Republican*, admiringly noted the company's return. "What a contrast they present now to what they did when three years ago they marched from this place—then they left with full ranks—now they return but a remnant. They have given full evidence of their loyalty, and proved their courage on many hard-fought fields where the bones of their dead comrades lie. We gladly welcome home these few hardy, bronzed and weather-beaten soldiers, after their long and arduous campaign."[12]

Lt. Harvey H. Clover, who commanded Company K after Edward Scofield's wounding, detailed some of the unit's losses. With 30 men present at muster-out, Clover observed that 27 others had been discharged for medical disability, 6 had transferred to the Invalid Corps, and 3 remained in hospital. Six men remained in Rebel prisons, and 5 had

Company	County	Original Designation	Mustered-out*	Transferred to 190th/191st P.V.	Aggregate
A	Cambria	Cambria Guards	17	28	45
B	Indiana	Indiana National Guards	28	12	40
C	Butler	Dickson Guards	24	12	36
D	Butler	Connoquenessing Rangers	16	29	45
E	Indiana	Washington Blues (I)	26	13	39
F	Fayette	Union Volunteers	22	12	34
G	Armstrong	Independent Blues	20	14	34
H	Westmoreland	Westmoreland Guards	13	25	38
I	Westmoreland	Washington Blues (II)	14	27	41
K	Jefferson	Brady Guards	30†	17	47
Field and staff unattached to companies (e.g., chaplain and surgeon)			1	1	2
TOTAL			211	190	401[13]

*Includes men detached from companies and promoted to field and staff positions (e.g., colonel, major, quartermaster) but not those listed as sick or otherwise absent at muster-out.

†Clover's figure, see above. Bates (*Pennsylvania Volunteers*, 1:873–875) lists 29 in Company K at muster-out.

deserted. Seventeen men (3 reenlistees from the original Brady Guards, 14 replacements with time left to serve), were destined for the 190th Pennsylvania. Thirty-one others had died from wounds or disease.[14]

Factoring in replacements with time left to serve, on paper the Eleventh Reserves ended the war with about 400 men. But as noted earlier, ordnance returns preceding the 1864 campaign (albeit incomplete) gave the regiment a "musket strength" of 323. Many soldiers not accounted for on that list were probably detached or detailed elsewhere before (and possibly during) the May fighting.

The legacy of the Eleventh Pennsylvania Reserves was sustained for a while in the veteran 190th and, to a lesser extent, the 191st, the latter receiving a handful of transferees from Samuel Jackson's old command. Most, however, went into Company A of the 190th, now captained by former lieutenant Richard Birkman of Indiana County's Washington Blues. Both regiments were formed on the Cold Harbor battlefield and brigaded together within a new division of the V Corps.

In the weeks that followed, the new units distinguished themselves in fighting near Charles City on 13 June. They helped capture an entire North Carolina regiment outside Petersburg a few days later. But in a mid-August echo of Gaines' Mill, the Wilderness, and the first phase of Bethesda Church, the two regiments took part in an attack on the Weldon Railroad and advanced too far into enemy territory. Surrounded, they were forced to surrender. But as with the Eleventh Reserves two years earlier, the few survivors of the debacle banded together. They kept the unit in the war while the rest languished (and many died) in a ramshackle Rebel prison at Salisbury, North Carolina.

In April 1865, this scratch force was among the mass of Union troops nipping at the flanks of Lee's army near Appomattox Court House. Suddenly, "over the brow of the hill in front came a horseman, then another, and another. The first bore a white flag." The order came to cease firing, and word passed that the Army of Northern Virginia was negotiating its surrender.[15]

Chapter 14

"He Will Sit with a Small Mirror, and Look at His Reflection"

An Epilogue to the Eleventh Pennsylvania Reserves

The first reunion of the Eleventh Reserves took place in Philadelphia on the Fourth of July 1866, at ceremonies honoring Pennsylvania's Civil War veterans. After a parade of the state's volunteer units, their regimental flags were presented to George Meade, then Andrew Curtin. The worn, often shot-riddled colors were guarded overnight and shipped the next morning to Harrisburg, where they were to be permanently displayed.[1]

The original banner of the Eleventh Reserves was missing from the presentation, although it was again in Federal hands. Union troops occupying Richmond in 1865 found it among a number of captured colors. The large Horstmann Brothers flag showed traces of battle damage from Gaines' Mill, and its captors had removed the staff, but was otherwise in excellent shape.

The War Department returned it to Pennsylvania in 1905. Its first destination was the Harrisburg Executive Library and Museum building, where the state's battle flags had been housed since 1895. The colors stayed there for nine more years, when officials decided to move them to the rotunda of a new capitol building. The transfer ceremony was held on Flag Day 1914, during which aged, often emotional survivors from each regiment took their respective colors, wrapped in protective silk, to the new repository.[2]

The Eleventh Reserves' representative that day was seventy-five-year-old John T. Kelly. The onetime blacksmith, twenty-two with dark hair and hazel eyes when he signed on as a private with the Dickson Guards in 1861, had been a sergeant at muster-out. His honor at representing the regiment in Harrisburg was probably tinged with a bit of resentment. The government a few months earlier denied him a $5 increase to his monthly disability stipend of $25. The decision hinged on confusion over how the army in 1864 determined that the regiment had served its full three years—lesser service length meant lower pension rates. "Our Record as a Regt, and as a fighting Division had no Superiors in the army," Kelly wrote in protest to the commissioner of pensions, using stationery from his post in the Grand Army of the Republic veterans organization. "There was no Splitting of hairs then by the Govt or by us."[3]

Kelly ultimately prevailed in this contest, but he was not alone in his complaints. Although the government provided pensions for its veterans, their widows, and other dependents, the applicants' success rates varied. Charles Minnemyer in 1883, for example, failed to convince official examiners that he had been disabled during the Wilderness, as there was no record of him sustaining any injury there.[4]

Several of the Eleventh Reserves' veterans who were mustered-out in June 1864 proved willing to go back to war for a price. Not long after returning to Armstrong County, former Independent Blues Pvt. James McIlwain accepted an offer to serve as a substitute for a drafted man. Assigned to the garrison at Pittsburgh's draft depot, one day late in October McIlwain was stationed as a sentinel at the rear of the guardhouse.

There the corporal of the guard found McIlwain "so drunk on his post as to be entirely incapable of performing his duty." The court-martial sentence was harsh: hard labor for six months, twelve days of each to be spent wearing a ball and chain. A provision that he forfeit $10 pay during each month of confinement was later dropped. McIlwain spent his confinement at Fort Mifflin and was discharged in 1865. He returned home to his wife Emma and fathered six more children. He did not seek a pension before he died in 1883.[5]

Thompson Carney, the Cambria Guards' fiddler shot in the groin at Gaines' Mill, also returned to the war in both volunteer and substitute roles. While recuperating at home in Garman's Mills, he successfully applied for a pension for his gunshot wound in early 1863. He received $4 a month, his doctor stating that Carney's "hip joint is considerably stiffened, is still sore and painful, Especially during damp weather." Additionally, Carney "soon becomes tired in walking, or standing for any length of time."

Such ailments notwithstanding, in mid-1864 Carney signed on in a 100-day battalion, making corporal and upping his enlistment to one year when his company reorganized in mid-September. He evidently had second thoughts, for he subsequently vanished and was carried on the rolls as a deserter. By January 1865 he was willing to serve again, this time as a substitute for a drafted man. Although he signed up under his own name, enlistment officers at Hollidaysburg knew nothing about the desertion charges and sent him on to the Carlisle draft depot. From there Carney went to the Twenty-ninth Pennsylvania Volunteers, serving for a time in Raleigh, North Carolina, before being mustered out in July.

Perhaps because his pension arrangements had already been made, the desertion charges caught up with Carney only late in life. By 1889, arguing for more money, he was complaining of the effects caused by a shell wound to the left ankle suffered at Gaines' Mill but not hitherto reported. In December 1895, with Carney now receiving $12 a month, the commissioner of pensions asked the army for the old soldier's service record. The resulting document included details of the desertion charges. Whether the issue was brought to Carney's attention is unclear, but he died four days after Christmas at Strongstown, Pennsylvania.[6]

Carney's comrades from the original Cambria Guards met different fates. At their return, the *Alleghanian* reported that the survivors "are all in excellent health and spirits. They look not as if soldiering had disagreed with them, but rather as though it had done them much good, physically and otherwise."[7] This was not the case with onetime drummer

Thomas Litzinger, who came back as a lieutenant and adjutant of the Eleventh Reserves. He had never recovered from the illness contracted in Richmond's prisons and was so wasted by disease on his return that friends failed to recognize him.

Early in 1865 he married Emily Rush, with whom he had corresponded during the war. His wartime letters to her frequently referred to illness, but documents filed with her widow's pension requests state that "he never mentioned the character of the disease until after their nuptials, when she learned it was chronic diarrhoea." He died in mid-1867, a doctor attributing the death to "tubercular deposits in the bowels . . . probably induced by exposure in service."[8]

Relatively little has survived in government files about Robert McCoy, who arrived home two days after the rest of the company. The onetime second lieutenant returned from Crawford's staff a lieutenant colonel. An 1864 note in his service file seeks permission to "visit my home in Muncy, Lycoming County, Penna.," but after muster-out he resumed his legal career in Ebensburg for a while. In June 1867, he was breveted simultaneously a colonel and a brigadier general of volunteers for gallantry at the Wilderness, Spotsylvania, and Bethesda Church. In 1868 at Harrisburg he gave a deposition in a Cambria Guardsman's pension claim. He did not apply for a pension himself, nor did his descendants seek a government headstone. One source gives his death date as 1893.[9]

Many of the Eleventh's survivors became active in the first germinations of Civil War veterans' organizations. In Ebensburg, the *Democrat & Sentinel* reported on an 1866 soldiers' meeting in the county, in which delegates to a "soldiers' state convention" were elected who would "oppose the doctrine of Negro Equality and Suffrage." John Scanlan, John C. McBride, William Elder, and William Sechler of the Cambria Guards, James Oatman of the Indiana National Guards, and J. C. Murray of the Independent Blues all signed documents emerging from the session. One resolution passed at the convention maintained "that we hold the same belief now that we did when we took up arms in 1861, that the war was a war for the Union, and for no other purpose."[10]

Such sentiments would have found no home with former major Robert Litzinger. He continued his business partnership in Cambria County with abolitionist and Republican congressman Abraham Barker, the pair at one point setting up a saw mill in Strongstown. By 1885 Litzinger was living in Johnstown, apparently retired. He spent his last years in Ashville, living on a plot containing a frame house and barn near the Pennsylvania Railroad tracks. When he died in 1922, his modest estate included the home, appraised at $600; $691.74 in a Bank of Cresson, Pennsylvania, checking account; a pair of $50 Liberty Bonds, and four shares in the Pennsylvania Central Light, Heat and Power Company, worth $60 each.[11]

In spite of the illnesses that plagued his service in the Eleventh Reserves and the emergency units of subsequent years, Robert Litzinger did not apply for a government pension to supplement his means. Nor did another former major of the Eleventh Pennsylvania Reserves, Fayette County's Peter Johns, disabled the night before Fredericksburg. Johns' widow, however, sought one after her husband died in 1876 of "acute jaundice." Besides her own statements of family need—Mrs. Johns bore sons in 1861 and 1864—her husband's doctor testified that the late officer had suffered from "chronic diarrhoea and functional disease of the liver" traceable to his army service.[12]

Daniel Porter, Johns' onetime rival for the major's post and later the regiment's lieutenant colonel, returned to Indiana County to nurse his ill wife and resume his legal career. He was elected district attorney on the Republican ticket in 1865, and nine years later lost a bid for the state senate to a Jefferson County Democrat. He remained active in veterans' organizations for the rest of his life. Having received a brevet colonelcy a month before Appomattox, Porter the next year led a soldiers' convention that petitioned Congress for uniform treatment in bounty payments. In 1874 he received a lieutenant colonel's commission in the Pennsylvania militia, and four years later he founded the county's Grand Army of the Republic Post #28.

Like the Eleventh's other former majors, Daniel Porter did not file for a pension, but he helped other old soldiers with their applications. His first wife, Sarah, died at some point after the war, and Porter later wed Mary Butler. He was about forty-five when he died in May 1884. He was buried in Indiana borough's Oakland Cemetery.[13]

Rowland Jones, the Cambria Guards lieutenant shot in the penis at Second Bull Run, was discharged from the Veteran Reserve Corps on Christmas Eve 1864. As of the same date, he began drawing a $7.50 monthly pension, upped to $11.25 nine years later. He settled in Washington, D.C., in 1865, where the former law student worked as a clerk in the Treasury Department and was a dedicated employee until his health rapidly failed in the mid-1870s. His supervisor cautioned him about working too hard, but Jones stayed at his job. A justice of the peace who first met Jones in summer 1865 "noticed from the first of my acquaintance the serious effect of physical or mental fatigue, which has increased with the years. The pain and prostration was severe, and at times distressing even to witness."

Jones' terrible injury did not prevent him from marrying Julia W. Moore in 1867. Perhaps surprisingly, he fathered several children, the last born in November 1876 as his health was collapsing. A surgeon who examined him in 1877 found Jones' "right testis is not half the size of the other; partial paralysis of right side of the body with considerable atrophy of the muscles; has some cough; says he had several hemorrhages from the lungs; dullness on percussion with harsh respiration over upper part of the right lung, but he has not the appearance of a person suffering from tubercular disease; no evidence of vicious habits." His wife testified that Jones "required constant attention—could not walk one step without assistance, neither could he feed himself, dress or undress." In 1877, his pension increased to $31.25, then (after initial rejection) to $50 in 1883. He died early in 1885.[14]

Hannibal Sloan, who ended the war commanding the Indiana National Guards, returned to his law studies after muster-out. In September 1867, he was admitted to the bar, and three years later his service in the Eleventh Reserves helped him win election to the state's House of Representatives as a Democrat, notwithstanding the district's overwhelming Republican makeup. In 1888 he again triumphed across party lines, winning a seat in the state senate, representing Indiana and Jefferson Counties. His prosperity as a politician evidently dissuaded him from seeking a pension.

Sloan married Loretta F. Bonner in 1869 and they had six children. A late nineteenth-century account described him as "a man of fine personal appearance, over six feet in height, straight as an arrow and martial-looking." A newspaper of the era called him "a gentleman of solid sense, broad intelligence and much experience in parliamentary bodies. Both his public and private life are without stain, and he is recognized as one of the truest friends of the agricultural and laboring classes. He is affable and unassuming, and meets men of high degree or humble station with equal cordiality and respect." He died, aged fifty-five, in mid-1894 and was buried in Blairsville.[15]

Sloan's old sergeant, Henderson C. Howard, returned home and eventually attained a militia colonel's rank. He prospered in business and served as county treasurer. In 1879, the Medal of Honor winner married Catherine Dalby, who gave birth to a son, Ross D. Howard. In 1885 they moved to Fort Collins, Colorado. Howard in 1915 joined John Kelly and others struggling to convince the pension board that their regiment had served the full three years. Quoting his discharge papers, he argued that the officer who signed them in June 1864 "certainly would not have mustered us out of the service of the U.S. if he had not been satisfied that our term of service had expired." Howard died late in 1919, aged eighty. In applying for a widow's pension, Catherine Howard observed that her husband's unit had been "Company B, 11th Pennsylvania Reserves,— known as 'The Bloody Eleventh.'"[16]

The company's other Medal of Honor winner, Charles Shambaugh, plagued by the loss of his leg, had a harder time after the war. "I know he has been unable to wear his artificial limb at times on account of the great tenderness of the stump," his doctor wrote in 1870. "I know he cannot wear an ordinary artificial limb and that the appliance he does use is heavy, clumsy, unsightly, and a great injury to his general health, from its constant strain on the muscles and nerves of the hip and back." The stress was so bad, the doctor added, that the former soldier "is obliged to use large and frequent doses of morphine and atrophine to enable him to attend to his ordinary daily duties and the use of these drugs are not only seriously injuring his general health but are affecting his eyesight most unfavorably." Shambaugh remained near Washington, D.C., working as a watchman at the War Department. His first marriage ended in divorce and his second in his wife's death; Shambaugh left a third wife, Catherine, when he died in 1913.[17]

William Hazlett, another of the charter members of the Indiana National Guards, returned to farming after muster-out in 1864. He eventually moved to Kansas with his wife, Elizabeth Fyock, whom he married in 1859. The former soldier suffered from a number of ailments in his later years. Although he had been wounded twice—at Glendale and again in the Wilderness—he told pension examiners that his biggest problem was with his back. This injury, he reported, came about during the chaos at Gaines' Mill, at which time he had been detailed to work as a teamster. Apparently seeking cover, he jumped into a ditch, and several like-minded comrades fell on top of him. By 1897, he was receiving a $12 monthly pension for his service-related disabilities, but he was also plagued with kidney and digestive trouble, among other problems. He died in 1905; he and his wife left no children.[18]

Dickson Guards Sgt. John Kelly, the 1914 flag bearer, had married within weeks of his return to Butler in 1864. A Presbyterian minister united Kelly with Eliza J. Shira in a ceremony at her father's North Washington township home. Eliza bore two sons and two daughters between 1869 and 1880. In 1866, Kelly's horse threw him and kicked him in the head hard enough to leave a dent near his left temple. An 1890 law made veterans elegible for pensions for debilitating, non-service-related injuries and illnesses, and Kelly was one of several from the Eleventh Reserves to file under its provisions. Suffering from what his doctor described as "sudden and alarming attacks of prostration," Kelly lived until 1918, drawing the $30 per month he successfully fought for in 1914. Eliza survived him by a decade.[19]

Kelly's old Dickson Guards comrade Aaron Kepler died at age eighty in Lancaster in 1921. Throughout his life he suffered from constant pain and cramps caused by the bullet that transfixed his right thigh at Gaines' Mill. Another Butler County soldier, Connoquenessing Ranger Robert McBride, studied theology and was a minister in Cincinnati by 1881, when he published his recollections of army life in both the Eleventh Reserves and the 190th Pennsylvania.[20]

McBride's corporal, teenage diarist Jesse Fry, also survived the war, settling in Venango County. In Greenville, late in 1868, the former Company D member married a Dempseytown woman, Mary Jane Dyson, the Philadelphia-born daughter of English immigrants. She gave birth to a son in 1872. Two years earlier, her soldier-husband joined the Captain William Evans Post, #167, one of several Oil City-area Grand Army of the Republic chapters that sprang up after the war. The Frys were living in Rouseville in August 1895 when the former soldier suffered a case of food poisoning, which he blamed on bad maple syrup. The illness triggered nine days of constant vomiting, a condition that, an examining surgeon wrote, "aggravated a predisposition to appoplexy [*sic*]." The resulting stroke left Fry partly paralyzed on one side. The pension bureau gave him $10 a month, then $12 until his death early in 1909. Mary Jane was receiving a widow's stipend of $40 a month when she died, about six weeks shy of her ninety-second birthday, in 1939.[21]

Connoquenessing Ranger and onetime sergeant John Gansz ended the war a private in the same company; the man arrested at home as a deserter was honorably discharged in June 1864 and immediately afterward began receiving a small disability pension because of the gunshot wound at Gaines' Mill. Gansz spent the rest of his life farming at different residences in Butler, Westmoreland, and Fayette Counties. In early 1871 he was married in the Baptist Church on Sandusky Street, Allegheny. His wife Caroline bore four sons between 1872 and 1878. In 1875 he suffered a severe hernia while unloading wood and began wearing a truss. He was receiving $30 a month by the time of his death in 1918.[22]

Diarist and Company E corporal James McGinley returned to Indiana County at war's end, but three years in the army had made him want to roam. He went first to Indiana, then Michigan, before finally settling down in Fort Collins, Colorado with his wife, the former Clarissa A. Jones, who bore nine children. He reported a host of ailments on his pension applications, including chronic diarrhea, rheumatism, and heart trouble, all reportedly dating from his Libby Prison and Belle Isle experiences. He was receiving $24 a month by the time of his death from stomach cancer in mid-1916 at age seventy-four.[23]

Daniel R. Coder, who led McGinley's unit for part of the regiment's tenure and ended the war a brevet major, returned home minus several teeth from the wound at Second Bull Run and with a gash in his leg from walking on the bayonet at Bristoe Station in the winter of 1864. The mouth wound evidently prevented or dissuaded him from taking up his former position as a schoolteacher, and he found work as a carpenter instead. His wife, Ellen, gave birth to a daughter, Mabel, in 1882.[24]

The former captain was a widower living in Meadville, working alongside one T. B. Stewart in the building trade when late in 1893 or early in 1894 he hurt his right hand while removing a nail. "It bled a little," Stewart recalled, "and this same injury afterward developed into a cancer requiring the amputation of the hand." The operation, done in March, 1895, removed the hand and forearm "about midway between the wrist & elbow." A medical board in June found that the "Stump has healed but is still enlarged and flabby." By this time, Coder had only one tooth left in his upper jaw and a few stumps in his lower one. As he was impoverished and entirely disabled, his monthly pension was elevated from $6 to $30.[25] Coder died in February 1896. A relative was named guardian of Mabel, not yet sixteen, but an effort to get a pension for the captain's daughter was rejected "on the grounds of the acknowledged inability to show that Soldier's death was due to his military service."[26]

Company F Capt. James Hayden, taken prisoner during the first day of the Wilderness, was eventually exchanged and discharged. If the former printer returned to Fayette County, he stayed only briefly before settling in Pittsburgh from 1865 to 1870, then moving to Maryland. In his pension request, Hayden did not cite the hand and ankle wounds suffered at Fredericksburg but noted that he had "been afflicted with diabetes since February 1863. Believe it was caused by an attack of intermittent fever contracted on Belle Isle, Va., in August 1862, and is more marked as I advance in life." The former Union Volunteers officer was described as feeble when he died in 1931 at age eighty-nine. His wife, the former Letita Virginia Savage, whom he married in 1875, preceded him in death by about four years. She had given birth to seven children, only four of whom were living by 1915.[27]

Hayden's old sergeant, Eugenius Tibbs, remained psychologically shattered by the war, yet he could not accept his service ending with his medical discharge in May 1864 when he was released from the Washington insane asylum. On 16 September, he signed on for one year as a private in Company I of the Thirteenth Pennsylvania Cavalry, a regiment known as the "Irish Dragoons" and the same one that experienced so much bad luck earlier in the year fighting guerrillas. In rejoining the service, Tibbs may have hidden the fact that his earlier discharge was given as a "consequence of Insanity." His recruiters may also have refrained from asking probing questions.

No details of his cavalry career are extant in Tibbs' pension or military service files, but when the unit was mustered out in July 1865, he was unable to make his way home. Somehow he came to the attention of the Washington, D.C., provost marshal, who in mid-August brought Tibbs back to the Government Hospital for the Insane. The doctors who examined him found him in "much more excitement than he exhibited on his previous admission." His condition improved by early December, and in January 1866 he was discharged again into his wife's care for the trip back to Fayette County.[28]

Uniontown physician Frederick C. Robinson took Tibbs under his care. By 1871, he reported to the pension board, which had allotted Tibbs a small monthly sum, that the former soldier "continues to get worse, the paroxysms returning more frequently and continuing for a longer period each time." Tibbs was subsequently committed to a Pennsylvania asylum for about two years.

An army surgeon who examined Tibbs after his release wrote: "He is perfectly incoherent in conversation—unresponsive in his actions—wayward in his conduct and refuses to engage in any occupation or perform any manual labor." By 1877, he was described as "delusional and feeble minded—wandering or standing around without object in view[;] depending mostly upon his wife to support himself and family." The latter now included three more daughters. The last, born in November 1873, was evidently conceived during some break in his confinement in the asylum, from which he was "recently discharged" as of late September that year.[29]

In about 1895, one of his daughters began to care for him in her Chicago home. "He is never dangerous or violent," her husband wrote in a deposition given in June 1903, shortly before Tibbs' death, "though there are times when he will become Very much excited and agitated over some trivial matter, and at such times we generally get him quieted down by gentle talk and reasoning." The stooped, wizened, white-haired veteran needed constant care and help. "He does not read or write, though I have seen him take a newspaper & sit for hours looking at the pictures, or he will Sit with a small mirror, and look at his reflection."

The surgeon who examined him that March for a pension increase also left a description. "Claimant has contracted eye brows, extremely anxious expression in the face, startles at every move of the attendants, head shakes continuously . . . gives fairly accurate account of some events of his life, but is suddenly distracted from the subject, becoming confused, losing the subject and mumbling incoherently as if talking to an imaginary person, occasion[al]ly starting with seeming alarm."[30]

Union Volunteers Pvt. Isaac Miller and his wife Rachel headed west at some point after he was exchanged and sent home; pension investigators never definitely established the locale, but it seems to have been in Illinois. Here, Rachel bore a third child, Jacob, sometime before she died in March 1867. The place and cause of her death were never recorded; Miller told her mother that Rachel died of homesickness. He brought Jacob back to Fayette County and left him with his own mother, Catherine Miller, to raise. What happened to his other two children is unrecorded.[31]

Miller did not stay a widower long. Seven months after Rachel's death, he married a fifteen-year-old Fayette County girl, Mary Johnson, the ceremony taking place in the house of a justice of the peace. "It was not a planned affair," Mary stated in a deposition she gave in 1916, "nobody knew of our intention to get married." She was pregnant. After the ceremony, Miller took Mary to his mother's house to live, but months before she gave birth he was off again to the west. "He wanted to take me," Mary recalled, "and my folks would not hear to [sic] it, my mother would not. He however went and always said he would return to me."

He never did, nor did he write to find out about his new daughter, Mary Agnes (the child died at age four). The next summer, word came that Miller had found another woman. Then a rumor circulated that he was in prison for stealing cattle. Then Mary heard that he was dead.

The last report at least was untrue. It is unclear how or if his marriage to Mary was dissolved, but in October 1871 Isaac Miller married Catherine (Kate) Morgan Conner, the widow of a man killed in a railroad accident, before a justice of the peace in La Salle County, Illinois. They moved to Stanberry, Missouri, and raised ten children. Meanwhile, Mary in 1875 wed another Union veteran, John Weyand, who had served in the 148th Pennsylvania and later in the Nineteenth Veteran Reserve Corps regiment. They lived together in Somerset County until he died in 1897.

Isaac Miller's third wife died the same year, but the old soldier's rambling life continued until 1905. Now about seventy-three, virtually toothless, nearly blind and deaf, and suffering from rheumatism and kidney problems, he was living in the National Military Home at Leavenworth, Kansas, drawing a $12 pension. That September, he went to visit his friend J. E. Hallowell, who lived in Elwood, near St. Joseph. Miller told Hallowell he was distraught and depressed, and confessed he was thinking about killing himself. He made good on the thought on 7 September, when at 10 A.M. Hallowell found Miller convulsing on a woodshed floor. Miller had swallowed strychnine—the bottle was found in his pocket—and when he regained consciousness he asked to be allowed to take more. A local doctor could do little for Miller, who died late in the afternoon. The coroner authorized the use of $25 in county funds to pay for his burial.[32]

Former Kittanning mill manager James Speer, who succeeded Samuel Jackson as captain of Company G, settled in Allegheny, becoming a bank cashier. In 1872 an Episcopal bishop officiated at his marriage to Annie R. Robinson; the couple does not appear to have had any children. By 1879 Speer's three wounds had so affected his mobility that, by his account, he was unable to perform manual labor. An examining surgeon found him only one-fourth incapacitated. The gunshot wounds in his right thigh and left shoulder were assessed as each being worth $2.50 per month; the bullet wound in his right wrist "entails no disability." With adjustments and increases over the years, he was receiving $20 per month when he died early in 1911.[33]

Andrew Ivory of Company G drew a monthly pension of $5.33⅓ (from the gunshot wound suffered at Fredericksburg) starting shortly after his discharge in 1863. The figure dropped for several years after an 1864 examination in which the doctor felt Ivory's injury would eventually improve. It failed to get better, however, and in 1887 a doctor noted that due "to relaxation of ligaments of the knee joint" Ivory "walks as though he wore an artificial leg." The former private-turned-lieutenant also suffered from piles first contracted in the service, and the same doctor described Ivory as having "engorged" hemorrhoid vessels and four external tumors "about the size of peas" in the area. Ivory was receiving $40 a month at the time of his death in 1908.[34]

Discharged after being wounded in both legs at Gettysburg, Company H Lt. James Fulton returned to a medical practice in Westmoreland County. He married in 1865 and fathered eight children. He was living in a house on a 50-by-150-foot site in New Florence and was receiving a $17 per month pension by the time of his death in 1894. Although his practice let him acquire a few other properties, including a cottage at Ridgeview Park, which the family rented out, he left many debts for his family to settle. The first attempt by his wife, Nancy Fulton, to secure a widow's pension failed, though by 1898 she was receiving $8 per month, with $2 per month for three children still underage. For a while at least, money troubles plagued the family, which, a pension examiner once reported, "had evidently been accustomed to living in what might now be said to be an extravagant manner." Nancy Fulton's death in 1912 closed out her husband's government files.[35]

After being captured for the second time in the war, half-blind, partly deaf Company H Capt. Benjamin Job was first sent to Richmond, then forwarded to a prison camp at Macon, Georgia. Released early in 1865 and discharged from the army on a half-disability pension, he settled in Turtle Creek, Pennsylvania. In 1866 he married Sarah Agnes McClelland in the town's First Parish Church. They had seven children between December 1866 and May 1883, three dying in childhood or infancy.

Job's sightless left eye appeared normal to army surgeons examining him for a pension increase in 1892. What convinced them was that, with the right eye closed, "he does not flinch or move eye lids or eye when a pen is 'jabbed' suddenly toward the open eye." Although the musket ball in his head still caused him pain and he suffered from rheumatism, Job worked as a builder, his bad eyesight causing him to lose some fingers in a sawmill accident. The old soldier whom Rebel bullets and shells failed to kill was receiving a $40 pension when he died, aged seventy-eight, at about two in the morning on 29 November 1919. The cause of death was listed as "Septicemia (Tubercular) cervical region, left groin[,] right leg[,] below knee." Pleurisy was given as a secondary cause. Sarah survived him by six years.[36]

Former Company I Capt. Eli Waugaman returned to his wagon-making job in Derry township, Westmoreland County, still suffering from rheumatism and the shell wounds picked up at Spotsylvania and now developing heart trouble. He married in November 1864, his wife Annie bearing at least two children: a girl named Susan, born circa 1869, and a son, Dick Coueler Waugaman, born in August 1885 and mentally disabled from childhood. In 1897, their ex-soldier father died two days after Christmas, the official cause of death being "rheumatism of the heart." In 1905, Annie obtained a government pension for her son.[37]

Waugaman's former lieutenant, David Berry, was too affected by wartime illnesses and injuries to immediately resume work as a blacksmith after muster-out. His son, who ran the Black Lick, Indiana County, forge during Berry's wartime absence, continued to operate it while his father drew $3.75

a month as a quarter-disabled invalid. By 1871, the senior Berry was well enough to resume light work, but by 1885, when he applied for additional government aid, he was incapacitated by severe varicose veins and other ailments. A pension examiner wrote that the old soldier "had not been able to do ⅓ a mans work. Says the reason he did not apply for Pension [separate from his earlier invalid claim] before was that when he returned he was pretty well fixed and had an idea only those wounded were entitled. When he ascertained otherwise [he] let it go until he lost his property." The government upped his invalid status to half-disabled, doubling his monthly allowance. When he died of stomach cancer in 1893, he left his widow, Olive, with what a neighbor later described as "284 acres of ridge land which is assessed at $3 per acre, nearly all of this land is rough and rocky and not yet cleared, for this reason yields little or no income and is not saleable." He also left a small farm house assessed at $200 and a half lot worth $20. His widow's income from the farm amounted to less than $25 a year, causing her to seek a pension herself. She received $8 per month until she died in 1905.[38]

James George, who commanded the Brady Guards in 1863 until his severe hernia forced him to resign, returned to newspaper life in Brookville, drawing $10 per month because of the wagon-lifting injury. By 1900 the former Company K officer was also struggling with varicose veins, rheumatism, and heart disease. His appeal for an increase in pension that year was rejected, but later efforts succeeded. He was drawing $30 a month when he died in September 1915 after a cerebral hemorrhage. His wife, Jane, died the following February. They were preceded in death by their four children.[39]

For a while, James George employed his old comrade Joseph P. Miller, who finished the war in the 190th Pennsylvania. Miller had passed through service in the Eighth Pennsylvania and Eleventh Reserves with only a "varicocele of left side"—noticed after prison in Richmond—but on the Jerusalem Plank Road outside Petersburg on 1 September 1864 a shell fragment broke his left arm. He survived the war and later wed a Brookville woman, Mara L. O'Neal, though the marriage quickly ended in divorce.

He moved to the Pittsburgh area, where in 1874 he married Jennie (or Jane) Frye, the widow of a Nebraska man who had died in 1860. They had two children. By 1895, they were living in Sharon, Wisconsin, the veteran struggling with failing eyesight but still setting type and running presses for the *Sharon Reporter* newspaper. After he died in 1897, his wife learned for the first time of her husband's previous marriage. As she wrote to the commissioner of pensions in April, 1898:

Sir, enclosed I send you A Copy of Decree in the case of Joseph P. Miller vs. Mara L. Miller which I had never heard of untill I received your letter of March 16 and the shock so overcame me that I was not able to atend to any kind of business for quite awhile. To think that I had lived with him for almost 24 years and right among his people and had never bin toald about it you can have some idie of the effect it would have on A Womman of my age for I am almost 61 years oald and now that I have found it out after he has bin bin [sic] in his grave for almost A year I shal always cherish his memory for he was A kind and Loving Husband.[40]

Another printer, and the last captain of the Brady Guards, Edward Scofield moved to Oconto, Wisconsin, in 1868. There he married Agnes Potter, raised three children, and became a major figure in the Wisconsin lumber industry. His wife died in 1919. Tuberculosis killed him six years later at age eighty-two. If he was wounded in the action near Spotsylvania (at which he was erroneously reported dead), he did not seek a pension for it. But he did ask the government for assistance when his health severely declined two years before his death.[41]

Elijah Bish was another Brady Guardsman who ended up in the 190th. After the war, he came back to Knox township, soon to be called Knox-dale, where he found work as a carpenter. In 1865, he married Sarah A. Walters in Uniontown; about seven years later the couple had a daughter, Eliza Ann. Bish died of cancer in 1899, Sarah surviving him by twenty-eight years.[42]

Thomas Sallade, another Company K member who reenlisted in the 190th Pennsylvania, settled after the war near Pittsburgh. In Sharpsburgh in 1866 he married Rebecca Hultz, who bore six children between 1869 and 1880. Drawing a pension for the gunshot wound suffered at Gaines' Mill, Sallade found steady work as a carpenter. But by 1891, when he was named foreman on the Sharpsburg Bridge project, the pain and instability in his leg forced him to give up the job. Nine years later, doctors removed 150 varicose nodules from his leg, giving him some comfort, though not enough to restore him to the carpentry trade. By 1906, now sixty-three, he was working a six-hour shift running an elevator at night. He died in Pittsburgh in 1925.[43]

After service in the Eleventh Reserves and a role in the capture of John Hunt Morgan, Bvt. Brig. Gen. Thomas Gallagher returned to the Pennsyl-vania militia as a major general. He served two terms in the state legislature, prospered in business, and with his wife raised six children. Yet the New Alexandria merchant's kidney trouble, which first appeared in 1862, never abated. It was compounded by heart disease, and his family physician would later write that such a combination "in the last few years of his life rendered his existence very miserable indeed."

Gallagher died on 4 November 1883. His family fell on hard times shortly afterwards. "Since his death," a lawyer for the family wrote, "all his property has been swept away and his wife and children are left without a house . . . and on the very verge of starvation." In 1886 an act of Congress granted Elizabeth Gallagher a widow's pension. She received $30 per month until her death in 1898.[44]

Those who filed affidavits on Elizabeth's behalf stressed that her husband never sought recompense for himself, despite the wound at South Mountain and, especially, the disabling kidney ailment which, they all testified, he had contracted while serving his country. Former captain Thomas Spires recalled having once asked Gallagher why he did not seek a pension. The Eleventh's former colonel replied that his old soldiers needed it more than he did.[45]

In contrast, Everard Bierer, onetime captain of Company F, definitely felt the government owed him for the wound suffered at South Mountain. The musket ball he took there, in the left arm, could not be immediately removed. When he came home on a subsequent medical leave a local newspaper reported: "The ball is still in the arm, which is now very much swollen and inflamed. The result of the injury cannot be told at present."[46]

Yet Bierer's pension file shows the ex-colonel debating an examiner's interpretation of a surgeon's report, which indicated "only such a degree and character of disability on your part as Seems to me insufficient for pension." Worse, the pension board was fully aware of his initial dishonorable dismissal, while his honorable discharge somehow had not made it to their attention.[47]

In October 1865, he moved his family to a farm near Hiawatha, Brown County, Kansas, where he set up another law office. Disgusted by Grant's first term as president, he switched back to being a Democrat.[48] By 1876, he was still trying to get a pension, arguing that his injured left arm was useless for manual labor. Two neighbors affirmed "that he is incapacitated to use his said Arm in the performance of Manual labor. That they know he Superintends the Business of his said Farm, and performs Some manual labor Such as Trimming his Hedges, Nailing up loose Boards on his fences, Trimming his fruit trees, feeding his stock &c which he mainly performs by the use of his Right arm."[49] He evidently succeeded this time, for in 1893 his family sought an increase to an existing pension. His wife Ellen described severe, almost constant pains in her husband's upper body and noted his dependence on her and a servant girl to dress and bathe.[50]

Struggling with cancer in 1910, Bierer hung on until the day after Christmas, dying at age eighty-four. On New Year's Day, one of the old soldier's sons and his wife brought Ellen, then seventy-eight, first to Kansas City, then on to Guthrie, Oklahoma. The children applied to get their mother a widow's pension. She received monthly payments of $12 until her death in 1913.[51]

Having so earnestly sought a general's star, Bierer may have envied Samuel Jackson, who like Gallagher ended up with a brigadier's brevet. But Jackson's return to domestic life was shattered in September 1864, by the death of his wife Martha. With two small daughters to care for, he married again four years later, on Christmas Day, the Reverend James Elder presiding over his vows with Mary E. Wilson. The second marriage produced four more children between 1870 and 1882.[52]

Jackson was a key figure at regimental reunions—the Eleventh Reserves' first major gathering after 1866 seems to have been one that was held 25 September 1879, in Indiana borough. In 1887, he led an effort to dedicate a monument at Gettysburg marking the site of the charge to the Wheat-field. With design and text proposals approved by the Commonwealth of Pennsylvania, the veterans' committee contracted with Rhode Island's Smith Granite Company to produce a suitable marker. The monument came in time for the dedication ceremony in September 1889, by which time the Wheatfield episode had grown ever larger in the regiment's collective mind.[53]

Years earlier, in 1877, Jackson had corresponded with artist Peter F. Rothermel, who was doing research for a painting depicting the wheat-field action. "The gallantry of Genl. Crawford in leading this charge had much to do with its success," Jackson wrote at the time, "and he is certainly entitled to great commendation as it was this charge that saved the Union lines from being severed and that turned the tide of that great battle in our favor."[54]

But Crawford's role—along with that of the rest of McCandless' First Brigade—shrank in memory by the time of the 1889 ceremony. With old comrades in attendance, Jackson and Sloan related fresh interpreta-tions of that fateful July day's events. Jackson had ordered the Eleventh Reserves to charge on his own initiative, though he was "assured that the regiments of the First Brigade which had been laying in rear of us on Little

Round Top, had joined us in the charge." Sloan, now a state senator, put forth a resolution that made it sound as though the regiment had cut its way single-handedly through most of Lafayette McLaws' division.

> *First.* That Colonel Jackson with his regiment, the Eleventh Pennsylvania Reserves, and the artillery held that part of Little Round Top on the afternoon of the 2d of July, 1863, at the supreme crisis of the battle.
>
> *Second.* That Colonel Jackson assumed all the responsibility of issuing the order to his regiment and did make the charge successfully, driving back the enemy which had defeated the Third Army Corps and two divisions and one brigade . . . of the Fifth Army Corps, and this with a force of less than four hundred men.
>
> *Third.* That the First Brigade of the Pennsylvania Reserve Corps did not reach the position in the front of the wheat-field and woods until some time after it had been occupied by the Eleventh Regiment under command of Colonel Jackson.
>
> *Fourth.* General Crawford was not seen by our regiment until after the First Brigade had come up and formed line of battle on the right and left of the Eleventh Regiment. . . .
>
> *Fifth.* And that when General Crawford did join the line of battle, he gave the credit for leading the charge to the Eleventh Regiment, and did compliment Colonel Jackson . . . on the wonderful results attained by the charge made by his regiment under his orders.

Sloan's sixth and final point was an indignant one. "At that time," it read, "no man dreamed that the action of the Eleventh in leading the charge on that day and saving the day to the Union army would ever be belittled or ignored, both of which has been done." Why the men of the Eleventh Reserves considered themselves so treated was unstated. The resolution found favor with men who not only believed a distorted version of their own history, but who were convinced that their service had been overlooked.[55]

In 1891, Jackson successfully applied for a disability pension, citing rheumatism (a surgeon actually diagnosed it as sciatica) and kidney stones. By 1895, the latter problem had advanced to a point which, his doctor wrote, "would entirely disable and disqualify him from manual labor both present and future." Jackson died at about 7 P.M. on 8 May 1907. Mary died early in 1916. In 1925 one of their sons, John, published his father's 1862 diary. Another son, Frank, later gave the Eleventh Reserves colonel's engraved, jeweled sword to the Western Pennsylvania Historical Society. By the end of the twentieth century, it was no longer in the society's possession; its present location is undocumented.[56]

Wounds forced Samuel Crawford out of action early in 1865. Breveted a major general after the volunteer army's postwar dismantling he served as lieutenant colonel (and after 1869 colonel) of the Second U.S. Infantry of the small Regular Army. The thigh wound suffered at Antietam was often swollen and frequently discharged pus and pieces of bone. He retired from the army in 1873 and died in Philadelphia in November 1892, following a stroke. Twenty years earlier, George Meade passed away in the same city, his wound-weakened system losing a fight with pneumonia and jaundice.[57]

In 1867, Hugh Torrance was breveted a captain for "gallant conduct at the battle of South Mountain, Md.," one of the many unofficial postwar promotions bestowed by a generous government. But the former quarter-master, now back in Blairsville, was still experiencing effects from the wound he received in Maryland; it seems to have aggravated the epilepsy from which he suffered at Camp Tennally. Torrance's once-quiet character changed as well, a neighbor later recalling, "When he came home finally discharged he was irritable and nervous."[58]

The former blacksmith returned to his forge, but by his own testimony "I found out after trying it some month or so that I was in no condition to work—lightness of the head, could not keep my head down to shoe a horse. When I raised myself up I'd swing like I was going to fall, became dizzy." He also became increasingly excitable.

With a two-year-old child to support—he and his wife ultimately raised seven children—Torrance opened a general store, but many simple duties left him exhausted or dizzy. Worse, he started suffering "peculiar attacks" during which he would "go into a sleep and once I was found on the floor in the store unconsciousness." By 1899, he reported that "on an average I have one [seizure] a week for the year—sometimes 3 or 4 a week—I am unconscious—know nothing when under the spell of this Epileptic Seisure."

By then, not only did his old wound cause him pain, but he also blamed it for diminished hearing and memory. Additionally, Torrance started to suffer fits of dementia, which today might be diagnosed as post-traumatic stress disorder. Noise triggered these attacks. "He has to run away from home whenever the boys celebrate 4th of July," his wife stated in a document filed with the Bureau of Pensions. "If we can keep him quiet, no excitement, he feels fairly well but let the least noise come and he raves like a Maniac. Will run away, wants to strike people, has no control over himself, seems to want to injure someone." Torrance himself testified that loud or sudden noises brought on periods during which "I abuse my clothing and abuse my bed . . . am liable to run away or do something I should not do, am perfectly conscious of what I am doing but cannot control myself."[59]

His neighbors were increasingly scared of the ex-officer. One neighbor stated that when the seizures came on Torrance "he runs away from home, wants to fight any body. . . . The man is going crazy fast. . . . I see him in them [his fits of dementia] but am afraid of him and get out of the way."[60]

Torrance died on 27 May 1902, at a time when his family was living in Bairdstown, Westmoreland County. Despite his illnesses, the ex-quarter-master had several properties to his name. Before his death, he sold the Blairsville home, "comfortably but not expensively furnished," to one of his sons for about $2,000, to be paid off in small, interest-free monthly installments. His widow sold the Bairdstown home for $2,150 and got $800 for another lot on which an old brick house stood. Another Bairdstown site brought $35, and thirteen vacant Blairsville plots were valued at $325.[61]

The regiment's last major, James Burke, also endured severe problems with epilepsy, which he traced to the shell wound suffered at Spotsylvania. He returned home to his mother Veronica Maguire's house and settled down, eventually marrying; his wife, Margaret, died childless late in 1883. Burke's mother seems to have lived with the young couple. She herself never wed; the man who reputedly fathered her soldier-child died in 1870.

For a time in the 1880s Burke boarded with a Pittsburgh family. They tended the former Cambria Guards officer during his seizures, holding his head and wrists while "the cold perspiration would stand in large beads or drops on his forehead." The widower had trouble getting pension increases. His letters to the government strove to prove that his claim of a head wound was legitimate, and that he was not a "dead beat." Burke's health steadily failed until he died in Ebensburg in September 1892. Within two years, his aged mother was reduced to selling off her furniture and begging for assistance from neighbors. They helped her file for a pension as a dependent mother. "Unless she receives her pension very soon," a neighbor wrote on her behalf, she "will have to be placed in the County Alms House." Veronica Maguire received $12 per month until she died in 1902.[62]

Andrew Lewis' wife Maria applied for an army widow's pension in October 1862. It was granted—$20 per month—retroactive to the Cambria Guards captain's death after Gaines' Mill. Later she moved the remnants of her family—her children Jackey and Mary Frances—to Lebanon, Pennsylvania.

In spite of his father's wishes, Jackey never attended West Point. In February 1887, when he married Elizabeth Allwein, the younger Lewis was living on Weidman Street, working as a bricklayer and stonemason. He enjoyed writing poetry and became involved in St. Mary's Catholic church as a youth; he sang in its choir all his life. He and his wife raised several children, and by the mid-1890s, the extended family was living together in a roomy house at 748 Mifflin Street.

In mid-October 1895, Maria Lewis became seriously ill with dysentery. Just before she died she saw her daughter, now fifty and described as "a maiden lady," near her bedside. "Mary," she said, "I think you will soon follow me." Mary Frances died eight weeks later of what the local newspaper called "a complication of diseases." Jackey's wife died in 1916; he stayed on at the Mifflin Street home until his own death a few days before Christmas 1928.

Today, most of the Lewis family lies buried around an obelisk in Lebanon's St. Mary's Cemetery, but Andrew Lewis' last resting place is unknown. If a headboard had been set up over his shallow grave on the Gaines' Mill battlefield, weather may have obliterated any writing on it. By the end of the war, rain had partly uncovered the corpses, which were eventually moved to what became Cold Harbor National Cemetery.

The former officer's remains probably lie in the mass grave there, alongside hundreds of unidentified Union dead. It is a peaceful place, a short drive from Bethesda Church, where Lewis' old regiment fought its last battle. Nor is it far from Mechanicsville and Dr. Gaines' land, where men who already styled themselves the "Bloody Eleventh" began to earn the name.[63]

Notes

Introduction

1. References to the regiment as the "Bloody Eleventh" occur in the letter by "J." cited in "The Cambria Guards at Washington," *Alleghanian*, 1 August 1861, 3, and the letter by "Veritas," *Democrat & Sentinel*, 23 August 1861, 2. An inkling of a "bloody" unit's social status may be drawn from the Third Colorado Cavalry, "contemptuously called the Bloodless Third" until it participated in the infamous 1864 attack on a Cheyenne village at Sand Creek. Evan S. Connell, *Son of the Morning Star: Custer and the Little Bighorn* (San Francisco: North Point Press, 1984), 176.

2. Coco, *Civil War Infantryman*, 10; Fox, *Regimental Losses*, 8, 260; Dyer, *Compendium*, III:1582.

3. One brigade remained behind near Washington when the rest of the division rejoined the Army of the Potomac prior to Gettysburg. In 1864, two of those stray regiments rejoined the division, though their parent brigade ceased to exist.

4. Bates, *Pennsylvania Volunteers*, I:845–54; Sypher, *History of the Pennsylvania Reserve Corps*, passim. Several county histories contain a few pages on the regiment; some anecdotal information is included in Caldwell, *History of Indiana County Pennsylvania*, 266–68. Pfanz, *Second Day*, is one recent campaign history that details the Eleventh Reserves' performance in battle.

5. The USAMHI has photocopies and transcripts of the Lantzy, Lewis, and Sallade letters. Michael Barton published transcripts of the Lewis documents in *Western Pennsylvania Historical Magazine* 60 (October 1977):371–90. A typescript of the Reverend Adam Torrance's letter is owned by the Division of History, Pennsylvania Historical and Museum Commission, PSA; the author consulted a copy in the files of the GNMP.

6. The USAMHI has a copy of McBride's *In the Ranks*, as well as copies of the Fair letters, the Fry diary, and a typescript of the Minnemyer diary. The Historical Society of Pennsylvania owns the original of Kepler's 1900 memoir; a typescript (without page numbers) was donated to the RNBP in July 1996 by Jane L. Davis of Westerville, Ohio.

7. The USAMHI has a copy of Jackson's *Diary* as well as copies of McIlwain's letters. The Ivory letters are owned by the Library of Virginia, Richmond. The McElhaney letter was obtained by a private collector; a transcript was published on the Internet site (www.ebay.com) from which it was auctioned.

8. Joseph H. Gilmore to J. W. McGinley, 20 December 1890, photocopy in files of the RNBP, which received its copy of the original diary and correspondence courtesy of Byron McGinley of Olathe, Kansas.

9. Kepler typescript, HSP; "Swear Him and Let Him Go," *Alleghanian*, 3 October 1861, 1. Postbellum distortions of events at Gettysburg are detailed in the final chapter.

10. See, e.g., the differences between Thirteenth Pennsylvania Reserves private Cordello Collins' original letters and the edited missive printed on page 2 of the 23 August 1862 *Warren Mail*, as detailed in Reinsberg, "Bucktail Voice," 239–41.

11. T. O'Brien, Department of Veterans Affairs, to author, 16 June and 20 July 2000.

12. John F. Reynolds' papers and correspondence are in the collections of the Shadek-Fackenthal Library, Franklin and Marshall College, Lancaster, Pa.; some important transcriptions are contained in Nichols, *Toward Gettysburg*. Meade's wartime correspondence is

compiled in the two-volume *Life and Letters of George Gordon Meade*. The Philadelphia-based Historical Society of Pennsylvania holds a collection of his original papers. The Civil War battle reports were originally published in *The War of the Rebellion: A Compilation of the Official Records of the Union and Confederate Armies*.

13. Reinsberg, "Descent of the Raftsmen's Guard," 2.

14. Polley, *Hood's Texas Brigade*, 56. Polley's remarks echo those of the Duke of Wellington, uttered decades earlier, about the battle of Waterloo. See Keegan, *Face of Battle*, 117.

15. Kenner Garrard to G. K. Warren, 31 October 1877, in Ladd and Ladd, eds., *John Bachelder's History of the Battle of Gettysburg*, 468.

16. Nicholson, *Pennsylvania at Gettysburg*, I:264.

17. Meade, *Life and Letters*, II:314.

18. Welsh, *Medical Histories*, xvii.

19. John A. Speer, "A Voice from the Soldiers," *Greensburgh Herald*, 1 April 1863, 3. Speer was a Company G sergeant and had been discharged on a surgeon's certificate on 17 May 1862. Bates, *Pennsylvania Volunteers*, I:868.

20. "The 11th Reserves," *Pennsylvania Argus*, 15 June 1864, 3.

21. At the time this practice started, units were apparently forming under "line" numbers subsequently given to the Reserves, and accordingly had their designations reshuffled. The unit that ultimately became the Seventy-fifth Pennsylvania may have lost its initial line number to the Eleventh Reserves, for the order book for the Seventy-fifth's Company D refers to its original parent body as the "Fortieth Pennsylvania." The order book is in NA-RG94, stack location 9W3/10/7/D.

22. This is based on the following documents in NA-RG94-11P: volunteer enlistment form for Frederick Rexroud, 26 February 1864; Adjutant General's Office to John Cuthbertson, 21 March 1864; and copy of an extract from Special Orders No. 160, 27 April 1864.

23. Examples of the river's name spelled with an extra "n" (e.g., "Connoquennessing") appear in "Departure of the Cambria Guards from Camp Wright," *Alleghanian*, 25 July 1861, 3, and the Record of Recruits, Connoquennessing Rangers, 19 June 1861, in NA-RG94-11MR.

24. Boatner, *Civil War Dictionary*, 612, and Boatner, *Military Customs and Tradition*, 88–89.

25. From Krick's introduction to O'Shea and Greenspan, *Battle Maps of the Civil War*, 7.

Chapter 1. A County Divided

1. Storey, *History of Cambria County*, I:193; Caldwell, *Illustrated Historical Atlas*, 13–14.

2. Jonathan Oldbuck, "Ebensburg Borough," part of a series of local profiles appearing under the rubric "Cambria County," *Alleghanian*, 26 July 1860, 2.

3. For an example of the *Democrat & Sentinel*'s views on slavery, see "Facts" on page 2 of its 25 January 1860 issue. The *Democrat & Sentinel* came into being in 1853, upon the merger of two papers: the *Mountain Sentinel* (founded in 1836 as the *Mountaineer and Cambria and Somerset Advertiser* but better known simply as the *Mountaineer*) and the *Mountain Democrat*, founded in 1852. William B. Sipes was its first editor and proprietor; Robert Litzinger was its printer, but by late 1853 Richard White and H. C. Devine were listed as editors and proprietors; Charles Wimmer became printer. The *Democrat & Sentinel* closed its doors in late 1866; its press equipment was sold off at an early 1867 sheriff's sale. The purchasers, Robert L. Johnston and Philip Collins, on 31 January 1867, used the machinery to produce the first issue of the new *Cambria Freeman*. Storey, *History of Cambria County*, I:377–81.

4. Not to be confused with the *Mountaineer and Cambria and Somerset Advertiser*, this incarnation of the *Mountaineer* began publishing on 4 February 1858. Philip S. Noon was its first "editor and proprietor," stepping down on 22 September 1858 to pursue his legal career without distraction. He was succeeded by his brother, James Chrysostom Noon. As he had with the *Democrat & Sentinel*, Robert Litzinger served as printer/publisher of the fledgling

Mountaineer. Storey, *History of Cambria County,* I:388. For an example of the *Mountaineer's* political views, see "Are Northern Men Cowards?" *Mountaineer,* 1 February 1860, 2.

5. The *Alleghanian* began on 23 August 1853 as a Whig party organ; one of its early numbers contained an attack on a Col. John Piper, who successfully sued for libel. The paper continued until 1855, when the press equipment was sold to a Dr. A. Rodrigue, credited with founding the town of Lecompton, who took it to Kansas. "Arriving in that then turbulent Territory, the office was seized by a body of border ruffians, and [the equipment was] thrown into the Missouri River. The stock was subsequently fished out, however, and was afterward used, first, to spread abroad the pestilential heresy of pro-Slaveryism, and next, as a counter-vailing good, to preach the doctrines of Abolitionism." The *Alleghanian* name was resurrected on 25 August 1859, with J. Todd Hutchinson as publisher. Storey, *History of Cambria County,* I:386, citing an undated 1866 *Alleghanian* article "The Press in Ebensburg." The distance cited here is as given in "Air-Line Distance Table," Caldwell, *Illustrated Historical Atlas,* 6.

6. Untitled article, *Mountaineer,* 18 May 1859, 2.

7. Untitled article, *Democrat & Sentinel,* 18 January 1860, 2.

8. "Negro Equality," *Alleghanian,* 1 November 1860, 2.

9. "Fama Semper Vivat," *Alleghanian,* 24 October 1861, 2.

10. "Death of C. D. Murray, Esq.," *Alleghanian,* 19 June 1862, 2.

11. Storey, *History of Cambria County,* I:186–92; Randy Wells, "Slavery Issue Pushes County to Civil War," *Indiana Gazette,* 15 February 2000, M-1.

12. Untitled article, *Democrat & Sentinel,* 7 December 1859, 2.

13. "Brown, No More," *Mountaineer,* 7 December 1859, 2.

14. "The Harper's Ferry Tragedy," *Alleghanian,* 27 October 1859, 2. A month before Brown's raid, the *Alleghanian* condemned the Buchanan administration for allowing more slaves to be imported despite a federal ban on the trade—"a traffic condemned alike by the laws of God and man." From "The Slave Trade," *Alleghanian,* 22 September 1859, 2.

15. See "Who Is to Blame," *Cambria Tribune,* 28 October 1859, 2. The *Tribune* was founded on 7 December 1853, as the successor to a Whig campaign paper called the *Cambrian,* which operated the year before to promote Gen. Winfield Scott's presidential campaign. The paper's name changed to that of the *Johnstown Tribune* on 14 October 1864. Storey, *History of Cambria County,* I: 371–72.

16. Article credited to *Somerset Herald,* "The Execution of John Brown," *Cambria Tribune,* 16 December 1859, 2.

17. Article credited to *State Journal,* "What John Brown Has Done for Virginia," *Alleghanian,* 8 December 1859, 2.

18. "Cambria County Redeemed! Official Returns," *Alleghanian,* 15 November 1860, 2.

19. "Quite Natural," *Democrat & Sentinel,* 26 December 1860, 2.

20. Untitled article, ibid.

21. "The Meeting," and "Public Sentiment of Cambria," *Democrat & Sentinel,* 24 April 1861, 2; Smith, *Price of Patriotism,* 4–5; "Ebensburg Aroused," *Democrat & Sentinel,* 24 April 1861, 2; "The War News in Ebensburg," *Alleghanian,* 25 April 1861, 2; "Little Cambria in Motion—The Voice of her People," *Alleghanian,* 25 April 1861, 3. For accounts of other war gatherings, see letters and notices in *Democrat & Sentinel,* 24 April 1861, 2, and *Alleghanian,* 25 April 1861, 2.

22. Ledoux, *Catholic Vital Records,* I:182, 187, II:56, 62, 75; Caldwell, *Illustrated Historical Atlas,* 10, 14; Storey, *History of Cambria County,* II:3–5, III:500–501.

23. "Close of the Second Volume," *Mountaineer,* 8 February 1860, 2; "The Cambria Guards," *Democrat & Sentinel,* 12 June 1861, 3; Black Lick Township, Cambria County, Pennsylvania 1860 Federal Census, as posted at http://www.geocities.com/Heartland/Hollow/5913/census/blac1860.html; Storey, *History of Cambria County,* I:381, 388. Of Litzinger's tenure and fiscal situation at the *Mountaineer,* the paper in June 1859 observed: "Mr. L[itzinger] has, for the last year, had charge of the publishing department of this paper, and to the faithfulness with which he discharged his duties we, and we know all our subscribers, will bear testimony

willingly. Still, up to this time he has not been what is technically called publisher. In taking charge of the Mountaineer, we did not desire to make it an object of pecuniary benefit. We wished to make it a fearless exponent of democratic principles, and felt satisfied that in doing this the democracy of the county would amply sustain us. Nor have we been mistaken. The Mountaineer is now established beyond peradventure, and is a paying institution. Adhering to the resolution formed on taking charge of the paper, and believing fully that the laborer is worthy of his hire, we have made arrangements with Mr. Litzinger, giving him the entire proceeds of the office, merely reserving an amount of the profits, sufficient to pay for the wear and tear of materials." From "New Arrangement," *Mountaineer,* 8 June 1859, 2.

24. Caldwell, *Illustrated Historical Atlas,* 46; A. A. Barker, "Salutatory," *Alleghanian,* 26 September 1861, 2; "The People's Mass Meeting," *Cambria Tribune,* 16 December 1859, 2; "Ebensburg Bor. Officers," under the "'Alleghanian' Directory" rubric, *Alleghanian,* 8 September 1859, 1.

25. Barton, "Civil War Letters of Captain Andrew Lewis and His Daughter," 371; "The Cambria Guards," *Democrat & Sentinel,* 12 June 1861, 3; "Death of Capt. Andrew Lewis," *Alleghanian,* 7 August 1862, 2; "Ebensburg Bor. Officers," under the "'Alleghanian' Directory" rubric, *Alleghanian,* 8 September 1859, 1; Caldwell, *Illustrated Historical Atlas,* 10.

26. "Death of Capt. Andrew Lewis," *Alleghanian,* 7 August 1862, 2; Andrew Lewis pension file (cert. 2,265), NA-RG15; Madeline Paine Moyer to author, 5 November 1999 and 6 April 2000; Barton, "Civil War Letters of Captain Andrew Lewis and His Daughter," 371, 390; "Tribute of Respect," *Alleghanian,* 28 August 1862, 3.

27. Andrew Lewis to wife, 8 September 1861, USAMHI; Madeline Paine Moyer to author, 5 November 1999; Barton, "Civil War Letters of Captain Andrew Lewis and His Daughter," 372.

28. Lewis, *Family Reunion,* 104; Andrew Lewis to wife, 8 September 1861, USAMHI. Madeline Paine Moyer to author, 5 November 1999.

29. "Military Company," *Alleghanian,* 22 September 1859, 2.

30. "Ebensburg Aroused," *Democrat & Sentinel,* 24 April 1861, 2; "The War News in Ebensburg," *Alleghanian,* 25 April 1861, 2; "Little Cambria in Motion—The Voice of Her People," *Alleghanian,* 25 April 1861, 3; "Commissioned Officers List, Eleventh Regiment of Infantry in the Reserve Corps," 25 July, 1861, microfilm roll #3689, folder 12, 40th Regt., PSA-RG19. Born in 1815, Robert L. Johnston was admitted to the bar in 1841, served as county treasurer in 1845–47, and as prothonotary in 1851–54. A Whig until 1854, when he joined the Democrats, he ran unsuccessfully for state senator in 1849 and Congress in 1864 and 1866. He was elected presiding judge in 1883 when Cambria County was organized as a separate judicial district. Caldwell, *Illustrated Historical Atlas,* 15, 20. The "Citizen Guards," a three-month company from Johnstown, commanded by Captain John P. Linton, was apparently also known to some as the "Cambria Guards." It became Company F of the Third Pennsylvania. See Storey, *History of Cambria County,* II:16–17 and Sauers, *Advance the Colors,* I:249.

31. Barton, "Civil War Letters of Captain Andrew Lewis and His Daughter," 371; "Commissioned Officers List, Eleventh Regiment of Infantry in the Reserve Corps," 25 July 1861, microfilm roll #3689, folder 12, 40th Regt., PSA-RG19; Andrew Lewis to wife, 6 June 1862, USAMHI.

32. "The War News in Ebensburg," *Alleghanian,* 25 April 1861, 2; statement by Robert A. McCoy, 19 October 1868, and undated affidavit by William Semmon, M.D., in Rowland M. Jones pension file (cert. 307,949), NA-RG15; "Company A, 11th Reserves," *Democrat & Sentinel,* 13 July 1864, 2; and "The Cambria Guards," *Democrat & Sentinel,* 12 June 1861, 3; Robert A. McCoy military service file, NA-RG94-CSR. A so-called third lieutenant was initially also named, the position filled by John Scanlan. See "The War News in Ebensburg," *Alleghanian,* 25 April 1861, 2. Scanlan was given the rank of sergeant when the company formally entered state service, according to a roster published in the *Democrat & Sentinel,* 19 June 1861, 3.

33. Untitled article, *Democrat & Sentinel,* 1 May 1861, 2; "War Movements," *Alleghanian,* 2 May 1861, 2.

34. "James Kearns, better known as 'Peatty' Kearns, returned to his home, in this place, a few days ago, from the Confederate Army, where he had just served out his enlistment of one year.—Peatty was in Virginia at the breaking out of the rebellion, and, finding he could not escape, joined the rebels, and was at Bull's Run, Falling Waters, and a number of other skirmishes, escaping all unscathed—alleging that he never fired his gun at our forces, in any of these encounters. When his term of enlistment expired, he re-enlisted, obtained the fifty dollars 'Scrip,' procured a permit to pass the pickets to look after a stray horse, and immediately made his way to this place. He expresses himself perfectly satisfied with 'secesh' and avows his intention of joining the 54th Penna. Regiment, with the expectation of paying the rebels another visit, when he will be better prepared for the meeting." From "A Secesh Soldier in Our Midst," *Cambria Tribune*, 27 June 1862, 3.

35. For a statewide study of attitudes against the war, see Shakman, *Pennsylvania Antiwar Movement*, passim.

36. "The Meeting," *Democrat & Sentinel*, 24 April 1861, 2.

37. "Local and Personal," *Alleghanian*, 2 May 1861, 2; "A Liar and Scoundrel," *Democrat & Sentinel*, 1 May 1861, 2; "Who Are Union Men?" *Democrat & Sentinel*, 15 May 1861, 2.

38. Heseltine, *Lincoln and the War Governors*, 150, 172; "Bad Treatment of Our Volunteers," *Democrat & Sentinel*, 12 June 1861, 2.

39. Donald, *Lincoln*, 265–67.

40. Heseltine, *Lincoln and the War Governors*, 31–32.

41. Ibid., 144, 150.

42. "A Call for Troops," *Cambria Tribune*, 19 April 1861, 2; Heseltine, *Lincoln and the War Governors*, 172; Woodward, *Our Campaigns*, 13–14; Catton, *Coming Fury*, 329; Egle, *Life and Times of Andrew Gregg Curtin*, 263. For an example of the War Department rejecting regiments and the controversy such decisions caused, see the 19 May 1861 correspondence between Cameron and Ohio Gov. W. Dennison in *Official Records*, series 3, 1, p. 217.

43. Minnigh, *History of Company K*, 3; "New Military Bill," *Cambria Tribune*, 17 May 1861, 2; Heseltine, *Lincoln and the War Governors*, 172; Sauers, *Advance the Colors*, I:80.

44. *Official Records*, series 3, 1, p. 202.

45. Ibid., pp. 219, 228; "Items: Local and Otherwise," *Cambria Tribune*, 21 June 1861, 3.

46. "The Cambria Guards Called Out," *Alleghanian*, 13 June 1861, 3.

47. Ibid.; Chapman, *Valley of the Conemaugh*, 133; Andrew Lewis, in a 25 June 1862 letter to his wife (USAMHI) gives details about Thomas Litzinger's family, indicating that his father was dead. Thus Robert Litzinger, then ill but very much alive, was not Thomas' father. The rail distances cited here are as given in "Useful Table," *Alleghanian*, 22 September 1859, 2.

48. Benjamin F. Taylor in the *Chicago Journal*, reprinted in "A Ride Through Pennsylvania," *Cambria Tribune*, 24 June 1864, 1; letter by "K.," *Alleghanian*, 20 June 1861, 3; "The Cambria Guards Called Out," *Alleghanian*, 13 June 1861, 3.

49. Letter by "K.," *Alleghanian*, 20 June 1861, 3.

50. "A Day at Camp Wright," *Alleghanian*, 18 July 1861, 3.

51. George Swetnam, "The Camp We Forgot," *Pittsburgh Press*, 16 September 1962, 6. The approximate distance between the two camps is cited in a notation on F. J. Logan letter #2, Beale Family Correspondence, Historical Society of Western Pennsylvania, MFF #4, folder 3, translations and notes.

52. "Epistolary Advice," *Alleghanian*, 20 June 1861, 3; "For the Soldiers on the 'Fourth,'" *Alleghanian*, 27 June 1861, 3; "Liberal," *Alleghanian*, 27 June 1861, 3; letter by "K.," *Alleghanian*, 27 June 1861, 3.

53. "Muster Roll," *Alleghanian*, 20 June 1861, 3; "Non Est," *Alleghanian*, 27 June 1861, 3.

54. "Extract from a Private Letter Dated Camp Wright, June 22, 1861," *Alleghanian*, 27 June 1861, 3; "Honorable Exoneration," *Alleghanian*, 20 June 1861.

55. "In Town," *Alleghanian*, 27 June 1861, 3; "From Our Volunteers," *Alleghanian*, 4 July 1861, 3.

56. "From Our Volunteers," *Alleghanian*, 4 July 1861, 3. General Orders No. 15 of the War Department, Adjutant General's Office, dated 4 May 1861, stated: "Each regiment will consist

of ten companies, and each company will be organized as follows: Minimum—1 captain, 1 first lieutenant, 1 second lieutenant, 1 first sergeant, 4 sergeants, 8 corporals, 2 musicians, 1 wagoner, 64 privates; aggregate, 83. Maximum—1 captain, 1 first lieutenant, 1 second lieutenant, 1 first sergeant, 4 sergeants, 8 corporals, 2 musicians, 1 wagoner, 82 privates; aggregate, 101." *Official Records,* series 3, 1, p. 152.

57. "From Our Volunteers," *Alleghanian,* 4 July 1861, 3.

58. Letter by "Romeo," *Democrat & Sentinel,* 3 July 1861, 2.

59. Letter by "Veritas," *Democrat & Sentinel,* 26 June 1861, 2; letter by "S.," *Democrat & Sentinel,* 19 June 1861, 2. "S." may have been William Sechler, a schoolmaster whom the newspaper later described as a frequent correspondent. See "In Town," *Democrat & Sentinel,* 10 July 1861, 3.

60. The Company A roll given in Bates, *Pennsylvania Volunteers,* I:857 states that Henry C. Wissel deserted 21 July 1861. Probably because Wissel deserted before being sworn into Federal service, he is not listed on the "Roll of Company 'A,' 11th Regt. Penna. Reserves" contained in NA-RG94-11MR. There is no reference to Wissel, or his desertion, on two other relevant documents in NA-RG94-11MR: an undated "Deserted and Dropped from the Rolls" list, and a 4 April 1863 report on desertions compiled by then Lt. Col. Samuel Jackson, addressed to Col. James B. Fry of the office of the provost marshal general.

Notes to
Pages 15–20

■

314

Chapter 2. Soldiers in Dead Earnest

1. Smith, *Price of Patriotism,* 2, 3, 16.

2. Ibid., 3–4; Randy Wells, "Slavery Issue Pushes County to Civil War," *Indiana Gazette,* 15 February 2000, M-1, M-5; Stephenson, *Indiana County,* IV:374.

3. Stephenson, *Indiana County,* I:185, 567, 592, 626–27.

4. Smith, *Price of Patriotism,* 4, 6, 17; Manners, *Veterans' Grave Registration Record,* 331; Stephenson, *Indiana County,* I:626; notes on typed transcript of undated letters on the death of Harvey Fair, signed by "Lib" and "your affectionate sister Lizzie," RNBP; "Executed with John Brown," *National Tribune,* 9 July 1891, clipping, no page number, in files of RNBP; Bates, *Pennsylvania Volunteers,* I:859; William M. Hazlett pension file (cert. 622,980), NA-RG15. Another Hazlett, James L., joined what would become Company E of the Eleventh Reserves (Bates, I:864). His name is spelled "Haslett" on the enlistment form in NA-RG94-11P, but this was apparently written by another, as the new recruit signed the document by making "his mark" with an X. (William M. Hazlett also made "his mark" on forms in his pension file.)

5. Bates, *Pennsylvania Volunteers,* I:857, 864; "Indiana County," *Alleghanian,* 20 June 1861, 3; "The Remains of Captain Nesbitt" [*sic*], a story credited to the *Blairsville Record,* 2 October 1862, reprinted in *Indiana Weekly Democrat,* 9 October 1862, 3; "Roll of Company 'E,' 11th Regt. Penna. Reserves" in NA-RG94-11MR. In the above-cited "Remains of Captain Nesbitt," the writer makes no reference to James; refers to Nathaniel (at least a year younger than James) as "Jr."; and states that Nathaniel was laid to rest alongside "his brother, who perished about a year ago by disease while in the army." This cannot refer to James Nesbit, as Smith, in *Price of Patriotism,* 9, finds him alive and in Indiana County as late as 1889.

6. Daniel R. Coder pension file (cert. 430,414), NA-RG15; Hugh A. Torrance pension file (cert. 672,261), NA-RG15.

7. Smith, *Price of Patriotism,* 6.

8. Samuel Kistler pension file (cert. 1,808), NA-RG15; "Commissioned Officers List, Eleventh Regiment of Infantry in the Reserve Corps," 25 July 1861, microfilm 3689, folder 12, 40th Regt., PSA-RG19; Van Atta, *Bicentennial History,* 225; Boucher and Hedley, *Old and New Westmoreland,* II:327; Albert, *History of the County of Westmoreland,* 511, 519; Mains, *Newspaper Accounts of Births, Marriages & Deaths,* 131; Jennifer Wilson, Westmoreland County Historical Society, to author, 15 July 1999.

9. "Commissioned Officers List, Eleventh Regiment of Infantry in the Reserve Corps," 25 July 1861, microfilm 3689, folder 12, 40th Regt., PSA-RG19; Eli Waugaman pension file (cert. 2,694,399), NA-RG15; Thomas Spires pension file (cert. 21,454), NA-RG15; David Berry pension file (cert. 444,948), NA-RG15.

10. Aaron Kepler typescript, HSP; Aaron Kepler pension file (cert. 99,274), NA-RG15; "Roll of Company 'C,' 11th Regt. Penna. Reserves," NA-RG94-11MR; *History of Butler County*, I:234. Dickson's name is often rendered as Dixon in regimental files; his age at muster-in is recorded in Brig. Gen. C. H. Bridges to Commissioner of Pensions, 15 December 1928, in William Hardcastle pension file (cert. 1,627,700), NA-RG15.

11. William Stewart pension file (cert. 288,713), NA-RG15; "Commissioned Officers List, Eleventh Regiment of Infantry in the Reserve Corps," 25 July 1861, microfilm 3689, folder 12, 40th Regt., PSA-RG19.

12. "Roll of Company 'D,' 11th Regt. Penna. Reserves," NA-RG94-11MR; William Stewart pension file (cert. 288,713), NA-RG15; Record of Recruits, Connoquennessing [*sic*] Rangers, 19 June 1861, NA-RG94-11MR.

13. "Record of Recruits, Connoquennessing [*sic*] Rangers," NA-RG94-11MR; John Gansz to Andrew Curtin, 9 August 1862, and other documents in Gansz military service file, NA-RG94-CSR; John Gansz pension file (cert. 214,192), NA-RG15.

14. Everard Bierer pension file (cert. 719, 091), NA-RG15; Wiley, *Biographical and Portrait Cyclopedia of Fayette County*, 138, 142.

15. Peter Johns pension file (cert. 228,559), NA-RG15; Hadden, *History of Uniontown*, 544, 682; Ellis, *History of Fayette County*, 151, 152, 154, 189; John DeFord pension file (cert. 1,113,071), NA-RG15.

16. Letter by E. R. Brady, *Indiana Democrat*, 2 October 1862, 1; Evans Brady pension file (cert. 2,264), NA-RG15; "Roll of Company 'K,' 11th Regt. Penn. Reserves," NA-RG94-11MR; "Our Soldiers," *Indiana Messenger*, 9 July 1862, 3.

17. James George pension file (cert. 799,683), NA-RG15; Joseph Miller pension file (cert. 472,014), NA-RG15; Edward Scofield pension file (cert. 1,118,071), NA-RG15.

18. Jackson, *Diary*, 11, 51; Samuel Jackson pension file (cert. 667,873), NA-RG15; James Speer pension file (cert. 172,716), NA-RG15; "The 11th Reserves," *The Mentor* 1, no. 5 (8 January 1863): 35.

19. Sears, *Civil War Papers of George B. McClellan*, 10; Boatner, *Civil War Dictionary*, 522–23; letter by "Romeo," *Democrat & Sentinel*, 3 July 1861, 2; Welsh, *Medical Histories*, 209.

20. Nichols, *Toward Gettysburg*, 77; Woodward, *Our Campaigns*, 21.

21. Gilham, *Gilham's Manual*, 33; letter by "H.," *Democrat & Sentinel*, 10 July 1861, 2; "From Our Volunteers," *Alleghanian*, 4 July 1861, 3. Camp Wright was originally to be named for McCall, according to a notation on F. J. Logan letter #2, Beale Family Correspondence, Historical Society of Western Pennsylvania, MFF #4, folder 3, transcriptions and notes.

22. Bates, *Pennsylvania Volunteers*, I:857, 860, 862, 864, 866, 868, 870–71, 873; "Indiana County," *Alleghanian*, 20 June 1861, 3; "Departure of the Cambria Guards from Camp Wright," *Alleghanian*, 25 July 1861, 3 (which transposes the names and captains of Companies F and G).

23. An example of how the officer-election process worked appears in a 12 August 1861 letter by Union Army Western Department commander Maj. Gen. John C. Frémont to Col. J. McNeil, of the U.S. Reserve Corps based at Saint Louis. In it, Frémont gave directions for the reorganization of the city's Home Guard: "The companies will, in the first place, elect their company officers, who will thereupon nominate their field officers, and submit their names for approval to the general commanding the department." *Official Records*, 3, p. 437.

24. Thomas Gallagher pension file (cert. 222,972), NA-RG15. Thomas Gallagher service file, NA-RG94-CSR; Boucher and Jordan, *History of Westmoreland County*, I:431, 432, and II:11; Sypher, *History of the Pennsylvania Reserve Corps*, 89; Gallagher family genealogical data in the files of the Westmoreland County Historical Society.

25. Boucher and Hedley, *Old and New Westmoreland,* III:215; Jordan, *History of Westmoreland County,* II:10; "From Tents to Barracks—How the Cambria Guards Changed Quarters," *Alleghanian,* 18 July 1861, 3; letter by "H.," *Democrat & Sentinel,* 4 September 1861, 2; Jackson, *Diary,* 17.

26. *Revised Regulations for the Army of the United States,* 130; Christopher Herbert to Elizabeth Gallagher, 14 November 1885, in Thomas Gallagher pension file (cert. 222,972), NA-RG15.

27. Letter by "Romeo," *Democrat & Sentinel,* 17 July 1861, 2; Gilham, *Gilham's Manual,* 82–140.

28. Gilham, *Gilham's Manual,* 189–216; Hardee, *Rifle and Light Infantry Tactics,* I:174, 185, 197–208; letter by "E.," *Alleghanian,* 15 August 1861, 3; letter by "J.," *Alleghanian,* 8 August 1861, 3; "A Day at Camp Wright," *Alleghanian,* 18 July 1861, 3; Griffith, *Battle Tactics of the Civil War,* 100.

29. Special Order No. 4, dated Camp Worth, 1 [?] September 1861, transcribed in Company D order/miscellaneous book, Fortieth Pennsylvania Infantry (Seventy-fifth Pennsylvania Infantry), NA-RG94, stack location 9W3/10/7/D.

30. Gilham, *Gilham's Manual,* 33, 36; Casey, *Infantry Tactics,* I:15–16; Sauers, *Advance the Colors,* I:25; Coco, *Civil War Infantryman,* 97; letter by "H.," *Democrat & Sentinel,* 18 September 1861, 3.

31. Gilham, *Gilham's Manual,* 238.

32. Ibid., 218–19, 225, 226.

33. Letter by "H.," *Democrat & Sentinel,* 10 July 1861, 2; letter by "K.," *Alleghanian,* 18 July 1861, 3; Bates, *Pennsylvania Volunteers,* I:854–55; Gilham, *Gilham's Manual,* xiii, xxiv.

34. *Official Records,* 21, p. 878; Jacob Heffelfinger to Samuel Heffelfinger, 9 May 1862, in McLaughlin, ed., "'Dear Sister Jennie,'" 138.

35. Letter by "H.," *Democrat & Sentinel,* 10 July 1861, 2; and letter by "K.," *Alleghanian,* 18 July 1861, 3.

36. "Farewell Meeting," *Democrat & Sentinel,* 12 June 1861, 3; "Havelocks, &c," *Alleghanian,* 13 June 1861, 3; "Havelocks," *Alleghanian,* 20 June 1861, 3; letter by "Romeo," *Democrat & Sentinel,* 3 July 1861, 2.

37. Untitled article, *Alleghanian,* 25 July 1861, 3.

38. Minnigh, *History of Company K,* 5.

39. Reinsberg, "Descent of the Raftsmen's Guard: A Roll Call," 2; letter by "H.," *Democrat & Sentinel,* 7 August 1861, 2; "Departure of the Cambria Guards from Camp Wright," *Alleghanian,* 25 July 1861, 3.

40. "Calling Out the Militia," *Cambria Tribune,* 3 May 1861, 4; Minnigh, *History of Co. K,* 6; Frassanito, *Antietam,* 175; Wiley, *Life of Billy Yank,* 59.

41. Letter by "C.," *Cambria Tribune,* 24 May 1861, 2.

42. Letter by "Romeo," *Democrat & Sentinel,* 17 July 1861, 2; Philip Lantzy to father, mother, brothers and sisters, 7 December 1861, USAMHI; Philip Lantzy to brother, 31 July 1861, USAMHI; Cordello Collins to parents, 1 November 1861, in Reinsberg, "Bucktail Voice," 237.

43. Griffith, *Battle Tactics of the Civil War,* 117–35, 189.

44. Shields, *From Flintlock to M-1,* 14, 17–19.

45. Ibid., 14, 16, 48, 51–54.

46. Calvin Goddard, "Small Arms," *Encyclopedia Britannica* (Chicago: Benton, 1957), 20:805.

47. Shields, *From Flintlock to M-1,* 50.

48. *Official Records,* 2, pp. 620–22.

49. Letter by "Romeo," *Democrat & Sentinel,* 17 July 1861, 2; "Camp Wright," *Alleghanian,* 18 July 1861, 3.

50. Letter by "H.," *Democrat & Sentinel,* 7 August 1861, 2; Shields, *From Flintlock to M-1,* 65, 67; Coates and Thomas, *Introduction to Civil War Small Arms,* 11; "Collecting the Arms," *Cambria Tribune,* 26 July 1861, 3, which quotes the *Harrisburg Telegraph* of 20 July 1861.

51. Letter by "Romeo," *Democrat & Sentinel*, 3 July 1861, 2.

52. "Local Items," *Democrat & Sentinel*, 24 July 1861, 3; "Extract from a Private Letter Dated Camp Wright, June 22 1861," *Alleghanian*, 27 June 1861, 3; Thompson Carney pension file (cert. 104,562); letter by "H.," *Democrat & Sentinel*, 10 July 1861, 2; letter by "Romeo," *Democrat & Sentinel*, 17 July 1861, 2. The *Democrat & Sentinel*'s remark about the harvest impeding recruiting appears in an untitled item on page 3 of the 17 July 1861 issue.

53. "The Cambria Guards," *Democrat & Sentinel*, 24 July 1861, 2; letter by "H.," *Democrat & Sentinel*, 7 August 1861, 2. The distance was computed using a Pennsylvania Railroad distance/rate chart printed in *Alleghanian*, 22 September 1859, 2.

54. Jonathan Oldbuck, "Carroll Township," *Alleghanian*, 2 August 1860, 2; Bates, *Pennsylvania Volunteers*, I:857.

55. Chapman, *Valley of the Conemaugh*, 130–31.

56. Although originally in Carroll Township, the Lantzy homestead's site is today "located near Spangler in Barr Township." Lantzy, *Genealogy*, 1. Details about the Lenzi/Lantzy family are drawn from the entry for John Lantzy given in *Biographical and Portrait Cyclopedia of Cambria County*, 155–57, and a series of detailed genealogy charts compiled by Charles A. Lantzy of Mechanicsburg, Pa., in the files of the Cambria County Historical Society. Sources for variant spellings of the last name include "Lantcy" in Sypher, *Pennsylvania Reserve Corps*, 685; "Lantzey" in Bates, *Pennsylvania Volunteers*, I:857; and "Philip Lancy," which appears on the "list of enternments [*sic*]" recorded by Lt. Col. Samuel Jackson in a report dated 22 September 1862, NA-RG94-11MR.

57. Jonathan Oldbuck, "Carroll Township," *Alleghanian*, 2 August 1860, 2.

58. Philip Lantzy to brother, 31 July 1861, USAMHI.

59. Philip Lantzy to father and mother, 27 July 1861, USAMHI.

60. Letter by "H.," *Democrat & Sentinel*, 7 August 1861, 2.

61. Letter by "J.," *Alleghanian*, 8 August 1861, 3.

62. Letter by "H.," *Democrat & Sentinel*, 7 August 1861, 2.

63. Letter by "E.," *Alleghanian*, 15 August 1861, 3; Griffith, *Battle Tactics of the Civil War*, 100; letter by "J.," *Alleghanian*, 8 August 1861, 3.

64. Davis and Wiley, *Civil War Times Photographic History of the Civil War: Fort Sumter to Gettysburg*, 1162–65; Woodward, *Our Campaigns*, 39.

65. "Scipio," *Alleghanian*, 3 October 1861, 3; letter by "K.," *Alleghanian*, 15 August 1861, 3; Helm, *Tenleytown, D.C.*, i–ii, 41–45.

66. Letter by "K.," *Alleghanian*, 15 August 1861, 3.

67. George McClellan to wife, 20 August 1861, in Sears, *Civil War Papers of George B. McClellan*, 89; Jacob Heffelfinger to sister, 22 August 1861, in McLaughlin, ed., "'Dear Sister Jennie,'" 118.

68. Philip Lantzy to brother, 22 August 1861, USAMHI.

69. Quoted in Woodward, *Our Campaigns*, 39.

70. Philip Lantzy to brother, 22 August 1861, USAMHI; Billings, *Hardtack and Coffee*, 353, 360.

71. Philip Lantzy to brother, 22 August 1861, USAMHI.

72. Mary Lewis to father, 19 September 1861 and 16 March 1862, in Barton, "Civil War Letters," 377–78; Madeline Paine Moyer to author, 6 April 2000.

73. Andrew Lewis to wife, 8 September 1861, USAMHI. Madeline Paine Moyer to author, 5 November 1999.

74. Barton, 373–74n4. Lewis brought his family's letters to his home during a leave in February 1862. Barton, "Civil War Letters," 372.

75. *Revised Regulations for the Army of the United States*, 243; Billings, *Hardtack and Coffee*, 111.

76. Letter by "H.," *Democrat & Sentinel*, 11 September 1861, 3.

77. Quoted in Cubbison, "That Gallant Company," 15.

78. Kepler typescript, RNBP; Billings, *Hardtack and Coffee*, 138–39.

79. Letter by "H.," and Letter by "Veritas," *Democrat & Sentinel*, 4 September 1861, 2.

80. Andrew Lewis to wife, 8 September 1861, USAMHI; Coolins and Owen, *Mr. Lincoln's Forts*, 143 (quoting Leo W. Fuller, Seventh Pennsylvania Reserves), 147; letter by "Veritas," *Democrat & Sentinel,* 5 October 1861, 3; letter by "K.," *Alleghanian*, 3 October 1861, 3; Woodward, *Our Campaigns*, 39; Boatner, *Civil War Dictionary*, 43; Jacob Heffelfinger to sister, 25 September 1861, in McLaughlin, ed., "'Dear Sister Jennie,'" 122–23; "Report of names of Pioneers in the Eleventh Regiment PRVC with Spade & pick opposite names of those to whom they are charged," undated document signed by Thomas Gallagher, NA-RG94-11MR; Helm, *Tenleytown, D.C.*, 118.

81. Coolins and Owen, *Mr. Lincoln's Forts*, 143, 147; letter by "H.," *Democrat & Sentinel*, 11 September 1861, 3; letter by "Veritas," *Democrat & Sentinel*, 4 September 1861, 2; letter by "Romeo," *Democrat & Sentinel,* 25 September 1861, 2.

82. Letter by "E.," *Alleghanian*, 15 August 1861, 3; letter by "S.," *Democrat & Sentinel*, 14 August 1861, 2. It is important to note that "S." refers to "Companies A. & C." getting rifles; however, I have chosen to trust the letter by "E." cited above and the letter by "J.," *Alleghanian*, 8 August 1861, 3, both of which name Company K as the second flank unit. Surviving regimental documents and contemporary newspapers do not seem to resolve this issue, and ordnance inventories do not exist for this period.

83. Coates and Thomas, *Introduction to Civil War Small Arms*, 14–17; Shields, *From Flintlock to M-1*, 70.

84. Coates and Thomas, *Introduction to Civil War Small Arms*, 16; Shields, *From Flintlock to M-1*, 73.

85. Coates and Thomas, *Introduction to Civil War Small Arms*, 8–10; Shields, *From Flintlock to M-1*, 38, 62, 64.

86. Coates and Thomas, *Introduction to Civil War Small Arms*, 10, 71; Shields, *From Flintlock to M-1*, 64; Gilham, *Gilham's Manual*, 59; Stewart, *Pickett's Charge*, 100; J. Weller, "Civil War Minie Rifles Prove Quite Accurate," *American Rifleman* (July 1971): 36–40, cited in Coco, *Civil War Infantryman*, 65, Lord, *Civil War Collector's Encyclopedia*, II:164.

87. Sypher, *History of the Pennsylvania Reserve Corps,* 113.

88. Ibid., 111–13; Coco, *Civil War Infantryman*, 68; Coates and Thomas, *Introduction to Civil War Small Arms*, 22.

89. McCall's report is quoted in Sypher, *History of the Pennsylvania Reserve Corps,* 121. The 19 September date for issuance of the weapons appears in the letter by "Romeo," *Democrat & Sentinel,* 25 September 1861, 2. "Romeo" remarks that the entire regiment, not just the flank companies, was issued rifles, but this is an error.

90. Coolins and Owen, *Mr. Lincoln's Forts*, 143, 147; Andrew Lewis to wife, 8 September 1861, USAMHI; Caldwell, *History of Indiana County*, 267.

91. Letter by "K.," *Alleghanian*, 15 August 1861, 3; "The Cambria Guards at Washington," *Alleghanian*, 1 August 1861, 3; letter by "H.," *Democrat & Sentinel*, 11 September 1861, 2; *Official Records*, 5, p. 553.

92. Letter by "H.," *Democrat & Sentinel*, 11 September 1861, 3; Bates, *Pennsylvania Volunteers*, I:845.

93. John M. Loor to father, 8 August 1861, in John M. Loor pension file (cert. 262,128), NA-RG15.

94. From a fragment of John M. Loor to father, n.d., and John M. Loor to mother, 21 September 1861, both in John M. Loor pension file (cert. 262,128), NA-RG15.

95. "Standing Guard," *Alleghanian*, 4 July 1861, 1.

96. Letter by "Summit," *Democrat & Sentinel*, 4 September 1861, 2.

97. Letter by "K.," *Alleghanian,* 15 August 1861, 3.

98. Letter by "Veritas," *Democrat & Sentinel*, 23 August 1861, 2.

99. Bates, *Pennsylvania Volunteers*, I:845–46, 867; letter by "Veritas," *Democrat & Sentinel*, 23 August 1861, 2; letter by "H.," *Democrat & Sentinel*, 4 September 1861, 2.

100. Letter by "Veritas," *Democrat & Sentinel,* 4 September 1861, 2; "Original Roll of Field & Staff of 11th Infty Regt. Penna. Reserves," NA-RG94-11MR.

101. Letter by "K.," *Alleghanian,* 27 June 1861, 3; letter by "K.," *Alleghanian,* 20 June 1861, 3. "M'Lane's Erie Regiment" was mustered in at Camp Wayne, Erie, Pa., on 28 April 1861. After being stationed at Camps Wilkins and Wright, it was mustered out 25 July 1861. Dyer, *Compendium,* III:1577.

102. Philip Lantzy to friends, 17 December 1861, USAMHI.

103. Philip Lantzy to brother and brother-in-law, 8 [?] June 1862, USAMHI; Philip Lantzy to friends, 17 December 1861, USAMHI; Untitled entry, *Democrat & Sentinel,* 7 August 1861, 2.

104. Letter by "S.," *Democrat & Sentinel,* 19 June 1861, 2.

105. Letter by "K.," *Alleghanian,* 20 June 1861, 3.

106. Untitled article, *Alleghanian,* 25 July 1861, 3; Woodward, *Our Campaigns,* 23–24, 36.

107. Lowry, *Tarnished Eagles,* 208–12.

108. "Accident to a Cambria Volunteer," *Alleghanian,* 18 July 1861, 3. Three companies from Cambria County served in the Third Pennsylvania. "Third Regiment," *Alleghanian,* 18 July 1861, 3.

109. Letter by "H.," *Democrat & Sentinel,* 4 September 1861, 2; letter by "H.," *Democrat & Sentinel,* 18 September 1861, 3.

110. Letter by "J.," *Alleghanian,* 8 August 1861, 3; Dyer, *Compendium,* I:277; Boatner, *Civil War Dictionary,* 609.

111. Boatner, *Civil War Dictionary,* 539; D. H. Hill quoted in Murfin, *Gleam of Bayonets,* 179.

112. Quoted in John J. Hennessy, "I Dread the Spring," in Gary Gallagher, ed., *Wilderness Campaign,* 69–70.

113. Letter by "K.," *Alleghanian,* 3 October 1861, 3; letter by "E.," *Alleghanian,* 14 November 1861, 3.

114. Charles A. Dana, *Recollections of the Civil War* (1898; repr., New York: Collier, 1963), 171–72, quoted in John J. Hennessy, "I Dread the Spring," in Gary Gallagher, ed., *Wilderness Campaign,* 69; Jackson, *Diary,* 5; Nichols, *Toward Gettysburg,* 145; Billings, *Hardtack and Coffee,* 349.

115. Catton, *Stillness at Appomattox,* 51; Nichols, *Toward Gettysburg,* 78.

116. George Meade to wife, 12 October 1861, in Meade, *Life and Letters,* I:223.

117. Sauers, *Advance the Colors,* I:91–94, 99–101, 254–55.

118. George Meade to wife, 14 October 1861, in Meade, *Life and Letters,* I:224; Sauers, *Advance the Colors,* I:112, 256.

119. Fox, *Regimental Losses,* 261; Nichols, *Toward Gettysburg,* 76–77; Dyer, *Compendium,* III:1583. At least some element of the Bucktails seems to have been present by late September. "Kaine's [*sic*] Rifles . . . form the right and the 11th the left [of the brigade]." Letter by "K.," *Alleghanian,* 3 October 1861, 3.

120. Sypher, *History of the Pennsylvania Reserve Corps,* 116; Sauers, *Advance the Colors,* I:15, 80, 112. The Fourth Pennsylvania Reserves, also on picket duty at the time of the ceremony, was also represented by its color guard. Sauers, *Advance the Colors,* I:93.

121. Philip Lantzy to father, mother, sisters and brothers, 15 September 1861, USAMHI.

122. Thomas Sallade to John Bell, 12 September 1861, USAMHI; Thomas Sallade pension file (cert. 112,245), NA-RG15.

Chapter 3. No More Bull Run Affairs

1. Letter by "E.," *Alleghanian,* 17 October 1861, 3; *Official Records,* 2, p. 123; Jacob Heffelfinger to sister, 4 August [*sic*], 1861, in McLaughlin, ed., "'Dear Sister Jennie,'" 114–15, 116.

The August date seems to be an error of the letter-writer or a transcriber; the action it describes corresponds with the 4 September episode at Great Falls.

2. *Official Records,* 5, p. 127, and 51:1, pp. 39–40.

3. Johnson and Anderson, *Artillery Hell,* 26–27.

4. Jacob Heffelfinger to sister, 4 August [*sic,* see note 1, above] 1861, in McLaughlin, ed., "'Dear Sister Jennie,'" 115; *Official Records,* 5, p. 127, and 51:1, pp. 39–40.

5. *Official Records,* 5, pp. 165–68.

6. Philip Lantzy to father, mother, sisters and brothers, 15 September 1861, USAMHI; letter by "J," *Alleghanian,* 1 August 1861, 3; letter by "Veritas," *Democrat & Sentinel,* 23 August 1861, 2.

7. Andrew Lewis to wife, 8 September 1861, USAMHI.

8. Everard Bierer to George Meade, 22 October 1861, NA-RG94-11MR.

9. "List of names of Recruits of Eleventh (11) Regiment P.R.C. Sworn into State Service and not Sworn into U.S. Service," undated document signed by Thomas F. Gallagher, NA-RG94-11MR.

10. Letter by "Veritas," *Democrat & Sentinel,* 9 October 1861, 2; letter by "E.," *Alleghanian,* 17 October 1861, 3.

11. Letter by "Veritas," *Democrat & Sentinel,* 9 October 1861, 2; letter by "E.," *Alleghanian,* 17 October 1861, 3.

12. Letter by "E.," *Alleghanian,* 17 October 1861, 3; Philip Lantzy to parents, 16 November 1861, USAMHI.

13. Philip Lantzy to parents, 16 November 1861, USAMHI; letter by "Veritas," *Democrat & Sentinel,* 9 October 1861, 2.

14. Letter by "Veritas," *Democrat & Sentinel,* 9 October 1861, 2; Joseph Polley letter, 1 October 1863, quoted in Commager, *Blue and the Gray,* 473.

15. Letter by "E.," *Alleghanian,* 17 October 1861, 3; letter by "Veritas," *Democrat & Sentinel,* 9 October 1861, 2. "Veritas" mistakenly refers to "Major Johnson" in his text.

16. McBride, *In the Ranks,* 53–54.

17. Nichols, *Toward Gettysburg,* 78; Aaron Kepler typescript, RNBP; letter by "E.," *Alleghanian,* 17 October 1861, 3.

18. Letter by "E.," *Alleghanian,* 31 October 1861, 3.

19. *Official Records,* 5, p. 32; George Meade to wife, 18 October 1861, in *Life and Letters,* I:224.

20. Letter by "E.," *Alleghanian,* 31 October 1861, 3; George Meade to wife, 21 October 1861, in *Life and Letters,* I:224.

21. *Official Records,* 5, p. 32.

22. Ibid., 33–34; George Meade to wife, 21 October 1861, in *Life and Letters,* I:225.

23. Letter by "E.," *Alleghanian,* 31 October 1861, 3. For more on the battle of Ball's Bluff and Stone's fate, see Sears, *Controversies and Commanders,* 29–50.

24. George Meade to wife, 24 October and 28 November 1861, in *Life and Letters,* I:225–26, 232.

25. Philip Lantzy to brothers and sisters, 17 February 1862, USAMHI.

26. David Berry pension file (cert. 444,948), NA-RG15.

27. "Charges and Specifications preferred against Captain Thomas H. Spires, Co. 'I,' 11th Regiment Penna. R.V.C. [Reserve Volunteer Corps] attached to the 2nd Brigade McCall[']s Division, Army of the Potomac," undated document in NA-RG94-11P.

28. Special Orders No. 151, dated Headquarters, McCall's Division, Camp Pierpont, 24 October 1861; and Special Orders No. 335, dated Headquarters, Army of the Potomac, 21 December 1861, in NA-RG94-11P. On page 3 of its 31 October 1861 issue, under the heading "Found Asleep on Duty," the *Alleghanian* reprinted an item from the *Latrobe Inquirer* giving a brief mention of the 16 October episode. It noted that Spires "has been court-martialed and his commission taken from him." Spires vigorously denied this version of events in a subsequent item, published under the heading "Not True," *Alleghanian,* 21 November 1861, 3. Data

on the Spires court-martial does not seem to exist outside the regimental collection of personal papers. Spires' file within the National Archives' collection of Combined Military Service Records makes no mention of the trial. Nor is there a reference to a trial involving Spires in the archives' index (M1105) to courts-martial contained in Record Group 153.

29. Special Orders No. 24 [?] dated Headquarters, Army of the Potomac, Washington, 3 September 1861, and Special Orders No. 113, dated Headquarters, Army of the Potomac, Washington, 22 October 1861, in NA-RG94-11P; Smith, *Price of Patriotism,* 54; Sauers, *Advance the Colors,* I:276.

30. Thomas Gallagher and James Speer to George Meade, 28 October 1861, NA-RG94-VSF; Special Orders No. 113, dated Headquarters, Army of the Potomac, Washington, 22 October 1861, NA-RG94-11P; Bates, *Pennsylvania Volunteers,* I:846; and Robert Litzinger service file, NA-RG94-CSR.

31. James C. Burke pension file (cert. 398,014), NA-RG15; "Company A, 11th Reserves," *Democrat & Sentinel,* 13 July 1864, 2.

32. Letter by E. R. Brady, *Indiana Democrat,* 2 October 1862, 1; Thomas Gallagher pension file (cert. 222,972), NA-RG15; Thomas Gallagher service file, NA-RG94-CSR.

33. This section draws upon various items from NA-RG94-11MR, including vouchers from late 1861 and early 1862; a 7 November 1861 note signed by Gallagher, no addressee, written from Head Quarters, 11th Reg. P.R.V.C., Camp Pierpont; and documents headed "The Company Fund in account with Captain Andrew Lewis, Co. A, 11th Regt. PRVC, for the period ending 31st Dec. 1861," and "Company Post Fund of Company K 11th Regt. P.R.V.C. Received and disbursed by Captain E. R. Brady, during the Quarter ending January 1st, 1862."

34. Abel, *Singing the New Nation,* 133. The vouchers for the instruments and shipping charges, dated Camp Pierpont, 22 December 1862 [*sic*] and 15 January 1862, are in NA-RG94-11MR. The year on the earlier voucher must be an error as the regimental band was dissolved on 3 August 1862. Bates, *Pennsylvania Volunteers,* I:855. Bates (I:855, 875) gives the names of ten musicians who were evidently specially recruited for the regimental band, mustered-in on 1 October 1861; the names of surviving musicians selected from within the regiment itself are listed on Special Orders No. 100 [?], pt. 3, from Headquarters, V Army Corps, 3 August 1862, NA-RG94-11MR.

35. Jacob Heffelfinger to father, 15 November 1861, in McLaughlin, ed., "'Dear Sister Jennie,'" 124. A photo of Lantzy wearing this hat is in the James Beck Collection, USAMHI.

36. Philip Lantzy to father, mother, sisters and brothers, 28 October 1861, USAMHI; letter by "E.," *Alleghanian,* 31 October 1861, 3.

37. *Official Records,* 5, pp. 9, 448–49, and series 2, 2, p. 1286; Boatner, *Civil War Dictionary,* 52; George Meade to wife, 28 November 1861, in *Life and Letters,* I:232; Welsh, *Medical Histories,* 23–24.

38. *Official Records,* 5, pp. 448–49, 913–14; George Meade to wife, 2 December 1861, in *Life and Letters,* I:233.

39. *Official Records,* 5, p. 455, and series 2, 2, pp. 1292–94; George Meade to wife, 8 December and 11 December 1861, *Life and Letters,* I:234, 235; letter by "E.," *Alleghanian,* 26 December 1861, 3; Philip Lantzy to father, mother, brothers and sisters, 7 December 1861, USAMHI; Aaron Kepler typescript, RNBP.

40. George Meade to wife, 8 December 1861, in *Life and Letters,* I:234.

41. *Official Records,* 5, p. 999.

42. R. H. Fair to brother, 15 December 1861, USAMHI.

43. *Official Records,* 5, pp. 490–91.

44. Ibid., 474.

45. Murdoch, "Pittsburgh Rifles and the Battle of Dranesville," 301–2; *Official Records,* 5, pp. 473–74; Philip Lantzy to brother, 22 December 1861, USAMHI.

46. *Official Records,* 5, pp. 489, 494.

47. Ibid., 66; George Meade to wife, 21 December 1861, in *Life and Letters,* I:237; Sauers, *Advance the Colors,* I:81.

48. Philip Lantzy to brother, 22 December 1861, USAMHI; Samuel Jackson to George Meade, 20 December 1861, NA-RG94-11MR.

49. *Official Records*, 5, p. 84; Aaron Kepler typescript, RNBP; Bates, *Pennsylvania Volunteers,* I:846.

50. Philip Lantzy to father, mother, brothers and sisters, 7 December 1861, USAMHI; Bates, *Pennsylvania Volunteers,* I:857. The Company A muster roll in NA-RG94-11MR notes only that Wise "Died of disease—Dec. 1861."

51. R. H. Fair to brother, 15 November 1861, USAMHI.

52. "Sergt. R. H. Fair," *Indiana Messenger,* 13 August 1862, 3; Smith, *Price of Patriotism,* 24.

53. "Terrible Accident," *Alleghanian,* 6 February 1862, 3.

54. Bates, *Pennsylvania Volunteers,* I:867; Thomas Gallagher to George Meade, 13 February, 1862, in NA-RG94-11MR; John W. DeFord pension file (cert. 1,113,071), NA-RG15. Reports mentioning personnel detailed for various tasks are in NA-RG94-11MR. Data on McKearns is drawn from the Company F muster roll in NA-RG94-11MR, and "Charges and Specifications preferred against Private James K. P. McKarnes [*sic*], 11th Regiment, Penna. Reserve Corps.," document signed by Lt. Samuel T. Cushing, NA-RG94-11P.

55. Thomas F. Gallagher to George Meade, dated Headquarters 11th Regt. P.R.V.C., Camp near Falmouth, 18 May 1862, NA-RG94-11MR.

56. Jackson, *Diary,* 3, 8. The target practice reports, each dated between 28 January and 20 February 1862, and signed by either Gallagher or Jackson, are in NA-RG94-11MR.

57. Captain Fleming (initials indecipherable), "Picket officer Left Flank," to George Meade, 19 January 1862, NA-RG94-11MR; Cubbison, "That Gallant Company," 15; Jackson, *Diary,* 8. Alt eventually deserted on 14 May 1863, according to an undated "Deserted and dropped from the Rolls" list contained in NA-RG94-11MR.

58. Robert Litzinger medical records file, NA-RG94-CMR; Robert Litzinger service file, NA-RG94-CSR; Aaron Kepler typescript, RNBP; J. S. DeBenneville pension file (cert. 97,513), NA-RG15; Jackson, *Diary,* 9; James Fulton pension file (cert. 491,097), NA-RG15.

59. Undated "Charge and Specification against assistant Surgeon D. W. Ballantine, 11th Regt. P.R.V.C.," NA-RG94-11P; Special Orders No. 44, pt. 2, dated Headquarters, Army of the Potomac, Washington, 11 February 1862, NA-RG94-11P.

60. Philip Lantzy to brother, 18 February 1862, USAMHI; Special Orders No. 45, pt. 5, dated Headquarters, Army of the Potomac, Washington, 15 February 1862, NA-RG94-11P.

61. "Resignation of Maj. Litzinger," *Alleghanian,* 17 April 1862, 3; Litzinger to Gallagher, 28 March, 1862, Litzinger service file, NA-RG94-CSR; Special Orders No. 63, pt. 10, dated Headquarters, Army of the Potomac, Washington, 7 March 1862, NA-RG94-11P; Special Orders No. 70, pt. 4, dated Headquarters, Army of the Potomac, Washington, 11 March 1862, NA-RG94-11P.

62. Philip Lantzy to brother, 19 April 1862, USAMHI.

63. Philip Lantzy to brother, 20 June 1862, USAMHI; George Meade to wife, 4 April 1862, in *Life and Letters,* I: 256; Sears, *Gates of Richmond,* 100, 102–3.

64. "From the Cambria Guards," *Alleghanian,* 3 April 1862, 3; Andrew Ivory to daughter, 7 May 1862, Library of Virginia; Andrew Ivory pension file (cert. 16,097), NA-RG15; Sears, *Gates of Richmond,* 15–16.

65. "From the Cambria Guards," *Alleghanian,* 3 April, 1862, 3; Jacob Heffelfinger to sister, 18 March, 1862, in McLaughlin, "'Dear Sister Jennie,'" 129; Jackson, *Diary,* 14-15.

66. Bates, *Pennsylvania Volunteers,* I:847. Christopher Herbert to Elizabeth Gallagher, 14 November 1885, in Thomas Gallagher pension file (cert. 222,972), NA-RG15.

67. Jackson, *Diary,* 15, 16; Philip Lantzy to brother, 22 March 1862, USAMHI.

68. Boatner, *Civil War Dictionary,* 187–88; Sears, *Gates of Richmond,* 100, 102–5.

69. George Meade to wife, 8 and 9 April 1862, in *Life and Letters,* I:257, 259; Adam S. Bright to uncle, 19 April 1862, in Truxall, *Respects to All,* 20; letter by "W.," *Alleghanian,* 1 May 1862, 3.

70. Letter by "W.," *Alleghanian,* 1 May 1862, 3.

71. Ibid.; Aaron Kepler typescript, HSP; George Meade to wife, 13 April 1862, in *Life and Letters,* I:259; McBride, *In the Ranks,* 27.

72. Letter by "W.," *Alleghanian,* 1 May 1862, 3; Woodward, *Our Campaigns,* 63.

73. Reynolds quoted in Nichols, *Toward Gettysburg,* 84; Jacob Heffelfinger to sister, 15 April 1862, in McLaughlin, ed., "'Dear Sister Jennie,'" 133.

74. George Meade to wife, 19 April 1862, in *Life and Letters,* I:261; Philip Lantzy to brother, 19 April 1862, USAMHI; letter by "W.," *Alleghanian,* 22 May 1862, 3.

75. "The Eleventh Regiment, P.R.C.," *Alleghanian,* 1 May 1862, 3. Bates, *Pennsylvania Volunteers,* I:847. Jackson, *Diary,* 18, 20.

76. Aaron Kepler typescript, RNBP.

77. Nichols, *Toward Gettysburg,* 85; Andrew Ivory to daughter, 27 April 1862, Library of Virginia; letter by "W.," *Alleghanian,* 22 May 1862, 3.

78. Letter by "W.," *Alleghanian,* 22 May 1862, 3; "Report of men still absent from the 11th Regt. P.R.V.C. having been detailed under Order No. (blank) as Bridge Builders," document dated Headquarters 11th Regt. PRVC, Camp opposite Fredericksburg, 29 May 1862, NA-RG94-11MR; Woodward, *Our Campaigns,* 71; Nichols, *Toward Gettysburg,* 85–86; George Meade to wife, 30 April and 10 May 1862, in *Life and Letters,* I:263, 265.

79. Adam S. Bright to uncle, 12 May 1862, in Truxall, *Respects to All,* 21; George Meade to wife, 30 April and 10 May 1862, in *Life and Letters,* I: 263, 265; Andrew Ivory to daughter, 7 May 1862, Library of Virginia.

Chapter 4. One of the Awfulest Battles

1. Andrew Lewis to wife, 6 June, 1862, USAMHI. Besides those sources specifically cited, troop movement details and background data presented in this chapter are principally drawn from Sears, *Gates of Richmond,* passim; the unpublished 1960 Edwin C. Bearss map set in the files of RNBP; Esposito, ed., *West Point Atlas,* I, maps 42–45 and corresponding text; and conversations and correspondence during 1999–2000 with Robert E. L. Krick, RNBP.

2. Philip Lantzy to father, mother, sisters and brothers, 24 May 1862, USAMHI; John M. Loor to father, 6 May and 10 May 1862, in Loor pension file (cert 262,128), NA-RG15.

3. Thomas Gallagher to George Meade, 11 May 1862, NA-RG94-11MR; "The 11th Reserves—Unofficial Report of the Killed and Wounded, and Prisoners, at Richmond," *Pittsburgh Gazette,* 22 July 1862, no page number, clipping in files of RNBP.

4. Sears, *Gates of Richmond,* 104–6.

5. Ibid., 103–5; George Meade to wife, 23 May 1862, in *Life and Letters,* I:267.

6. Philip Lantzy to father, mother, sisters and brothers, 24 May 1862, USAMHI.

7. *Official Records,* 11:1, pp. 27, 30–31, and 12:1, p. 523; George Meade to wife, 30 May 1862, in *Life and Letters,* I:269.

8. *Official Records,* 11:1, p. 31.

9. Livermore, *Numbers and Losses,* 81; Sears, *Gates of Richmond,* 111–45.

10. Sears, *Gates of Richmond,* 160.

11. Philip Lantzy to brother and brother-in-law, 8 [?] June 1862, USAMHI.

12. Andrew Lewis to wife, 6 June 1862, USAMHI.

13. Woodward, *Our Campaigns,* 72–73; George Meade to wife, 11 June 1862, in *Life and Letters,* I:272.

14. Woodward, *Our Campaigns,* 73–74; James McGinley diary, 10–12 June 1862, RNBP; McGinley pension file (cert. 813,072), NA-RG15; Kepler typescript, HSP; Woodward, *Our Campaigns,* 73–74; Sears, *Gates of Richmond,* 163.

15. George Meade to wife, 11 June 1862, in *Life and Letters,* I:273; Boatner, *Civil War Dictionary,* 609, 733; Sauers, "Pennsylvania Reserves," 25; Nichols, *Toward Gettysburg,* 88.

16. *Official Records,* 11:1, p. 1028.

17. McGinley diary entries for 12–17 June 1862, RNBP.

18. *Official Records,* 11:1, pp. 52, 165.

19. *Official Records,* 11:2, p. 384; Sears, *Gates of Richmond,* 213, 254; W. C. McClellan to sister, 2 April 1863, quoted in Wiley, *Johnny Reb,* 313.

20. *Official Records,* 11:2, p. 384; Woodward, *Our Campaigns,* 84.

21. *Official Records,* 11:1, p. 1058, and 11:2, pp. 384, 398–99.

22. George Meade to wife, 18 June 1862, in *Life and Letters,* I:275; *Official Records,* 11:2, p. 384; E. Porter Alexander, *Fighting for the Confederacy: The Personal Recollections of General Edward Porter Alexander,* ed. Gary Gallagher (Chapel Hill: University of North Carolina Press, 1989), 95, quoted in Sears, *Gates of Richmond,* 202.

23. *Official Records,* 11:2, p. 490.

24. Andrew Lewis to wife, 15 June 1862, USAMHI.

25. James X. McIlwain to wife, 15 June 1862, USAMHI; James X. McIlwain pension file (cert. 381,783), NA-RG15. The latter contains examples of Emma McIlwain making "her mark" on her 19 May 1891 "Secondary Proof of Marriage" form and a 16 September 1916 letter to the Commissioner of Pensions witnessed by W. R. Remaley. James McIlwain's age and description are noted on a list of men on leave compiled by Dan S. Porter and addressed to Lt. Wm. A. Hoyt, 20 December 1863, NA-RG94-11MR. A letter in NA-RG94-11P dated 17 May 1862 (much of the text obliterated by an ink stain) details McIlwain to serve as saddler in Meade's brigade.

26. James X. McIlwain to wife, 22 June 1862, USAMHI.

27. George Meade to wife, 18 June 1862, in *Life and Letters,* I:276, 277; James X. McIlwain to wife, 22 June 1862, USAMHI.

28. Adam S. Bright to uncle, 24 June 1862, in Truxall, *Respects to All,* 23–24; George Meade to wife, 20 June 1862, in *Life and Letters,* I:277; Kepler typescript, HSP; Philip Lantzy to brother, 20 June 1862, USAMHI.

29. Kepler typescript, HSP.

30. George Meade to wife, 22 June and 24 June 1862, in *Life and Letters,* I:278; Andrew Lewis to wife, 25 June 1862, USAMHI; "A Curious Letter to General M'Call," *Richmond Examiner,* 30 June 1862, 1.

31. Bates, *Pennsylvania Volunteers,* I:847; Andrew Lewis to wife, 25 June 1862, USAMHI.

32. Kepler typescript, HSP.

33. Sauers, "Pennsylvania Reserves," 24, 29–30; *Official Records,* 11:2, p. 399.

34. Bates, *Pennsylvania Volunteers,* I:847; *Official Records,* 11:2, p. 835.

35. E. A. Pollard, *Lost Cause,* 284; *Official Records,* 11:2, p. 399; McGinley diary entry for 26 June 1862, RNBP; letter by James C. Burke, *Alleghanian,* 31 July 1862, 3; letter by Daniel D. Jones, *Alleghanian,* 21 August 1862, 3; Bates, *Pennsylvania Volunteers,* I:847; Thomas Gallagher report to George McCall, a document quoted in the letter by "A.M.R.," *Alleghanian,* 28 August 1862, 1.

36. *Southern Historical Society Papers* 21 (1893):125; Edgar Allen Jackson to mother, 1 July 1862, quoted in Sears, *Gates of Richmond,* 207.

37. Letter by Daniel D. Jones, *Alleghanian,* 21 August 1862, 3.

38. Wiley, *Billy Yank,* 69, 71–72; Walter Clark, *Under the Stars and Bars* (Augusta, Ga.: no publisher cited, 1900), 45, quoted in Coco, *Civil War Infantryman,* 92.

39. Priest, *Antietam,* 30; Jacob Heffelfinger to sister, 11 August 1862, in McLaughlin, ed., "'Dear Sister Jennie,'" 206; "The Second Anniversary of Co. K, 11th Regt. P.R.C.—May 15th, 1863," *Brookville Republican,* 27 May 1863, 1; Grant quoted in John Keegan, *Mask of Command,* 183; Coco, *Civil War Infantryman,* 139; Keegan, *Face of Battle,* 205.

40. Woodward, *Our Campaigns,* 153–54.

41. Frank Holsinger, "How Does One Feel under Fire," in Commager, *Blue and the Gray,* 306–7.

42. Kepler typescript, HSP; Jacob Heffelfinger to sister, 11 August 1862, in McLaughlin, ed., "'Dear Sister Jennie,'" 206.

43. *Official Records,* 11:1, p. 222 and 11:2, p. 624; letter by Daniel D. Jones, *Alleghanian,* 21 August 1862, 3 ; Sears, *Gates of Richmond,* 207; "Incidents of the Contest," *Richmond Examiner,* 1 July 1862, 1.

44. Pollard, *Lost Cause,* 284; Kepler typescript, HSP; Jacob Heffelfinger to sister, 11 August 1862, in McLaughlin, ed., "'Dear Sister Jennie,'" 206.

45. Letter by James C. Burke, *Alleghanian*, 31 July 1862, 3; letter by Daniel D. Jones, *Alleghanian*, 21 August 1862, 3; Gallagher to McCall, as quoted by "A.M.R.," *Alleghanian*, 28 August 1862, 1; *Official Records*, 11:2, p. 386.

46. *Official Records*, 11:2, p. 399; Cordello Collins to parents, 19 July 1862, as reprinted in the *Warren (Penn.) Mail*, 23 August 1862, 2, in Reinsberg, ed., "Bucktail Voice," 241.

47. Livermore, 82. For more on the Confederate penchant for the tactical offensive, see Grady McWhiney and Perry D. Jamieson, *Attack and Die: Civil War Military Tactics and the Southern Heritage* (Tuscaloosa: University of Alabama Press, 1982).

48. *Official Records*, 11:2, pp. 222, 386.

49. *Official Records*, 11:1, p. 165 and 11:2, p. 400; Sears, *Gates of Richmond*, 210–11.

50. *Official Records*, 11:2, p. 386.

51. Gallagher to McCall, as quoted by "A.M.R.," *Alleghanian*, 28 August 1862, 1; letter by James C. Burke, *Alleghanian*, 31 July 1862, 3.

52. Gallagher to McCall, as quoted by "A.M.R.," *Alleghanian*, 28 August 1862, 1; Jackson, *Diary*, 32; Kepler typescript, HSP; John M. Loor pension file (cert. 262,128), NA-RG15.

53. Sauers, "Pennsylvania Reserves," 29–30; *Official Records*, 11:2, p. 386.

54. *Official Records*, 11:2, p. 401; Sears, *Gates of Richmond*, 240.

55. Sauers, "Pennsylvania Reserves," 30; *Official Records*, 11:2, pp. 400–401.

56. "More of the Yankee Prisoners—Scenes and Incidents in the City," *Richmond Examiner*, 30 June 1862, 1; letter by Evans R. Brady, *Indiana Democrat*, 2 October 1862, 1. Sarah Watt's house near the Gaines' Mill battlefield today is administered by the National Park Service. She owned twenty-eight slaves according to the 1860 United States Population Census, Slave Schedules for St. Paul's Parish, Hanover County, Virginia, M653, roll 139, NA.

57. *Official Records*, 11:2, p. 348; Bates, *Pennsylvania Volunteers*, I:847.

58. Sauers, "Pennsylvania Reserves," 30, 31; Gallagher to McCall, as quoted by "A.M.R.," *Alleghanian*, 28 August 1862, 1.

59. Gallagher to McCall, as quoted by "A.M.R.," *Alleghanian*, 28 August 1862, 1; Bates, *Pennsylvania Volunteers*, I:848; "Company B," *Indiana Messenger*, 16 July 1862, 3; letter by Hannibal K. Sloan, *Indiana Democrat*, 17 July 1862, 3.

60. *Official Records*, 11:2, pp. 420, 433, 444.

61. Gallagher to McCall, as quoted by "A.M.R.," *Alleghanian*, 28 August 1862, 1; letter by George W. Kremer, *National Tribune*, 14 February 1884 [no page notation], clipping in files of RNBP; Bates, *Pennsylvania Volunteers*, I:848.

62. Gallagher to McCall, as quoted by "A.M.R.," *Alleghanian*, 28 August 1862, 1; letter by Daniel D. Jones, *Alleghanian*, 21 August 1862, 3.

63. *Official Records*, 11:2, pp. 420, 444–45, 483.

64. Besides Hood's own *Advance and Retreat*, for more on the man and his campaigns, see Buell, *Warrior Generals*; Wiley Sword, *The Confederacy's Last Hurrah: Spring Hill, Franklin and Nashville* (Lawrence: University of Kansas Press, 1992); and Richard M. McMurry, *John Bell Hood and the War for Southern Independence* (Lincoln, Neb.: Bison Books, 1992).

65. Hood, *Advance and Retreat*, 26–27.

66. Captain (then-Lt.) W. T. Hill, quoted in Polley, *Texas Brigade*, 65.

67. *Official Records*, 11:2, p. 445.

68. Gallagher to McCall, as quoted by "A.M.R.," *Alleghanian*, 28 August 1862, 1; letter by Daniel D. Jones, *Alleghanian*, 21 August 1862, 3; letter by James C. Burke, *Alleghanian*, 31 July 1862, 3.

69. Kepler typescript, HSP; Burke, *Alleghanian*; Jones, *Alleghanian*; "Further Particulars—Official List of Casualties," *Alleghanian*, 24 July 1862, 3, citing the *Pittsburgh Gazette*; Thompson Carney pension file (cert. 104,562), NA-RG15; letter by William Leavy, *Alleghanian*, 7 August 1862, 2; Philip Lantzy to father, mother, sisters and brothers, 7 August 1862, USAMHI.

70. Benjamin Job pension file (cert. 889,728), NA-RG15; Thomas Spires pension file (cert. 21,454), NA-RG15; James Speer pension file (cert. 172,716), NA-RG15; "11th Reserves," *Indiana Messenger*, 23 July 1862, 3.

71. Jacob Heffelfinger to sister, 19 January 1863, in McLaughlin, ed., "'Dear Sister Jennie,'" 217.

72. Kepler typescript, HSP; Kepler pension file (cert. 99,274), NA-RG15; Thompson Carney pension file (cert. 104,562), NA-RG15.

73. Letter by James C. Burke, *Alleghanian*, 31 July 1862, 3; letter by Daniel D. Jones, *Alleghanian*, 21 August 1862, 3; Philip Lantzy to father, mother, sisters and brothers, 7 August 1862, USAMHI; "Letter from Maj. Johns," *Genius of Liberty*, 31 July 1862, 4.

74. O. T. Hanks, "Sketch History of Captain B. F. Bentons Company," handwritten ms., Stephen F. Austin State University, quoted in James I. Robertson Jr., *Stonewall Jackson*, 482–83.

75. *Official Records*, 11:2, p. 445.

76. Gallagher to McCall, as quoted in letter by "A.M.R.," *Alleghanian*, 28 August 1862, 1; Thomas Sallade pension file (cert. 112,246), NA-RG15.

77. *Official Records*, 11:2, pp. 349–50, 388–89, 401, 446, 457.

78. Ibid., pp. 445–46.

79. Bates, *Pennsylvania Volunteers*, I:848; letter by George W. Kremer, *National Tribune*, 14 February 1884, no page, clipping in files of the RNBP.

80. Gallagher to McCall, as quoted in letter by "A.M.R.," *Alleghanian*, 28 August 1862, 1; Bates, *Pennsylvania Volunteers*, I:848.

81. *Official Records*, 11:2, p. 445; Bates, *Pennsylvania Volunteers*, I:848.

82. Gallagher to McCall, as quoted in letter by "A.M.R.," *Alleghanian*, 28 August 1862, 1; Philip Lantzy to father, mother, sisters and brothers, 7 August 1862, USAMHI; letter by Daniel D. Jones, *Alleghanian*, 21 August 1862, 3; McBride, *In the Ranks*, 21.

83. *Official Records*, 11:2, p. 446; O. T. Hanks, "Sketch History of Captain B. F. Bentons Company," quoted in Robertson, *Stonewall Jackson*, 483; letter by Daniel D. Jones, *Alleghanian*, 21 August 1862, 3; E. M. Law, "On the Confederate Right at Gaines' Mill," in Johnson and Buel, eds., *Battles and Leaders*, II:364; William R. Hamby, quoted in Polley, *Hood's Texas Brigade*, 61.

84. Gallagher to McCall, as quoted in letter by "A.M.R.," *Alleghanian*, 28 August 1862, 1; Jackson, *Diary*, 39; Daniel S. Porter to "Capt. Baird," 11 July 1862, NA-RG94-11MR. The latter shows that between 30 June and 11 July 1862, Porter reported the return of four men from Company A, four men from Company E, seven men from Company F, nineteen men from Company G, and nine men from Company K. The report does not differentiate those who escaped capture at Gaines' Mill from returnees from details, hospital, etc.

85. Letter by Daniel D. Jones, *Alleghanian*, 21 August 1862, 3; "More of the Yankee Prisoners—Scenes and Incidents in the City," *Richmond Examiner*, 30 June 1862, 1

86. W. T. Hill, quoted in Polley, *Hood's Texas Brigade*, 66–67 (Hill mistakenly identifies the Union regiment as the "Sixth New Jersey"); Simpson quoted in E. M. Law, "On the Confederate Right at Gaines' Mill," in Johnson and Buel, eds., *Battles and Leaders*, II:364n.

87. E. M. Law, "On the Confederate Right at Gaines' Mill," in Johnson and Buel, eds., *Battles and Leaders*, II:365; *Official Records*, 11:2, pp. 32, 34; Bates, *Pennsylvania Volunteers*, I:849; "11th Reserves," *Indiana Messenger*, 23 July 1862, 3; "The 11th Reserves—Unofficial Report of the Killed and Wounded, and Prisoners, at Richmond," *Pittsburgh Gazette*, 22 July 1862, no page number, clipping in files of RNBP; McGinley diary entry for 17 June 1862, RNBP; letter by George W. Kremer, *National Tribune*, 14 February 1884, no page number, clipping in files of RNBP.

88. Thomas Green Penn to mother, 27 June 1862, quoted in Robertson, *Stonewall Jackson*, 483; Kepler typescript, HSP; William R. Hamby, quoted in Polley, *Hood's Texas Brigade*, 61.

89. "The Fight at Gaines' Mills—An Officer's Statement," *Richmond Examiner*, 2 July 1862, 1; "The 11th Regiment Reserves," *Pittsburgh Gazette*, 25 June 1862, no page number, clipping in files of RNBP.

90. *Official Records*, 11:2, p. 446.

91. *Official Records*, 11:2, pp. 388–89.

92. Fox, *Regimental Losses*, 260; letter by James C. Burke, *Alleghanian*, 31 July 1862, 3.

Chapter 5. Another Way to Take Richmond

1. Untitled entry, *Democrat & Sentinel,* 9 July 1862, 2.

2. Kepler typescript, HSP.

3. Letter by James C. Burke, *Alleghanian,* 31 July 1862, 3.

4. Letter by James C. Burke, *Alleghanian,* 31 July 1862, 3. "Death of Captain Andrew Lewis," *Alleghanian,* 7 August 1862, 2; Kepler typescript, HSP; Sypher, *History of the Pennsylvania Reserve Corps,* 508.

5. Daniel Porter to Maria Lewis, 24 July 1862, USAMHI; J. S. DeBenneville pension file (cert. 97,513), NA-RG15.

6. "The Battles on the Richmond Lines," *Richmond Examiner,* 30 June 1862, 1.

7. Bates, *Pennsylvania Volunteers,* I:849; "More of the Yankee Prisoners—Scenes and Incidents in the City," *Richmond Examiner,* 30 June 1862, 1.

8. Bates, *Pennsylvania Volunteers,* I:849; Jackson, *Diary,* 32; "Incidents of the Contest," *Richmond Examiner,* 1 July 1862, 1; "Colors Brought In" and "The Bucktails Played Out," *Richmond Enquirer,* 1 July 1862, 1.

9. Letter by George W. Kremer, *National Tribune,* 14 February 1884, no page, clipping in files of RNBP; Kepler typescript, HSP.

10. *Official Records,* series 2, 5, pp. 905–6; 6, pp. 262–63, 544–45, 573; Robert W. Waitt, *Libby Prison,* Official Publication #12, Richmond Civil War Centennial Committee, 1961–65, transcribed at www.mdgorman.com/libby_prison__robert_w_waitt.htm; Aaron Kepler typescript, HSP.

11. "More of the Yankee Prisoners—Scenes and Incidents in the City," *Richmond Examiner,* 30 June 1862, 1; James McGinley diary entry for 28 June 1862, RNBP.

12. Bates, *Pennsylvania Volunteers,* I:849; Jackson, *Diary,* 32; letter by George W. Kremer, *National Tribune,* 14 February 1884, no page notation, clipping in files of RNBP.

13. Letter by George W. Kremer, *National Tribune,* 14 February 1884, no page notation, clipping in files of RNBP.

14. Letter by George W. Kremer, *National Tribune,* 14 February 1884, clipping (no page notation) in files of RNBP; *Official Records,* series 2, 5, p. 387; letter by D. P. K. Lavan, *National Tribune,* 10 February 1884, clipping, no page citation, in files of RNBP.

15. "Belle's Island Prison Depot," *Richmond Examiner,* 4 August 1862, 2; Waitt, *Libby Prison.*

16. Lemuel Dobbs pension file (cert. 522,302), NA-RG15.

17. "At Home," *Alleghanian,* 28 August 1862, 3; Philip Lantzy to father, mother, sisters and brother, 7 August 1862, USAMHI; Adam Bright to uncle, 8 August 1862, in Truxall, *Respects to All,* 29.

18. "More of the Yankee Prisoners—Scenes and Incidents in the City," *Richmond Examiner,* 30 June 1862, 1; "Yankee Counterfeiting of Confederate Money," *Richmond Examiner,* 2 July 1862, 1.

19. "More of the Yankee Prisoners—Scenes and Incidents in the City," *Richmond Examiner,* 30 June 1862, 1.

20. Letter by William Leavy, *Alleghanian,* 7 August 1862, 2; Kepler typescript, HSP.

21. Letter by James C. Burke, *Alleghanian,* 31 July 1862, 3.

22. White quotes his own remark, which he states he wrote in a previous letter to the same recipient, in a letter to Brig. Gen. W. A. Hammond, 31 March 1863, NA-RG94-MOF.

23. William H. White to Brig. Gen. S. P. Graham, 20 September 1863, in White pension file (cert. 332,088), NA-RG15.

24. William H. White to Brig. Gen. W. A. Hammond, 31 March 1863, NA-RG94-MOF; S. T. Denny to Surgeon General U.S.A., 4 September 1863, NA-RG94-MOF; Captain A. Judson Clark to Captain Geo. E. Randolph, 1 October 1863, NA-RG94-MOF; extract from Special Orders No. 434, 28 September 1863, NA-RG94-MOF; William H. White to Brig. Gen. S. P. Graham, 20 September 1863, and William H. White death certificate, both in White pension file (cert. 332,088), NA-RG15.

25. *Official Records,* series 2, 5, p. 386.

26. Meade, *Life and Letters,* I:296; "Letter from Gen. McCall," *Indiana Messenger,* 23 July 1862, 3; Welsh, *Medical Histories,* 209. William R. Hamby, quoted in Polley, *Hood's Texas Brigade,* 61–62.

27. *Official Records,* series 2, 5, p. 386; Letter by James C. Burke, *Alleghanian,* 31 July 1862, 3.

28. Letter by James C. Burke, *Alleghanian,* 31 July 1862, 3.

29. "Treatment of Yankee Officers in Richmond," *Richmond Examiner,* 5 July 1862, 1; *Official Records,* series 2, 5, p. 386; Jackson, *Diary,* 33; "Letter from Maj. Johns," *Genius of Liberty,* 31 July 1862, 4.

30. Jackson, *Diary,* 33; James McGinley diary entry for 21 July 1862, RNBP.

31. Jackson, *Diary,* 33, 34, 35, 37, 38.

32. Ibid., 36 (Jackson [37] also recorded a visit by Whaley to Major Johns on Monday, 21 July); *Official Records,* 11:2, 397.

33. Daniel Porter reported that between 30 June and 11 July he received the return of four men from Company A, four men from Company E, seven men from Company F, 19 men from Company G, and nine men from Company K. Porter to Captain Baird, 11 July 1862, NA-RG94–11MR.

34. James McIlwain to wife, 6 July 1862, USAMHI.

35. "Sergt. R. H. Fair," *Indiana Messenger,* 13 August 1862, 3; Sutor's letter is quoted in Cubbison, "That Gallant Company," 17; "Company B," *Indiana Messenger,* 16 July 1862, 3.

36. Smith, *Price of Patriotism,* 24; undated letters on the death of Harvey Fair, signed by "Lib" and "your affectionate sister Lizzie" (apparently by a sister of Fair), RNBP; "Sergt. R. H. Fair," *Indiana Messenger,* 13 August 1862, 3.

37. Sears, *Gates of Richmond,* 255–57.

38. *Official Records,* 51:1, p. 114; James McIlwain to wife, 6 July 1862, USAMHI.

39. *Official Records,* 51:1, p. 114; Sears, *Gates of Richmond,* 255–57.

40. *Official Records,* 51:1, p. 114; Sears, *Gates of Richmond,* 298–99.

41. *Official Records,* 51:1, p. 114; Sears, *Gates of Richmond,* 298–99; Welsh, *Medical Histories,* 225.

42. *Official Records,* 51:1, p. 114; Smith, *Price of Patriotism,* 25; "Our Soldiers," *Indiana Messenger,* 9 July 1862, 3; Cubbison, "That Gallant Company," 18; Henderson Howard pension file (cert. 885,935), and Charles Shambaugh pension file (cert. 20,341), NA-RG15; *Story of American Heroism,* 136; Sears, *Gates of Richmond,* 298–99.

43. Letter from Hannibal Sloan, *Indiana Democrat,* 17 July 1862, 3; "Company B," *Indiana Messenger,* 16 July 1862, 3; "Our Soldiers," *Indiana Messenger,* 9 July 1862, 3; "Executed with John Brown," *National Tribune,* 9 July 1891, clipping, no page number, in files of RNBP; Bates, *Pennsylvania Volunteers,* I:858, 859; *Official Records,* 51:1, p. 114; William Hazlett pension file (cert. 622,980), NA-RG15; Cubbison, "That Gallant Company," 18; Sears, *Gates of Richmond,* 298–99.

44. Letter by Hannibal Sloan, *Indiana Democrat,* 17 July 1862, 3; "Our Soldiers," *Indiana Messenger,* 9 July 1862, 3; "Rebel Flag," *Indiana Messenger,* 20 August 1862, 3.

45. Pvt. Leo Faller quoted in Cubbison, "That Gallant Company," 19; Adam S. Bright to uncle and aunt et al., 7 July 1862, in Truxall, *Respects to All,* 25–26.

46. Pollard, *Lost Cause,* 617–19.

47. Jackson, *Diary,* 37; untitled article, *Alleghanian,* 31 July 1862, 2.

48. Benjamin Job pension file (cert. 889,728), NA-RG15.

49. Bell I. Wiley, *Billy Yank,* 157; Special Orders No. 100 [?], pt. 3, from Headquarters, V Army Corps, 3 August 1862, NA-RG94–11MR; Bates, *Pennsylvania Volunteers,* I:855, 875; letter by Hannibal Sloan, *Indiana Democrat,* 17 July 1862, 3.

50. Meade, *Life and Letters,* I:296; Jackson, *Diary,* 34; Welsh, *Medical Histories,* 225–26.

51. Letter by A. W. Stewart, *Indiana Messenger,* 6 August 1862, 3.

52. Daniel Porter to Andrew Curtin, 4 August 1862, PSA-RG19, microfilm 3690, folder 1, 40th Regt.

53. Woodward, *Our Campaigns,* 121.

54. Special Order form (no number) from Headquarters, Seymour's Division, PRVC, 16 July 1862, in NA-RG94–11MR.

55. See, e.g., the Summary Statements of Quarterly Returns of Ordnance and Ordnance Stores included in Record Group 156 (Records of the Office of the Chief of Ordnance), National Archives Microfilm Publication M1281.

56. Philip Lantzy to brother and sister-in-law, 24 August 1862, USAMHI.

Chapter 6. Shot Down Like Sheep

1. The Second Bull Run/Second Manassas campaign was a complex one of intense movement, by both sides, involving often widely scattered forces. Besides those sources specifically cited, troop movement details and background data presented in this chapter are principally drawn from Hennessy, *Return to Bull Run;* Esposito, ed., *West Point Atlas,* I, maps 57–62 and corresponding text; the NPS Second Manassas map series; and notes and correspondence during 1999–2000 with Frank A. O'Reilly, FSNMP.

2. Hennessy, *Return to Bull Run,* 8–10.

3. Ibid., 10.

4. Bates, *Pennsylvania Volunteers,* I:849.

5. *Official Records,* series 2, 4, pp. 437, 445.

6. Philip Lantzy to father, mother, sisters and brothers, 7 August 1862, USAMHI; Sauers, *Advance the Colors,* I:108.

7. Thomas Sallade pension file (cert. 172,245), NA-RG15; Philip Lantzy to brother and sister-in-law, 24 August 1862, USAMHI; Welsh, *Medical Histories,* 209.

8. Jackson, *Diary,* 40, 41; Lewis A. Johnston to Elizabeth Gallagher, 6 November 1885, and undated statement by Joseph L. Cook, M.D., Thomas F. Gallagher pension file (cert. 222,972), NA-RG15; Extract from Special Orders No. 236, 14 August 1862, NA-RG94-11P.

9. Bates, *Pennsylvania Volunteers,* I:871; Special Orders No. 247, 18 September 1862, in NA-RG94-11P; Thomas Spires pension file (cert. 21,454), NA-RG15. Details about Dickson's service and resignation are contained in Brig. Gen. C. H. Bridges to Commissioner of Pensions, 15 December 1928, William G. Hardcastle pension file (cert. 1,627,700), NA-RG15.

10. Thomas D. Litzinger pension file (cert. 158,640), NA-RG15.

11. McGinley diary entries for 5, 6, and 13 August 1862, RNBP.

12. Sypher, *History of the Pennsylvania Reserve Corps,* 334–35; Samuel Jackson et al. to S. Williams, 14 August 1862, NA-RG94-11MR; Jackson, *Diary,* 41.

13. Jackson, *Diary,* 41–42.

14. Untitled document signed by D. S. Porter as "Captain Commanding 11th Reg. P.R.C.," executed "In obedience to Gen. Order No. 10," 18 August 1862, NA-RG94-11MR.

15. Bates, *Pennsylvania Volunteers,* I:849, 850; Woodward, *Our Campaigns,* 127.

16. Nichols, *Toward Gettysburg,* 79, 80, 81.

17. Ibid., 79, 80.

18. John Reynolds to sisters, 15 August 1862, Archives and Special Collections Dept., Franklin and Marshall College, MS group 6, series X, box 8, folder 2, Eleanor Reynolds scrapbook of J. F. Reynolds correspondence.

19. *Official Records,* 51:1, pp. 752–53.

20. Jackson, *Diary,* 42.

21. Welsh, *Medical Histories,* 181; Sypher, *History of the Pennsylvania Reserve Corps,* 416; Philip Lantzy to brother and sister-in-law, 24 August 1862, USAMHI.

22. Jackson, *Diary,* 42; Philip Lantzy to brother and sister-in-law, 24 August 1862, USAMHI; letter by J. P. Miller, *Brookville Republican,* 22 April 1863, 2.

23. Philip Lantzy to brother and sister-in-law, 24 August 1862, USAMHI.

24. Boatner, *Civil War Dictionary,* 102; McGinley diary, 23 August 1862, RNBP; Jackson, *Diary,* 42, 43.

25. *Official Records*, 12:3, p. 643; Reynolds to sisters, 15 August 1862, Archives and Special Collections Dept., Franklin and Marshall College, MS group 6, series X, box 8, folder 2, Eleanor Reynolds scrapbook of J. F. Reynolds correspondence.

26. Nichols, *Toward Gettysburg*, 110–11. Also see Sigel's testimony at the McDowell Court of Inquiry in *Official Records*, 12:1, p. 124.

27. Jackson, *Diary*, 43, 44; letter by E. R. Brady, *Indiana Democrat*, 2 October 1862, 1.

28. Jackson, *Diary*, 43–44; *Official Records*, 12:2, pp. 265, 377–78, 393; Second Manassas mapset, NPS.

29. Jackson, *Diary*, 44; letter from E. R. Brady, *Indiana Democrat*, 2 October 1862, 1.

30. Jackson, *Diary*, 44; *Official Records*, 12:2, pp. 266, 393–94, 397–98; Second Manassas map set, NPS.

31. *Official Records*, 12:3, p. 729; Second Manassas map set, NPS.

32. Jackson, *Diary*, 44; letter by E. R. Brady, *Indiana Democrat*, 2 October 1862, 1; *Official Records*, 12:2, pp. 393–94; Second Manassas map set, NPS.

33. *Official Records*, 12:2, pp. 393–94; letter by E. R. Brady, *Indiana Democrat*, 2 October, 1862, 1; letter by George Trimble quoted under "Letter from the Army," *Indiana Messenger*, 10 September 1862, 2; Bates, *Pennsylvania Volunteers*, I:859; James McGinley diary, 29 August 1862, RNBP; Jackson, *Diary*, 44.

34. Esposito, ed., *West Point Atlas*, I, map 62 and corresponding text; Hennessy, *Return to Bull Run*, 233–34; *Official Records*, 12:2, pp. 564–65; 12:2 (supplement), pp. 852, 903, 1010–11; 12:3, p. 730.

35. Bates, *Pennsylvania Volunteers*, I:849–50; Second Manassas map set, NPS.

36. Esposito, ed., *West Point Atlas*, I, map 62 and corresponding text; *Official Records*, 12:2, p. 519. For more on Porter's court-martial, see Sears, *Controversies and Commanders*, 53–73.

37. *Official Records*, 12:2, pp. 547, 565, 605; Hennessy, *Return to Bull Run*, 287–304; Buell, *Warrior Generals*, 103.

38. *Official Records*, 12:2, pp. 395, 481, and 51:1, p. 130; Sypher, *History of the Pennsylvania Reserve Corps*, 358; Welsh, *Medical Histories*, 181.

39. Nichols, *Toward Gettysburg*, 112; Jackson, *Diary*, 44. Bates, *Pennsylvania Volunteers*, I:850; letter by E. R. Brady, *Indiana Democrat*, 2 October 1862, 1.

40. *Official Records*, 12:2, pp. 394, 565.

41. Ibid., 394; Second Manassas map set, NPS.

42. *Official Records*, 12:2, p. 394; Nichols, *Toward Gettysburg*, 113.

43. *Official Records*, 12:2, pp. 394, 503.

44. Hennessy, *Return to Bull Run*, 375; Bates, *Pennsylvania Volunteers*, I:850; *Official Records*, 12:2, pp. 394, 502–3.

45. Hennessy, *Return to Bull Run*, 376.

46. Polley, *Hood's Texas Brigade*, 104–7; Hennessy, *Return to Bull Run*, 376–77; letter by E. R. Brady, *Indiana Democrat*, 2 October 1862, 1.

47. Hennessy, *Return to Bull Run*, 375–77; letter by George Trimble quoted under "Letter from the Army," *Indiana Messenger*, 10 September 1862, 2; Bates, *Pennsylvania Volunteers*, I:859; untitled item, *Democrat & Sentinel*, 10 September 1862, 2; statement by Robert McCoy dated 19 October 1868 on a Certificate of Disability form, and other documents in Rowland Jones pension file (cert. 307,949), NA-RG15.

48. Welsh, *Medical Histories*, 151; *Official Records*, 12:2, p. 395; Bates, *Pennsylvania Volunteers*, I:784. According to Anderson's papers in his service file (NA-RG94-CSR), he was forty-three as of 21 July 1861. He resigned his commission 10 February 1863. In 1889, his rank upon discharge was altered to that of colonel of volunteers, retroactive to 17 July 1862.

49. *Official Records*, 12:2, p. 395.

50. Bates, *Pennsylvania Volunteers*, I:858–59; "Henderson C. Howard," undated clipping in Civil War Scrapbook, Historical and Genealogical Society of Indiana County; Henderson C. Howard pension file (cert. 885,935), NA-RG15; letter from E. R. Brady, *Indiana Democrat*, 2 October 1862, 1; letter by George Trimble quoted under "Letter from the

Army," *Indiana Messenger,* 10 September 1862, 2; Charles Shambaugh pension file (cert. 20,341), NA-RG15.

51. Daniel R. Coder pension file (cert. 430, 414), NA-RG15; Bates, *Pennsylvania Volunteers,* I:862–64; Fox, *Regimental Losses,* 260; McBride, *In the Ranks,* 22; J. T. Stewart, *Indiana County, Pennsylvania* (Chicago: J. H. Beers, 1913), I:111.

52. As quoted by W. R. Hamby in Polley, *Hood's Texas Brigade,* 94–95.

53. *Official Records,* 12:2, p. 395; James McGinley diary entry for 30 August 1862, RNBP; letter by E. R. Brady, *Indiana Democrat,* 2 October 1862, 1.

54. Letter by E. R. Brady, *Indiana Democrat,* 2 October 1862, 1.

55. Ibid.

56. Jackson, *Diary,* 44.

57. "Experiences of a Prisoner," *National Intelligencer,* 27 September 1862, 2.

Chapter 7. Brave Comrades Falling

1. Lee recounted the reasons behind the Maryland campaign in an 1868 talk with William Allen, transcribed in Gallagher, ed., *Lee the Soldier,* 7; Esposito, ed., *West Point Atlas,* I, map 65 and corresponding text.

2. George Meade to wife, 4 September 1862, in *Life and Letters,* I:308.

3. Daniel Porter to "Capt. Baird," 7 August 1862, NA-RG94-11MR; Special Orders No. 18, Headquarters, IX Army Corps, 16 August 1862, NA-RG94-11MR; "At Home," *Alleghanian,* 28 August 1862, 3.

4. Philip Lantzy to brother and sister-in-law, 24 August 1862, USAMHI.

5. Letter by George Trimble, *Indiana Messenger,* 10 September 1862, 2.

6. Letter by E. R. Brady, *Indiana Democrat,* 2 October 1862, 1.

7. McGinley diary entry for 6 September 1862, RNBP; Jackson, *Diary,* 45; James Burke to Gen. John C. Black, 15 July 1886, in Burke pension file (cert. 398,014), NA-RG15.

8. Letter by Evans Brady, *Indiana Democrat,* 2 October 1862, 1.

9. Letter by George Trimble, *Indiana Messenger,* 10 September 1862, 2.

10. D. M. Perry, "Gen. McDowell's Hat," *National Tribune,* 1 December 1892, quoted in Hennessy, *Return to Bull Run,* 466.

11. *Official Records,* 12:1, p. 39.

12. Ibid., pp. 331–32.

13. Boatner, *Civil War Dictionary,* 187–88, 409.

14. *Official Records,* 11:2, p. 111.

15. Sauers, "Pennsylvania Reserves," 38–39, and n45; *Official Records,* 11:2, pp. 114, 393–98; George McCall, *Pennsylvania Reserves on the Peninsula* (Philadelphia, 1862).

16. Nichols, *Toward Gettysburg,* 123; *Official Records,* 19:2, p. 216 and 51:1, p. 791; "Our Cambria County Militia," *Alleghanian,* 25 September 1862, 3.

17. *Official Records,* 19:2, pp. 214, 217.

18. Ibid., p. 217.

19. Jackson, *Diary,* 46.

20. Christopher Herbert to Elizabeth Gallagher, 14 November 1885, in Thomas Gallagher pension file (cert. 222,972), NA-RG15.

21. "Our Cambria County Militia," *Alleghanian,* 25 September 1862, 3; *Official Records,* 27:2, p. 215.

22. *Official Records,* 19:2, pp. 250, 252.

23. Ibid., pp. 273–74.

24. Jackson, *Diary,* 46; George Meade to wife, 13 September 1862, in *Life and Letters,* I:310.

25. Reynolds to sisters, 28 September 1862, Archives and Special Collections Dept., Franklin and Marshall College, MS Group 6, series X, box 8, folder 2, Eleanor Reynolds scrapbook of J. F. Reynolds correspondence.

26. Newspaper clippings headed "Gen. Reynolds" and "From All Accounts," no dates, no source or page citations, but grouped with correspondence dated 14 October 1862, Archives and Special Collections Dept., Franklin and Marshall College, MS Group 6, series X, box 8, folder 2, Eleanor Reynolds scrapbook of J. F. Reynolds correspondence.

27. Jackson, *Diary*, 46; "Capt. E. Bierer," *Genius of Liberty*, 25 September 1862, 4; Record of Recruits, Connoquennessing [*sic*] Rangers, 19 June 1861, NA-RG94-11MR.

28. For a recent treatment of the Lost Order episode, see "Last Words on the Lost Order," in Sears, *Controversies and Commanders*, 109–30. Besides those sources specifically cited, troop movement details and background data presented in this chapter are principally drawn from Esposito, ed., *West Point Atlas*, I, maps 65–69 and corresponding text; Murfin, *Gleam of Bayonets* (featuring troop movement maps by James D. Bowlby), passim; Harsh, *Taken at the Flood*, passim; Sears, *Landscape Turned Red*, passim; and conversations and correspondence during 2000 with Keith Snyder and Ted Alexander of Antietam National Battlefield.

29. Jackson, *Diary*, 47.

30. Boatner, *Civil War Dictionary*, 20.

31. James McIlwain to wife, 14 September 1862, USAMHI.

32. Letter by Joseph Potter Miller, *Brookville Republican*, 5 August 1863, 1; Woodward, *Our Campaigns*, 149; Jackson, *Diary*, 47; Sears, *Landscape Turned Red*, 135–36; Harsh, *Taken at the Flood*, 265.

33. *Official Records*, 19:1, pp. 170, 221, 241, 274; Sears, *Landscape Turned Red*, 136; Welsh, *Medical Histories*, 195; Carman, "Maryland Campaign" ms.

34. Woodward, *Our Campaigns*, 152; David L. Thompson, quoted in Sears, *Landscape Turned Red*, 136.

35. James McGinley diary entry for 14 September 1862, RNBP; Frassanito, *Antietam*, 256.

36. *Official Records*, 19:1, pp. 267, 272–74, and 51:1, pp. 142, 148; Jackson, *Diary*, 47; Sears, *Landscape Turned Red*, 136; Woodward, *Our Campaigns*, 152; Hardin, *History of the Twelfth Regiment*, 117; Murfin, *Gleam of Bayonets*, 178–79; Carman, "Maryland Campaign" ms.

37. Woodward, *Our Campaigns*, 152; *Official Records*, 19:1, p. 274, and 51:1, p. 153.

38. *Official Records*, 19:1, pp. 267, 274, and 51:1, pp. 149, 153, 154; *Official Military Atlas*, map 3, plate 27; Murfin, *Gleam of Bayonets*, 179; Carman, "Maryland Campaign" ms.

39. *Official Records*, 19:1, pp. 272, 1035; Sears, *Landscape Turned Red*, 137; Murfin, *Gleam of Bayonets*, 180, 181; Carman, "Maryland Campaign" ms.

40. *Official Records*, 19:1, pp. 274–75, 1035, and 51:1, pp. 149, 153, 154; "Capt. E. Bierer," *Genius of Liberty*, 25 September 1862, 4; Hugh Torrance pension file (cert. 672,261), NA-RG15; Bates, *Pennsylvania Volunteers*, I:850; Evans Brady pension file (cert. 2,264), NA-RG15; "The Second Anniversary of Co. K., 11th Regt. P.R.C.—May 15th, 1863," *Brookville Republican*, 27 May 1863, 1; Sypher, *History of the Pennsylvania Reserve Corps*, 374–75; Carman, "Maryland Campaign" ms. Speer's absence at this time is established in a letter (no addressee) by Pittsburgh doctor Julian Rogers, dated 19 September 1862, seeking "an extension of his leave of absence," and "that he is still incapable of performing his duty as a soldier on account of wounds received at the battle of Gaines Hill [*sic*]," NA-RG94-11P.

41. *Official Records*, 19:1, pp. 274–75; Bates, *Pennsylvania Volunteers*, I:850, 858; Carman, "Maryland Campaign" ms.

42. Thomson and Rauch, *History of the Bucktails*, 205; court-martial case file mm22, NA-RG153; Henry C. Stone military service file, NA-RG94-CSR; "The Remains of Captain Nesbitt," *Indiana Democrat*, 9 October 1862, 3.

43. *Official Records*, 51:1, p. 154; "Capt. E. Bierer," *Genius of Liberty*, 25 September 1862, 4; "Roll of Co. A" and "Roll of Co. G.," NA-RG94-11MR; Carman, "Maryland Campaign" ms.; James McIlwain to wife, 16 September 1862, USAMHI.

44. *Official Records*, 19:1, p. 1036; James McGinley diary entry for 14 September 1862, RNBP.

45. "Visit to Our Soldiers," *Alleghanian*, 16 October 1862, 2.

46. "The Second Anniversary of Co. K., 11th Regt. P.R.C.—May 15th, 1863," *Brookville Republican*, 27 May 1863, 1; *Official Records*, 19:1, p. 267, and 51:1, p. 153.

47. *Official Records,* 19:1, p. 268; "The Second Anniversary of Co. K., 11th Regt. P.R.C.—May 15th, 1863," *Brookville Republican,* 27 May 1863, 1; "Visit to Our Soldiers," *Alleghanian,* 16 October 1862, 2.

48. "The Remains of Captain Nesbitt," *Indiana Democrat,* 9 October 1862, 3.

49. *Official Records,* 19:1, p. 268; Bates, *Pennsylvania Volunteers,* I:850; Jackson, *Diary,* 47.

50. Woodward, *Our Campaigns,* 153.

51. *Official Records,* 19:1, p. 216.

52. Stotelmyer, *Bivouacs of the Dead,* 3–5; Lord, *Civil War Collector's Encyclopedia,* IV:137.

53. Woodward, *Our Campaigns,* 153.

54. Jackson, *Diary,* 47.

55. *Official Records,* 19:1, p. 217.

56. James McIlwain to wife, 16 September 1862, USAMHI.

57. *Official Records,* 19:1, pp. 268–69; Harsh, *Taken at the Flood,* 351.

58. Jackson, *Diary,* 47; *Official Records,* 19:1, pp. 217–18, 922, 937; Sears, *Landscape Turned Red,* 176; Polley, *Hood's Texas Brigade,* 115, 118; Harsh, *Taken at the Flood,* 351–52, 358.

59. National Park Service marker text (unnumbered, but adjacent to marker no. 24), Antietam Battlefield National Historical Site; *Official Records,* 19:1, pp. 217–18, and 51:1, pp. 150, 153, 154–55; Jackson, *Diary,* 47; Polley, *Hood's Texas Brigade,* 115.

60. *Official Records,* 19:1, p. 218; Sears, *Landscape Turned Red,* 181; Murfin, *Gleam of Bayonets,* 211–13.

61. Sears, *Landscape Turned Red,* 182, 191, 192; Murfin, *Gleam of Bayonets,* 212.

62. Text of marker no. 24, Antietam Battlefield National Park; *Official Records,* 19:1, pp. 218, 270; Sears, *Landscape Turned Red,* 184; Murfin, *Gleam of Bayonets,* 213.

63. *Official Records,* 19:1, p. 218; Sears, *Landscape Turned Red,* 182; Murfin, *Gleam of Bayonets,* 213–14.

64. *Official Records,* 19:1, p. 923; Murfin, *Gleam of Bayonets,* 219–21.

65. *Official Records,* 51:1, pp. 150–51, 153–54; "Visit to Our Soldiers," *Alleghanian,* 16 October 1862, 2.

66. *Official Records,* 19:1, pp. 932–33, and 51:1, pp. 150–51, 153–54.

67. Letter by "G.," *American Citizen,* 11 May 1864, 2; Samuel Jackson to James Kirk, 27 September 1862, NA-RG94-MR; Daniel Kistler pension file (cert. 1,808), NA-RG15. The Company C roll in NA-RG94-11MR states that Kuhn died on 18 September but Jackson's letter reads in part that Kuhn "died (from effects of wounds) on the 21st day of Sept. 1862."

68. Daniel Porter to Abraham Moore, Esq., in *Indiana Messenger,* 1 October 1862, 2.

69. From the text of marker no. 31, Antietam Battlefield National Park. The plaque, destroyed in late 1987, was located on the east side of the Hagerstown Pike. Keith Snyder of the park's staff provided the author with a copy of its original text.

70. Daniel Porter to Abraham Moore, Esq., *Indiana Messenger,* 1 October 1862, 2.

71. Jackson, *Diary,* 48; Stotelmyer, *Bivouacs of the Dead,* 6.

72. David Hunter Strother quoted in Stotelmyer, *Bivouacs of the Dead,* 7.

73. "Visit to Our Soldiers," *Alleghanian,* 16 October 1862, 2; Jackson, *Diary,* 51; "Co. A., 11th Penna. Reserves," *Alleghanian,* 16 October 1862, 3; Company A roll, NA-RG94-11MR; Samuel Jackson, "List of enternments [*sic*]" 22 September 1862, NA-RG94-11MR.

74. Bates, *Pennsylvania Volunteers,* I:868, 869, 874–75; Stotelmyer, *Bivouacs of the Dead,* 3, 6–7, 19–20, 21, 22, 25, 103, 127.

75. *Official Records,* 11:2, p. 114.

Chapter 8. Butchered Like So Many Animals

1. *Official Records,* 21, p. 878.

2. *Official Records,* 14, p. 389; Boatner, *Civil War Dictionary,* 188, 190, 664, 733; Woodward, *Our Campaigns,* 176.

3. Samuel Jackson to James T. Kirk, 24 September 1862, NA–RG94–11MR.

4. Jackson, *Diary*, 49, 53; court-martial case file KK 271, NA–RG153.

5. The endorsement appears on a 25 July 1862 letter signed by Tenth Pennsylvania Reserves surgeon B. Roher recommending a leave of absence for Kirk, in the James T. Kirk military service file, NA–RG94–CSR; Kirk pension file (cert. 230,107), NA–RG15.

6. James T. Kirk pension file (cert. 230,107), NA–RG15.

7. James T. Kirk to Seth Williams, 12 October 1862, in Kirk military service file, NA–RG94–CSR

8. Jackson, *Diary*, 49–50.

9. Samuel Jackson to James T. Kirk, 27 September 1862, NA–RG94–11MR.

10. Aaron Kepler pension file (cert. 99,274), NA–RG15.

11. Samuel Jackson to James T. Kirk, 27 September 1862, NA–RG94–11MR.

12. Jackson, *Diary*, 50–51; Adam Torrance military service file, NA–RG94–CSR.

13. Jackson, *Diary*, 51–53.

14. This segment is based on three documents in the Hugh A. Torrance pension file (cert. 672,261) in NA–RG15: a 27 July 1899 deposition by Torrance, a 12 April 1897 War Department form summarizing Torrance's military and medical records, and an undated but circa 1897 typewritten statement by Webster Davis to the Commissioner of Pensions.

15. Statement by J. S. DeBenneville, 22 September 1861, Hugh A. Torrance military service file, NA–RG94–CSR.

16. Hugh A. Torrance pension file (cert. 672,261) NA–RG15; Hugh A. Torrance to adjutant general, 12 November 1862, Torrance military service file, NA–RG94–CSR.

17. Robert Abbott McCoy to Truman Seymour, 24 September 1862, NA–RG94–11P.

18. Special Orders No. 247, 18 September 1862, NA–RG94–11P; Bates, *Pennsylvania Volunteers*, I:871.

19. Robert McElhaney pension file (cert. 452,875), NA–RG15; Robert McElhaney to Sarah A. Billingsley, 27 September 1862. A private collector purchased the latter document on 23 November 2000 on the Internet auction site www.ebay.com, which posted a transcript and scanned images of the letter. It is hoped that copies of the original will soon be made available to various archival collections.

20. Letter by "T.D.," *Alleghanian*, 13 November 1862, 3; Thomas D. Litzinger pension file (cert. 158,640), NA–RG15.

21. *Official Records*, 12:3, p. 311 and 25:2, p. 31; letter by "T.D.," *Alleghanian*, 13 November 1862, 3.

22. Anthony E. Stocker, M.D., to "Capt. Liebeman, provost marshal," 29 September 1862 (two letters of the same date), NA–RG94–11MR; Bates, *Pennsylvania Volunteers*, I:850.

23. Everard Bierer to Simon Cameron, 23 August 1861, in Peter A. Johns military service file, NA–RG94–CSR.

24. Everard Bierer to George Meade, 27 May 1862, NA–RG94–11MR.

25. Everard Bierer to Andrew Curtin, 30 January 1862, microfilm 3689, folder 12, 40th Regt. PSA–RG19; Boatner, *Civil War Dictionary*, 471.

26. Extracts from Special Orders 195 (19 August 1862) and 210 (28 August 1862), NA–RG94–11P; copy of Special Orders No. 210 (written in Bierer's distinctive handwriting), 28 August 1862, signed by Edwin M. Stanton, PSA–RG19, microfilm 3689, folder 12. For biographical data on Covode, see "From the Archives," *Western Pennsylvania Historical Magazine* 60 (1977):195. For biographical data on Cowan, see Albert, *History of the County of Westmoreland*, 334–36.

27. T. J. Coffey to E. M. Stanton, 30 August 1862, PSA–RG19, microfilm 3689, folder 12.

28. Everard Bierer to Andrew Curtin, 31 August 1862, PSA–RG19, microfilm 3689, folder 12, 40th Regt.

29. Everard Bierer to Abraham Lincoln, 4 September 1862, NA–RG94–11P.

30. "Capt. E. Bierer," *Genius of Liberty*, 25 September 1862, 4; Everard Bierer to E. Stezer, 2 October 1862, microfilm 3689, folder 12, 40th Regt., PSA–RG19.

31. Everard Bierer to Andrew Curtin, 11 November 1862, microfilm 3690, folder 1, 40th Regt., PSA-RG19.

32. Bates, *Pennsylvania Volunteers,* IV:1165–66.

33. Esposito, ed., *West Point Atlas,* I, map 70 and corresponding text; James McGinley diary, 2–8 November 1862, RNBP.

34. Jacob Heffelfinger to sister, 24 November 1862, in McLaughlin, ed., "'Dear Sister Jennie,'" 215; James McGinley diary, 11 November 1862, RNBP; letter by Samuel Jackson, *Greensburgh Herald,* 29 April 1863, 3.

35. Boatner, *Civil War Dictionary,* 310–13. Besides those sources specifically cited, troop movement details and background data presented in this chapter are principally drawn from O'Reilly, *"Stonewall" Jackson at Fredericksburg,* passim; Esposito, ed., *West Point Atlas,* I, maps 70–73 and corresponding text; the NPS Fredericksburg map set; and conversations and correspondence during 1999–2000 with Frank A. O'Reilly, FSNMP.

36. Boatner, *Civil War Dictionary,* 313; Sears, *Chancellorsville,* 4–5; O'Reilly, *"Stonewall" Jackson at Fredericksburg,* 1, 11.

37. James Fulton pension file (cert. 491,097), NA-RG15.

38. Jackson, *Diary,* 60, 61; *Official Records,* 21, p. 521.

39. *Official Records,* 21, pp. 514, 516, 517, 521.

40. Foote, *Civil War,* II: 27–28; Jackson, *Diary,* 61; *Official Records,* 21, p. 521.

41. Fredericksburg map set, NPS; Bates, *Pennsylvania Volunteers,* I:851; *Official Records,* 21, p. 453.

42. Jackson, *Diary,* 61; James Speer to W. J. Carson, 18 February 1863, NA-RG94-11MR.

43. Court-martial case file, file MM 22, NA-RG153.

44. O'Reilly, *"Stonewall" Jackson at Fredericksburg,* 26, 36; Fredericksburg map set, NPS; *Official Records,* 21, pp. 521–22; Adam Torrance to wife, 5 July 1863, PSA.

45. *Official Records,* 21, p. 514.

46. Bates, *Pennsylvania Volunteers,* I:852; McBride, *In the Ranks,* 22; Company D roll and Record of Recruits, Connoquennessing [*sic*] Rangers, 19 June 1861, NA-RG94-11MR.

47. Woodward, *Our Campaigns,* 191.

48. *Official Records,* 21, 510; Fredericksburg map set, NPS.

49. O'Reilly, *"Stonewall" Jackson at Fredericksburg,* 52.

50. Ibid., 64–65, 76.

51. Bates, *Pennsylvania Volunteers,* I:851; O'Reilly, *"Stonewall" Jackson at Fredericksburg,* 78–79.

52. Bates, *Pennsylvania Volunteers,* I:851; *Official Records,* 21, p. 522; Sypher, *History of the Pennsylvania Reserve Corps,* 416–17; O'Reilly, *"Stonewall" Jackson at Fredericksburg,* 80. The *Official Records* (21, p. 59), which lists Anderson as commander of the Third Brigade by the time the battle ended, also lists Col. Joseph W. Fisher of the Fifth Reserves as Conrad Jackson's immediate replacement. Documents in Fisher's service file, however, show him absent at this time in Columbia, Lancaster County, Pennsylvania. From there he wrote headquarters on 9 December requesting an extension to a medical leave that had begun on the first of the month. He appended a note from his doctor, who found "him to be laboring under Bronchitis, and to the best of my judgment, at least Twenty days will be necessary to restore the party diseased to a healthful condition and render him fit for service." A muster-roll extract also lists the colonel as "absent sick on leave of absence" for November and December 1862. Joseph W. Fisher to Seth Williams, 9 December 1862; unaddressed statement by S. [?] Armor, M.D., 9 December 1862; and November-December 1862 Field and Staff Muster Roll card, Joseph W. Fisher military service file, NA-RG94-CSR.

53. O'Reilly, *"Stonewall" Jackson at Fredericksburg,* 80; S. M. Elder to R. J. Tomb, reprinted under "Letters from Our Army. Company H, 12th Reserves," *Indiana Messenger,* 24 December 1862, 2; *Official Records,* 21, pp. 454, 519, 521.

54. Meade, *Life and Letters,* II:314; *Official Records,* 21, p. 522.

55. Nichols, *Toward Gettysburg,* 151–53; Sypher, *History of the Pennsylvania Reserve Corps,* 414–15; *Official Records,* 21, p. 362.

56. Bates, *Pennsylvania Volunteers,* I:851–52, 858; letter by J. P. Miller, *Brookville Republican,* 22 April 1863, 2; James P. Speer pension file (cert. 172,716); "The 11th Reserves," *The Mentor,* vol. 1, no. 5 (8 January 1863): 35; James A. Hayden pension file (cert. 615,996), NA-RG15.

57. O'Reilly, *"Stonewall" Jackson at Fredericksburg,* 94.

58. *Official Records,* 21, p. 522; Foote, *Civil War,* II:42; Adam S. Bright to uncle, 27 December 1862, in Truxall, *Respects to All,* 35.

59. *Official Records,* 21, p. 140; Fox, *Regimental Losses,* 260; Sypher, *History of the Pennsylvania Reserve Corps,* 419.

60. Daniel Porter to mother, reprinted under "Letters from Our Army. From Company B," *Indiana Messenger,* 24 December 1862, 2; Bates, *Pennsylvania Volunteers,* I:861, 866, 874; Stephenson, *Indiana County 175th Anniversary History,* I:655.

61. Lewis A. Johnston to Joseph H. Barrett, 11 March and 24 June 1864, in Johnston pension file (cert. 29,761), NA-RG15.

62. Andrew Ivory pension file (cert. 16,097), NA-RG15.

63. Unsigned report dated Marson House hospital, 23 December 1862, NA-RG94-11P; Co. B roll, NA-RG94-11MR; Bates, *Pennsylvania Volunteers,* I:859. The other William Conner, of Lancaster, enlisted in Company E in September 1862, giving his age as nineteen and his occupation as "laborer." He made his mark with an "X" on the enlistment form, which described him as having hazel eyes, auburn hair, a fair complexion, and a height of five feet, five inches. NA-RG94-11P. Bates (*Pennsylvania Volunteers,* I:865) states that upon the Eleventh Reserves' muster-out in June 1864, Conner was transferred, along with other veterans with time left in service, to the 190th Pennsylvania.

64. Nichols, *Toward Gettysburg,* 153; George Meade to wife, 17 December 1862, in *Life and Letters,* I:338–39.

65. "Pennsylvania Reserves—Sacrificed Again," *Democrat & Sentinel,* 31 December 1862, 4; "The Battle," *Democrat & Sentinel,* 24 December 1862, 2; "Oh! Abraham, Resign!!" poem attributed to "a New Contributor," *Democrat & Sentinel,* 24 December 1862, 1.

66. Jackson, *Diary,* 63; Daniel Porter to mother, reprinted under "Letters from Our Army. From Company B," *Indiana Messenger,* 24 December 1862, 2.

Chapter 9. A Regiment Worth Its Weight in Gold

1. Sauers, *Advance the Colors,* I:83; *Official Records,* 21, p. 879; Bates, *Pennsylvania Volunteers,* I:852; Jackson, *Diary,* 63; Boatner, *Civil War Dictionary,* 321; Thomas F. Gallagher military service file, NA-RG94-CSR.

2. Boatner, *Civil War Dictionary,* 321; Boucher and Jordan, *History of Westmoreland County,* I:432

3. James P. Speer to W. J. Carson, 18 February 1863, NA-RG94-11MR; Peter A. Johns pension file (cert. 228,559), NA-RG15.

4. The undated petitions, addressed "To His Excellency, Gov. A. G. Curtin," are in microfilm 3689, folder 12, 40th Regt., PSA-RG19.

5. Bates, *Pennsylvania Volunteers,* I:852; Hadden, *History of Uniontown,* 682; Peter A. Johns pension file (cert. 228,559), NA-RG15; Special Orders No. 145, 30 March 1863, microfilm 3689, folder 12, 40th Regt., PSA-RG19; J. W. Fisher to Henry S. Jones, 30 March 1863, and other documents in Peter A. Johns military service file, NA-RG94-CSR.

6. John R. Baker to M. J. McMahon, 21 December 1862, NA-RG94, Volunteer Service file P-696, V.S. 64, box 579.

7. *Official Records,* 21, pp. 877–78, and 25:2, p. 182.

8. *Official Records,* 21, pp. 878–79.

9. Jackson, *Diary,* 63–64.

10. Sears, *Chancellorsville,* 3–4; Adam S. Bright to uncle, 27 January 1863, in Truxall, *Respects to All,* 37.

11. Boatner, *Civil War Dictionary*, 573; Adam S. Bright to uncle, 27 January 1863, in Truxall, *Respects to All*, 38; Cordello Collins to mother, 28 January 1863, in Reinsberg, "Bucktail Voice," 246.

12. Boatner, *Civil War Dictionary*, 409; *Official Records*, 25:2, pp. 10, 49–50; Nichols, *Toward Gettysburg*, 160.

13. *Official Records*, 25:2, pp. 54, 63, 83; 87–88, 90–91; Sypher, *History of the Pennsylvania Reserve Corps*, 428.

14. Sypher, *History of the Pennsylvania Reserve Corps*, 433; Bates, *Pennsylvania Volunteers*, I:852; Boatner, *Civil War Dictionary*, 199; Jesse Fry pension file (cert. 2,680,982); Fry diary, 18–21 February 1863, USAMHI; Lowry, *Story the Soldiers Wouldn't Tell*, 73–75, citing National Archives Record Group 393, vol. 298, records of the XXII Corps Provost Marshal; James McGinley diary, 21 and 22 February 1863, RNBP.

15. Letter by J. P. Miller, *Brookville Republican*, 22 April 1863, 2; Samuel Jackson to W. J. Carson, 13 and 19 June 1863, NA-RG94-11MR.

16. Records of the Judge Advocate General's Office (Army), entry 15, Court-martial case file, file MM 22, NA-RG 153; Henry C. Stone military service file, NA-RG94-CSR; Bates, *Pennsylvania Volunteers*, I:870.

17. Fourth Quarter 1862 and First Quarter 1863 inventory reports contained in Summary Statements of Quarterly Returns of Ordnance and Ordnance Stores included in Record Group 156 (Records of the Office of the Chief of Ordnance), National Archives Microfilm Publication M1281, roll 4.

18. Letter by J. P. Miller, *Brookville Republican*, 22 April 1863, 2.

19. McGinley diary, 23 April 1863, RNBP; Jesse Fry diary, 28 February 1863, USAMHI.

20. Nicholson, *Pennsylvania at Gettysburg*, I:255; James P. George pension file (cert. 799,683), NA-RG15; Bates, *Pennsylvania Volunteers*, I:873.

21. James Hayden deposition, 24 December 1870, and other documents in Eugenius Tibbs pension file (cert. 111,904), NA-RG15.

22. Bates, *Pennsylvania Volunteers*, I:852; Boatner, *Civil War Dictionary*, 207; Catton, *Stillness at Appomattox*, 70, quoting Harold A. Small, ed., *The Road to Richmond: The Civil War Memoirs of Major Abner R. Small, of the 16th Maine Volunteers* (Berkeley, Calif., 1939), 149; Warner, *Generals in Blue*, 99–100; Welsh, *Medical Histories*, 80–81; Robert M. Green, comp., *History of the One Hundred Twenty-fourth Regiment Pennsylvania Volunteers* (Philadelphia, 1907), 120, cited in Priest, *Antietam*, 25.

23. Esposito, ed., *West Point Atlas*, I, map 93 and corresponding text.

24. Sauers, *Advance the Colors*, 83; Woodward, *Our Campaigns*, 204–5, 207; Jesse Fry diary, 23 June 1863, USAMHI; *Official Records*, 27:1, p. 144; letter by J. Potter Miller, *Brookville Republican*, 5 August 1863, 1; Eugenius Tibbs pension file (cert. 111,904).

25. Meade, *Life and Letters*, I:388; *Official Records*, 25:2, pp. 112, 118, and 27:3, p. 214.

26. Sears, *Controversies and Commanders*, 180; *Official Records*, 27:1, p. 61; Boatner, *Civil War Dictionary*, 190; letter by J. Potter Miller, *Brookville Republican*, 5 August 1863, 1.

27. Nicholson, *Pennsylvania at Gettysburg*, I:255.

28. Ibid., I:260.

29. Letter by J. Potter Miller, *Brookville Republican*, 5 August 1863, 1; McGinley diary, 30 June 1862, RNBP.

30. Nicholson, *Pennsylvania at Gettysburg*, I:256.

31. Letter by J. Potter Miller, *Brookville Republican*, 5 August 1863, 1; McGinley diary, 1 July 1863, RNBP; Nicholson, *Pennsylvania at Gettysburg*, I:256–57; Pfanz, *Second Day*, 547n31 (citing a later edition of Nicholson's work [Harrisburg: William Stanley Ray, 1904], I:116).

32. Letter by J. Potter Miller, *Brookville Republican*, 5 August 1863, 1; McGinley diary, 1 July 1863; Nicholson, *Pennsylvania at Gettysburg*, I:257; Adam Torrance to wife, 5 July 1863, PSA.

33. Besides those sources specifically cited, troop movement details and background data presented in this chapter are principally drawn from Pfanz, *Second Day*, passim; Esposito, ed.,

West Point Atlas, I, maps 96–98 and corresponding text; John Bachelder's 1876 set of Gettysburg maps; Ladd and Ladd, *Bachelder's History,* passim; Pfanz, *Ewell,* 302–21; Freeman, *Lee's Lieutenants,* 561–611; and conversations and correspondence during 2000 with John Heiser, GNMP.

34. Nichols, *Toward Gettysburg,* 205, 206. Nicholson, *Pennsylvania at Gettysburg,* I:257.

35. Adam Torrance to wife, 5 July 1863, PSA; *Official Records,* 27:1, pp. 652–53; Pfanz, *Second Day,* 391.

36. Adam Torrance to wife, 5 July 1863, PSA; Esposito, ed., *West Point Atlas,* I, maps 96–98 and corresponding text; Bates, *Pennsylvania Volunteers,* I:852; Jesse Fry diary, 2 July 1863, USAMHI.

37. For discussions of Sickles' decision, see, e.g., Foote, *Civil War,* II:494–97; Pfanz, *Second Day,* 102–3, 124; and Sears, *Controversies and Commanders,* 212–14.

38. Pfanz, *Second Day,* 292, 296–302, 392, 397; *Official Records,* 27:1, p. 653; Bachelder's Gettysburg map set; Adam Torrance to wife, 5 July 1863, PSA.

39. Pfanz, *Second Day,* 392; Adam Torrance to wife, 5 July 1863, PSA; letter by J. Potter Miller, *Brookville Republican,* 5 August 1863, 1.

40. Pfanz, *Second Day,* 393; letter by J. Potter Miller, *Brookville Republican,* 5 August 1863, 1.

41. Nicholson, *Pennsylvania at Gettysburg,* I:258; Samuel Crawford to A. Jacobs, (n.d.) December 1863, Crawford Papers, vol. 3, Library of Congress Manuscript Division; *Official Records,* 27:1, pp. 684–85; Pfanz, *Second Day,* 393–97; Adam Torrance to wife, 5 July 1863, PSA. Semmes was mortally wounded on 1 July, but the brigade retained his name for the rest of the battle. *Official Records,* 27:2, p. 283 and Boatner, *Civil War Dictionary,* 731. Wheaton, who took temporary command of the Third Division of the Union VI Corps during the battle, was succeeded at brigade command by Col. David Nevin. *Official Records,* 27:1, pp. 684–85.

42. Minnigh, *History of Company K,* 26; Pfanz, *Second Day,* 395, 396, 546n23; Samuel Jackson to P. F. Rothermel, 5 July 1877, PSA; Nicholson, *Pennsylvania at Gettysburg,* I:258; J. L. Parker, *Henry Wilson's Regiment* (Boston: Rand Avery, 1887), 313.

43. Pfanz, *Second Day,* 396–98; Minnigh, *Company K,* 24–25; Woodward, *Our Campaigns,* 213; Bates, *Pennsylvania Volunteers,* I:852–53; letter by J. Potter Miller, *Brookville Republican,* 5 August 1863, 1; Nicholson, *Pennsylvania at Gettysburg,* I:258–59; Samuel Crawford to Professor A. Jacobs, (n.d.) December 1863, Samuel Crawford Papers, vol. 3, Library of Congress Manuscript Division; Samuel Jackson to P. F. Rothermel, 5 July 1877, PSA.

44. Pfanz, *Second Day,* 398; Sypher, *History of the Pennsylvania Reserve Corps,* 461; *Official Records,* 27:1, pp. 684–85.

45. Letter by J. Potter Miller, *Brookville Republican,* 5 August 1863, 1; *Official Records,* 27:1, p. 657; Samuel Crawford to A. Jacobs, (n.d.) December 1863, Crawford Papers, vol. 3, Library of Congress Manuscript Division; Minnigh, *History of Company K,* 25.

46. *Official Records,* 27:1, p. 654; Adam Torrance to wife, 5 July 1863, PSA; Nicholson, *Pennsylvania at Gettysburg,* I:259.

47. Adam Torrance to wife, 5 July 1863, PSA; James Fulton pension file (cert. 491,097), NA-RG15; letter by J. Potter Miller, *Brookville Republican,* 5 August 1863, 1; *Official Records,* 27:1, p. 657; Benjamin A. Job pension file (cert. 889,728), NA-RG15; Bates, *Pennsylvania Volunteers,* I:858.

48. *Official Records,* 27:1, pp. 654–55.

49. Adam S. Bright to uncle, 16 July 1863, in Truxall, *Respects to All,* 46; Thompson and Rauch, *History of the Bucktails,* 273; Nicholson, *Pennsylvania at Gettysburg,* 212; Fry diary, 3 July 1863, USAMHI; Sypher, *History of the Pennsylvania Reserve Corps,* 470–71.

50. *Official Records,* 27:1, p. 654; letter by J. Potter Miller, *Brookville Republican,* 5 August 1863, 1.

51. *Official Records,* 27:1, pp. 654–55, 657–58.

52. *New York Herald* quoted in letter by J. Potter Miller, *Brookville Republican,* 5 August 1863, 1; Woodward, *Our Campaigns,* 217; Adam Torrance to wife, 5 July 1863, PSA; Bates, *Pennsylvania Volunteers,* I:853; *Official Records,* 27:1, pp. 180, 655.

53. Samuel Crawford to A. Jacobs, (n.d.) December 1863, Samuel Crawford Papers, vol. 3, Library of Congress Manuscript Division.

Chapter 10. Duty in the Context of the Cartridge Box

1. Jesse Fry diary, 4 and 5 July 1863, USAMHI. The corps' movements during the post-Gettysburg campaign are summarized in *Official Records*, 27:1, pp. 145–50.

2. Thompson and Rauch, *History of the Bucktails*, 277; Woodward, *Our Campaigns*, 221–22; Fry diary, 12 July 1863, USAMHI.

3. Bates, *Pennsylvania Volunteers*, I:853; Woodward, *Our Campaigns*, 222–23.

4. *Official Records*, 27:1, pp. 148, 150, and 29:1, p. 222; Woodward, *Our Campaigns*, 224; Thompson and Rauch, *History of the Bucktails*, 277.

5. James McGinley diary, 24–26 July 1863, RNBP; Woodward, *Our Campaigns*, 226. The Meade anecdote is included in the latter title; a slightly different rendering appears in Nicholson, *Pennsylvania at Gettysburg*, I:216.

6. Letter by J. P. Miller, *Brookville Republican*, 22 April 1863, 2.

7. Boatner, *Civil War Dictionary*, 175.

8. Letter by "Harry," *Greensburgh Herald*, 15 April 1863, 2.

9. Letter by Samuel M. Jackson, *Greensburgh Herald*, 29 April 1863, 3.

10. Letter by Lemuel D. Dobbs, *Brookville Republican*, 26 August 1863, 1; letter by Lemuel D. Dobbs, *Brookville Republican*, 30 September 1863, 1. A similar exchange occurred in the pages of the *Greensburgh Democrat* and *Greensburgh Herald* between soldier-correspondents from the Eleventh Reserves. See the letter by "High Private in Reserve Corps," *Greensburgh Herald*, 7 September 1863, 3.

11. John I. Faller to brother, 19 October 1863, in Flower, *Dear Folks at Home*, 108.

12. Bates, *Pennsylvania Volunteers*, I: 873–74; extract from General Orders No. 39, 1 September 1863, in NA-RG94-11MR; Catton, *Stillness at Appomattox*, 143–44.

13. James Elliott pension file (cert. 632,761), NA-RG15.

14. Lemuel Dobbs pension file (cert. 522,302), NA-RG15.

15. Bierer's letter to Foster, dated 28 October 1863, in NA-RG94-11P recounts the details of his earlier correspondence with the latter, as well as the episode concerning the looking glass and accusations arising from it.

16. Bierer describes the lieutenant as "a personal Enemy to me" and relates details of the case in a 19 September 1864 letter to Secretary of the Interior John P. Usher, asking for assistance with his pension request, in Bierer pension file (cert. 719,091), NA-RG15. As with Spires' trial, data on the Bierer proceedings does not seem to exist within the National Archives' collection of courts-martial data in Records Group 153; nor (as of 1 November 1999) within the updated index of courts-martial records being compiled by Thomas and Beverly Lowry of Woodbridge, Va. Bierer's military service file (in NA-RG94-CSR) does, however, note that he was initially dishonorably discharged, and it also contains a copy of the order revoking the dishonorable discharge.

17. Bierer quotes the document in his 19 September 1864 letter to Secretary of the Interior John P. Usher, Bierer pension file (cert. 719,091), NA-RG15.

18. Everard Bierer to Joseph H. Barrett, 7 June 1864, Bierer pension file (cert. 719,091), NA-RG15.

19. As noted above, a copy of these orders exists in Bierer's service records file. Bierer transcribes the document in an 18 August 1864 letter to Joseph H. Barrett, Bierer pension file (cert. 719,091), NA-RG15.

20. Everard Bierer to J. G. Foster, 28 October 1863, in NA-RG94-11P. This letter recounts the details of Bierer's earlier correspondence with Foster.

21. James P. Speer pension file (cert. 172,716), NA-RG15; Bates, *Pennsylvania Volunteers*, I:853, 854, 855.

22. J. S. DeBenneville pension file (cert. 97,513), NA-RG15; Sypher, *History of the Pennsylvania Reserve Corps,* 508; Bates, *Pennsylvania Volunteers,* I:855.

23. Eli Waugaman pension file (cert. 2,694,399), NA-RG15.

24. From a 26 January 1887 surgeon's report in the James C. Burke pension file (cert. 398,014), NA-RG15.

25. This section is based on Lewis A. Johnston to Joseph H. Barrett, 11 March and 24 June 1864, and other documents in the Johnston pension file (cert. 29,761), NA-RG15.

26. McGinley diary, 30 July–29 August 1863, RNBP.

27. Samuel M. Jackson to James B. Fry, 4 April 1863, NA-RG94-11MR; John Gansz to Andrew Curtin, 16 August 1863, and other documents in Gansz military service file, NA-RG94-CSR.

28. For background on the campaign, see Henderson, *Road to Bristoe Station,* passim; and Esposito, ed., *West Point Atlas,* I, map 118 and corresponding text.

29. Welsh, *Medical Histories,* 81; Record of Recruits, Connoquennessing [*sic*] Rangers, 19 June 1861, NA-RG94-11MR; Charles Minnemyer military service file, NA-RG94-CSR; Bates, *Pennsylvania Volunteers,* I:855.

30. Charles Minnemyer diary transcript, 12–15 October 1863, USAMHI.

31. Adam S. Bright to uncle, 24 October 1863, in Truxall, *Respects to All,* 49; Bates, *Pennsylvania Volunteers,* I:859, 860; Woodward, *Our Campaigns,* 236–37; Thompson and Rauch, *History of the Bucktails,* 282; Hardin, *History of the Twelfth Regiment,* 164, 167–69; Charles Minnemyer diary transcript, 12–15 October 1863, USAMHI; *Official Records,* 29:1, p. 242.

32. Hardin, *History of the Twelfth Regiment,* 169–71; *Official Records,* 29:1, pp. 577–78; Thompson and Rauch, *History of the Bucktails,* 282; Charles Minnemyer diary transcript, 19 October 1863, USAMHI; McGinley diary, 19 October 1863, RNBP; Woodward, *Our Campaigns,* 237–38; John Gansz to W. W. Dudley, 15 February 1882, Gansz pension file (cert. 214,192), NA-RG15.

33. *Official Records,* 27:1, p. 656; Summary Statement of Ordnance and Ordnance Stores for Third Quarter, 1863, NA-RG156, Microfilm Publication 1281, roll 5.

34. Adam S. Bright to uncle, 17 December 1863, in Truxall, *Respects to All,* 50–51; Esposito, ed., *West Point Atlas,* I, map 119 and accompanying text; Woodward, *Our Campaigns,* 238, 240; Thompson and Rauch, *History of the Bucktails,* 283–84; Hardin, *History of the Twelfth Regiment,* 172–73; John J. Hennessy, "I Dread the Spring: The Army of the Potomac Prepares for the Overland Campaign," in Gallagher, *Wilderness Campaign,* 66.

35. Adam S. Bright to uncle, 17 December 1863, in Truxall, *Respects to All,* 50–51; Hardin, *History of the Twelfth Regiment,* 173; McGinley diary, 30 November 1863, RNBP; Thompson and Rauch, *History of the Bucktails,* 284–85; Woodward, *Our Campaigns,* 240; Hennessy, "I Dread the Spring," in Gallagher, *Wilderness Campaign,* 66.

36. Adam S. Bright to uncle, 17 December 1863, in Truxall, *Respects to All,* 50–51; McGinley diary, 30 November 1863, RNBP; Hennessy, "I Dread the Spring," in Gallagher, *Wilderness Campaign,* 67; David Berry pension file (cert. 444,948), NA-RG15.

Chapter 11. Winter 1863–1864

1. Woodward, *Our Campaigns,* 240.

2. Letter by "Veteran Volunteer," *American Citizen,* 23 March 1864, 2.

3. Samuel M. Jackson to Fred C. Locke, 11 December 1863, Samuel Jackson military service file, NA-RG94-CSR; Daniel S. Porter to William A. Hoyt, 20 December and 31 December 1863, NA-RG94-11MR.

4. Hennessy, "I Dread the Spring," in Gallagher, ed., *Wilderness Campaign,* 75–77; Minnemyer diary transcript, 18 April 1864, USAMHI; Adam Torrance military service file, NA-RG94-CSR; Bates, *Pennsylvania Volunteers,* I:855; "Original Roll of Field and Staff of 11th Infty Regt. Penna. Reserves," in NA-RG94-11MR; McBride, *In the Ranks,* 59–60; John A. Delo pension file (cert. 129,322), NA-RG15; John A. Delo military service file, NA-RG94-CSR.

5. Daniel R. Coder affidavit, 26 November 1881, and Hugh A. Torrance affidavit, 27 December 1881, Daniel R. Coder pension file (cert. 430,414), NA-RG15.

6. George G. Ingersoll affidavit, 11 June 1896, Daniel R. Coder pension file (cert. 430,414), NA-RG15.

7. Minnemyer diary transcript, 20 January 1864, USAMHI; Record of Recruits, Connoquennessing [*sic*] Rangers, 19 June 1861, NA-RG94-11MR; Daniel R. Coder pension file (cert. 430,414), NA-RG15; Bates, *Pennsylvania Volunteers,* I:862.

8. "Correspondents Wanted," *Brookville Republican,* 27 April 1864, 1; Company K muster roll, NA-RG94-11MR.

9. *Official Records,* 29:1, p. 978; Hardin, *History of the Twelfth Regiment,* 174; Welsh, *Medical Histories,* 152.

10. *Official Records,* 51:1, pp. 212–13.

11. *Official Records,* 33, p. 660.

12. Daniel S. Porter to Fred T. Locke, 7 January 1864, Daniel S. Porter to George G. Meade, 15 December 1861, and "Casualty Sheet" in Daniel S. Porter service file, NA-RG94-CSR; Stephenson, *Indiana County 175th Anniversary History,* IV:374–75; Bates, *Pennsylvania Volunteers,* I:853, 855.

13. Archibald Stewart to Fred T. Locke, 4 March 1864, Archibald Stewart military service file, NA-RG94-CSR.

14. Letter by "A Veteran Volunteer," *American Citizen,* 23 March 1864, 2.

15. McBride, *In the Ranks,* 24–27; McBride enlistment form, NA-RG94-11P.

16. "Roll of Volunteers (Form B)," documents for Allegheny City, Pa., and Greensburg, Pa., dated (n.d.) February, 5 February, 25 February, and 31 March 1864, NA-RG94-11MR.

17. Letter, signature indecipherable, from surgeon in charge of U.S. Army General Hospital, Camden Street, Baltimore, to Surg. Josiah Simpson, 11 February 1864, NA-RG94-11P.

18. Extract from Special Orders No. 552, War Department, Adjutant General's Office, Washington, 14 December 1863, in NA-RG94-11P.

19. *Official Records,* 33, p. 637.

20. *Official Records,* 33, pp. 924–25, 982, 1032.

21. W. C. Talley to Samuel Jackson, 24 April and 27 April 1864, NA-RG94-11MR.

22. Catton, *Stillness at Appomattox,* 70.

23. *Official Records,* 29:2, pp. 83, 90, and 33, pp. 637–38.

24. *Official Records,* 33, pp. 733, 881–82, 1035.

25. Bates, *Pennsylvania Volunteers,* I:870, V:291; Company H roll, NA-RG94-11MR; and the following documents in NA-RG94-11P: George Dunn volunteer enlistment form, 29 August 1862; John Jones, James Fries [?], W. H. Markle, A. M. Fulton, and James A. Hunter to Andrew Curtin, 4 February 1864; Henry Dunn to Andrew Curtin, 5 February 1864; and the response to their letters by a secretary to Curtin (signature illegible), 25 February 1864.

26. Summary Statement of Ordnance and Ordnance Stores for Fourth Quarter, 1863, and First Quarter, 1864, NA-RG156, Microfilm Publication 1281, roll 5.

27. *Official Records,* 33, p. 276; Adam S. Bright to uncle, 15 April 1864, in Truxall, *Respects to All,* 55.

28. Letter, signature illegible, dated Govt. Hospital for the Insane, near Washington, D.C., 20 January 1871, Eugenius Tibbs pension file (cert. 111,904), NA-RG15. Tibbs' military service file in NA-RG94-CSR includes a 15 April 1864 letter by Eleventh Reserves surgeon William Lyons (no addressee) makes no mention of the 1 June 1863 episode. Instead, it gives 22 November 1863 as the date on which Tibbs' condition started, "prior to which time he was perfectly rational."

Chapter 12. An Awful Sight of Men Cut Up

1. Letter by John S. Sutor, J. J. Oatman, and H. Prothero, *Greensburgh Herald,* 23 September 1863, 1; James McGinley diary, 10 September 1863, RNBP; letter by "G," *American Citizen,*

11 May 1864, 2; Frank W. Jackson, "Colonel Samuel M. Jackson and the Eleventh Pennsylvania Reserves," *Western Pennsylvania Historical Magazine* 18 (1935): 46–47.

2. McBride, *In the Ranks*, 28–29, 31. McBride's assertion that Elliott died at Andersonville is not borne out by the National Park Service's Andersonville prisoner database (presently searchable via an Internet site, http://montezuma.corinthian.net/mccc/aville.html, operated by the Macon County, Ga., Chamber of Commerce). The Park Service records do, however, include a John H. Elliott from the Eighty-third Pennsylvania, captured on 5 May 1864, who died later that year.

3. *Official Records*, 33, pp. 1035–36. Besides those sources specifically cited, troop movement details and background data presented in this chapter are principally drawn from Esposito, ed., *West Point Atlas*, I, maps 117–35 and corresponding text; the NPS Wilderness map set; Rhea's *Battle of the Wilderness*, *The Battles for Spotsylvania Court House*, and *To the North Anna River*, passim; and conversations and correspondence in 2000 with Frank A. O'Reilly of FSNMP.

4. Minnemyer diary transcript, 30 April, 1 May, and 3 May 1864, USAMHI; *Official Records*, 36:2, p. 967; Sypher, *History of the Pennsylvania Reserve Corps*, 547.

5. Welsh, *Medical Histories*, 81; Wainwright, *Diary of Battle*, 347–48.

6. *Official Records*, 36:2, p. 360.

7. Minnemyer diary transcript, 3 May 1864, USAMHI.

8. McBride, *In the Ranks*, 62.

9. Minnemyer diary transcript, 4 May 1864, USAMHI; Wainwright, *Diary of Battle*, 348.

10. Steele, *Wilderness Campaign*, 47, 51, 469; Wainwright, *Diary of Battle*, 348; Minnemyer diary transcript, 4 May 1864, USAMHI; Eicher, *Civil War Battlefields*, 70.

11. *Official Records*, 36:1, p. 1.

12. Ibid., p. 539; Wainwright, *Diary of Battle*, 349–50; Steele, *Wilderness Campaign*, 102.

13. Steele, *Wilderness Campaign*, 114.

14. Rhea, *Battle of the Wilderness*, 127–28, 194.

15. Ibid., 138; *Official Records*, 36:2, pp. 417–20.

16. Elijah Bish, "Which Division Was Broken?" *National Tribune*, 9 January 1890, 3; Rhea, *Battle of the Wilderness*, 143, 166; Sypher, *History of the Pennsylvania Reserve Corps*, 511.

17. Elijah Bish pension file (cert. 492,859), NA-RG15.

18. Elijah Bish, "Which Division Was Broken?" *National Tribune*, 9 January 1890, 3; Rhea, *Battle of the Wilderness*, 166.

19. Elijah Bish, "Which Division Was Broken?" *National Tribune*, 9 January 1890, 3; Rhea, *Battle of the Wilderness*, 166; Bates, *Pennsylvania Volunteers*, I:854; Sypher, *History of the Pennsylvania Reserve Corps*, 511–12; Smith, *Price of Patriotism*, 88.

20. McBride, *In the Ranks*, 31; Record of Recruits, Connoquennessing [*sic*] Rangers, 19 June 1861, NA-RG94-11MR; Elijah Bish, "Which Division Was Broken?" *National Tribune*, 9 January 1890, 3; Bates, *Pennsylvania Volunteers*, I:854; Minnemyer diary transcript, 6 May 1864, USAMHI.

21. Elijah Bish, "Which Division Was Broken?" *National Tribune*, 9 January 1890, 3; Rhea, *Battle of the Wilderness*, 166–67; Bates, *Pennsylvania Volunteers*, I:854; Sypher, *History of the Pennsylvania Reserve Corps*, 511–12; Minnemyer diary transcript, 6 May 1864, USAMHI; Smith, *Price of Patriotism*, 88; Esposito, ed., *West Point Atlas*, I, maps 122 and 123 and corresponding text.

22. Rhea, *Battle of the Wilderness*, 166–67; Hardin, *History of the Twelfth Regiment*, 178. See also John I. Faller's different account of the events behind the Seventh Reserves' surrender in Flower, *Dear Folks at Home*, 116.

23. *Official Records*, 36:1, p. 124; Minnemyer diary transcript, 6 May 1864, USAMHI.

24. "Obituary—Capt. Daniel D. Jones," *Alleghanian*, 16 June 1864, 3; McBride, *In the Ranks*, 31; "Our Boys," *Alleghanian*, 23 June 1864, 3; Bates, *Pennsylvania Volunteers*, I:857, 866; William M. Hazlett pension file (cert. 622,980), NA-RG15; Record of Death and Interment, Archibald Stewart service file, NA-RG94-CSR.

25. Bates, *Pennsylvania Volunteers*, I:867; Special Examiner Theodore [illegible] to Commissioner of Pensions, 27 May 1916, and other documents in Isaac Miller pension file (cert. 696,867), NA-RG15.

26. Pass Book stub no. 376, 30 December 1863, in NA-RG94-11P; Isaac Miller pension file (cert. 696,867), NA-RG15.

27. Rachel Miller to "abrem linceln," 26 November 1864, NA-RG94-11P. Isaac Miller wrote: "I was in Andersonville Prison" at the bottom of his 11 January 1898 reply to a pension bureau questionnaire in his pension file (cert. 696,867) NA-RG15.

28. Letter to Rachel Miller marked "[For] Records," dated War Department, Washington City, 13 December 1864, in NA-RG94-11P.

29. Bates, *Pennsylvania Volunteers*, I:867.

30. McBride, *In the Ranks*, 32–33.

31. Rhea, *Battle of the Wilderness*, 250–51.

32. McBride, *In the Ranks*, 35; Minnemyer diary transcript, 6 and 7 May 1864, USAMHI. Steen was among those transferred to the 190th Pennsylvania after the Eleventh Reserves' muster-out; as a sergeant in Company C, he was killed during the 19 August 1864 fight along the Welden Railroad (McBride, *In the Ranks*, 35, 243).

33. *Official Records*, 36:1, pp. 190–91, 540–41; Rhea, *Battles for Spotsylvania Court House*, 25, 30–36.

34. *Official Records*, 36:1, pp. 191, 540–41; Rhea, *Battles for Spotsylvania Court House*, 45–60.

35. Sypher, *History of the Pennsylvania Reserve Corps*, 522–23; Rhea, *Battles for Spotsylvania Court House*, 60–63; Thompson and Rauch, *History of the Bucktails*, 300–301.

36. *Official Records*, 36:2, pp. 540–43.

37. Rhea, *Battles for Spotsylvania Court House*, 83–84; Pfanz, *Ewell*, 377; Freeman, *Lee's Lieutenants*, 675.

38. Thompson and Rauch, *History of the Bucktails*, 301; Hardin, *History of the Twelfth Regiment*, 180–81; Sypher, *History of the Pennsylvania Reserve Corps*, 522–23; Rhea, *Battles for Spotsylvania Court House*, 83–84; *Official Records*, 36:1, p. 1071, and 36:2, pp. 539–40, 543–45, 714. Ewell received Talley personally and, after reminiscing with him about his days stationed at Carlisle Barracks, offered to parole him. Talley declined; a Union cavalry raid a few days later repatriated him. Pfanz, *Ewell*, 378.

39. James C. Burke pension file (cert. 398,014), NA-RG15; Eli Waugaman pension file (cert. 2,694,399), NA-RG15; "Casualties in Co. K, 11th Pa. Reserves," *Brookville Republican*, 25 May 1864, 2; letter by J. P. George, *Brookville Republican*, 18 May 1864, 2; Edward Scofield pension file (cert. 2,495,338), NA-RG15.

40. *Official Records*, 36:2, pp. 543, 544–45, 715; Rhea, *Battles for Spotsylvania Court House*, 84–85.

41. Hardin, *History of the Twelfth Regiment*, 181; Esposito, ed., *West Point Atlas*, I, maps 127 and 128 and corresponding text; Bates, *Pennsylvania Volunteers*, I:854.

42. Thompson and Rauch, *History of the Bucktails*, 303–4; Sypher, *History of the Pennsylvania Reserve Corps*, 524–25; Rhea, *Battles for Spotsylvania Court House*, 112; John Gansz to W. W. Dudley, 15 February 1882, Gansz pension file (cert. 214,192), NA-RG15; Minnemyer diary transcript, 7, 8, 9, 10, and 19 May 1864, USAMHI.

43. Thompson and Rauch, *History of the Bucktails*, 303–4; Sypher, *History of the Pennsylvania Reserve Corps*, 524–25; Rhea, *Battles for Spotsylvania Court House*, 142–49; Minnemyer diary transcript, 10 May 1864, USAMHI.

44. Minnemyer diary transcript, 11 May 1864, USAMHI; McBride, *In the Ranks*, 40–41; Bates, *Pennsylvania Volunteers*, I:861.

45. *Official Records*, 36:2, p. 639.

46. Ibid., p. 640; Minnemyer diary transcript, 11 May 1864, USAMHI.

47. *Official Records*, 36:2, pp. 669–70; Rhea, *Battles for Spotsylvania Court House*, 282–84.

48. *Official Records*, 36:2, pp. 670, 671, 715; Minnemyer diary transcript, 12 May 1864, USAMHI; Rhea, *Battles for Spotsylvania Court House*, 284–90.

49. *Official Records*, 36:2, pp. 714, 715, 716; Esposito, ed., *West Point Atlas*, I, map 131 and corresponding text.

50. *Official Records*, 36:1, p. 606; Hardin, *History of the Twelfth Regiment*, 182–83; Minnemyer diary transcript, 16–18 May 1864, USAMHI.

51. *Official Records,* 36:1, pp. 600–601; Minnemyer diary transcript, 19 May 1864, USAMHI; Woodward, *Our Campaigns,* 251; Rhea, *To the North Anna River,* 181.

52. *Official Records,* 36:1, p. 142, and 36:3, pp. 15, 94; Minnemyer diary transcript, 20, 21, and 22 May 1864, USAMHI; Woodward, *Our Campaigns,* 251; Rhea, *To the North Anna River,* 273.

53. *Official Records,* 36:2, pp. 818–19; Thompson and Rauch, *History of the Bucktails,* 318.

54. Esposito, ed., *West Point Atlas,* I, map 135 and corresponding text; *Official Records,* 36:1, pp. 202–3 and 36:3, p. 301; Hardin, *History of the Twelfth Regiment,* 186; Freeman, *Lee's Lieutenants,* 688, 715; Minnemyer diary transcript, 23 May 1864, USAMHI; McBride, *In the Ranks,* 65; Woodward, *Our Campaigns,* 252; Rhea, *To the North Anna River,* 293–94, 304, 306, 317.

55. Minnemyer diary transcript, 26 May 1864, USAMHI; Rhea, *To the North Anna River,*, 328–29, 334, 443 n. 75.

56. Minnemyer diary transcript, 28 and 29 May 1864, USAMHI.

57. Baltz, *Cold Harbor,* 27, 29, 30, 32; *Official Records,* 36:3, pp. 300, 303.

58. Hardin, *History of the Twelfth Regiment,* 188; Minnemyer diary transcript, 30 May 1864, USAMHI.

59. *Official Records,* 36:3, pp. 335–36; Baltz, *Cold Harbor,* 4, 44.

60. Hardin, *History of the Twelfth Regiment,* 188–89; Sypher, *History of the Pennsylvania Reserve Corps,* 545, 546–47.

61. Baltz, *Cold Harbor,* 41–43; *Official Records,* 33, p. 851.

62. Thompson and Rauch, *History of the Bucktails,* 318–19; Minnemyer diary transcript, 30 May 1864, USAMHI; Hardin, *History of the Twelfth Regiment,* 189; Woodward, *Our Campaigns,* 253; "The Pennsylvania Reserves," *Alleghanian,* 16 June 1864, 1; Minnigh, *History of Company K,* 37.

63. Bates, *Pennsylvania Volunteers,* I:870; Benjamin A. Job pension file (cert. 889,728), NA-RG15; McBride, *In the Ranks,* 67.

64. Thompson and Rauch, *History of the Bucktails,* 319; Hardin, *History of the Twelfth Regiment,* 189–90, 191; Sypher, *History of the Pennsylvania Reserve Corps,* 545; Minnemyer diary transcript, 30 May 1864, USAMHI.

65. Thompson and Rauch, *History of the Bucktails,* 319–20; C. B. Christian, "The Color Bearer Killed," *Southern Historical Society Papers* 33 (January-December 1905): 59–60; McBride, *In the Ranks,* 66, 68; Sypher, *History of the Pennsylvania Reserve Corps,* 545–46; Hardin, *History of the Twelfth Regiment,* 190–91.

66. Hardin, *History of the Twelfth Regiment,* 191; Minnemyer diary transcript, 30 May 1864, USAMHI; *Official Records,* 36:1, p. 158 and 36:3, pp. 398, 389–90; Noah A. Trudeau, "'A Mere Question of Time': Robert E. Lee from the Wilderness to Appomattox Court House," in Gallagher, ed., *Lee the Soldier,* 535; Nicholson, *Pennsylvania at Gettysburg,* I:220; Sypher, *History of the Pennsylvania Reserve Corps,* 545–46.

67. Minnemyer diary transcript, 30 May 1864, USAMHI.

Chapter 13. A Remnant Returns

1. *Official Records,* 26:3, pp. 347, 387.

2. Minnemyer diary transcript, 31 May 1864, USAMHI; Woodward, *Our Campaigns,* 254–55; "The Pennsylvania Reserves," *Alleghanian,* 16 June 1864, 1.

3. Minnemeyer diary transcript, 31 May 1864, and margin notes, USAMHI; Woodward, *Our Campaigns,* 255, 256, 259; Bates, *Pennsylvania Volunteers,* V:279–81.

4. Woodward, *Our Campaigns,* 255–56; McBride, *In the Ranks,* 70–71.

5. Minnemyer diary transcript, 1 June 1864, USAMHI; Woodward, *Our Campaigns,* 256; Esposito, ed., *West Point Atlas,* I, map 136 and corresponding text.

6. Minnemyer diary transcript, 3 and 4 June 1864 (and margin notes), USAMHI; Woodward, *Our Campaigns,* 256–58.

7. "The Reserves," and "The 11th Reserves," *Pennsylvania Argus,* 15 June 1864, 3; Sypher, *History of the Pennsylvania Reserve Corps,* 547.

8. "The Eleventh Penna. Reserves," *Alleghanian,* 16 June 1864, 3. The numbers of return-ing men given by local newspapers often do not correspond exactly with those given in Bates, *Pennsylvania Volunteers,* I:854–75. Barring mistakes, a possible explanation is that not all the men released from duty returned together from Pittsburgh. That said, though Bates' work contains errors and omissions (as do the original documents preserved in the National Archives and the Pennsylvania State Archives), I have used it as the source for the figures given here in the following pages.

9. "Home Again!" *Alleghanian,* 23 June 1864, 3; Bates, *Pennsylvania Volunteers,* I:854–57.

10. Smith, *Price of Patriotism,* 96; Bates, *Pennsylvania Volunteers,* I:854–55, 857–60, 864–66.

11. Bates, *Pennsylvania Volunteers,* I:854–55, 860–64; "Grand Celebration," *American Citi-zen,* 22 June 1864, 3; "Evansburg Celebration," *American Citizen,* 6 July 1864, 3.

12. "Co. K, 11th Pa. Reserves," *Brookville Republican,* 22 June 1864, 2.

13. Bates, *Pennsylvania Volunteers,* I:854–75 and V:288–303.

14. Letter by H. H. Clover, *Brookville Republican,* 22 June 1864, 2; Bates, *Pennsylvania Vol-unteers,* I:873–75.

15. Bates, *Pennsylvania Volunteers,* V:279–81.

Chapter 14. "He Will Sit with a Small Mirror"

1. "The Flags," *American Citizen,* 18 July 1866, 1; Sauers, *Advance the Colors,* I:31.

2. Sauers, *Advance the Colors,* I:32–34, 108.

3. John T. Kelly to Commissioner of Pensions, 9 January 1914, Kelly pension file (cert. 843,602), NA-RG15.

4. Kelly pension file (cert. 843,602), NA-RG15. At this writing, Minnemyer's pension folder is among those affected by the February 2000 fire in the Department of Veterans Affairs records holding area at Suitland, Md. Reference to his pension rejection is contained in the margin notes on the C. Minnemyer diary transcript, USAMHI, adjacent to his 7 May 1864 entries.

5. James X. McIlwain pension file (cert. 381,783), NA-RG15.

6. Thompson Carney pension file (cert. 104,562), NA-RG15.

7. "Home Again!" *Alleghanian,* 23 June 1864, 3.

8. Thomas Litzinger pension file (cert. 158,640), NA-RG15.

9. "Lieut. Col. Robt. A. M'Coy," *Alleghanian,* 23 June 1864, 3; "Company A, 11th Reserves," *Democrat & Sentinel,* 13 July 1864, 2; Robert A. McCoy military service file, NA-RG94-CSR; Rowland M. Jones pension file (cert. 307,949), NA-RG15; Boatner, *Civil War Dictionary,* 529.

10. "Soldiers State Convention," *Democrat & Sentinel,* 9 August 1866, 2.

11. See the item concerning a fatal accident at the Barker-Litzinger saw mill, headlined "Killed," in the *Democrat & Sentinel,* 12 July 1866, 3; Caldwell, *Historical Atlas,* 10; "Appraise-ment for Transfer Inheritance Tax Purposes" and "Appointment of Transfer Inheritance Tax Appraisers" forms regarding the estate of Robert Litzinger, in the files of Register of Wills, Cambria County, Pennsylvania.

12. Peter A. Johns pension file (cert. 228,559), NA-RG15.

13. Manners, *Veteran's Grave Register Record,* 292; Stephenson, *Indiana County 175th Anniversary History,* IV:374–75. Records of government-issued headstones in NA-RG92 note the 1889 issuance of one for Porter's grave, though the date of death listed there conflicts with that given in other sources.

14. Rowland M. Jones pension file (cert. 307,949), NA-RG15.

15. Wiley, ed., *Biographical and Historical Cyclopedia of Indiana and Armstrong Counties,* 145–47; Manners, *Veteran's Grave Registration Record,* 331.

16. "Col. Henderson C. Howard," unsourced, undated but circa 1919 clipping in Civil War Scrapbook, Historical and Genealogical Society of Indiana County; Henderson C. Howard to

Commissioner of Pensions, 5 January 1915, and other documents in Howard pension file (cert. 885,935), NA-RG15.

17. *Story of American Heroism,* 136; Charles Shambaugh pension file (cert. 20,341), NA-RG15.

18. William M. Hazlett pension file (cert. 622,980), NA-RG15.

19. John T. Kelly pension file (cert. 843,602), NA-RG15.

20. Aaron Kepler pension file (cert. 99,274), NA-RG15. At this writing, McBride's pension folder is among those affected by the February 2000 fire in the Department of Veterans Affairs records holding area at Suitland, Md. T. O'Brien, Dept. of Veterans Affairs, to author, 20 July 2000.

21. Jesse Fry pension file (cert. 2,680,982), NA-RG15; G. E. Duncan to Editor, *Oil City Blizzard,* 19 January 1939, Jesse Fry papers, USAMHI.

22. John Gansz pension file (cert. 214,192), NA-RG15.

23. James McGinley pension file (cert. 813,072), NA-RG15.

24. Daniel R. Coder pension file (cert. 430,414), NA-RG15.

25. Affidavit of T. B. Stewart, 12 June 1895, and surgeon's certificate, 12 June 1895, Daniel R. Coder pension file (cert. 430,414), NA-RG15.

26. Original Pension of Minor Children form, Coder pension file (cert. 430,414), NA-RG15.

27. James A. Hayden pension file (cert. 615,996), NA-RG15.

28. Letter, signature illegible, dated Govt. Hospital for the Insane, near Washington, D.C., 20 January 1871, and other documents in Eugenius Tibbs pension file (cert. 111,904), NA-RG15.

29. Eugenius Tibbs pension file (cert. 111,904), NA-RG15.

30. Charles E. May deposition, 22 June 1903; and other documents in Eugenius Tibbs pension file (cert. 111,904), NA-RG15.

31. Isaac Miller pension file (cert. 696,867), NA-RG15.

32. Ibid.

33. James P. Speer pension file (cert. 172,716), NA-RG15.

34. Andrew Ivory pension file (cert. 16,097), NA-RG15.

35. James Fulton pension file (cert. 491,097), NA-RG15.

36. Benjamin A. Job pension file (cert. 889,728), NA-RG15.

37. Eli Waugaman pension file (cert. 2,694,399), NA-RG15.

38. David Berry pension file (cert. 444,948), NA-RG15.

39. Pensioner-Dropped form dated 2 October 1915; Form 3–389 questionnaire dated 2 January 1915; James P. George pension file.

40. Joseph P. Miller pension file (cert. 472,014), NA-RG15.

41. "Casualties in Co. K, 11th Pa. Reserves," *Brookville Republican,* 25 May 1864, 2; letter by J. P. George, *Brookville Republican,* 18 May 1864, 2; Edward Scofield pension file (cert. 2,495,338), NA-RG15.

42. Elijah Bish pension file (cert. 492,859), NA-RG15.

43. Thomas Sallade pension file (cert. 112,245), NA-RG15.

44. Boucher and Jordan, *History of Westmoreland County,* I:431, 432, and II:11; Wiley, *Biographical and Historical Cyclopedia of Westmoreland County,* 31; Thomas Gallagher pension file (cert. 222,972), NA-RG15.

45. Thomas Spires affidavit, 8 December 1885, Thomas Gallagher pension file (cert. 222,972), NA-RG15

46. "Capt. E. Bierer," *Genius of Liberty,* 25 September 1862, 4.

47. Everard Bierer to Secretary of the Interior John P. Usher, 19 September 1864, Bierer pension file (cert. 719,091), NA-RG15.

48. Wiley, *Biographical and Portrait Cyclopedia of Fayette County,* 142.

49. Affidavit signed by James Mathers and David Copeland, dated "State of Kansas, Brown County, Ad 1876," Bierer pension file (cert. 719,091), NA-RG15.

50. General Affidavit signed by Ellen Bierer, dated 16 April 1893, Bierer pension file (cert. 719,091), NA-RG15.

51. "1910 Deaths—Brown County, Kansas," file compiled and edited by Pat Hollingsworth and posted at http://www.rootsweb.com/usgenweb/ks/brown/deaths/1910.html; Bierer pension file (cert. 719,091), NA-RG15.

52. Samuel Jackson pension file (cert. 667,873), NA-RG15.

53. Nicholson, *Pennsylvania at Gettysburg,* I:vii; John Heiser, of the Gettysburg National Military Park, provided additional data from the park's files during a 23 February 2000 telephone conversation with the author.

54. Samuel Jackson to P. F. Rothermel, 5 July 1877, PSA.

55. Undated clippings regarding Hannibal Sloan in the "Civil War Scrapbook," *Historical and Genealogical Society of Indiana County;* Nicholson, *Pennsylvania at Gettysburg,* I:259, 263, 264.

56. Samuel M. Jackson pension file (cert. 667,873), NA-RG15; Frank W. Jackson, "Colonel Samuel M. Jackson and the Eleventh Pennsylvania Reserves," *Western Pennsylvania Historical Magazine* 18 (1935): 47; Author's telephone conversation, 11 February 2000, with Linda Pelan, assistant registrar, museum department, Western Pennsylvania Historical Society.

57. Welsh, *Medical Histories,* 81–82, 225–26.

58. General Order 65, 22 June 1867, copy in Hugh Torrance military service file, NA-RG94-CSR; William Stitt deposition, 27 July 1899, Hugh A. Torrance pension file (cert. 672,261), NA-RG15.

59. Depositions of Hugh A. Torrance and Harriet Torrance, 27 July 1899, and other documents in Torrance pension file (cert. 672,261), NA-RG15. For more on stress-induced mental illness among Civil War veterans, see Eric T. Dean, "'We Will All be Lost and Destroyed': Post-Traumatic Stress Disorder and the Civil War," *Civil War History* 37 (1991): 138–53.

60. William Stitt deposition, 27 July 1899, in Hugh A. Torrance pension file (cert. 672,261), NA-RG15.

61. Widow's Pension application, 28 April 1908, and statement by J. J. Fritz, 15 August 1903, Hugh A. Torrance pension file (cert. 672,261), NA-RG15.

62. James C. Burke pension file (cert. 398,014), NA-RG15.

63. Andrew Lewis pension file (cert. 2,265), NA-RG15; Madeline Paine Moyer to author, 17 May 2000; newspaper clippings from *The Report* (Lebanon, Pa.), 21 October and 16 December 1895, and other undated newspaper items provided the author by Madeline Paine Moyer; Robert E. L. Krick, e-mails to author, 29 October 1999 and 10 February 2000; Eicher, *Civil War Battlefields,* 124–26.

Bibliography

Selected Books and Articles

Abel, F. Lawrence, *Singing the New Nation: How Music Shaped the Confederacy, 1861–1865* (Mechanicsburg, Pa.: Stackpole, 2000).

Albert, George Dallas, ed., *History of the County of Westmoreland, Pennsylvania* (Philadelphia: L. H. Everts, 1882).

Baltz, Louis J. III, *The Battle of Cold Harbor* (Lynchburg: H. E. Howard, 1994).

Barton, Michael, ed., "The Civil War Letters of Captain Andrew Lewis and His Daughter," *Western Pennsylvania Historical Magazine* 60 (October 1977): 371–90.

Bates, Samuel P., *History of Pennsylvania Volunteers, 1861–1865,* 6 vols. (Harrisburg: B. Singerly, 1869).

Billings, John D., *Hardtack and Coffee: The Unwritten Story of Army Life, 1861–1865* (Boston: G. M. Smith, 1887).

Biographical and Historical Cyclopedia of Westmoreland County (Philadelphia: John M. Gresham & Co., 1890).

Biographical and Portrait Cyclopedia of Cambria County, Pennsylvania (Philadelphia: Union Publishing, 1896).

Boatner, Mark M. III, *The Civil War Dictionary* (New York: McKay, 1959).

———, *Military Customs and Tradition* (New York: McKay, 1956).

Boucher, John, and John W. Jordan, *History of Westmoreland County, Pennsylvania,* 2 vols. (New York: Lewis, 1906). Boucher is listed as author of vol. 1; Jordan as editor of vol. 2.

Boucher, John, and Fenwick Y. Hedley, eds., *Old and New Westmoreland,* 4 vols. (New York: American Historical Society, 1918). Boucher is listed as editor of vols. 1–2; Hedley as editor of vols. 3–4.

Caldwell, J. A., ed., *History of Indiana County Pennsylvania, 1745–1880* (Newark, Ohio: J. A. Caldwell, 1880).

———, *Illustrated Historical Combination Atlas of Cambria County, Pennsylvania: From actual surveys by and under the directions of J. A. Caldwell* (Philadelphia: Atlas Publishing Co., 1890).

———, *The Coming Fury* (New York: Doubleday, 1961).

Casey, Silas, *Infantry Tactics for the Instruction, Exercise and Manoeuvres of the Soldier, A Company, Line of Skirmishers, Battalion, Brigade, or Corps D'Armee* (New York: D. Van Nostrand, 1862).

Catton, Bruce, *A Stillness at Appomattox* (New York: Doubleday, 1953).

Chapman, Thomas J., *The Valley of the Conemaugh* (Altoona, Pa: McCrum and Dern, 1865).

Coates, Earl J., and Dean S. Thomas, *An Introduction to Civil War Small Arms* (Gettysburg: Thomas, 1990).

Coco, Gregory A., *The Civil War Infantryman* (Gettysburg: Thomas, 1996).

Commager, Henry S., *The Blue and the Gray* (New York: Fairfax Press, 1991).

Coolins, B. F., III, and Walton H. Owen II, *Mr. Lincoln's Forts* (Alexandria, Va.: White Mane, 1988).

Cubbison, Douglas R., "That Gallant Company," *Indiana County Heritage* 9 (summer 1984): 15–19.

Dana, Charles A., *Recollections of the Civil War* (New York: Collier, 1963).

Davis, William C., and Bell I. Wiley, eds., *Civil War Times Photographic History of the Civil War: Fort Sumter to Gettysburg* (New York: Black Dog and Leventhal, 1994).

Dean, Eric T., "'We Will All Be Lost and Destroyed': Post-Traumatic Stress Disorder and the Civil War," *Civil War History* 37 (1991): 138–53.

Donald, David Herbert, *Lincoln* (New York: Simon and Schuster, 1995).

Dyer, F. H., *A Compendium of the War of the Rebellion,* 3 vols. (Des Moines, Iowa: Dyer, 1908).

Egle, William H., *Life and Times of Andrew Gregg Curtin* (Philadelphia: Thompson, 1896).

Eicher, David J., *Civil War Battlefields: A Touring Guide* (Dallas: Taylor, 1995).

Ellis, Franklin, ed., *History of Fayette County, Pennsylvania* (Philadelphia: L. H. Everts, 1882).

Esposito, Brig. Gen. Vincent J., chief ed., *The West Point Atlas of American Wars,* vol. 1 (New York: Holt, 1995).

Flower, Milton E., ed., *Dear Folks at Home: The Civil War Letters of Leo W. and John I. Faller with an Account of Andersonville* (Carlisle, Pa.: Cumberland County Historical Society and Hamilton Library Association, 1963).

Foote, Shelby, *The Civil War: A Narrative,* 3 vols. (New York: Random House, 1958–74).

Fox, William F., *Regimental Losses in the American Civil War 1861–1865* (Albany: Albany Publishing Co., 1889).

Frassanito, William A. *Antietam: The Photographic Legacy of America's Bloodiest Day* (Gettysburg: Thomas, 1978).

Freeman, Douglas Southall, *Lee's Lieutenants: A Study in Command* (New York: Scribner, 1998).

Gallagher, Gary, ed., *Lee the Soldier* (Lincoln: University of Nebraska, 1996).

———, *The Wilderness Campaign* (Chapel Hill: University of North Carolina, 1997).

Gilham, William, *Gilham's Manual for Volunteers and Militia* (Philadelphia: Charles Desilver, 1861).

Gresham, John M., and Samuel T. Wiley, eds., *Biographical and Portrait Cyclopedia of Fayette County, Pennsylvania* (Chicago: John M. Gresham, 1889).

Griffith, Paddy, *Battle Tactics of the Civil War* (New Haven: Yale University Press, 1989).

Hadden, James, *A History of Uniontown* (Evansville, Ind.: Unigraphic, 1978).

Hadden, R. Lee, *Reliving the Civil War: A Reenactor's Handbook,* 2d ed. (Mechanicsburg, Pa.: Stackpole, 1999).

Hardee, W. J., *Rifle and Light Infantry Tactics* (Philadelphia: Lippincott, 1861).

Hardin, Martin D., *History of the Twelfth Regiment, Pennsylvania Reserve Volunteer Corps* (New York: privately published, 1890).

Harsh, Joseph L., *Taken at the Flood: Robert E. Lee and Confederate Strategy in the Maryland Campaign of 1862* (Kent, Ohio: Kent State University Press, 1999).

Helm, Judith Beck, *Tenleytown, D.C.: Country Village into City Neighborhood* (Washington: Tennally Press, 1981).

Henderson, William D., *The Road to Bristoe Station* (Lynchburg: H. E. Howard, 1987).

Hennessy, John J. *Return to Bull Run: The Campaign and Battle of Second Manassas* (Norman: University of Oklahoma, 1993).

Heseltine, William B., ed., *Civil War Prisons* (Kent, Ohio: Kent State University Press, 1972).

———, *Lincoln and the War Governors* (New York: Alfred A. Knopf, 1948).

History of Butler County, Pennsylvania (Chicago: R. C. Brown and Co., 1895).

Hood, John Bell, *Advance and Retreat* (Edison, N.J.: Blue and Grey, 1985).

Jackson, Frank W., "Colonel Samuel M. Jackson and the Eleventh Pennsylvania Reserves," *Western Pennsylvania Historical Magazine* 18 (1935): 45–47.

Jackson, John H., ed., *Diary of General S. M. Jackson for the Year 1862* (Apollo, Pa.: privately printed, 1925).

Johnson, Curt, and Richard C. Anderson Jr., *Artillery Hell: The Employment of Artillery at Antietam* (College Station: Texas A&M University Press, 1995).

Johnson, Robert, and Clarence C. Buel, eds., *Battles and Leaders of the Civil War,* 4 vols. (New York: Thomas Yoseloff, 1956).

Keegan, John, *The Face of Battle* (New York: Penguin, 1976).

———, *The Mask of Command* (New York: Penguin, 1988).

Kreidberg, Lt. Col. Marvin, *History of the Military Mobilization of the United States Army,* U.S. Army pamphlet #20–212 (Washington: Department of the Army, June 1955).

Ladd, David L. and Audrey J., eds., *John Bachelder's History of the Battle of Gettysburg* (Dayton, Ohio: Morningside House, 1997).

Lantzy, Charles A., ed., *Genealogy on the Battle of Antietam, MD, and the Battle of Gettysburg, PA* (Mechanicsburg, Pa.: privately printed, 1997).

Ledoux, Rev. Albert H., ed., *Catholic Vital Records of Central Pennsylvania* (Ebensburg, Pa.: privately printed, 1993–96), in files of Cambria County Historical Society, Ebensburg, Pa.

Lewis, Kathleen Ann, *Family Reunion: The Story of the Lewis and Rogers Families* (Lebanon, Pa.: Sowers, 1979).

Livermore, Thomas L., *Numbers and Losses in the Civil War in America, 1861–65* (Carlisle, Pa.: John Kallman, 1996).

Lord, Francis A., *The Civil War Collector's Encyclopedia,* 5 vols. (Edison, N.J.: Blue and Grey, 1995).

Lowry, Thomas P., *Don't Shoot That Boy! Abraham Lincoln and Military Justice* (Mechanicsburg, Pa.: Stackpole, 1999).

———, *The Story the Soldiers Wouldn't Tell: Sex in the Civil War* (Mechanicsburg, Pa.: Stackpole, 1994).

———, *Tarnished Eagles: The Courts-Martial of Fifty Union Colonels and Lieutenant Colonels* (Mechanicsburg, Pa.: Stackpole, 1997).

Mains, Mary Jane, *Newspaper Accounts of Births, Marriages & Deaths 1808–1929 Westmoreland County, Pennsylvania,* privately printed, in the files of the Westmoreland County Historical Society, Greensburg, Pa.

Manners, Herbert, ed., *[Indiana County] Veteran's Grave Register Record* (privately compiled, 1937), in files of the Historical and Genealogical Society of Indiana County.

McBride, the Rev. Robert E., *In the Ranks: From the Wilderness to Appomattox Court-House* (Cincinnati: Walden & Stowe, 1881).

McClelland, Russ, "Forward, Bucktails, Forward!" *Game News,* August 1983, 3–8.

McElfresh, Earl B., *Maps and Mapmakers of the Civil War* (New York: Harry N. Abrams, 1999).

McLaughlin, Florence C., ed., "'Dear Sister Jennie—Dear Brother Jacob.' The Correspondence Between a Northern Soldier and His Sister in Mechanicsburg, Pa., 1861–1864," *Western Pennsylvania Historical Magazine* 60 (1977): 109–43, 203–40.

Meade, George, ed., *Life and Letters of George Gordon Meade*, 2 vols. (New York: Charles Scribner's Sons, 1913).

Minnigh, H. N., *History of Company K, 1st Penn'a Reserves* (Duncansville, Pa.: "Home Print" Publisher, 1891).

Moehling, Eugene P., and Arleen Keylin, eds., *The Civil War Extra: From the Pages of the Charleston Mercury and the New York Times* (New York: Arno, 1975).

Murdoch, Alexander, "The Pittsburgh Rifles and the Battle of Dranesville," *Western Pennsylvania Historical Magazine,* 53, no. 3 (July 1970): 299–304.

Murfin, James V., *The Gleam of Bayonets: The Battle of Antietam and Robert E. Lee's Maryland Campaign, September, 1862* (Baton Rouge: Louisiana State University, 1993).

Musick, Michael P., "The Little Regiment: Civil War Units and Commands," *Prologue: The Quarterly of the National Archives* (summer 1995), 152–71.

Nevins, Allan, ed., *A Diary of Battle: The Personal Journals of Colonel Charles S. Wainwright, 1861–1865* (New York: Harcourt, Brace and World, 1962).

Nicholas, Alexander F., ed., *Second Brigade of the Pennsylvania Reserves at Antietam: Report of the Antietam Battlefield Memorial Commission of Pennsylvania and Ceremonies at the Dedication of the Monuments Erected by the Commonwealth of Pennsylvania to Mark the Position of Four Regiments of the Pennsylvania Reserves Engaged in the Battle* (Harrisburg: Harrisburg Publishing Company, state printer, 1908).

Nichols, Edward J., *Toward Gettysburg: A Biography of General John F. Reynolds* (University Park: Pennsylvania State University Press, 1958).

Nicholson, John P., ed., *Pennsylvania at Gettysburg: Ceremonies at the Dedication of the Monuments Erected by the Commonwealth of Pennsylvania to Mark the Positions of the Pennsylvania Commands Engaged in the Battle,* 2 vols. (Harrisburg: E. K. Meyers, state printer, 1893).

O'Reilly, Frank A., *"Stonewall" Jackson at Fredericksburg: The Battle of Prospect Hill* (Lynchburg: H. E. Howard, 1993).

O'Shea, Richard (text), and Greenspan, David (maps), *American Heritage Battle Maps of the Civil War* (Tulsa, Okla.: Council Oak Books, 1992).

The Official Military Atlas of the Civil War (New York: Fairfax, 1983).

Pfanz, Donald C., *Richard S. Ewell: A Soldier's Life* (Chapel Hill: University of North Carolina, 1998).

Pfanz, Harry W., *Gettysburg: The Second Day* (Chapel Hill: University of North Carolina Press, 1987).

Polley, J. B., *Hood's Texas Brigade* (Dayton, Ohio: Morningside House, 1988).

Priest, John Michael, *Antietam: The Soldiers' Battle* (New York: Oxford University Press, 1989).

———, *Before Antietam: The Battle for South Mountain* (New York: Oxford University Press, 1992).

———, *Nowhere to Run: The Wilderness, May 4 and 5, 1864* (Shippensburg, Pa.: White Mane, 1995).

Reinsberg, Mark, "Descent of the Raftsmen's Guard: A Roll Call," *Western Pennsylvania Historical Magazine* 53 (1970): 1–32.

Reinsberg, Mark, ed., "A Bucktail Voice: Civil War Correspondence of Pvt. Cordello Collins," *Western Pennsylvania Historical Magazine* 48 (1965): 235–48.

Revised Regulations for the Army of the United States, 1861 (Philadelphia: J. G. L. Brown, 1861).

Rhea, Gordon C., *The Battle of the Wilderness, May 5–6, 1864* (Baton Rouge: Louisiana State University, 1994).

————, *The Battles for Spotsylvania Court House and the Road to Yellow Tavern, May 7–12, 1864* (Baton Rouge: Louisiana State University, 1997).

————, *To the North Anna River: Grant and Lee, May 13–25, 1864* (Baton Rouge: Louisiana State University, 2000).

Robertson, James I. Jr., *Stonewall Jackson: The Man, the Soldier, the Legend* (New York: Macmillan, 1997).

Sauers, Richard A., *Advance the Colors: Pennsylvania Civil War Battle Flags*, 2 vols. (Harrisburg: Capitol Preservation Committee, 1987).

————, "The Pennsylvania Reserves: George McCall's Division on the Peninsula," in William J. Miller, ed., *The Peninsula Campaign of 1861: Yorktown to the Seven Days*, vol. 1 (Campbell, Calif.: Savas Woodbury, 1997), 19–45.

Schildt, John W., *Union Regiments at Antietam* (Chewsville, Md.: Antietam Publications, 1997).

Sears, Stephen W., *Chancellorsville* (Boston: Houghton Mifflin, 1996).

————, *Controversies and Commanders: Dispatches from the Army of the Potomac* (Boston: Houghton Mifflin, 1999).

————, *Landscape Turned Red: The Battle of Antietam* (Boston: Houghton Mifflin, 1983).

————, *To the Gates of Richmond: The Peninsula Campaign* (Boston: Houghton Mifflin, 1992).

Sears, Stephen W., ed., *The Civil War Papers of George B. McClellan* (New York: Da Capo, 1992).

Shakman, Arnold M., *The Pennsylvania Antiwar Movement, 1861–1865* (Cranbury, N.J.: Associated University Presses, 1980).

Shields, Joseph W., *From Flintlock to M-1* (New York: Coward-McCann, 1954).

Smith, Wayne, *The Price of Patriotism: Indiana County in the Civil War* (Indiana, Pa.: Historical and Genealogical Society of Indiana County, 1999).

Snow, William P., *Lee and His Generals* (Avenel, N.J.: Gramercy, 1996).

Southern Historical Society Papers, 52 vols. (Richmond: Southern Historical Society, 1876–1959). Electronic version of this title published in 1998 by Guild Press, Carmel, Ind.

Steele, Edward, *The Wilderness Campaign* (Harrisburg: Stackpole, 1960).

Stephenson, Clarence D., *Indiana County 175th Anniversary History*, 5 vols. (Indiana, Pa.: A. G. Halldin, 1978–95).

Steuart, Bradley W., *Pennsylvania West 1870 Census Index*, 2 vols. (Bountiful, Utah: Precision Indexing, 1993).

Stewart, George W., *Pickett's Charge* (New York: Fawcett, 1963).

Stewart, Joshua Thompson, *Indiana County, Pennsylvania; her people, past and present, embracing a history of the county comp. by Prof. J. T. Stewart, and a genealogical and biographical record of representative families . . .* , 2 vols. (Chicago: J. H. Beers, 1913).

The Story of American Heroism: Thrilling Narratives of Personal Adventures During the Great Civil War, as Told by the Medal Winners and Roll of Honor Men (New York: Werner Company, 1896).

Stotelmyer, Steven R., *The Bivouacs of the Dead: The Story of Those Who Died at Antietam and South Mountain* (Baltimore: Toomey, 1992).

Sypher, Josiah R., *A History of the Pennsylvania Reserve Corps* (Lancaster, Pa.: Elias Barr, 1865).

Truxall, Aida Craig, ed., *"Respects to All": Letters of Two Pennsylvania Boys in the War of the Rebellion* (Pittsburgh: University of Pittsburgh Press, 1962).

Van Atta, Robert B., *A Bicentennial History of the City of Greensburg* (Greensburg, Pa.: Chas. M. Henry, 1999).

Walkinshaw, Lewis Clark, *Annals of Southwestern Pennsylvania*, 4 vols. (New York: Lewis Historical Publishing, 1939).

The War of the Rebellion: A Compilation of the Official Records of the Union and Confederate Armies, 128 vols. (Washington: Government Printing Office, 1880–1901). Electronic version: *The Civil War CD-ROM: The War of the Rebellion* (Carmel, Ind.: Guild Press, 1996).

Welsh, Jack D., *Medical Histories of Union Generals* (Kent, Ohio: Kent State University Press, 1996).

Wiley, Bell I., *The Life of Billy Yank: The Common Soldier of the Union* (Baton Rouge: Louisiana State University Press, 1978).

———, *The Life of Johnny Reb: The Common Soldier of the Confederacy* (Baton Rouge: Louisiana State University Press, 1978).

Wiley, Samuel T., ed., *Biographical and Historical Cyclopedia of Indiana and Armstrong Counties, Pennsylvania* (Philadelphia: John M. Gresham & Co, 1891).

Woodward, Evan Morrison, *Our Campaigns: The Second Regiment Pennsylvania Reserve Volunteers, 1861–1864*, ed. Stanley W. Zamonski (Shippensburg, Pa.: Burd Street Press, 1995).

Manuscripts and Archival Collections

Franklin and Marshall College, Shadek-Fackenthal Library, Lancaster, Pa.
John F. Reynolds papers and correspondence.

Historical Society of Pennsylvania, Philadelphia, Pa.
Aaron Kepler memoir typescript. Copy at RNBP.

Historical Society of Western Pennsylvania, Pittsburgh, Pa.
Beale Family Correspondence, MFF #4, folder 3, translations and notes, F. J. Logan letter #2.

Library of Congress, Manuscript Division, Washington, D.C.
Samuel Crawford Papers, vol. 3, Samuel Crawford to Professor A. Jacobs, [n.d.] December 1863.

Library of Virginia, Richmond, Va.
Ivory Family Letters, 1862. Accession 37651, Personal Papers Collection.

National Archives and Records Administration, Washington, D.C.
Record Group 15, Records of the Veterans Administration, 1773–1976, pension files.
Record Group 92, Records of the Quartermaster General's Office.

Record Group 94, Records of the Adjutant General's Office:
    Carded Medical Records (entry 534).
    Compiled Military Service Records (entry 519).
    Eleventh Pennsylvania Reserves Personal Papers (boxes 117 and 118,
        7W2/R6/C19/SE).
    Eleventh Pennsylvania Reserves Miscellaneous Regimental Papers (box 4236,
        8W3/R6/C17/SC).
    Medical Officers files, box 630.
    Volunteer Service file, P-696, V.S. 64, box 579.
Record Group 153, Records of the Judge Advocate General's Office (Army), entry
    15, Court-Martial Case file.
Record Group 156, Records of the Office of the Chief of Ordnance.

Pennsylvania State Archives, Harrisburg, Pa.
Adam Torrance Papers, Division of History, Pennsylvania Historical and Museum
    Commission.
Record Group 19 (adjutant general's correspondence).
Record Group 26 (governor's correspondence).
Rothermel Papers, Division of History, Pennsylvania Historical and Museum
    Commission.

United States Army Military History Institute, Carlisle, Pa.
Civil War Times Illustrated Collection, Jesse Fry diary.
David Bell Papers, Thomas W. Sallade letter.
Harrisburg Civil War Round Table Collection, Andrew Lewis letters; Philip Lantzy
    letters, photocopies, and transcripts.
Lewis Leigh Collection, James X. McIlwain letters.
Save the Flags Collection. Charles Minnemeyer, typescript of diary entries.

United States Department of the Interior, Richmond, Va.
RNBP Collection, James W. McGinley diary; undated letters on the death of Har-
    vey Fair, signed by "Lib" and "your affectionate sister Lizzie" (apparently by a
    sister of Fair).

Washington County Free Library, Hagerstown, Md.
David A. Lilley Memorial Collection, Western Maryland Room, "The Maryland
    Campaign of 1862" by Gen. Ezra A. Carman, handwritten ms. (The author
    consulted a transcript, without page numbering, of the Carman work pro-
    vided courtesy of Steven R. Stotelmyer, Sharpsburg, Md.)

Selected Maps
Battle of Cold Harbor maps drafted by Edwin C. Bearss (U.S. Department of the
    Interior/National Park Service, 1960).
Battle of Fredericksburg maps drafted by Frank A. O'Reilly (U.S. Department of
    the Interior/National Park Service, 1997).
Battle of Gaines' Mill unpub. maps drafted by Edwin C. Bearss, 1960, on file at
    RNBP.
Battle of Gettysburg maps drafted by John Bachelder (New York: Endicott and Co.,
    1876).

Battle of Mechanicsville unpub. maps drafted by Edwin C. Bearss, 1960, on file at RNBP.

Battle of the Wilderness maps drafted by Edwin C. Bearss (U.S. Department of the Interior/National Park Service, 1962).

Second Bull Run/Manassas maps drafted by the Eastern National Park and Monument Association (U.S. Department of the Interior/National Park Service, 1985).

Newspapers

Alleghanian
Brookville Republican
Butler American Citizen
Cambria Tribune
Democrat & Sentinel
Greensburgh Herald
Indiana Messenger
Indiana Weekly Democrat
Kittanning Mentor
Mountaineer
National Intelligencer (Washington, D.C.)
New York Times
Pennsylvania Argus (Greensburg)
Richmond Enquirer
Richmond Examiner